A diction

simplified spelling

Based on the publications of the United States Bureau of Education and the rules of the American Philological Association and the Simplified Spelling Board

Frank H. Vizetelly

Alpha Editions

This edition published in 2019

ISBN : 9789353894696

Design and Setting By
Alpha Editions
email - alphaedis@gmail.com

A DICTIONARY OF SIMPLIFIED SPELLING

Based on the Publications of the United States Bureau of Education and the Rules of the American Philological Association and the Simplified Spelling Board

Compiled from the
FUNK & WAGNALLS NEW STANDARD DICTIONARY
OF THE ENGLISH LANGUAGE

By
FRANK H. VIZETELLY, Litt.D., LL.D.
Member of the Advisory Council of the Simplified Spelling Board;
Author of "Essentials of English Speech and Literature, etc.

FUNK & WAGNALLS COMPANY
NEW YORK and LONDON
1915

PREFACE

A FEW years ago, a writer to one of our great dailies expressed the hope that the advocates of simplified spelling would issue a manual containing, " in one alphabetical order and convenient for quick consultation, all the terms on the simplification of which they have agreed," instead of referring the public to the half hundred bulletins they have issued for the information it requires. Three years have passed by since this suggestion was made, and notwithstanding the fact that many inquiries for a manual of this kind have been received none has yet been issued. The purpose of the compiler of this book is to provide such an alphabetical guide. The vocabulary consists of the simpler forms of spelling that have been recommended for adoption from time to time by the American Philological Association and the Simplified Spelling Board, many of which were announced by the United States Department of Education in its Bulletin Number 202, and others, particularly the simplifications of the three hundred words recommended by the Simplified Spelling Board in the Board's Circular Number 5, as the bulletin entitled " Simplified Spelling for the Use of Government Departments " issued from the office of the Public Printer, Sept. 4, 1906, by direction of the President of the United States under date of Aug. 27, 1906, and the Simplified Spelling Board's "Alfabetic List," Circular Number 23, issued March 6, 1909.

In the compilation of this book the writer is not concerned with the reasons why this or that word should be simplified. This phase has already received the attention of many of the foremost scholars in English linguistry. All he has aimed to do is to provide in one volume a guide to the forms that words take when the rules for simplification recommended by these scholars are applied.

This Dictionary aims to supply the need of those persons who have been sufficiently interested in the Simplified Spelling Movement as to ask for an alphabetical list of words simplified according to rule. The vocabulary is not exhaustive, but the number of words it contains is sufficiently large to cover the various classes of simplifications recommended by the rules already referred to. It may be enlarged at will. The rules, classified according to number and to the societies that have recommended them, will be found printed elsewhere. To indicate words that are simplified according to the rules promulgated by the American Philological Association, the symbol ^{P} is printed immediately after the word. Words simplified in harmony with the rules recommended by the Simplified Spelling Board are indicated by the letter ^{S} printed in the same manner. Where the form of the word is affected by the rules of both Societies both letters are used, as **colleag,** $^{P\&S}$.

To provide supporters of the Simplified Spelling Movement with the adequate means for determining how each simplified word should be divided at the end of a line, every word is syllabicated, showing, wherever necessary, the primary stress (indicated by the prime mark (′) after the accented syllable), the secondary stress (indicated by the secondary mark (″) after the accented syllable), and the hyphen (-) which indicates syllabic division in such parts of a word as are not accented. The reader will understand that any word may be divided wherever primary or secondary accent is indicated as well as wherever the hyphen is shown. As compound words in great number may be formed by the combining of one word with another (as, *table-cloth, door-nail, dormer-window, friction-clutch, road-house, high-ball, stomach-pump*), these are not, in general, included. As an additional convenience, the grammatical character of each word is indicated, being followed by an abbreviation, printed in italic type, indicating its particular part in speech; as, *a.* for adjective; *n.* for noun; *v.* for verb; *adv.* for adverb, etc. In every case the abbreviation is that commonly used for the same purpose in dictionaries.

As Circular Number 26, published March 24, 1913, and containing additional rules of the Simplified Spelling Board, was issued after the editorial work on "Funk & Wagnalls New Standard Dictionary" had been completed, the rules that it announced could not be applied. In the following pages, therefore, only such words as the Board itself selected for examples, illustrating the application of the rules, are included.

The compiler ventures to hope that the following pages will be found to adequately supply the need for which they have been compiled, and prove acceptable to supporters of the Simplified Spelling Movement as well as to the people who would have given that movement their support had they been able to secure a simple, yet comprehensive, manual for their guidance. It should be borne in mind that the spellings printed in the pages that follow are not mandatory in any sense of the word; they are recorded there as recommended for the use of the general public by eminent scholars who have devoted years of labor to the subject of the amelioration of spelling of English words.

F. H. V.

NEW YORK, *September*, 1915.

THE AMERICAN PHILOLOGICAL ASSOCIATION

President, Prof. Edward Capps, Princeton University; *Vice-Presidents*, Prof. Carl D. Buck, University of Chicago, and Prof. Edward P. Morris, Yale University; *Secretary* and *Treasurer*, Prof. Frank G. Moore, of Columbia University, New York. Initiation fee, $5; annual dues, $3. Total membership, 690. The association was organized in 1869. Its object is " the advancement and diffusion of philological knowledge."

TEN RULES FOR SIMPLIFIED SPELLING

Recommended by the American Philological Association

THE Philological Society of England and the American Philological Association took joint action on the amendment of English spelling in 1883, and on the basis of it twenty-four joint rules were printed in the proceedings of the American association for that year (see next page). It was known that the application of these rules was difficult, and that an alfabetic list of amended words must be made. A pamflet of the English society and a paper in the Transactions of the American association for 1881 ar official context for interpretation. The corrections ar in the interest of etymological and historical truth, and ar to be confined to words which the changes do not much disguize from general readers.

In the following list, as in the twenty-four rules, many amendabl words hav been omitted for reasons such as these:—(1) The changed word would not be easily recognized, as *nee* for *knee:* or, (2), letters ar left in strange positions, as in *edg* for *edge*, *casq* for *casque*. (3) The word is of frequent use. Final *g*=*j*, *v*, *q*, *z*, and syllabic *l* and *n*, ar strange to our print but abundant in our speech. Many of them ar in the list: *hav*, *freez*, *singl*, *eatn*, etc.; but *iz* for *is*, *ov* for *of*, and many other words, as wel as the final *z*=*s* of inflections, ar omitted. (4) The wrong sound is suggested, as in *vag* for *vague*, *acer* for *acre*. (5) A valuabl distinction is lost: *casque* to *cask*, *dost* to *dust*. (6) The derivation is obscured: *nun* for *none*, *dun* for *done*, *munth* for *month*. (7) The change leads in the wrong direction.

Words doutful in pronunciation or etymology, and words undecided by the associations, however amendabl, ar omitted. Inflections ar printed in italics.

The rules proper ar as follows:

1. e.—Drop silent *e* when fonetically useless, writing *-er* for *-re*, as in *live*, *single*, *eaten*, *rained*, *theatre*, etc.
2. ea.—Drop *a* from *ea* having the sound of short *e*, as in *feather*, *leather*, etc.
3. o.—For *o* having the sound of *u* in *but* write *u* in *above* (abuv), *tongue* (tung), and the like.
4. ou.—Drop *o* from *ou* having the sound of *u* in but, in *trouble*, *rough* (ruf), and the like; for *-our* unaccented write *-or*, as in *honour*.

5. u, ue.—Drop silent *u* after *g* before *a*, and in nativ English words, and drop final *ue: guard, guess, catalogue, league*, etc.
6. Dubl consonants may be simplified when fonetically useless: *bailiff* (not *hall*, etc.), *battle* (batl), *written* (writn), *traveller*, etc.
7. d.—Change *d* and *ed* to final *t* when so pronounced, as in *looked* (lookt), etc., unless the *e* affects the preceding sound, as in *chafed*, etc.
8. gh, ph.—Change *gh* and *ph* to *f* when so sounded: *enough* (enuf), *laughter* (lafter), etc.; *phonetic* (fonetic), etc.
9. s.—Change *s* to *z* when so sounded, especially in distinctiv words and in *-ise: abuse*, verb (abuze), *advertise* (advertize), etc.
10. t.—Drop *t* in *tch: catch, pitch*, etc.

TWENTY-FOUR RULES

Recommended by the American Philological Association

THE following rules, jointly approved by the Philological Society of England and the American Philological Association, were reported in the Ninth Report of the Transactions of the American Philological Association in 1883, and were commended for immediate use:

1. e.—Drop silent *e* when fonetically useless, as in *live, vineyard, believe, bronze, single, engine, granite, eaten, rained*, etc.
2. ea.—Drop *a* from *ea* having the sound of ĕ, as in *feather, leather, jealous*, etc. Drop *e* from *ea* having the sound of a, as in *heart, hearken.*
3. eau.—For *beauty* uze the old *beuty.*
4. eo.—Drop *o* from *eo* having the sound of ĕ, as in *jeopardy, leopard.*
   For *yeoman* write *yoman.*
5. i.—Drop *i* of *parliament.*
6. o.—For *o* having the sound of ŭ in *but* write *u* in *above* (abuv), *dozen, some* (sum), *tongue* (tung), and the like.
   For *women* restore *wimen.*
7. ou.—Drop *o* from *ou* having the sound of ŭ, as in *journal, nourish, trouble, rough* (ruf), *tough* (tuf), and the like.
8. u.—Drop silent *u* after *g* before *a*, and in nativ English words, as *guarantee, guard, guess, guest, guild, guilt.*
9. ue.—Drop final *ue* in *apologue, catalogue*, etc.; *demagogue, pedagogue*, etc.; *league, colleague, harangue, tongue*, (tung).
10. y.—Spel *rhyme* rime.
11. Dubl consonants may be simplified:
    Final *b, d, g, n, r, t, f, l, z*, as *ebb, add, egg, inn, purr, butt, bailiff, dull, buzz* (not *all, hall*).
    Medial before another consonant, as *battle, ripple, written* (writn).
    Initial unaccented prefixes, and other unaccented syllabls, as in *abbreviate, accuse, affair*, etc., *curvetting, traveller*, etc.
12. b.—Drop silent *b* in *bomb, crumb, debt, doubt, dumb, lamb, limb, numb, plumb, subtle, succumb, thumb.*

13. c.—Change *c* back to *s* in *cinder, expence, fierce, hence, once, pence, scarce, since, source, thence, tierce, whence.*
14. ch.—Drop the *h* of *ch* in *chamomile, choler, cholera, melancholy, school, stomach.* Change to *k* in *ache* (ake), *anchor* (anker).
15. d.—Change *d* and *ed* final to *t* when so pronounced, as in *crossed* (crost), *looked* (lookt), etc., unless the *e* affects the preceding sound, as in *chafed chanced.*
16. g.—Drop *g* in *feign, foreign, sovereign.*
17. gh.—Drop *h* in *aghast, burgh, ghost.*
    Drop *gh* in *haughty, though* (tho), *through* (thru).
    Change *gh* to *f* where it has that sound, as in *cough, enough, laughter, tough,* etc.
18. l.—Drop *l* in *could.* 19. p.—Drop *p* in *receipt.*
20. s.—Drop *s* in *aisle, demesne, island.*
    Change *s* to *z* in distinctiv words, as in *abuse* verb, *house* verb, *rise* verb, etc.
21. sc.—Drop c in *scent, scythe* (sithe). 22. tch.—Drop t, as in *catch, pitch, witch,* etc.
23. w.—Drop *w* in whole. 24. ph.—Write *f* for *ph,* as in *philosophy, sphere,* etc.

THE SIMPLIFIED SPELLING BOARD

The Simplified Spelling Board was organized in March, 1906, for "the purpose of expediting this natural process (the simplification of English spelling) of change which has been going on for centuries, and, as far as may be possible, of guiding it in the direction of simplicity and economy" and to "urge educated people everywhere to aid in the gradual simplification of English spelling, and thus to make the English language more and more easy to acquire and to use." (***Simplified Spelling Board, Circular No. 1, March 21, 1906.***) The number of adherents to its principles exceeds 75,000.

THIRTY-ONE RULES

Recommended by the Simplified Spelling Board

The following are the rules under which the simplifications containd in the list are groupt. They are condenst from the circulars mentiond, and are arranged in the alfabetic order of the letter or letters, or the suffix, affected.

'*RULE*' here means simply a recommendation that applies to a number of words having the same irregularity of spelling. To facilitate acceptance it was deemd expedient in some cases to restrict the rule to a limited number of the words in the class. Any one who chooses to extend the rule at once to all the words of a given class is of course free to do so.

After each rule is given a list, either of all the words affected (if they are not many), or of all the words mentiond in the original rule, or of a few examples of the large number coverd by the rule. In the latter case "Ex." ('Examples') is prefixt, and "etc." is added. If the official recommendation applies to all words containing the letter, sequence of letters, or suffix, affected, in the pronunciation indicated, the word RULE is printed in capitals. For some small classes and for isolated amendments no rule is here given.

1. **ae, æ** or **e,** not final. RULE: Choose **e.** Ex.: ***Anesthetic, chimera, era, esthetic, ether, medieval, paleontology,*** etc.

2. **-bt,** with **b** silent. RULE: Omit **b.** *Debt, dettor, dout, indetted, redout, redouted, redoutable.*

3. **ea** pronounced as short **e.** RULE: Drop **a.** Ex.: *Hed, spred, sted, tred, thret, helth, welth, dremt, ment, plesant,* etc.

4. **ea** pronounced as **â,** before **r.** RULE: Drop **e.** *Harken, hart, harth.*

5. **-ed** or **'d** pronounced **-d.** RULE: Use simple **d** in all cases (reducing a double consonant). Ex.: *Aimd, armd, burnd, deemd, dimd, feld, fild, hangd, raind, stird, veild,* etc.

6. **-ed** or **-t,** the preceding single consonant being doubled before **-ed** (*-pped, -ssed*) and left single before **-t** (*-pt, -st*). RULE: Choose **-t** in all cases. Ex.: *Dipt, dript, dropt, stept, stopt, blest, prest, mist, blusht, washt, wisht, lockt, packt,* etc.

7. **-ence** or **-ense** (Latin *-ensa*). *RULE:* Choose **-ense.** *Defense, offense, pretense.* Also *license* (Latin *-entia*).

8. **-ette** or **-et.** RULE: Choose **-et.** Ex.: *Coquet, epaulet, etiquet, omelet, quartet, quintet, septet, sextet,* etc.

9. **gh** or **f.** *RULE:* Choose **f.** *Draft,* not *draught.*

10. **-gh** silent: (1) **-ough** or **-ow** (pronounced **au**). *RULE:* Choose **-ow.** *Plow.* (2) **-ough** or **-o** (pronounced **ō** or **o**). RULE: Choose **-o.** *Altho, tho, thoro, boro, -boro* (in place-names), *furlo.* (3) **-ough** or **-o** (pronounced **û**): *Through, thro' thro.* RULE: Choose *thro,* but advance it now to *thru.*

11. **-ice** unstrest, pronounced **-is.** RULE: Spell **-is.** Ex.: *Artifis, coppis, cornis, crevis, edifis, justis, notis, servis,* etc.

12. **-ile** unstrest, pronounced **-il.** RULE: Omit **e.** Ex.: *Agil, futil, servil,* etc. Retain **-ile** when the **i** is not pronounced short,

13. **-ine** unstrest, pronounced **-in.** RULE: Omit **e.** Ex.: *Determin, doctrin, engin, examin, genuin, imagin, pristin,* etc. Retain **-ine** when the **i** is not pronounced short.

14. **-ise** unstrest, pronounced **-is.** RULE: Omit **e.** *Anis, mortis, practis, premis, promis, treatis.*

15. **-ise** or **-ize** (from Greek), suffix of verbs. RULE: Choose **-ize.** Ex.: *Civilize, criticize, exorcize, legalize, organize,* etc.

16. **-ite** unstrest, pronounced **-it.** RULE: Omit **e.** Ex.: *Apposit, definit, infinit, opposit, preterit, requisit,* etc. Retain **-ite** when the **i** is not pronounced short.

17. **-ive** unstrest, pronounced **-iv.** RULE: Omit **e.** Ex.: *Activ, adjectiv, detectiv, executiv, motiv, nativ, progressiv,* etc.

18. **-ll** or **-l** (**-ill** or **-il**). RULE: Choose **-l.** *Distil, fulfil, instil;* like *until, compel, impel,* etc.

19. **-ll-** or **-l-** (**-ill-** or **-il-**, **-ull-** or **-ul-**) before **-ful** or **-ness.** RULE: Choose **-l.** *Skilful, wilful, dulness, fulness.*

20. **-mb** with **b** silent. *RULE:* Omit **b.** *Crum, dum, lam, lim, num, thum.*

21. **-mn** with **n** silent. *RULE:* Omit **n.** *Autum, colum, solem.*

22. **oe, œ,** or **e,** not final. RULE: Choose **e.** Ex.: *Ecumenical, esophagus, phenix, subpena,* etc.; like *economy, solecism,* etc.

23. **-our** or **-or.** *RULE:* Choose **-or.** Ex.: *Ardor, candor, clamor, color, favor, flavor, honor, humor, labor, rumor, tumor, valor, vigor,* etc.; also, *arbor, harbor, neighbor,* etc.

24. **ph** or **f.** *RULE:* Choose **f.** *Fantasm, fantasy, fantom, sulfate, sulfur;* like *fancy, frantic, frenzy, coffer, coffin,* etc., which originally had *ph.*

25. **ph** pronounced **f.** RULE: Use **f.** *Camfor, cifer; alfabet, diafram, pamflet; autograf, bibliografy, biografy, fonograf, fotograf, paragraf, telegraf, telefone.*

26. **-rr** or **-r.** RULE: Choose **r.** *Bur, pur;* like *cur, fur, blur, slur, spur, car, far, fir, stir,* etc.

27. **-re** or **-er.** RULE: Choose **-er.** Ex.: *Accouter, center, fiber, meter, miter, niter, saltpeter, scepter, sepulcher, somber, specter, theater,* etc.; like *diameter, number,* etc.

28. **s** or **z** (in the root). RULE: Choose **z.** *Apprize, assize, comprize, enterprize, raze, surprize, teazel.* (See also Rule 15.)

29. **s** medial, silent. *RULE:* Drop **s.** *Aile, ile, ilet, iland.*

30. **-ue** silent, after **-g.** RULE: Omit **-ue.** *Catalog, decalog, demagog, pedagog, prolog, colleag, leag, harang, tung.*

31. **-ve** after **l** or **r.** RULE: Omit **-e.** Ex.: *Delv, shelv, twelv, selvs, carv, curv, nerv, serv, deserv, reserv, starv,* etc.

THIRTY ADDITIONAL RULES

Recommended in Circular No. 26, issued March 24, 1913

1. **ch** pronounst **c** (chiefly in words of Greek origin). RULE: Drop **h.** Ex. *Cameleon, caos, caracter, casm, clorid, clorin, colera, cord* (in music), *corus, cromatic, crome, cromo, cronic, cronicle, cronology, arcaic, arcangel, conc, distic, eco, epoc, escatology, hemistic, mecanic, melancoly, monarc, monocrome, monostic, saccarin, scolar, scolastic, scolium, scool, stomac, stricnin, syncronus, tecnic, tecnology, trocaic,* etc.

   Retain, for the present, *ch* before *e, i,* and *y,* where, by a conventional assumption, *c* suggests the sound of *s.* Ex. *chemic, chemist, chemistry, chirografy, chyle, alchemy, archeology, architect, archives, bronchial, catechism, lichen, monarchy, orchestra, pachyderm, scheme, trochee,* etc.

2. **-ck** pronounst **c,** after an unstrest vowel, in words of two or more syllables. RULE: Drop **k.** Ex. *Bannoc, barrac, bulloc, cammoc, cassoc, charloc, derric, haddoc, hammoc, hassoc, hemloc, hilloc, hummoc, mammoc, mattoc, paddoc, polloc, puttoc, ruddoc, rulloc, shamroc, tussoc, wedloc, bailiwic,* etc. So also: *Haversac, napsac, nicnac, ransac* (where there is a secondary stress).

3. **-e** final, silent, after a single consonant preceded by a short vowel, strest, or by any strest vowel whose sound is not conventionally associated with the silent final *-e.* RULE: Drop **e.** Ex. *Bad, hav, giv, liv, forgiv, misgiv,* etc.; *ar, gon, wer.*

The rule can not be applied to the unstrest syllables *-ace*, *-ade*, *-age*, *-ate*, until it shal be determind what letters shal be adopted to indicate the weak or "obscure" vowels in question.

4. **-ea-** pronounst as long **ā** before *r*. Rule: Drop **e.** Ex. *Harken, hart, harten, harth, harty.*

5. **-ew** pronounst as long **u** after *l* or *r*, or *ch*. Rule: Change to **-u.** Ex. *Blu, clu, flu, slu, bru, cru, dru, gru, scru, thru, chu,* etc.

   Inflections: (1) **-ewed** becomes **-ued.** Ex. *Brued, chued, scrued.* (2) **-ews** becomes **-ues.** *Brues, chues, crues, scrues.* See 27.

6. **-ey** unstrest, pronounst like short final *y*. Rule: Drop e. Ex. *Abby, ally, attorny, barly, chimny, cockny, donky, gally, hackny, hony, jersy, jocky, jurny, kersy, kidny, lacky, lampry, linsy-woolsy, medly, mony, monky, motly, parly, parsly, pully, trolly, turky, vally, volly, whisky.*

7. **-ff** final, pronounst **f.** Rule: Drop one **f.** Ex. *Bluf, buf, chaf, chuf, clif, cuf, dof, duf, gaf, gruf, huf, luf, mif, muf, ruf, snif, snuf, staf, stif, stuf, tif, whif,* etc.; *bailif, caitif, distaf, mastif, midrif, plaintif, pontif, sherif, tarif,* etc. Retain *off*. See the general rule, paragraf 30.

8. **-gh** pronounst **f,** in *-augh, -aught* or *-ough.* Rule: Change to **-f** (changing also **au** to **a,** and **ou** to **o** or **u**). Ex. *Draft, laf, lafter, chuf, cluf, cof, enuf, ruf, sluf, tuf, trof,* etc.; and hence *laffing, coffing, sluffing, ruffen, tuffen, ruffer, tuffer,* etc.

9. **-gh** silent. Rule: Drop **gh.** Ex. *Aut, caut, dauter, distraut, fraut, hauty, slauter, taut,* etc.; *drout.*

10. **gn-** pronounst **n.** Rule: Drop **g.** Ex. *Narl, narld, narly, nash, nat, naw, neis, nome, nomic, nomon, nostic,* etc. See **kn-.**

11. **-gn** in *-eign* pronounst like *ein* in *vein, skein, seine, feint.* Rule: Drop **g.** Ex. *Dein, fein, rein.*

    h silent. See **ph, rh-, -rrh-.**

12. **kn-** pronounst **n.** Rule: Drop **k.** Ex. *Nack, nag, nap, napsac, nave, nead, nee, neel, neeling, nel, nelt, nicnac, nife, nit, nitting, nob, nock, nocker, nocking, nop, noll, not, notting, nuckle, nurl, nurld,* etc. Keep *k* in kno (*know*) and knoledge (*knowledge*) (see 20).

13. **-ll** final, after a short strest vowel. Rule: Drop one **l.** Ex. *Shal, bel, cel, del, dwel, el, fel, hel, sel, shel, smel, spel, swel, tel, wel, bil, chil, dil, dril, fil, fril, gil, gril, hil, kil, mil, pil, quil, ril, shril, sil, skil, spil, squil, stil, swil, thil, thril, til, wil, dol, bul, ful, pul, cul, dul, gul, hul, mul, nul, skul,* etc. Also, of course, forms like *distil, fulfil, instil,* and derivates like *skilful, wilful, dulness, fulness.* See the general rule, paragraf 30.

14. **-nced,** after a strest vowel, pronounst like **nst.** Rule: Change to **-nst.** Ex. *Advanst, chanst, danst, glanst, lanst, pranst, transt, enhanst, commenst, fenst, convinst, evinst, minst, winst, bounst, flounst, pounst, trounst, announst, denounst, enounst, pronounst, renounst,* etc.

15. **-nced,** after an unstrest vowel, pronounst like **nst.** Rule: Change to **-nst.** Ex. *Balanst, circumstanst, distanst, evidenst, experienst, influenst, instanst,* etc.

16. **-oe** pronounst **o.** Rule: Drop **e.** Ex. *Do, flo, fo, ho, ro, slo, to, wo,* etc.

17. **-ou-** pronounst like *u* in *but.* Rule: Drop **o.** Ex. *Cuntry, just, tuch, yung, yunker; chuf, cluf, ruf, tuf* (see paragraf 8). But *couple, cousin, double, trouble* ar left unchanged. For unstrest *-ou-* see **-ous.**

18. **-ou-** before *r,* pronounst like **u** in *burn.* Rule: Drop **o.** Ex. *Adjurn, curteus, curtesy; jurnal, jurny, sojurn, turnament, turny.* But *courage, flourish, nourish* ar left unchanged.

-ough. See 8. **-ought.** See 9.

19. **-ous,** unstrest, pronounst like *-us* unstrest. Rule: Change to **-us.** Ex. *Acrimonius, amfibius, anomalus, auriferus, bilius, bituminus, callus, commodius, coniferus, credulus, cutaneus, devius, enormus, envius, famus, felonius, frivolus, frugivorus, glorius, graminivorus, grievus, harmonius, herbivorus, hideus, illustrius, imperius, industrius, infamus, invidius, jelus, joyus, luminus, malarius, multifarius, mischievus, odius, odorus, parsimonius, plenteus, porus, ravenus, rebellius, resinus, ridiculus, rigorus, serius, spontaneus, tedius, vaporus, varius, vigorus, villanus, voluminus,* etc. Also many words in *-ceous* and *-cious,* and *-uous,* which now take the forms *-ceus, -cius, -uus.* Ex. *Cretaceus, farinaceus, rosaceus,* etc.; *audacius, fallacius, gracius,* etc.; *arduus, impetuus, sinuus, strenuus,* etc.

20. **-ow,** strest or unstrest, pronounst like **o,** long (ō) or short (o). Rule: Change to **-o.** Ex. *Blo, bo, cro, flo, glo, gro, kno, lo, mo, ro, sho, slo, sno, so, sto, stro, thro, to,* etc.; *belo, besto,* etc.; *bello, billo, fello, furro, hallo, hollo, mello, pillo, sallo, willo,* etc.

Inflections: (1) **-owed** becomes **-oed.** Ex. *Croed, floed, gloed, moed, roed, soed, belloed, folloed, furroed,* etc. (2) **-ows** becomes **-oes.** Ex. *Bloes, croes, floes, gloes, groes, moes, roes, soes, toes, belloes, felloes, halloes,* etc. (3) **-own** remains.

21. **ph** pronounst **f.** Rule: Change to **f.** Ex. *Fantasm, fantasmagoria, fantasy, fantom, farmacy, fenix, fesant, filology, filosofy, flem, flox, fosforus, fotograf, fotosfere, frase, fraseology, frenology, fysic, fysics, fysician, fysiology, etc.*; *alfabet, diafram, pamflet, autograf, paragraf, telegraf, bibliografy, biografy, fonetic, telefone; aferesis, atmosfere, blasfeme, cenotaf, chirografy, diafanus, dolfin, elefant, emfasis, emfatic, esofagus, geografy, grafic, hemisfere, hieroglyf, homofone, homograf, hyfen, mefitic, metamorfosis, morfia, morfology, nymf, orfan, parafrase, perifery, porfyry, profet, profetic, sarcofagus, sfere, sferic, sfinx, sofist, sofisticate, strofe, tyfoid, tyfus,* etc.; also (*ph* not of Greek origin), *lymf, lymfatic, triumf, trofy,* etc.; *calif, cifer, gofer,* etc.

22. **-rced** pronounst like **rst.** Rule: Change to **-rst.** Ex. *Amerst, forst, enforst, pierst,* etc. See **-nced.** Such spellings wer once common (Spenser, Lodge, Raleigh, etc.).

23. **rh-** pronounst like **r** (**h** silent). Rule: Drop **h.** Ex. *Rapsody, retoric, reum, reumatism, rinoceros, rizome, rododendron, romboid, rombus, rubarb, rime, rythm,* etc.

24. **-rrh-** medial, pronounst like **r** (**h** silent). Rule: Change to **-rr-** after a strest vowel, to **-r-** after an unstrest vowel. Ex. *Catarral, diarea, hemorage*, etc.

25. **-some** pronounst like *-sum*. Rule: Change to **-sum**. Ex. *Adventuresum, blithesum, burdensum, buxum* (*bucsum*), *cumbersum, darksum, dolesum, frolicsum, fulsum, gamesum, gladsum, handsum, irksum, lightsum, loathsum, lonesum, longsum, meddlesum, mettlesum, noisum, quarrelsum, tiresum, toilsum, toothsum, troublesum, wearisum, winsum*, etc.

26. **-ss** final, in monosyllables, pronounst like **s**. Rule: Drop one **s**. Ex. *Bas, bras, clas, cros, glas, gras, las, mas, pas, bles, ches, cres, dres, les, mes, pres, stres, tres, blis, his, kis, mis, bos, cros, dros, flos, gros, los, mos, tos, bus, fus, mus, pus, trus*, etc.

27. **-ue** final, after *l* or *r*, pronounst like long **u**. Rule: Change to **-u**. Ex. *Blu, clu, flu, glu*, etc.; *ru, tru*, etc.; *accru, constru, imbru*. Inflections unchanged: *Blued, blues, glued*, etc. See 5.

28. **wr-**, with **w** silent. Rule: Drop **w**. Ex. *Rack, raith, rangle, rap, rath, reak, reath, reathe, reck, ren, rench, rest, restle, retch, retched, riggle, right, ring, rinkle, rist, rite, riter, rithe, riting, ritten, rong, roth, rought, rung*, etc. *wr-* may be kept where one wishes to avoid an apparent conflict with similar words, as in *write, wright, wring*, etc.

29. **-zz** final. Rule: Drop one **z**. Ex. *Buz, fiz, friz, siz, whiz*. See 30.

30. Double consonant, final, namely, **-bb, -dd, -ff, -gg, -ll, -nn, -rr, -ss, -tt, -zz**. Rule: Use a single consonant. Ex. *Eb, ad, od, cuf, eg, el, er, bur, whir, bas, bos, pres, net, set, buz*, etc.

A Dictionary of Simplified Spelling

a-ban'dond[P&S], *pa.* Abandoned.

a-basht'[P&S], *pp.* Abashed.

a-bat'a-bl[P], *a.* Abatable.

ab'by[S], *n.* Abbey.

ab'di-ca-bl[P], *a.* Abdicable.

ab'di-ca"tiv[S], *a.* Abdicative.

ab'di-tiv[S], *a.* Abditive.

ab-hord'[P&S], *pp.* Abhorred.

-abl[P], *suffix.* -able.

ab'la-tiv[P&S], *a.* & *n.* Ablative.

a-bol'ish-a-bl[P], *a.* Abolishable.

a-bol'isht[P&S], *pp.* Abolished.

a-bom'i-na-bl[P], *a.* Abominable.

a-bor'tiv[P&S], *a.* Abortive.

ab-ra'siv[S], *a.* & *n.* Abrasive.

a-brest'[P&S], *adv.* Abreast.

a-bridg'ment[S], *n.* Abridgement.

ab-solv'[P&S], *vt.* Absolve.

ab-solv'a-bl[P], *a.* Absolvable.

ab-solvd'[P&S], *pp.* Absolved.

ab-sorb'a-bl[P], *a.* Absorbable.

ab-sorbd'[P&S], *pp.* Absorbed.

ab-sorp'tiv[P&S], *a.* Absorptive.

ab-staind'[P&S], *pp.* Abstained.

ab-strac'tiv[P&S], *a.* Abstractive.

a-bu'siv[P&S], *a.* Abusive.

a-bu'siv-ly[S], *adv.* Abusively.

a-bu'siv-ness[S], *n.* Abusiveness.

a-buv'[P], *a., n., adv.* & *prep.* Above.

a-buze'[P], *vt.* Abuse.

ac-cel'er-a-tiv[P&S], *a.* Accelerative.

ac-cept'a-bl[P], *a.* Acceptable.

ac-cept'a-bl-ness[P], *n.* Acceptableness.

ac-cep'tiv[S], *a.* Acceptive.

ac-ces'si-bl[P], *a.* Accessible.

ac-ces'siond[S], *pp.* Accessioned.

ac-claim'a-bl[P], *a.* Acclaimable.

ac-claimd'[S], *pp.* Acclaimed.

ac-cli'ma-ta-bl[P], *a.* Acclimatable.

ac-cli'ma-tiz"a-bl, -tis"a-bl[P], *a.* Acclimatizable, acclimatisable.

ac-com'mo-da-bl[P], *a.* Accommodable.

ac-com'mo-da-bl-ness[P], *n.* Accommodableness.

ac-com'mo-da"tiv[P&S], *a.* Accommodative.

ac-com'mo-da"tiv-ness[S], *n.* Accommodativeness.

ac-com'ple-tiv[S], *a.* Accompletive.

ac-com'plis[S], *n.* Accomplice.

ac-com'plish-a-bl[P], *a.* Accomplishable.

ac-com'plisht[P&S], *pa.* Accomplished.

ac-compt'a-bl[P], *a.* Accomptable.

ac-cord'a-bl[P], *a.* Accordable.

ac-cost'a-bl[P], *a.* Accostable.

ac-count'a-bl[P], *a.* Accountable.

ac-count'a-bl-ness[P], *n.* Accountableness.

ac-cou'ter[S], *vt.* Accoutre.

ac-cou'terd[S], *pp.* Accoutered.

ac-cre'tiv[S], *a.* Accretive.

ac-cru'[S], *v.* & *n.* Accrue.

ac-cum'pa-ni-ment[P], *n.* Accompaniment.

ac-cum'pa-ny[P], *vt.* & *vi.* Accompany.

ac-cu′mu-la-bl[P], *a.* Accumulable.
ac-cu′mu-la-tiv[P&S], *a.* Accumulative.
ac-cu′mu-la-tiv-ly[S], *adv.* Accumulatively.
ac-cu′mu-la-tiv-ness[S], *n.* Accumulativeness.
ac-curst′[P&S], *pa.* Accursed.
ac-cus′a-bl[P], *a.* Accusable.
ac-cu′sa-tiv[P&S], *a.* & *n.* Accusative.
ac-cu′sa-tiv-ly[S], *adv.* Accusatively.
ac-cus′tom-a-bl[P], *a.* Accustomable.
ac-cus′tomd[P&S], *pa.* Accustomed.
a-cef′a-lous[P], *a.* Acephalous.
a-cer′vu-lin[S], *a.* Acervuline.
a-cet′y-lid[S], *n.* Acetylide.
a-chiev′[P], *vt.* & *vi.* Achieve.
a-chiev′a-bl[P], *a.* Achievable.
a-chievd′[P&S], *pp.* Achieved.
a-chro″ma-tiz′a-bl[P], *a.* Achromatizable.
a-cid′i-fi″a-bl[P], *a.* Acidifiable.
ac-knowl′edg-ment[S], *n.* Acknowledgement.
a-cog′ni-tiv[S], *a.* Acognitive.
a′cornd[S], *a.* Acorned.
ac-quir′a-bl[P], *a.* Acquirable.
ac-quis′i-bl[P], *a.* Acquisible.
ac-quis′i-tiv[P&S], *a.* Acquisitive.
ac″ri-mo′ni-us[S], *n.* Acrimonious.
ac′ro-log[S], *n.* Acrologue.
ac′tion-a-bl[P], *a.* Actionable.
ac′tiv[P&S] *a.* Active.
ac′tiv-ly[S], *adv.* Actively.
ac′tiv-ness[S], *n.* Activeness.
ad[P&S], *vt.* & *vi.* Add.
ad″a-man′tin[S], *a.* Adamantine.
a-dapt′a-bl[P], *a.* Adaptable.
a-dap′ta-tiv[S], *a.* Adaptative.
a-dap′tiv[P&S], *a.* Adaptive.
add′a-bl[P], **add′i-bl**[P], *a.* Addable, addible.
ad′di-tiv[S], *a.* Additive.
ad-drest′[P&S], *pp.* Addressed.
ad-duce′a-bl[P], **ad-du′ci-bl**[P], *a.* Adduceable, adducible.
ad-duc′tiv[S], *a.* Adductive.
ad′e-qua-tiv[S], *a.* Adequative.
ad-es′siv[S], *n.* Adessive.
ad-he′siv[P&S], *a.* Adhesive.
ad′jec-tiv[P&S], *a.* & *n.* Adjective.
ad′jec-tiv-ly[S], *adv.* Adjectively.
ad-joind′[P&S], *pp.* Adjoined.
ad-journd′[S], *pp.* Adjourned.
ad-judge′a-bl[P], *a.* Adjudgeable.
ad-ju′di-ca″tiv[S], *a.* Adjudicative.
ad-junc′tiv[P&S], *a.* Adjunctive.
ad-jurn′[P&S], *vt.* & *vi.* Adjourn.
ad-jurnd′[P&S], *pp.* Adjourned.
ad-just′a-bl[P], *a.* Adjustable.
ad-jus′tiv[S], *a.* Adjustive.
ad′l[P], *vt.* & *vi.* Addle.
ad′ld[P], *pp.* Addled.
ad-lu′mi-din[S], *n.* Adlumidine.
ad-lu′min[S], *n.* Adlumine.
ad-me′sure[S], *vt.* Admeasure.
ad-me′zure[P], *vt.* Admeasure.
ad-min′is-terd[P&S], *pp.* Administered.
ad-min′is-tra-bl[P], *a.* Administrable.
ad-min′is-tra″tiv[P&S], *a.* Administrative.
ad′mi-ra-bl[P], *a.* Admirable.
ad′mi-ra″tiv[S], *a.* Admirative.
ad′mi-ra″tiv-ly[S], *adv.* Admiratively.
ad-mis′si-bl[P], *a.* Admissible.
ad-mis′siv[S], *a.* Admissive.
ad-mit′ta-bl[P], **ad-mit′ti-bl**[P], *a.* Admittable, admittible.
ad-mixt′[P&S], *pp.* Admixed.
ad-mon′isht[P&S], *pp.* Admonished.
ad-mon′i-tiv[P&S], *a.* Admonitive.
ad-mo′tiv[S], *a.* Admotive.
a-dopt′a-bl[P], *a.* Adoptable.
a-dopt′a-tiv[S], *a.* Adoptative.
a-dop′tiv[P&S], *a.* Adoptive.
a-dop′tiv-ly[S], *adv.* Adoptively.
a-dor′a-bl[P], *a.* Adorable.
a-dor′a-bl-ness[P], *n.* Adorableness.

a-dornd'[P&S], *pp.* Adorned.
ad-scrip'tiv[S], *a.* Adscriptive.
a-dul'ter-in[P&S], *a.* & *n.* Adulterine.
ad-um'bra-tiv[S], *a.* Adumbrative.
ad-vanst'[S], *pa.* Advanced.
ad-van'tage-a-bl[P], *a.* Advantageable.
ad-ven'tiv[S], *a.* Adventive.
ad-ven'ture-sum[P&S], *a.* Adventuresome.
ad-ver'sa-tiv[P&S], *a.* Adversative.
ad-ver'sa-tiv-ly[S], *adv.* Adversatively.
ad'ver-tize[P], *vt.* & *vi.* Advertise.
ad-ver'tiz-ment[P], *n.* Advertisement.
ad'ver-tiz"ing[S], *n.* Advertising.
ad-viz'a-bl[P], *a.* Advisable.
ad-vize'[P], *vt.* & *vi.* Advise.
ad-vized'[P], *pa.* Advised.
ad-vize'ment[P], *n.* Advisement.
ad-viz'er[P], *n.* Adviser.
ad-vi'zo-ry[P], *a.* Advisory.
adz[P&S], *v.* & *n.* Adze.
a-fer'e-sis[S], *n.* Apheresis, aphæresis.
af'fa-bl[P], *a.* Affable.
af'fa-bl-ness[P], *n.* Affableness.
af-fect'i-bl[P], *a.* Affectible.
af-fec'tiv[P&S], *a.* Affective.
af-fil'i-a-bl[P], *a.* Affiliable.
af-fin'i-ta-tiv[S], *a.* Affinitative.
af-fin'i-ta-tiv-ly[S], *adv.* Affinitatively.
af-fin'i-tiv[S], *a.* Affinitive.
af-firm'a-bl[P], *a.* Affirmable.
af-firm'a-tiv[P&S], *a.* & *n.* Affirmative.
af-firm'a-tiv-ly[S], *adv.* Affirmatively.
af-firmd'[P&S], *pp.* Affirmed.
af-fixt'[P&S], *pp.* Affixed.
af-flic'tiv[P&S], *a.* Afflictive.
af-flic'tiv-ly[S], *adv.* Afflictively.
af-ford'a-bl[P], *a.* Affordable.
af-for'ma-tiv[S], *n.* Afformative.
af-fric'a-tiv[S], *n.* Affricative.
af-frunt'[P], *vt.* & *n.* Affront.
af-frun'tiv[P], *a.* Affrontive.
a-frunt'[P], *adv.* Afront.
a-fyl'lous[P], *a.* Aphyllous.
a-gast'[P&S], *a.* Aghast.
a-gen'tiv[S], *a.* Agentive.
ag-glom'er-a-tiv[S], *a.* Agglomerative.
ag-glu'ti-na-bl[P], *a.* Agglutinable.
ag-glu'ti-na-tiv[P&S], *a.* Agglutinative.
ag'gran-diz"a-bl[P], **-dis"a-bl**[P], *a.* Aggrandizable, aggrandisable.
ag'gra-va"tiv[S], *a.* & *n.* Aggravative.
ag'gre-ga"tiv[S], *a.* Aggregative.
ag-gres'siv[P&S], *a.* Aggressive.
ag-grest'[S], *pp.* Aggressed.
ag-griev'[P], *vt.* & *vi.* Aggrieve.
ag-grievd'[P&S], *pa.* Aggrieved.
ag'il[P&S], **-ile**[S], *a.* Agile.
ag'i-ta-bl[P], *a.* Agitable.
ag"i-ta'tiv[S], *a.* Agitative.
-a-gog[P], *suffix.* -Agogue.
a-gree'a-bl[P], *a.* Agreeable.
a-gree'a-bl-ness[P], *n.* Agreeableness.
a-hed'[P&S], *adv.* Ahead.
aid'a-bl[P], *a.* Aidable.
aild[P&S], *pp.* Ailed.
aile[P&S], *n.* Aisle.
aimd[P&S], *pp.* Aimed.
aird[P&S], *pp.* Aired.
ake[P&S], *v.* & *n.* Ache.
ak'ing[S], *n.* Aching.
a-larmd'[P&S], *pp.* Alarmed.
a-lar'umd[S], *a.* Alarumed.
al'ca-liz"a-bl[P], *a.* Alcalizable.
al'co-hol-iz"a-bl[P], **-is"a-bl**[P], *a.* Alcoholizable, alcoholisable.
al'fa[P], *n.* Alpha.
al'fa-bet[P&S], *n.* Alphabet.
al"fa-bet'ic[S], *a.* Alphabetic.
al"fa-bet'i-cal[S], *a.* Alphabetical.
al'fa-bet-ize[S], *vt.* Alphabetize.
al'gra-fy[S], *n.* Algraphy.
a'lien-a-bl[P], *a.* Alienable.
a'liend[S], *pp.* Aliened.
al"i-men'ta-tiv[S], *a.* Alimentative.
al"i-men'ta-tiv-ness[S], *n.* Alimentativeness.
al"i-men'tiv[S], *a.* Alimentive.

al″i-men′tiv-ness[P&S], *n.* Alimentiveness.
al′ka-li-fi″a-bl[P], *a.* Alkalifiable.
al′ka-lin[S], *a.* Alkaline.
al′ka-liz″a-bl[P], **-lis″a-bl**[P], *a.* Alkalizable, -lisable.
al-layd′[P&S], *pp.* Allayed.
al-lege′a-bl[P], *a.* Allegeable.
al-le′vi-a-tiv[S], *a.* & *n.* Alleviative.
al-li′a-bl[P], *a.* Alliable.
al-lit′er-a-tiv[P&S], *a.* Alliterative.
al-lot′ta-bl[P], *a.* Allottable.
al-low′a-bl[P], *a.* Allowable.
al-low′a-bl-ness[P], *n.* Allowableness.
al-lowd′[P&S], *pp.* Allowed.
al-loyd′[P&S], *pp.* Alloyed.
al-lu′siv[P&S], *a.* Allusive.
al-lu′siv-ly[S], *adv.* Allusively.
al-lu′siv-ness[S], *n.* Allusiveness.
al′ly[S], *n.* Alley.
al′man-din[S], *n.* Almandine.
al-red′y[P&S], *adv.* Already.
al′ter-a-bl[P], *a.* Alterable.
al′ter-a-bl-ness[P], *n.* Alterableness.
al′ter-a-tiv[P&S], *a.* & *n.* Alterative.
al′terd[P&S], *pp.* Altered.
al-ter′na-tiv[P&S], *a.* & *n.* Alternative.
al-tho′[P&S], *conj.* Although.
al′u-min[P], *n.* Alumine.
a-mal′ga-ma-bl[P], *a.* Amalgamable.
a-mal′ga-ma-tiv[S], *a.* Amalgamative.
am″a-ran′thin[P&S], *a.* Amaranthine.
a-mass′a-bl[P], *a.* Amassable.
a-mast′[P&S], *pp.* Amassed.
am′a-tiv[P&S], *a.* Amative.
am′a-tiv-ness[S], *n.* Amativeness.
am′bl[P], *v.* & *n.* Amble.
am′bld[P], *pp.* Ambled.
am′bu-la-tiv[S], *a.* Ambulative.
am′busht[P&S], *pp.* Ambushed.
a-me′lio-ra-bl[P], *a.* Ameliorable.
a-me′lio-ra-tiv[S], *a.* Ameliorative.
a-me′na-bl[P], *a.* Amenable.
a-me′na-bl-ness[P], *n.* Amenableness.
a-mend′a-bl[P], *a.* Amendable.
a-mend′a-bl-ness[P], *n.* Amendableness.
a-merce′a-bl[P], **a-mer-ci-a-bl**[P], *a.* Amerceable, amerciable.
a-merst′[S], *pp.* Amerced. [tine.
am″e-thys′tin[P&S], **-ine**[S], *a.* Amethys-
am-fib′i-a[P], *n. pl.* Amphibia.
am-fib′i-an[P], *a.* & *n.* Amphibian.
am-fib′i-ous[P], *a.* Amphibious.
am-fib′i-us[S], *a.* Amphibious.
am′fi-brach[P], *n.* Amphibrach.
am″fi-the′a-ter[P], *n.* Amphitheater.
a′mi-a-bl[P], *a.* Amiable.
a′mi-a-bl-ness[P], *n.* Amiableness.
am′i-ca-bl[P], *a.* Amicable.
am′i-ca-bl-ness[P], *n.* Amicableness.
a-mis′si-bl[P], *a.* Amissible.
am-nic′o-lin[S], *a.* & *n.* Amnicoline.
a-mor′fous[P], *a.* Amorphous.
a-mor′tiz-a-bl[P], **-tis-a-bl**[P], *a.* Amortizable, -tisable. [-ible.
a-mov′a-bl[P], **-i-bl**[P], *a.* Amovable,
am″phi-the′a-ter[S], *n.* Amphitheatre.
am′pl[P], *a.* Ample.
am′pli-a-tiv[S], *a.* Ampliative.
am′pl-ness[P], *n.* Ampleness.
am′pli-fi-ca″tiv[P&S], *a.* Amplificative.
a-mung′[P], *prep.* Among.
a-mungst′[P], *prep.* Amongst.
a-mus′a-bl[P], *a.* Amusable.
a-mu′siv[P&S], *a.* Amusive.
an′a-glyf[P], *n.* Anaglyph.
an′a-log[P&S], *n.* Analogue.
an′a-lyz″a-bl[P], **-lys″a-bl**[P], *a.* Analyzable, -lysable.
an′a-lyz″a-bl-ness[P], **-lys″a-bl-ness**[P], *n.* Analyzableness, -lysableness.
an′a-lyze[P&S], *vt.* Analyse.
an′a-pest[S], *n.* Anapæst.
an′a-tin[S], *a.* Anatine. [-ise.
a-nat′o-mize[P&S], *vt.* & *vi.* Anatomize,
an″chi-the′ri-in[S], *a.* & *n.* Anchitheriine.

an'chor-a-bl[P], *a.* Anchorable.
an'chord[S], *pa.* Anchored.
an'de-sin[S], *n.* Andesine.
a-ne'mi-a[S], *n.* Anæmia.
a-ne'mic[S], *a.* Anæmic.
an"es-the'si-a[S], *n.* Anæsthesia.
an"es-thet'ic[S], *a.* & *n.* Anæsthetic.
an'gerd[P&S], *pp.* Angered.
an'gl[P], *v.* & *n.* Angle.
an'gld[P], *pp.* Angled.
an'guisht[P&S], *pp.* Anguished.
an-hal'o-nin[S], *n.* Anhalonine.
an'i-lin[S], *a.* & *n.* Aniline.
an'i-ma-bl[P], *a.* Animable.
an'i-ma-bl-ness[P], *n.* Animableness.
an"i-mad-ver'siv[S], *a.* Animadversive.
an"i-mad-ver'siv-ness[S], *n.* Animadversiveness.
an"i-mal'cu-lin[S], *a.* Animalculine.
an'i-ma"tiv[S], *a.* Animative.
an'is[P&S], *n.* Anise.
an'ker[P], *v.* & *n.* Anchor.
an'ker-age[P], *n.* Anchorage.
an'kerd[P], *pp.* Anchored.
an'kl[P], *n.* Ankle.
an'na-lin[S], *n.* Annaline.
an-neald'[P&S], *pp.* Annealed.
an-nex'a-bl[P], *a.* Annexable.
an-nex'iv[S], *a.* Annexive.
an-next'[P&S], *pp.* Annexed.
an-ni'hi-la-bl[P], *a.* Annihilable.
an-ni'hi-la-tiv[S], *a.* Annihilative.
an'no-ta"tiv[S], *a.* Annotative.
an'no-tin[S], *a.* & *n.* Annotine.
an-nounst'[S], *pp.* Announced.
an-noyd'[P&S], *pp.* Annoyed.
an-nuld'[P&S], *pp.* Annulled.
an-nul'la-bl[P], *a.* Annullable.
an-nun'ci-a-bl[P], *a.* Annunciable.
an-nun'ci-a-tiv[S], *a.* Annunciative.
a-nom'a-lus[S], *a.* Anomalous.
an'ser-in[S], *a.* Anserine.
an'swer-a-bl[P], *a.* Answerable.
an'swer-a-bl-ness[P], *n.* Answerableness.
an'swerd[P&S], *pp.* Answered.
an'themd[S], *pp.* Anthemed.
an"thro-pof'a-gy[P&S], *n.* Anthropophagy.
an-tic'i-pa-ta-bl[P], *a.* Anticipatable.
an-tic'i-pa-tiv[P&S], *a.* Anticipative.
an"ti-cor-ro'siv[S], *a.* & *n.* Anticorrosive.
an"ti-fer-men'ta-tiv[S], *a.* & *n.* Antifermentative.
an-tif'o-ny[P], *n.* Antiphony.
an-tif'ra-sis[P], *n.* Antiphrasis.
an"ti-pu"tre-fac'tiv[S], *a.* Antiputrefactive.
an"ti-py'rin[S], *n.* Antipyrine.
an-tis'tro-fe[P], *n.* Antistrophe.
an"ti-tox'in[S], *n.* Antitoxine.
an"ti-tus'siv[S], *a.* & *n.* Antitussive.
ant'lerd[S], *a.* Antlered.
an'vild[S], *pp.* Anviled.
a-per'i-tiv[S], *a.* & *n.* Aperitive.
ap'l[P], *n.* Apple.
a-poc'a-lyps[P], *n.* Apocalypse.
a-poc'ry-fa[P], *n.* Apocrypha.
a-poc'ry-fal[P], *a.* Apocryphal.
ap'o-graf[P], *n.* Apograph.
ap'o-log[P], *n.* Apologue.
a-pos'tl[P], *n.* Apostle.
a-pos'tro-fe[P], *n.* Apostrophe.
a-pos'tro-fize[P], *vt.* & *vi.* Apostrophize.
ap'o-them[S], *n.* Apothegm.
ap-pald'[P&S], *pp.* Appalled.
ap-par'eld[P&S], *pp.* Appareled, -elled.
ap-peal'a-bl[P], *a.* Appealable.
ap-peald'[P&S], *pp.* Appealed.
ap-peard'[P&S], *pp.* Appeared.
ap-peas'a-bl[P], *a.* Appeasable.
ap-peas'iv[S], *a.* Appeasive.
ap-pel'la-bl[P], *a.* Appellable.
ap-pel'la-tiv[P&S], *a.* & *n.* Appellative.
ap-pel'la-tiv-ly[S], *adv.* Appellatively.
ap-pel'la-tiv-ness[S], *n.* Appellativeness.

ap″per-cep′tiv[S], *a.* Apperceptive.
ap″per-taind′[P&S], *pp.* Appertained.
ap′pe-ti-bl[P], *a.* Appetible.
ap′pe-ti-bl-ness[S], *n.* Appetibleness.
ap′pe-ti″tiv[S], *a.* Appetitive.
ap-plaus′iv[S], *a.* Applausive.
ap-plaus′iv-ly[S], *adv.* Applausively.
ap′pli-ca-bl[P], *a.* Applicable.
ap′pli-ca-bl-ness[P], *n.* Applicableness.
ap′pli-ca-tiv[P&S], *a.* Applicative.
ap′pli-ca-tiv-ly[S], *adv.* Applicatively.
ap-plo′siv[S], *a.* Applosive.
ap-point′a-bl[P], *a.* Appointable.
ap-poin′tiv[P&S], *a.* Appointive.
ap-por′tion-a-bl[P], *a.* Apportionable.
ap-por′tiond[P&S], *pp.* Apportioned.
ap-pos′a-bl[P], *a.* Apposable.
ap′pos-it[S], *a.* Apposite.
ap-pos′i-tiv[S], *a.* & *n.* Appositive.
ap-prais′a-bl[P], *a.* Appraisable.
ap-pre′ci-a-bl[P], *a.* Appreciable.
ap-pre′ci-a-tiv[P&S], *a.* Appreciative.
ap-pre′ci-a-tiv-ly[S], *adv.* Apprecia-tively.
ap-pre′ci-a-tiv-ness[S], *n.* Apprecia-tiveness.
ap″pre-hen′si-bl[P], *a.* Apprehensible.
ap″pre-hen′siv[P&S], *a.* Apprehensive.
ap-pren′tis[S], *v.* & *n.* Apprentice.
ap-pren′tist[S], *pp.* Apprenticed.
ap-prest′[S], *a.* Appressed.
ap-prize′[S], *vt.* Apprise.
ap-proach′a-bl[P], *a.* Approachable.
ap-proacht′[P&S], *pp.* Approached.
ap′pro-ba″tiv[S], *a.* Approbative.
ap′pro-ba″tiv-ness[S], *n.* Approbative-ness.
ap-pro′pri-a-bl[P], *a.* Appropriable.
ap-pro′pri-a-tiv[S], *a.* Appropriative.
ap-pro′pri-a-tiv-ness[S], *n.* Appro-priativeness.
ap-prov′a-bl[P], *a.* Approvable.
ap-prov′a-bl-ness[P], *n.* Approvable-ness.
ap-prox′i-ma-tiv[P&S], *a.* Approxima-tive.

ap-pul′siv[S], *a.* Appulsive.
ap-pul′siv-ly[S], *adv.* Appulsively.
a′prond[S], *pp.* Aproned.
a-quat′iv-ness[S], *n.* Aquativeness.
aq′ui-lin, -line[P&S], *a.* Aquiline.
ar[P], *v.* Are.
ar′a-bl[P], *a.* Arable.
ar′a-bl-ness[P], *n.* Arableness.
ar′bi-tra-bl[P], *a.* Arbitrable.
ar′bi-tra″tiv[S], *a.* Arbitrative.
ar′bor[P&S], *n.* Arbour.
ar′bord[S], *a.* Arbored.
ar-ca′ic[S], *a.* Archaic.
arc-an′gel[S], *n.* Archangel.
ar″che-ol′o-gy[S], *n.* Archæology.
ar′chi-tec-tiv[S], *a.* Architective.
archt[P&S], *pa.* Arched.
ar′dor[P&S], *n.* Ardour.
ar′e-tin[S], *a.* Aretine.
ar′gen-tin, *a.* Argentine.
ar-gu′i-tiv[S], *a.* Arguitive.
ar″gu-men′ta-tiv[P&S], *a.* Argumenta-tive.
ar″gu-men′ta-tiv-ly[S], *adv.* Argu-mentatively.
ar″gu-men′ta-tiv-ness[S], *n.* Argu-mentativeness.
a-rize′[P], *vi.* Arise.
a-riz′n[P], *pp.* Arisen.
armd[S], *pa.* Armed.
ar′mi-stis[S], *n.* Armistice.
ar′mor[P&S], *v.* & *n.* Armour.
ar′mord[P&S], *pa.* Armored, armoured.
a-roze′[P], *v.* Arose.
ar-raignd′[P&S], *pp.* Arraigned.
ar-range′a-bl[P], *a.* Arrangeable.
ar-rayd′[P&S], *pp.* Arrayed.
ar-rest′a-bl[P], *a.* Arrestable.
ar-res′tiv[S], *a.* Arrestive.
ar′ro-ga-tiv[S], *a.* Arrogative.
ar′ti-cl[P], *v.* & *n.* Article.
ar-tic′u-la-bl[P], *a.* Articulable.
ar-tic′u-la-tiv[S], *a.* Articulative.
ar′ti-fis[S], *n.* Artifice.

ar'ti-zan[P&S], *n.* Artisan.
as-bes'tin[P], *a.* Asbestine.
as-cend'a-bl[P], *a.* Ascendable.
as-cen'siv[S], *a.* Ascensive.
as"cer-tain'a-bl[P], *a.* Ascertainable.
as"cer-tain'a-bl-ness[P], *n.* Ascertainableness.
as"cer-taind'[P&S], *pp.* Ascertained.
as-cri'ba-bl[P], *a.* Ascribable.
as'falt[P&S], *v.* & *n.* Asphalt.
as-fyx'i-a[P], *n.* Asphyxia.
as-fyx'i-a-tiv[S], *a.* Asphyxiative.
askt[S], *pp.* Asked.
as-per'siv[S], *a.* Aspersive.
as-per'siv-ly[S], *adv.* Aspersively.
as-perst'[S], *pp.* Aspersed.
as-sail'a-bl[P], *a.* Assailable.
as-sail'a-bl-ness[P], *n.* Assailableness.
as-saild'[S], *pp.* Assailed.
as-sas'sin-a-tiv[S], *a.* Assassinative.
as-sault'a-bl[P], *a.* Assaultable.
as-say'a-bl[P], *a.* Assayable.
as-sayd'[P&S], *pp.* Assayed.
as-sem'bl[S], *v.* & *n.* Assemble.
as-sem'bld[P], *pp.* Assembled.
as-sen'tiv[S], *a.* Assentive.
as-sen'tiv-ness[S], *n.* Assentiveness.
as-sert'a-bl[P], **as-sert'i-bl**[P], *a.* Assertable, -ible.
as-ser'tiv[P&S], *a.* Assertive.
as-ser'tiv-ly[S], *adv.* Assertively.
as-ser'tiv-ness[S], *n.* Assertiveness.
as-sess'a-bl[P], *a.* Assessable.
as-sest'[P&S], *pp.* Assessed.
as-sev'er-a-tiv[S], *a.* Asseverative.
as-sign'a-bl[P], *a.* Assignable.
as-signd'[P&S], *pp.* Assigned.
as-sim'i-la-bl[P], *a.* Assimilable.
as-sim'i-la-tiv[P&S], *a.* Assimilative.
as-size'[S], *n.* Assize.
as-so'ci-a-bl[P], *a.* Associable.
as-so'ci-a-tiv[P&S], *a.* Associative.
as-so'ci-a-tiv-ly[S], *adv.* Associatively.
as-so'ci-a-tiv-ness[S], *n.* Associativeness.
as-sort'a-tiv[S], *a.* Assortative.
as-sor'tiv[S], *a.* Assortive.
as-sua'siv[S], *a.* Assuasive.
as-sum'a-bl[P], *a.* Assumable.
as-sump'tiv[P&S], *a.* Assumptive.
as-sump'tiv-ly[S], *adv.* Assumptively.
as-sur'a-bl[P], *a.* Assurable.
as'ter-iskt[S], *pp.* Asterisked.
as-ton'ish-a-bl[P], *a.* Astonishable.
a-ston'isht[P&S], *pp.* Astonished.
as-tric'tiv[S], *a.* & *n.* Astrictive.
as-tric'tiv-ness[S], *n.* Astrictiveness.
at'mos-fere[P], *n.* Atmosphere.
at"mos-fer'ic[P&S], *a.* Atmospheric.
a-to'na-bl[P], **a-tone'a-bl**[P], *a.* Atonable, atoneable.
at'ro-fy[P], *v.* & *n.* Atrophy.
at-tach'a-bl[P], *a.* Attachable.
at-tacht'[P&S], *pp.* Attached.
at-tack'a-bl[P], *a.* Attackable.
at-tackt'[P&S], *pp.* Attacked.
at-tain'a-bl[P], *a.* Attainable.
at-tain'a-bl-ness[P], *n.* Attainableness.
at-taind'[P&S], *pp.* Attained.
at-tem'perd[P&S], *pp.* Attempered.
at-tempt'a-bl[P], *a.* Attemptable.
at-tempt'iv[S], *a.* Attemptive.
at-ten'tiv[P&S], *a.* Attentive.
at-test'a-bl[P], *a.* Attestable.
at-test'a-tiv[S], *a.* Attestative.
at-tes'tiv[S], *a.* Attestive.
at-tor'ny[S], *n.* Attorney.
at-tract'a-bl[P], *a.* Attractable.
at-tract'a-bl-ness[P], *n.* Attractableness.
at-trac'tiv[P&S], *a.* Attractive.
at-trac'tiv-ly[S], *adv.* Attractively.
at-trac'tiv-ness[P], *n.* Attractiveness.
at-trib'u-ta-bl[P], *a.* Attributable.
at-trib'u-tiv[P&S], *a.* & *n.* Attributive.
at-trib'u-tiv-ly[S], *adv.* Attributively.
at-trib'u-tiv-ness[S], *n.* Attributiveness.
auc'tiond[S], *pp.* Auctioned.

au'di-bl[F], *a.* Audible.
au'di-tiv[S], *a.* Auditive.
au'gerd[S], *pp.* Augered.
aug-ment'a-bl[F], *a.* Augmentable.
aug-men'ta-tiv[F&S], *v.* & *n.* Augmentative.
aug-men'ta-tiv-ly[S], *adv.* Augmentatively.
aug-men'tiv[S], *a.* Augmentive.
au'gurd[S], *pp.* Augured.
au'ri-cl[F], *n.* Auricle.
au-rif'er-us[S], *a.* Auriferous.
aus-cul'ta-tiv[S], *a.* Auscultative.
aus'pis[S], *n.* Auspice.
aut[S], *n.* Aught.
au-thor'i-ta"tiv[F&S], *a.* Authoritative.
au'thor-iz"a-bl[F], **au'thor-is"a-bl**[F], *a.* Authorizable, -isable.
au"to-bi-og'ra-fer[F], *n.* Autobiographer.
au"to-bi-og'ra-fy[F], *n.* Autobiography.
au'to-graf[F&S], *v.*, *a.*, & *n.* Autograph.
au'to-graft[S], *pp.* Autographed.
au"to-mo'tiv[S], *a.* Automotive.
au"to-sug-ges'tiv[S], *a.* Autosuggestive.
au'tum[S], *n.* Autumn.
a-vail'a-bl[F], *a.* Available.
a-vail'a-bl-ness[F], *n.* Availableness.
a-vaild'[F&S], *pp.* Availed.
av'a-lanch[F], *n.* Avalanche.
av'a-ris[S], *n.* Avarice.
a-verd'[F&S], *pp.* Averred.
a-ver'ra-bl[F], *a.* Averrable.
a-ver'siv[S], *a.* Aversive.
a-vert'i-bl[F], *a.* Avertible.
a-voc'a-tiv[S], *a.* & *n.* Avocative.
a-void'a-bl[F], *a.* Avoidable.
a-vouch'a-bl[F], *a.* Avouchable.
a-voucht'[F&S], *pp.* Avouched.
a-vow'a-bl[F], *a.* Avowable.
a-vow'a-bl-ness[F], *n.* Avowableness.
a-vowd'[F&S], *pa.* Avowed.
a-vul'siv[S], *a.* Avulsive.
aw[F], *v.* & *n.* Awe.
a-wak'a-bl[F], *a.* Awakable.
a-wak'en-a-bl[F], *a.* Awakenable.
a-wak'end[F&S], *pp.* Awakened.
a-ward'a-bl[F], *a.* Awardable.
awd[F&S], *pp.* Awed.
awnd[S], *a.* Awned.
awn'ingd[S], *a.* Awninged.
aw'sum[F], *a.* Awsome; awesome
ax[F&S], *v.* & *n.* Axe.
ax'il[S], *a.* Axile.
ax'l[F], *n.* Axle.
axt[F], *pp.* Axed.
ay[F], *adv.* Aye.
az'u-rin[S], *n.* Azurine.

B

bab'l[F], *v.* & *n.* Babble.
bab'ld[F], *pp.* Babbled.
bach[F], *v.* & *n.* Batch.
back'slidn[F], *pp.* Backslidden.
backt[F&S], *a.* Backed.
bad[F&S], *v.* Bade.
badg'erd[S], *pp.* Badgered.
baf'l[F], *v.* & *n.* Baffle.
baf'ld[F], *pp.* Baffled.
bag"a-tel'[F], *n.* Bagatelle.
bagd[S], *a.* Bagged.
bail'a-bl[F], *a.* Bailable.
baild[F&S], *pp.* Bailed.
bai'li-wic[S], *n.* Bailiwick.
baiz[F], *v.* & *n.* Baize.
bal'anst[S], *pp.* Balanced.
bald[S], *pp.* Balled.
ba'lif[F&S], *n.* Bailiff.
balkt[F&S], *pp.* Balked.
balld[F], *pp.* Balled.
bal-loond'[S], *pp.* Ballooned.
balmd[S], *pp.* Balmed.
bal'us-terd[S], *a.* Balustered.
band[S], *pp.* Banned.

bangd[p&s], *pp.* Banged.
ban′gl[p], *v.* & *n.* Bangle.
ban′gld[p], *a.* Bangled.
ban′isht[p&s], *pp.* Banished.
bank′a-bl[p], *a.* Bankable.
bankt[p&s], *a.* Banked.
ban′nerd[s], *pp.* Bannered.
ban′noc[s], *n.* Bannock.
bans[s], *n. pl.* Banns.
bant′erd[p&s], *pp.* Bantered.
barbd[p&s], *pa.* Barbed.
bard[s], *pp.* Barred.
bare′hed″ed[p], *a.* Bareheaded.
bar′gaind[p&s], *pp.* Bargained.
bark[s], *n.* Barque.
barkt[s], *pa.* Barked.
bar′ly[s], *n.* Barley.
bar′na-cl[p], *v.* & *n.* Barnacle.
bar′rac[s], *n.* Barrack.
bar′reld[p&s], *pa.* Barreled, -elled.
bar′ri-erd[s], *pp.* Barriered.
bar′rowd[s], *pp.* Barrowed.
bar′terd[p&s], *pp.* Bartered.
bas[s], *a.* Bass.
bas[s], *n.* Bass.
baskt[p&s], *pp.* Basked.
bas′tiond[s], *pp.* Bastioned.
bat′ond[s], *a.* Batoned.
bat′tend[s], *pp.* Battened.
bat′terd[p&s], *pp.* Battered.
bat′tl[p], *v.* & *n.* Battle.
bat′tld[p], *pp.* Battled.
bau′bl[p], *n.* Bauble.
bawld[p&s], *pp.* Bawled.
bayd[s], *pp.* Bayed.
bay′o-net″ed[p], *pp.* Bayonetted.
beacht[s], *a.* Beached.
bea′cond[s], *pp.* Beaconed.
bea′dl[p], *n.* Beadle.
bea′gl[p], *n.* Beagle.
beakt[p&s], *a.* Beaked.
beamd[p&s], *pp.* Beamed.
bear′a-bl[p], *a.* Bearable.
beat′a-bl[p], *a.* Beatable.
beat′n[p], *pa.* Beaten.
bea′verd[s], *a.* Beavered.
be-calmd′[p&s], *pp.* Becalmed.
beck′ond[p&s], *pp.* Beckoned.
be-cum′[p], *vt.* & *vi.* Become.
be-cum′ing[p], *pa.* Becoming.
be-dab′l[p], *vt.* Bedabble.
be-dab′ld[p], *pa.* Bedabbled.
be-deckt′[p&s], *pp.* Bedecked.
be-dev′ild[p], *pp.* Bedeviled, -illed.
be-dewd′[p&s], *pp.* Bedewed.
be-dimd′[p&s], *pp.* Bedimmed.
be-diz′end[s], *pp.* Bedizened.
be-drag′l[p], *vt.* Bedraggle.
be-drag′ld[p], *pp.* Bedraggled.
be-drencht′[p&s], *pp.* Bedrenched.
bed′rid″n[p&s], *a.* Bedridden.
be-dropt′[p&s], *pp.* Bedropped.
bed′sted[p&s], *n.* Bedstead.
bee′tl[p], *v.*, *a* & *n.* Beetle.
beevs[p], *n. pl.* Beeves.
be-faln′[p], *pp.* Befallen.
be-fel′[p], *vt.* & *vi.* Befell.
be-fogd′[s], *pp.* Befogged.
be-foold′[p&s], *pp.* Befooled.
be-fould′[p&s], *pp.* Befouled.
be-frend′[p], *vt.* Befriend.
begd[p&s], *pp.* Begged.
beg′gard[s], *pp.* Beggared.
be-gon′[p], *interj.* Begone.
be-got′n[p], *pp.* Begotten.
be-ha′vior[p&s], *n.* Behaviour.
be-hed′[p&s], *vt.* Behead.
bel[p&s], *v.* & *n.* Bell.
be-la′bor[p&s], *vt.* Belabour.
be-la′bord[p&s], *pp.* Belabored; belaboured.
be-layd′[p&s], *pp.* Belayed.
belcht[p&s], *pp.* Belched.
beld[p&s], *a.* Belled.
bel′dam[p], *n.* Beldame.
be-lea′ger[p], *vt.* Beleaguer.
be-lea′gerd[p&s], *pp.* Beleaguered.
be-liev′[p], *vt.* & *vi.* Believe.

be-liev'a-bl[P], *a.* Believable.
be-lievd'[P&S], *pp.* Believed.
be-lit'l[P], *vt.* Belittle.
be-lit'ld[P], *pp.* Belittled.
bel'lo[S], *v. & n.* Bellow.
bel'loed[S], *pp.* Bellowed.
bel'loes[S], *n. sing. & pl.* Bellows.
bel'lowd[S], *pp.* Bellowed.
be-lo'[S], *adv.* Below.
be-longd'[P&S], *pp.* Belonged.
be-luv'[P], *vt.* Belove.
be-luvd'[P], *pp.* Beloved.
be-luv'ed[P], *a.* Beloved.
be-moand'[P&S], *pp.* Bemoaned.
be-mockt'[P&S], *pp.* Bemocked.
bencht[S], *pp.* Benched.
ben'e-fis[S], *n.* Benefice.
ben'e-fist[S], *pp.* Beneficed.
be-num'[P&S], *vt.* Benumb.
be-numd'[P&S], *pp.* Benumbed.
be-queathd'[P&S], *pp.* Bequeathed.
be-reav'[P], *vt.* Bereave.
be-reavd'[P&S], *pp.* Bereaved.
be-rib'bond[S], *pp.* Beribboned.
be-rime'[P], *vt.* Berhyme.
bertht[S], *pp.* Berthed.
be-seemd'[P&S], *pp.* Beseemed.
be-smeard'[P&S], *pp.* Besmeared.
be-span'gl[P], *vt.* Bespangle.
be-span'gld[P], *pp.* Bespangled.
be-spat'terd[P&S], *pp.* Bespattered.
be-spred'[P&S], *vt.* Bespread.
be-sprin'kl[P], *vt.* Besprinkle.
be-sprin'kld[P], *pp.* Besprinkled.
be-sted'[S], *vt.* Bestead.
be-stird'[P&S], *pp.* Bestirred.
be-sto'[S], *v.* Bestow.
be-stowd'[P&S], *pp.* Bestowed.
be-strad'l[P], *vt.* Bestraddle.
be-strad'ld[P], *pp.* Bestraddled.
be-strewd'[S], *pp.* Bestrewed.
be-to'kend[S], *pp.* Betokened.
be-trayd'[S], *pp.* Betrayed.
be-trotht'[P&S], *pa.* Betrothed.
bet'terd[P&S], *pp.* Bettered.
beu'te-ous[P], *a.* Beauteous.
beu'ti-ful[P], *a.* Beautiful.
beu'ti-fy[P], *vt. & vi.* Beautify.
beu'ty[P], *n.* Beauty.
bev'eld[P&S], *pa.* Beveled; bevelled.
bev'el-ing[P], *n.* Bevelling.
be-waild'[P&S], *pp.* Bewailed.
be-wich'[P], *vt.* Bewitch.
be-wil'derd[P&S], *pp.* Bewildered.
be-witcht'[P&S], *pp.* Bewitched.
be-wrayd'[P], *pp.* Bewrayed.
bi'ast[P&S], *pp.* Biased; biassed.
bibd[S], *pp.* Bibbed.
bib"li-og'ra-fer[P&S], *n.* Bibliographer.
bib"li-o-graf'ic[S], *a.* Bibliographic.
bib"li-og'ra-fy[P&S], *n.* Bibliography.
bi-cef'a-lous[P], *a.* Bicephalous.
bick'erd[P&S], *pp.* Bickered.
bi"cul'ord[P], *a.* Bicolored; bicoloured.
bid'da-bl[P], *a.* Biddable.
bid'da-bl-ness[P], *n.* Biddableness.
bil[P&S], *v. & n.* Bill.
bild[S], *vt. & vi.* Build.
bild[P&S], *a.* Billed.
bild'er[S], *n.* Builder.
bild'ing[S], *n.* Building.
bil'ius[S], *a.* Bilious.
bilkt[P&S], *pp.* Bilked.
bil'lo[S], *v. & n.* Billow.
bil'lowd[S], *pp.* Billowed.
bilt[S], *pa.* Built.
bin'na-cl[P], *n.* Binnacle.
bin'o-cl[P], *n.* Binocle.
bi-og'ra-fer[P&S], *n.* Biographer.
bi"o-graf'ic[S], *a.* Biographic.
bi"o-graf'i-cal[S], *a.* Biographical.
bi-og'ra-fy[P&S], *n.* Biography.
bi-part'i-bl[P], *a.* Bipartible.
bircht[S], *pp.* Birched.
bis-sex'til[P&S], **-tile**[S], *a. & n.* Bissextile.
bis'ter[P&S], *n.* Bister; bistre.
bit'n[P], *pp.* Bitten.
bi-tu'mi-nus[S], *a.* Bituminous.

bit'terd[S], *pp.* Bittered.
bi'valv[P&S], *a.* & *n.* Bivalve.
bi'valvd[S], *a.* Bivalved.
blabd[P&S], *pp.* Blabbed.
black'balld''[P], *pp.* Blackballed.
black'end[P&S], *pp.* Blackened.
black'-eyd''[P&S], *a.* Black-eyed.
black'gard[P&S], *v., a.* & *n.* Blackguard.
black''led'[P&S], *vt.* Blacklead.
black'maild''[P&S], *pp.* Blackmailed.
blackt[P&S], *pp.* Blacked.
blam'a-bl[P], *a.* Blamable.
blam'a-bl-ness[P], *n.* Blamableness.
blame'wur''thy[P], *a.* Blameworthy.
blancht[P&S], *pp.* Blanched.
blan'disht[P&S], *pp.* Blandished.
blankt[S], *pp.* Blanked.
blas-feme'[P&S], *vt.* & *vi.* Blaspheme.
blas'fe-mous[P], *a.* Blasphemous.
blas'fe-my[P], *n.* Blasphemy.
bla'zond[S], *pp.* Blazoned.
bleacht[P&S], *pp.* Bleached.
bleard[P&S], *pp.* Bleared.
blem'isht[P&S], *a.* Blemished.
blencht[P&S], *pp.* Blenched.
blend[P], *n.* Blende.
bles[S], *v.* Bless.
bless'ed[P], **blest**[P&S], *a.* Blessed; blest.
blind'wurm''[P], *n.* blindworm.
blinkt[P&S], *pp.* Blinked.
blis[S], *n.* Bliss.
blis'terd[P&S], *pp.* Blistered.
blithe'sum[P&S], *a.* Blithesome.
blo[S], *v.* & *n.* Blow.
blobd[S], *pp.* Blobbed.
bloch[P], *v.* & *n.* Blotch.
blocht[P&S], *pp.* Blotched.
block'hed''[P&S], *n.* Blockhead.
blockt[P&S], *pp.* Blocked.
bloes[S], *v.* & *n.* Blows.
blond[P], *a.* & *n.* Blonde.
bloomd[P&S], *pp.* Bloomed.
blos'somd[P&S], *pp.* Blossomed.
blotcht[S], *pp.* Blotched.
blu[S], *v.* & *a.* Blue.
blu[S], *imp.* Blew.
blub'berd[P&S], *pa.* Blubbered.
blubd[S], *pp.* Blubbed.
bludg'eond[S], *a.* Bludgeoned.
blue'-eyd''[P], *a.* Blue-eyed.
bluf[P&S], *v., a.* & *n.* Bluff.
bluf'a-bl[P], *a.* Bluffable.
bluft[P&S], *pp.* Bluffed.
blun'derd[P&S], *pp.* Blundered.
blun'der-hed''[P], *n.* Blunderhead.
blurd[P&S], *pp* Blurred.
blusht[P&S], *pp.* Blushed.
blus'terd[P&S], *pp.* Blustered.
bo[S], *v.* & *n.* Bow.
boat'a-bl[P], *a.* Boatable.
bob'bind[S], *pp.* Bobbined.
bobd[P&S], *pp.* Bobbed.
bob'taild''[P&S], *a.* Bobtailed.
boch[P], *v.* & *n.* Botch.
bocht[P], *pp.* Botched.
bod'is[S], *n.* Bodice.
bod'ist[S], *a.* Bodiced.
bod'y-gard''[P], *n.* Body-guard.
bogd[S], *pp.* Bogged.
bog'l[P], *vt.* & *vi.* Boggle.
bog'ld[P], *pp.* Boggled.
boild[P&S], *pp.* Boiled.
bold'end[S], *pp.* Boldened.
bol'sterd[S], *pp.* Bolstered.
bolt'hed''[P], *n.* Bolthead.
bom[P], *v.* & *n.* Bomb.
bom''ba-zine'[P], *n.* Bombasine.
bom'shel''[P], *n.* Bombshell.
bookt[P&S], *pp.* Booked.
book'wurm''[P], *n.* Bookworm.
boomd[P&S], *pp.* Boomed.
booz[P], *v.* & *n.* Booze; boose.
boozd[S], *pp.* Boozed.
booz'y[P], *a.* Boosy.
bor'a-bl[P], *a.* Borable.
bor'derd[P&S], *pp.* Bordered.
bor'o[S], *n.* Borough.
bor'rowd[P&S], *pp.* Borrowed.

bos[S], *v.* & *n.* Boss.
bo'somd[S], *pp.* Bosomed.
bost[P&S], *pp.* Bossed.
botcht[S], *pp.* Botched.
both'erd[P&S], *pp.* Bothered.
bot'l[P], *v.* & *n.* Bottle.
bot'ld[P], *pp.* Bottled.
bots[P], *n. pl.* Botts.
bot'tomd[S], *a.* Bottomed.
boul'derd[S], *pp.* Bouldered.
bounce'a-bl[P], Bounceable.
bounst[S], *pp.* Bounced.
boun'ti-a-bl[P], *a.* Bountiable.
bowd[P&S], *a.* Bowed.
bow'eld[S], *a.* Boweled.
bow'erd[S], *a.* Bowered.
bowld[S], *pp.* Bowled.
bow'lin[P], *n.* Bowline.
box'hauld''[P&S], *a.* Boxhauled.
boxt[P&S], *a.* Boxed.
bra-chyg'ra-fy[P], *n.* Brachygraphy.
bragd[P&S], *pp.* Bragged.
braild[S], *pp.* Brailed.
braind[P&S], *a.* Brained.
braizd[S], *pp.* Braized.
bram'bl[P], *v.* & *n.* Bramble.
bram'bld[P], *a.* Brambled.
brancht[P&S], *pp.* Branched.
bran'disht[S], *pp.* Brandished.
bran'gl[P], *v.* & *n.* Brangle.
bran'gld[P], *pp.* Brangled.
bras[S], *n.* Brass.
brast[S], *pp.* Brassed.
brat'tis[S], *v.* & *n.* Brattice.
brawld[P&S], *pp.* Brawled.
brawnd[S], *a.* Brawned.
brayd[P&S], *pp.* Brayed.
bra'zen[S], *v.* & *a.* Brazen.
bra'zend[S], *pp.* Brazened.
bra'zier[S], *n.* Brazier, brasier.
breacht[P&S], *pp.* Breached.
break'a-bl[P], *a.* Breakable.
break'a-bl-ness[P], *n.* Breakableness.
breamd[S], *pp.* Breamed.
breath'a-bl[P], *a.* Breathable.
breath'a-bl-ness[P], *n.* Breathableness.
breathd[P&S], *pp.* Breathed.
bred[P&S], *v.* & *n.* Bread.
bredth[P&S], *n.* Breadth.
breecht[P&S], *pp.* Breeched.
breez[P], *n.* Breeze.
breezd[S], *pp.* Breezed.
brek'fast[P&S], *v.* & *n.* Breakfast.
brest[P&S], *v.* & *n.* Breast.
breth[P&S], *n.* Breath.
brewd[P&S], *pp.* Brewed.
brickt[P&S], *pp.* Bricked.
bride'wel[P], *n.* Bridewell.
brieft[P&S], *pp.* Briefed.
bright'end[P&S], *pp.* Brightened.
brimd[P&S], *pp.* Brimmed.
brin'dl[P], *n.* Brindle.
brin'dld[P], *a.* Brindled.
briskt[S], *pp.* Brisked.
bris'tld[P], *a.* Bristled.
brit'l[P], *a.* Brittle.
broacht[P&S], *pp.* Broached.
broad'end[P&S], *pp.* Broadened.
broi'derd[P&S], *pp.* Broidered.
broild[P&S], *pp.* Broiled.
bro'min[P], *n.* Bromine.
bronz[P], *v.* & *n.* Bronze.
bronzd[P&S], *pp.* Bronzed.
brookt[S], *pp.* Brooked.
broomd[S], *pp.* Broomed.
browd[S], *pp.* Browed.
brownd[P&S], *pp.* Browned.
browz[P], *v.* Browse, browze.
browzd[S], *pp.* Browsed, browzed.
bru[S], *v.* & *n.* Brew.
brusht[P&S], *pp.* Brushed.
bub'l[P], *v.* & *n.* Bubble.
bub'ld[P], *pp.* Bubbled.
buck'l[P], *v.* & *n.* Buckle.
buck'ld[P], *pp.* Buckled.
buck'lerd[S], *a.* Bucklered.
buckt[P&S], *a.* Bucked.

buf$^{P\&S}$, *v., a. & n.* Buff
buft^{S}, *a.* Buffed.
bul$^{P\&S}$, *v. & n.* Bull.
bulbd$^{P\&S}$, *pp.* Bulbed.
bul'hed''^{P}, *n.* Bullhead.
bulk'hed''$^{P\&S}$, *n.* Bulkhead.
bulkt^{S}, *pp.* Bulked.
bul'loc^{S}, *n.* Bullock.
bum'bl^{P}, *v. & n.* Bumble.
bum'bld^{P}, *pp.* Bumbled.
bumd^{S}, *pp.* Bummed.
bumpt$^{P\&S}$, *pp.* Bumped.
bun^{S}, *n.* Bun: formerly spelled *bunn*.
buncht$^{P\&S}$, *pp.* Bunched.
bun'dl^{P}, *v. & n.* Bundle.
bun'dld^{P}, *pp.* Bundled.
bungd^{S}, *pp.* Bunged.
bun'gl^{P}, *v. & n.* Bungle.
bun'gld^{P}, *pp.* Bungled.
bunkt^{S}, *pp.* Bunked.
buoyd^{S}, *pp.* Buoyed.
bur$^{P\&S}$, *n.* Burr.
burd^{S}, *pp.* Burred.
bur'den-a-bl^{P}, *a.* Burdenable.
bur'dend$^{P\&S}$, *pp.* Burdened.
bur'den-sum$^{P\&S}$, *a.* Burdensome.
burg^{P}, *n.* Burgh.
bur'geond^{S}, *pp.* Burgeoned.
bur'i-a-bl^{P}, *a.* Buriable.
burk^{P}, *vt.* Burke.
burkt$^{P\&S}$, *pp.* Burked.
bur'lapt^{S}, *pp.* Burlapped.
burld$^{P\&S}$, *pp.* Burled.
burnd, burnt^{S}, *pp.* Burned.
bur'nisht$^{P\&S}$, *pp.* Burnished.
bur'rowd$^{P\&S}$, *pp.* Burrowed.
bur'thend$^{P\&S}$, *pp.* Burthened.
bus^{S}, *n.* Buss.
busht$^{P\&S}$, *pp.* Bushed.
bus'kind$^{P\&S}$, *a.* Buskined.
buskt^{S}, *a.* Busked.
bust$^{P\&S}$, *pp.* Bussed.
bus'tl^{P}, *v. & n.* Bustle.
bus'tld^{P}, *pp.* Bustled.
but^{P}, *v. & n.* Butt.
butch'erd^{S}, *pp.* Butchered.
but'-end''^{P}, *n.* Butt-end.
but'terd$^{P\&S}$, *pp.* Buttered.
but'tond$^{P\&S}$, *a.* Buttoned.
but'trest$^{P\&S}$, *pa.* Buttressed.
bux'um^{P}, *a.* Buxom.
buz$^{P\&S}$, *v. & n.* Buzz.
buzd$^{P\&S}$, *pp.* Buzzed.
by^{P}, *n.* Bye.
by'gon''^{P}, *a. & n.* Bygone.

C

ca-bald'$^{P\&S}$, *pp.* Caballed.
cab'ind$^{P\&S}$, *pa.* Cabined.
ca'bld^{S}, *pp.* Cabled.
cach^{P}, *v. & n.* Catch.
cack'l^{P}, *v. & n.* Cackle.
cack'ld^{P}, *pp.* Cackled.
ca-cof'o-ny^{P}, *n.* Cacophony.
ca-cog'ra-fy^{P}, *n.* Cacography.
cai'tif$^{P\&S}$, *a. & n.* Caitiff.
cal''a-mog'ra-fer^{P}, *n.* Calamographer.
cal'cu-la-bl^{P}, *a.* Calculable.
cal'cu-la-tiv^{S}, *a.* Calculative.
cald^{S}, *pp.* Called.
cal'en-dard^{S}, *pp.* Calendared.
cal'en-derd$^{P\&S}$, *pp.* Calendered.
cal'i-ber$^{P\&S}$, *n.* Calibre.
cal'i-berd^{S}, *a.* Calibered.
ca'lif$^{P\&S}$, **ka'lif**^{P}, *n.* Caliph, kaliph.
ca-lig'ra-fy^{P}, *n.* Calligraphy.
cal'i-per^{S}, *v. & n.* Calliper.
cal'i-perd^{S}, *pp.* Callipered.
calkt$^{P\&S}$, *pp.* Calked.
call'a-bl^{P}, *a.* Callable.
calld^{P}, *pp.* Called.
cal'li-graf^{P}, *n.* Calligraph.

cal'lus[s], *v.* & *a.* Callous.
calm'a-tiv[s], *a.* & *n.* Calmative.
calmd[s], *pp.* Calmed.
calv[P&S], *vt.* & *vi.* Calve.
calvd[P&S], *pp.* Calved.
ca-me'le-on[s], *n.* Chameleon.
cam'fene[P], *n.* Camphene.
cam'for[P&S], *n.* Camphor.
cam'ford[s], *pp.* Camphored.
cam'moc[s], *n.* Cammock.
cam'o-mile[P], *n.* Chamomile.
cam-pain'[s], *v.* & *n.* Campaign.
cam-paind'[s], *pp.* Campaigned.
campt[P&S], *pp.* Camped.
ca-nald'[P&S], *pp.* Canalled.
can'cel-a-bl, can'cel-la-bl[P], *a.* Cancelable, cancellable.
can"cel-a'tion[P], *n.* Cancellation.
can'celd[P&S], *pp.* Canceled, cancelled.
can'cel-ing[P], *pres. p.* Cancelling.
cand[s], *pp.* Canned.
can'dl[P], *v.* & *n.* Candle.
can'dld[P], *pp.* Candled.
can'dor[P&S], *n.* Candour.
can'kerd[P&S], *a.* Cankered.
can'nond[s], *pp.* Cannoned.
can'terd[P&S], *pp.* Cantered.
can'ti-cl[P], *n.* Canticle.
can'vast[s], *pp.* Canvased.
can'vast[s], *pp.* Canvassed.
ca'os[s], *n.* Chaos.
ca'pa-bl[P], *a.* Capable.
ca'pa-bl-ness[P], *n.* Capableness.
ca-par'i-sond[s], *pa.* Caparisoned.
ca'perd[P&S], *pp.* Capered.
cap'i-ta"tiv[s], *a.* Capitative.
capt[s], *pp.* Capped.
cap'taind[s], *pp.* Captained.
cap'tiv[P&S], *a.* & *n.* Captive.
cap'tivd[s], *pp.* Captived.
car'ac-ter[s], *v.* & *n.* Character.
car'bun-cl[P], *n.* Carbuncle.
card[s], *pp.* Carred.
ca-reend'[P&S], *pp.* Careened.
ca-reerd'[P&S], *pp.* Careered.
ca-rest'[P&S], *pp.* Caressed.
car"i-cog'ra-fy[P], *n.* Caricography.
car'i-ta"tiv[s], *a.* Caritative
car'min[s], *n.* Carmine.
car-min'a-tiv[P&S], *a.* & *n.* Carminative.
car'old[P&S], *pp.* Caroled, -olled.
car'ol-ing[P], *pres. p.* Carolling.
car'omd[s], *pp.* Caromed.
carpt[P&S], *pp.* Carped.
car'ri-a-bl, car'ry-a-bl[P], *a.* Carriable, carryable.
car'riage-a-bl[P], *a.* Carriageable.
car-toond'[s], *pp.* Cartooned.
car'un-cl[P&S], *n.* Caruncle.
carv[P&S], *vt.* & *vi.* Carve.
carvd[P&S], *pp.* Carved.
cash-ierd'[P&S], *pp.* Cashiered.
casm[s], *n.* Chasm.
casht[s], *pp.* Cashed.
cas'soc[s], *n.* Cassock.
cast[P], *n.* Caste.
cas'tl[P], *v.* & *n.* Castle.
cat'a-log[P&S], *v.* & *n.* Catalogue.
cat'a-logd[P&S], *pp.* Catalogued.
cat'a-log"er[P&S], *n.* Cataloguer.
cat'a-log"ing[s], *pres. p.* Cataloguing.
ca-tar'ral[s], *a.* Catarrhal.
ca-tas'tro-fe[P], *n.* Catastrophe.
catch'a-bl[P], *a.* Catchable.
cat'e-chize[P&S], *vt.* Catechise.
ca'terd[P&S], *pp.* Catered.
cat'er-wauld[P&S], *pp.* Caterwauled.
cat'hed"[s], *v.* & *n.* Cathead.
cat'l[P], *n.* Cattle.
cau'cus-ing[P], *pres. p.* Caucussing.
cau'cust[P&S], *pp.* Caucused, -cussed.
cau'dl[P], *v.* & *n.* Caudle.
cau'dld[P], *pp.* Caudled.
caus'a-bl[P], *a.* Causable.
caus'a-tiv[P&S], *a.* & *n.* Causative.
caus'a-tiv-ly[s], *adv.* Causatively.
caus'a-tiv-ness[s], *n.* Causativeness.

caut[s], *imp.* & *pp.* Caught.
cau'ter-ize[P&S], *vt.* Cauterise.
cau'tiond[s], *pp.* Cautioned.
cav'ernd[s], *a.* Caverned.
cav'ild[P&S], *pp.* Caviled, -illed.
cav'il-ing[P], *pa.* & *n.* Cavilling.
cawd[P&S], *pp.* Cawed.
cay-en'[P], *v.* & *n.* Cayenne.
ceast[P&S], *pp.* Ceased.
ce'drin[P&S], *a.* Cedrine.
ce-fal'ic[P], *a.* & *n.* Cephalic.
cef'a-lo-pod[P], *a.* & *n.* Cephalopod.
ceild[P&S], *pp.* Ceiled.
cel[P&S], *n.* Cell.
cel'a-tiv[s], *a.* Celative.
celd[P], *pp.* Celled.
cel'e-bra"tiv[s], *a.* Celebrative.
cel'lard[s], *a.* Cellared.
cen'a-cl[P], *n.* Cenacle.
cen'o-taf[P&S], *n.* Cenotaph.
cen'siv[s], *a.* Censive.
cen'sord[s], *pp.* Censored.
cen'sur-a-bl[P], *a.* Censurable.
cen'ter[P&S], *v.* & *n.* Centre.
cen'terd[s], *pp.* Centered.
cen'tu-pl[P], *v.* & *a.* Centuple.
ce-rog'ra-fy[P], *n.* Cerography.
cer'ti-fi"a-bl[P], *a.* Certifiable.
chaf[P&S], *v.* & *n.* Chaff.
chaf'ferd[s], *pp.* Chaffered.
chaft[P&S], *pp.* Chaffed.
cha-grind'[s], *pp.* Chagrined.
chaind[P&S], *a.* Chained.
chaird[P&S], *pp.* Chaired.
chal-cog'ra-fy[P], *n.* Chalcography.
chal'is[s], *n.* Chalice.
chalkt[P&S], *pp.* Chalked.
cham'berd[P&S], *a.* Chambered.
cham'ferd[s], *a.* Chamfered.
cham'piond[P&S], *pp.* Championed.
champt[s], *pp.* Champed.
change'a-bl[P], *a.* Changeable.
chan'neld[P&S], *pa.* Channeled, channelled.
chan'nel-ing[P], *n.* Channelling.
chanst[s], *pp.* Chanced.
chapt[P&S], *pa.* Chapped.
chap'terd[s], *pp.* Chaptered.
chard[P&S], *pp.* Charred.
char'ac-ter-iz"a-bl[P], *a.* Characterizable.
charge'a-bl[P], *a.* Chargeable.
charge'a-bl-ness[P], *n.* Chargeableness.
char'i-ta-bl[P], *a.* Charitable.
char'i-ta-bl-ness[P], *n.* Charitableness.
char'loc[s], *n.* Charlock.
charmd[P&S], *pp.* Charmed.
char'terd[P&S], *pa.* Chartered.
chas'a-bl, chase'a-bl[P], *a.* Chasable, chaseable.
chas'i-bl[P], *n.* Chasible.
chast'end[P&S], *pp.* Chastened.
chas-tize'[P&S], *vt.* Chastise.
chas'tiz-ment[P], *n.* Chastisement.
chas'u-bl[P], *n.* Chasuble.
chat'ta-bl[P], *a.* Chattable.
char'terd[P&S], *pp.* Chattered.
chawd[P&S], *pp.* Chawed.
cheap'end[P&S], *pp.* Cheapened.
cheat'a-bl[P], *a.* Cheatable.
cheat'a-bl-ness[P], *n.* Cheatableness.
check[s], *n.* Check, cheque.
checker[s], *v.* & *n.* Checker, chequer.
check'erd[s], *pa.* Checkered, chequered.
checkt[P&S], *pp.* Checked.
cheekt[s], *pp.* Cheeked.
cheerd[P&S], *pp.* Cheered.
cher'isht[P&S], *pp.* Cherished.
ches[s], *n.* Chess.
chewd[P&S], *pp.* Chewed.
chid'n[P&S], *pp.* Chidden.
chil[P&S], *v.*, *a.* & *n.* Chill.
chilld[P], **child**[P&S], *pa.* Chilled.
chi-me'ra[s], *n.* Chimæra.
chim'ny[s], *n.* Chimney.
chin'=cof"[P], *n.* Chin-cough.
chind[s], *a.* Chinned.
chinkt[s], *pp.* Chinked.

chipt[P&S], *pp.* Chipped.
chi'ro-graf[P], *n.* Chirograph.
chi-rog'ra-fy[P&S], *n.* Chirography.
chirpt[P&S], *pp.* Chirped.
chir'rupt[P&S], *pp.* Chirruped.
chis'eld[P&S], *pa.* Chiseled, -elled.
chis'el-ing[P], *pres. p.* Chiselling.
chlo'rid[P], *n.* Chloride.
chlo'rin[P], *n.* Chlorine.
chockt[S], *pp.* Chocked.
choos'a-bl, choose'a-bl[P], *a.* Choosable, chooseable.
choos'a-bl-ness, choose'a-bl-ness[P], *n.* Choosableness, chooseableness.
chopt[P&S], *pp.* Chopped.
cho'ro-graf[P], *n.* Chorograph.
cho-rog'ra-fy[P], *n.* Chorography.
choze[P], *v. & n.* Chose.
cho'zen[P], *pa.* Chosen.
chris'tend[S], *pp.* Christened.
chron'i-cl[P], *v. & n.* Chronicle.
chron'i-cld[P], *pp.* Chronicled.
chron'o-graf[P], *n.* Chronograph.
chu[S], *v. & n.* Chew.
chuck'l[P], *v. & n.* Chuckle.
chuck'ld[P], *pp.* Chuckled.
chuckt[P&S], *pp.* Chucked.
chuf[P&S], *n.* Chough; chuff.
chumd[P&S], *pp.* Chummed.
churcht[P&S], *pp.* Churched.
churnd[P&S], *pp.* Churned.
cic'a-tris[S], *n.* Cicatrice.
ci'fer[P&S], *v. & n.* Cipher.
ci'fered[P&S], *pa.* Ciphered.
cig"a-ret'[P&S], *n.* Cigarette.
cim'i-tar[P], *n.* Scimitar.
cincht[S], *pp.* Cinched.
cir'cl[P], *v. & n.* Circle.
cir'cld[P], *pp.* Circled.
cir'cu-la-bl[P], *a.* Circulable.
cir'cu-la"tiv[S], *a.* Circulative.
cir'cum-cize[P], *vt.* Circumcise.
cir"cum-nav'i-ga-bl[P], *a.* Circumnavigable.
cir"cum-scrib'a-bl[P], *a.* Circumscribable.
cir"cum-scrip'tiv[S], *a.* Circumscriptive.
cir"cum-scrip'tiv-ly[S], *adv.* Circumscriptively.
cir"cum-spec'tiv[S], *a.* Circumspective.
cir"cum-spec'tiv-ly[S], *adv.* Circumspectively.
cir'cum-stanst[S], *pp.* Circumstanced.
cir"cum-stan'ti-a-bl[P], *a.* Circumstantiable.
cir"cum-ven'tiv[S], *a.* Circumventive.
cir"cum-volv'[P&S], *vt.* Circumvolve.
cir"cum-volvd'[P&S], *pp.* Circumvolved.
cis'sors[P], *n. pl.* Scissors.
cit'a-bl[P], *a.* Citable.
ci'ta-tiv[S], *a.* Citative.
cit'rin[P&S], *a. & n.* Citrine.
civ'i-lize[S], *vt.* Civilise.
civ'i-liz"[or -lis"]a-bl[P], *a.* Civilizable, civilisable.
clackt[P&S], *pp.* Clacked.
claimd[P&S], *pp.* Claimed.
clam'berd[P&S], *pp.* Clambered.
clamd[S], *pp.* Clammed.
clam'or[S], *v. & n.* Clamor.
clam'ord[P&S], *pp.* Clamored.
clamp'erd[S], *pp.* Clampered.
clampt[S], *pp.* Clamped.
clan-des'tin[S], *a.* Clandestine.
clangd[S], *pp.* Clanged.
clan'gor[S], *v. & n.* Clangor.
clankt[P&S], *pp.* Clanked.
clap'perd[S], *pp.* Clappered.
clapt[P&S], *pp.* Clapped.
clas[S], *v. & n.* Class.
clasht[P&S], *pp.* Clashed.
claspt[P&S], *pp.* Clasped.
class'a-bl, class'i-bl[P], *a.* Classable, classible.
clas'i-fi"a-bl[P], *a.* Classifiable.
clast[P&S], *pp.* Classed.

clat'terd[P&S], *pp.* Clattered.
clav'i-cl[P], *n.* Clavicle.
clawd[P&S], *pp.* Clawed.
clayd[S], *pp.* Clayed.
cleand[P&S], *pp.* Cleaned.
cleans'a[or **-i**]**-bl**[S], *a.* Cleansable, cleansible.
cleard[P&S], *pa.* Cleared.
cleav[P], *v.* & *n.* Cleave.
cleav'a-bl[P], *a.* Cleavable.
cleavd[P&S], *pp.* Cleaved.
clencht[S], *pp.* Clenched.
clen'li-ness[P], *n.* Cleanliness.
clen'ly[P&S], *a.* & *adv.* Cleanly.
clense[S], *vt.* & *vi.* Cleanse.
clenz[P], *vt.* & *vi.* Cleanse.
clenzd[P], *pp.* Cleansed.
cler'gi-a-bl[P], **cler'gy-a-bl**[P], *a.* Clergyable.
clerkt[P&S], *pp.* Clerked.
clickt[P&S], *pp.* Clicked.
clif[S], *n.* Cliff.
climbd[P], *pp.* Climbed.
clincht[P&S], *pp.* Clinched.
clink'erd[S], *pp.* Clinkered.
clinkt[P&S], *pp.* Clinked.
clipt[P&S], *pp.* Clipped.
cloakt[P&S], *pp.* Cloaked.
clockt[S], *a.* Clocked.
clogd[S], *pp.* Clogged.
clois'terd[P&S], *pa.* Cloistered.
clo'rid[S], *n.* Chlorid.
clo'rin[S], *n.* Chlorin.
clos'a-bl[P], *a.* Closable.
clot'terd[S], *pp.* Clottered.
cloyd[P&S], *pp.* Cloyed.
cloze[P], *vt.* & *vi.* Close.
cloz'et[P], *v.*, *a.* & *n.* Closet.
clo'zure[P], *v.* & *n.* Closure.
clu[S], *v.* & *n.* Clew, clue.
clubd[P&S], *pp.* Clubbed.
clucht[P], *pp.* Clutched.
cluckt[P&S], *pp.* Clucked.
cluf[P&S], *n.* Clough.
clumpt[S], *pp.* Clumped.
clus'terd[P&S], *pp.* Clustered.
clutcht[S], *pp.* Clutched.
clut'terd[P&S], *pp.* Cluttered.
coacht[P&S], *pp.* Coached.
co-ac'tiv[P&S], *a.* Coactive.
co-ad'u-na-tiv[S], *a.* Coadunative.
co-ad'u-na-tiv-ly[S], *adv.* Coadunatively.
co-ag'u-la-tiv[S], *a.* Coagulative.
coald[P&S], *pp.* Coaled.
coars'end[S], *pp.* Coarsened.
coaxt[P&S], *pp.* Coaxed.
cobd[S], *pp.* Cobbed.
cob'l[P], *v.* & *n.* Cobble.
cob'ld[P], *pp.* Cobbled.
cob'webd''[S], *pa.* Cobwebbed.
cock'erd[S], *pp.* Cockered.
cock'l[P], *v.* & *n.* Cockle.
cock'ny[S], *n.* Cockney.
cockt[P&S], *pp.* Cocked.
co'co[S], *n.* Cocoa.
co'co-nut''[S], *n.* Cocoanut.
coc'til[S], *a.* Coctile.
cod'l[P], *vt.* Coddle.
cod'ld[P], *pp.* Coddled.
co-er'ci-bl[P], *a.* Coercible.
co-er'ci-bl-ness[P], *n.* Coercibleness.
co-er'civ[P&S], *a.* Coercive.
co-er'civ-ly[S], *adv.* Coercively.
co-er'civ-ness[S], *n.* Coerciveness.
co-e'val[S], *a.* Coæval.
co''ex-ten'siv[S], *a.* Coextensive.
co''ex-ten'siv-ly[S], *adv.* Coextensively.
co''ex-ten'siv-ness[S], *n.* Coextensiveness.
cof[P&S], *v.* & *n.* Cough.
cof'ferd[S], *pp.* Coffered.
cof'find[S], *pp.* Coffined.
cof'ing[S], *ppr.* Coughing.
coft[P], *pp.* Coughed.
cogd[S], *pp.* Cogged.
cog'i-ta-bl[P], *a.* Cogitable.
cog'i-ta''tiv[P&S], *a.* Cogitative.

cog'i-ta"tiv-ly[S], *adv.* Cogitatively.
cog'ni-tiv[S], *a.* Cognitive.
cog'ni-za-bl, cog'ni-sa-bl[P], *a.* Cognizable, cognisable.
cog'ni-za-bl-ness[P], *n.* Cognizableness.
cog-nos'ci-tiv[S], *a.* Cognoscitive.
cog-nos'ci-tiv-ly[S], *adv.* Cognoscitively.
co-he'si-bl[P], *a.* Cohesible.
co-he'siv[P&S], *a.* Cohesive.
co-he'siv-ly[S], *adv.* Cohesively.
co-he'siv-ness[S], *n.* Cohesiveness.
co-hor'ta-tiv[S], *a.* Cohortative.
coift[S], *pp.* Coifed.
coild[S], *pp.* Coiled.
coind[P&S], *pp.* Coined.
col'er[P], *n.* Choler.
col'er-a[P&S], *n.* Cholera.
col'er-ic[P], *a.* Choleric.
col-laps'[P], *v.* & *n.* Collapse.
col-lapst'[P&S], *pp.* Collapsed.
col'lard[P&S], *pa.* Collared.
col-la'tiv[S], *a.* Collative.
col'leag[P&S], *n.* Colleague.
col-lect'a-bl[P], **col-lect'i-bl**[P], *a.* Collectable, collectible.
col-lec'tiv[P&S], *a.* & *n.* Collective.
col'li-ga-tiv[S], *a.* Colligative.
col-liq'ua-tiv[S], *a.* Colliquative.
col-liq'ua-tiv-ness[S], *n.* Colliquativeness.
col-li'siv[S], *a.* Collisive.
col"lo-ca'tion-a-bl[P], *a.* Collocationable.
col'lo-ca-tiv[S], *a.* Collocative.
col'lo-graf[P], *n.* Collograph.
col-lu'siv[P&S], *a.* Collusive.
col'o-niz"a-bl[P], *a.* Colonizable.
col'o-nize[S], *vt.* & *vi.* Colonise.
col'or[S], *v.* & *n.* Colour.
col'ord[S], *pa.* Colored.
col'ter[S], *n.* Coulter.
col'terd[P], *a.* Coltered.
col'um[S], *n.* Column.
col'umd[S], *a.* Columned.
com-, *prefix.* See also under CUM-.
com-bat'a-bl[P], *a.* Combatable.
com'ba-tiv[P&S], *a.* Combative.
com'ba-tiv-ness[S], *n.* Combativeness.
combd[P&S], *a.* Combed.
com-bin'a-bl[P], *a.* Combinable.
com-bin'a-bl-ness[P], *n.* Combinableness.
com-bi'na-tiv[S], *a.* Combinative.
com'bl†[P], *vt.* Comble.
com-bus'ti-bl[P], *a.* & *n.* Combustible.
com-bus'tiv[S], *a.* Combustive.
co-mes'ti-bl[P], *a.* & *n.* Comestible.
com'i-ta"tiv[P], *a.* Comitative.
com"man-deerd'[S], *pp.* Commandeered.
com-mem'o-ra-bl[P], *a.* Commemorable.
com-mem'o-ra-tiv[S], *a.* Commemorative.
com-mend'a-bl[P], *a.* Commendable.
com-mend'a-bl-ness[P], *n.* Commendableness.
com-menst'[S], *pp.* Commenced.
com-men'su-ra-bl,[P] *a.* Commensurable.
com-men'su-ra-bl-ness[P], *n.* Commensurableness.
com-mer'cia-bl[P], *a.* Commerciable.
com-min'gl[P], *vt.* & *vi.* Commingle.
com-mis'er-a-bl[P], *a.* Commiserable.
com-mis'er-a-tiv[S], *a.* Commiserative.
com-mis'er-a-tiv-ly[S], *adv.* Commiseratively.
com-mis'siond[S], *pp.* Commissioned.
com-mis'siv[S], *a.* Commissive.
com-mis'siv-ly[S], *adv.* Commissively.
com-mit'a-bl[P], **com-mit'i-bl**[P], *a.* Committable, committible.
com-mixt'[P&S], *pp.* Commixed.
com-mo'di-us[S], *a.* Commodious.
com'mon-a-bl[P], *a.* Commonable.

com'mond[s], *pp.* Commoned.
com'mon-welth''[s], *n.* Commonwealth.
com-mo'tiv[s], *a.* Commotive.
com-mu'ni-ca-bl[p], *a.* Communicable.
com-mu'ni-ca-bl-ness[p], *n.* Communicableness.
com-mu'ni-ca''tiv[p&s], *a.* Communicative.
com-mu'ni-tiv[s], *a.* Communitive.
com-mut'a-bl[p], *a.* Commutable.
com-mut'a-bl-ness[p], *n.* Commutableness.
com-mu'ta-tiv[s], *a.* Commutative.
com-mu'ta-tiv-ly[s], *adv.* Commutatively.
com-pact'i-bl[p], *a.* Compactible.
com-pan'i-a-bl[p], *a.* Companiable.
com-pan'iond[s], *pp.* Companioned.
com-pan'ion-a-bl. See CUMPANIONABLE.
com'pa-ra-bl[p], *a.* Comparable.
com'pa-ra-bl-ness[p], *n.* Comparableness.
com-par'a-tiv[p&s], *a.* & *n.* Comparative.
com-par'a-tiv-ly[s], *adv.* Comparatively.
com-par'a-tiv-ness[s], *n.* Comparativeness.
com-pas'sion-a-bl[p], *a.* Compassionable.
com-pas'siond[s], *pp.* Compassioned.
com-pas'siv[s], *a.* Compassive.
com'past[p&s], *pp.* Compassed.
com-pat'i-bl[p], *a.* Compatible.
com-pat'i-bl-ness[p], *n.* Compatibleness.
com-peld'[p&s], *pp.* Compelled.
com-pel'la-ble[p], *a.* Compellable.
com-pel'la-tiv[s], *a.* & *n.* Compellative.
com-pen'sa-bl†[p], *a.* Compensable.
com-pen'sa-tiv[s], *a.* & *n.* Compensative.
com-pen'sa-tiv-ness[s], *n.* Compensativeness.
com-pet'i-tiv[p&s], *a.* Competitive.
com-pet'i-tiv-ly[s], *adv.* Competitively.
com-pet'i-tiv-ness[s], *n.* Competitiveness.
com-plain'a-bl[p], *a.* Complainable.
com-plaind'[p&s], *pp.* Complained.
com-plain'tiv[s], *a.* Complaintive.
com-plain'tiv-ness[s], *n.* Complaintiveness.
com''ple-men'ta-tiv[s], *a.* Complementative.
com-plet'a-bl[p], *a.* Completable.
com-ple'tiv[s], *a.* Completive.
com-plext'[s], *a.* Complexed.
com-plex'iv-ly[s], *adv.* Complexively.
com-pli'a-bl[p], *a.* Compliable.
com'pli-ca''tiv[s], *a.* Complicative.
com'plis[s], *n.* Complice.
com-plis'i-ty[s], *n.* Complicity.
com'pli-ment''a-bl[p], *a.* Complimentable.
com''pli-men'ta-tiv[s], *a.* Complimentative.
com-port'a-bl[p], *a.* Comportable.
com-pos'it[p&s], *a.* & *n.* Composite.
com-pos'i-tiv[s], *a.* Compositive.
com-pos'i-tiv-ly[s], *adv.* Compositively.
com-pos'si-bl[p], *a.* Compossible.
com''pre-hend'i-bl[p], *a.* Comprehendible.
com''pre-hen'si-bl[p], *a.* Comprehensible.
com''pre-hen'si-bl-ness[p], *n.* Comprehensibleness.
com''pre-hen'siv[p&s], *a.* Comprehensive.
com''pre-hen'siv-ness[s], *n.* Comprehensiveness.
com-press'i-bl[p], *a.* Compressible.
com''press'i-bl-ness[p], *n.* Compressibleness.

com-pres'siv[s], *a.* Compressive.
com-pres'siv-ly[s], *adv.* Compressively.
com-prest'[p], *pa.* Compressed.
com-pris'a-bl[p], **com-priz'a-bl**[p], *a.* Comprisable, comprizable.
com-prize'[s], *vt.* Comprise.
com"pro-duc'tiv[s], *a.* Comproductive.
com'pro-mize[s], *v.* & *n.* Compromise.
compt'a-bl[p], *a.* Comptable.
com-pul'sa-tiv[s], *a.* Compulsative.
com-pul'sa-tiv-ly[s], *adv.* Compulsatively.
com-pul'siv[p&s], *a.* Compulsive.
com-put'a-bl[p], *a.* Computable.
com-pu'ta-tiv[s], *a.* Computative.
com-pu'ta-tiv-ness[s], *n.* Computativeness.
co'na-tiv[s], *a.* & *n.* Conative.
conc[s], *n.* Conch.
con-ceald'[p&s], *pp.* Concealed.
con-ceiv'[p], *vt.* & *vi.* Conceive.
con-ceiv'a-bl[p], *a.* Conceivable.
con-ceiv'a-bl-ness[p], *n.* Conceivableness.
con-ceivd'[p&s], *pp.* Conceived.
con-cen'ter[s], *vt.* & *vi.* Concentre.
con-cen'terd[s], *pp.* Concentered.
con-cen'tra-tiv[s], *a.* Concentrative.
con-cen'tra-tiv-ness[s], *n.* Concentrativeness.
con-cep'ta-cl[p], *n.* Conceptacle.
con-cep'tiv[p&s], *a.* Conceptive.
con-cep'tiv-ness[s], *n.* Conceptiveness.
con-cernd'[p&s], *pa.* Concerned.
con-ces'si-bl[p], *a.* Concessible.
con-ces'siv[p&s], *a.* Concessive.
con-ces'siv-ly[s], *adv.* Concessively.
con-ces'siv-ness[s], *n.* Concessiveness.
con-cil'i-a-tiv[s], *a.* Conciliative.
con-clu'si-bl[p], *a.* Conclusible.
con-clu'siv[p&s], *a.* Conclusive.
con-clu'siv-ly[s], *adv.* Conclusively.
con-clu'siv-ness[s], *n.* Conclusiveness.
con-coc'tiv[p&s], *a.* Concoctive.
con-cres'ci-bl[p], *a.* Concrescible.
con-cres'civ[s], *a.* Concrescive.
con-cre'tiv[s], *a.* Concretive.
con-cre'tiv-ly[s], *adv.* Concretively.
con-cu'pis-ci-bl[p], *a.* Concupiscible.
con-cu'pis-ci-bl-ness[p], *n.* Concupiscibleness.
con-curd'[p&s], *pp.* Concurred.
con-cus'siv[p&s], *a.* Concussive.
con-cust'[s], *pp.* Concussed.
cond[s], *pp.* Conned.
con-dem'na-bl[p], *a.* Condemnable.
con-demd'[s], *pa.* Condemned.
con-dens'a-bl[p], **con-dens'i-bl**[p], *a.* Condensable, condensible.
con-dens'a-tiv[s], *a.* Condensative.
con-denst'[p&s], *pp.* Condensed.
con-dit'[s], *vt.* Condite.
con'dit[s], *n.* Conduit.
con-di'tiond[s], *pa.* Conditioned.
con-do'na-tiv[s], *a.* Condonative.
con-du'ci-bl[p], *a.* Conducible.
con-du'ci-bl-ness[p], *n.* Conducibleness.
con-du'civ[p&s], *a.* Conducive.
con-du'civ-ness[s], *n.* Conduciveness.
con-duct'i-bl[p], *a.* Conductible.
con-duc'tiv[s], *a.* Conductive.
con-fed'er-a-tiv[p&s], *a.* Confederative.
con-ferd'[p&s], *pp.* Conferred.
con-fer'ra-bl[p], *a.* Conferrable.
con-fes'siv[s], *a.* Confessive.
con-fest'[p&s], *pp.* Confessed.
con-fig'ur-a-tiv[s], *a.* Configurative.
con-fin'a-bl[p], *a.* Confinable.
con-firm'a-bl[p], *a.* Confirmable.
con-firm'a-tiv[s], *a.* Confirmative.
con-firm'a-tiv-ly[s], *adv.* Confirmatively.
con-firmd'[p&s], *pa.* Confirmed.

con-fis'ca-bl[P], *a.* Confiscable.
con"fis-cat'a-bl[P], *a.* Confiscatable.
con'fla-gra"tiv[S], *a.* Conflagrative.
con-flic'tiv[S], *a.* Conflictive.
con-form'a-bl[P], *a.* Conformable.
con-form'a-bl-ness[P], *n.* Conformableness.
con-formd'[P&S], *pa.* Conformed.
con-frunt'[P], *vt.* Confront.
con-fus'a-bl[P], *a.* Confusable.
con-fut'a-bl[P], *a.* Confutable.
con-fu'ta-tiv[S], *a.* Confutative.
con-geal'a-bl[P], *a.* Congealable.
con-geal'a-bl-ness[P], *n.* Congealableness.
con-geald'[P&S], *pp.* Congealed.
con-ġe'la-tiv[S], *a.* Congelative.
con-ges'tiv[S], *a.* Congestive.
con-glu'ti-na-tiv[P&S], *a.* Conglutinative.
con-grat'u-la-bl[P], *a.* Congratulable.
con'gre-ga"tiv[P], *a.* Congregative.
con'gre-ga"tiv-ness[S], *n.* Congregativeness.
con-gres'siv[S], *a.* Congressive.
co-nif'er-us[S], *a.* Coniferous.
con-jec'tiv[S], *a.* Conjective.
con-jec'tur-a-bl[P], *a.* Conjecturable.
con-joind'[P&S], *pa.* Conjoined.
con'ju-ga-bl[P], *a.* Conjugable.
con'ju-ga"tiv[S], *a.* Conjugative.
con-junc'tiv[P&S], *a.* & *n.* Conjunctive.
con-nect'a-bl[P], *a.* Connectable.
con-nec'tiv[P&S], *a.* & *n.* Connective.
con-nex'iv†[S], *a.* Connexive.
con-no'ta-tiv[S], *a.* Connotative.
con-no'ta-tiv-ly[S], *adv.* Connotatively.
con-no'tiv[S], *a.* Connotive.
con-no'tiv-ly[S], *adv.* Connotively.
con'querd[S], *pp.* Conquered.
con'scion-a-bl[P], *a.* Conscionable.
con'scion-a-bl-ness[P], *n.* Conscionableness.
con-sec'u-tiv[P&S], *a.* Consecutive.
con-sent'a-bl[P], *a.* Consentable.
con-sent'i-bl[P], *a.* Consentible.
con-serv'[P&S], *vt.* Conserve.
con-serv'a-bl[P], *a.* Conservable.
con-ser'va-tiv[P&S], *a.* & *n.* Conservative.
con-servd'[S], *pp.* Conserved.
con-sid'er-a-bl[P], *a.* Considerable.
con-sid'er-a-tiv[S], *a.* Considerative.
con-sid'erd[P&S], *pp.* Considered.
con-signd'[P&S], *pp.* Consigned.
con"sig-nif'i-ca-tiv[S], *a.* Consignificative.
con-sol'a-bl[P], *a.* Consolable.
con-sol'a-bl-ness[P], *n.* Consolableness.
con-sol'a-tiv[S], *a.* Consolative.
con-sol'i-da"tiv[S], *a.* Consolidative.
con-sort'a-bl[P], *a.* Consortable.
con'sta-bl[P], *n.* Constable.
con'sti-tu"tiv[P&S], *a.* & *n.* Constitutive.
con-strain'a-bl[P], *a.* Constrainable.
con-straind'[P&S], *pa.* Constrained.
con-stric'tiv[S], *a.* Constrictive.
con'stru[S], *v.* Construe.
con-stru'a-bl[P], *a.* Construable.
con-struct'i-bl[P], *a.* Constructible.
con-struc'tiv[P&S], *a.* & *n.* Constructive.
con-struc'tiv-ness[S], *n.* Constructiveness.
con-sub'stan-tiv[S], *a.* Consubstantive.
con-sult'a-bl[P], *a.* Consultable.
con-sult'a-tiv[S], *a.* Consultative.
con-sult'iv[S], *a.* Consultive.
con-sum'a-bl[P], *a.* Consumable.
con-sump'ti-bl[P], *a.* Consumptible.
con-sump'tiv[S], *a.* & *n.* Consumptive.
con-sump'tiv-ly[S], *adv.* Consumptively.
con-sump'tiv-ness[S], *n.* Consumptiveness.

con-tain'a-bl[P], *a.* Containable.
con-taind'[S], *pp.* Contained.
con-tam'i-na-bl[P], *a.* Contaminable.
con-tam'i-na-tiv[S], *a.* Contaminative.
con-tem'ni-bl[P], *a.* Contemnible.
con-tem'perd†[S], *pp.* Contempered.
con-tem'pla-bl[P], *a.* Contemplable.
con-tem'pla-tiv[P&S], *a.* Contemplative.
con-tem'pla-tiv-ly[S], *adv.* Contemplatively.
con-tem'pla-tiv-ness[S], *n.* Contemplativeness.
con-tempt'i-bl[P], *a.* Contemptible.
con-ter'mi-na-bl[P], *a.* Conterminable.
con-test'a-bl[P], *a.* Contestable.
con-test'a-bl-ness[P], *n.* Contestableness.
con-tex'tiv[S], *a.* Contextive.
con-tin'u-a-bl[P], *a.* Continuable.
con-tin'u-a-tiv[S], *a.* & *n.* Continuative.
con-tor'siv[S], *a.* Contorsive.
con-tor'tiv[S], *a.* Contortive.
con-tourd'[S], *pp.* Contoured.
con-tract'i-bl[P], *a.* Contractible.
con-tract'i-bl-ness[P], *n.* Contractibleness.
con-trac'til[P&S], *a.* Contractile.
con-trac'tiv[S], *a.* Contractive.
con-trac'tiv-ly[S], *adv.* Contractively.
con"tra-dict'a-bl[P], *a.* Contradictable.
con"tra-dic'tiv[S], *a.* Contradictive.
con"tra-dis-tinc'tiv[S], *a.* Contradistinctive.
con"tra-pos'i-tiv[S], *a.* & *n.* Contrapositive.
con-tras'tiv[S], *a.* Contrastive.
con-trib'ut-a-bl[P], *a.* Contributable.
con-trib'u-tiv[P&S], *a.* Contributive.
con-triv'a-bl[P], *a.* Contrivable.
con-trold'[P&S], *pp.* Controlled.
con-trol'la-bl[P], *a.* Controllable.
con-trol'la-bl-ness[P], *n.* Controllableness.
con-trol'ler[S], *n.* Comptroller.
con"tro-vert'i-bl[P], *a.* Controvertible.
con"va-nes'ci-bl[P], *a.* Convanescible.
con-vec'tiv[S], *a.* Convective.
con-vec'tiv-ly[S], *adv.* Convectively.
con-ve'na-bl[P], *a.* Convenable.
con-vers'a-bl[P], *a.* Conversable.
con-vers'a-bl-ness[P], *n.* Conversableness.
con"ver-sa'tion-a-bl[P], *a.* Conversationable.
con-vers'a-tiv[S], *a.* Conversative.
con-vers'i-bl[P], *a.* Conversible.
con-ver'siv[S], *a.* Conversive.
con-verst'[P&S], *pp.* Conversed.
con-vert'i-bl[P], *a.* Convertible.
con-vert'i-bl-ness[P], *n.* Convertibleness.
con-ver'tiv[S], *a.* Convertive.
con'vext[S], *pp.* Convexed.
con-vey'a-bl[P], *a.* Conveyable.
con-veyd'[P&S], *pp.* Conveyed.
con-vict'a-bl[P], **con-vict'i-bl**[P], *a.* Convictable, convictible.
con-vic'tiv[S], *a.* Convictive.
con-vic'tiv-ly[S], *adv.* Convictively.
con-vic'tiv-ness[S], *n.* Convictiveness.
con-vinc'i-bl[P], *a.* Convincible.
con-vinst'[S], *pp.* Convinced.
con-voc'a-tiv[S], *a.* Convocative.
con-volv'[S], *vt.* & *vi.* Convolve.
con-volvd'[S], *pp.* Convolved.
con-voyd'[P&S], *pp.* Convoyed.
con-vuls'i-bl[P], *a.* Convulsible.
con-vul'siv[P&S], *a.* Convulsive.
con-vul'siv-ly[S], *adv.* Convulsively.
con-vul'siv-ness[S], *n.* Convulsiveness.
con-vulst'[S], *pp.* Convulsed.
cood[P&S], *pp.* Cooed.
cook'a-bl[P], *a.* Cookable.
cookt[P&S], *pp.* Cooked.

coold[P&S], *pp.* Cooled.
co-op′er-a-tiv[S], *a.* & *n.* Cooperative.
co-op′er-a-tiv-ly[S], *adv.* Cooperatively.
co-op′er-a-tiv-ness[S], *n.* Cooperativeness.
coop′erd[S], *pp.* Coopered.
coopt[P&S], *pp.* Cooped.
cop′a-bl[P], *a.* Copable.
cop′perd[S], *pp.* Coppered.
cop′per-hed″[S], *n.* Copperhead.
cop′pis[S], *n.* Coppice.
cops[P], *v.* & *n.* Copse.
copt[S], *a.* Copped.
cop′u-la-tiv[P&S], *a.* & *n.* Copulative.
co-quet′[S], *v.* & *n.* Coquet, coquette.
cord[S], *n.* Chord.
cor′al-lin[S], *a.* & *n.* Coralline.
cor′beld[S], *pp.* Corbeled.
co-rel′a-tiv[S], *a.* Corelative.
corkt[P&S], *a.* Corked.
cornd[P&S], *pa.* Corned.
cor′nerd[S], *a.* Cornered.
cor′ni-cl[P], *n.* Cornicle.
cor′nis[S], *v.* & *n.* Cornice.
cor′nist[S], *pp.* Corniced.
cor′po-ra-tiv†[S], *a.* Corporative.
cor-rec′tiv[P&S], *a.* & *n.* Corrective.
cor-rec′tiv-ly[S], *adv.* Correctively.
cor-rel′a-tiv[P&S], *a.* & *n.* Correlative.
cor″re-spon′siv[S], *a.* Corresponsive.
cor″re-spon′siv-ly[S], *adv.* Corresponsively.
cor′ri-gi-bl[P], *a.* Corrigible.
cor′ri-gi-bl-ness[S], *n.* Corrigibleness.
cor-rob′o-ra-tiv[P&S], *a.* & *n.* Corroborative.
cor-rob′o-ra-tiv-ly[S], *adv.* Corroboratively.
cor-rod′i-bl[P], *a.* Corrodible.
cor-ro′si-bl[P], *a.* Corrosible.
cor-ro′si-bl-ness[P], *n.* Corrosibleness.
cor-ro′siv[P&S], *a.* & *n.* Corrosive.
cor-ro′siv-ly[P], *adv.* Corrosively.
cor-ro′siv-ness[P], *n.* Corrosiveness.
cor-rupt′i-bl[P], *a.* Corruptible.
cor-rupt′i-bl-ness[P], *n.* Corruptibleness.
cor-rup′tiv[S], *a.* Corruptive.
cor-rup′tiv-ly[P], *adv.* Corruptively.
co′rus[S], *n.* Chorus.
cos′mo-lin[S], *n.* Cosmoline.
cos′tiv[P&S], *a.* Costive.
cot′tond[S], *pp.* Cottoned.
coucht[P&S], *pp.* Couched.
count′a-bl[P], *a.* Countable.
coud[P], *v.* Could.
coun′cil-or[P], *n.* Councilor, councillor.
coun′seld[S], *pp.* Counseled, counselled.
coun′sel-or[P], *n.* Counsellor, counselor.
coun″ter-ac′tiv[S], *a.* & *n.* Counteractive.
coun″ter-ac′tiv-ly[S], *adv.* Counteractively.
coun′terd[S], *pp.* Countered.
coun′ter-fit[S], *v.*, *a.* & *n.* Counterfeit.
coun′ter-marcht[P&S], *pp.* Countermarched.
coun′ter-signd[P&S], *pp.* Countersigned.
coun″ter-vail′a-bl[P], *a.* Countervailable.
coun′ter-vaild[S], *a.* Countervailed.
coup′la-bl[P], *a.* Couplable.
couple. See CUPL.
courst[S], *pp.* Coursed.
court″mar′tiald[S], *pp.* Courtmartialed.
cover. See CUVER.
cov′erd[S], *pp.* Covered.
cov′et-a-bl[P], *a.* Covetable.
cov′et-iv-ness[S], *n.* Covetiveness.
cow′ard-is[S], *n.* Cowardice.
cowd[P&S], *pp.* Cowed.
cow′erd[P&S], *pp.* Cowered.
cowld[P&S], *pa.* Cowled.
coz′end[S], *pp.* Cozened.
co′zy[P], *a.* & *n.* Cosy.

crabd[S], *pp.* Crabbed.
crack'l[P], *v.* & *n.* Crackle.
crack'ld[P], *pp.* Crackled.
crackt[P&S], *pa.* Cracked.
cramd[P&S], *pp.* Crammed.
crampt[P&S], *pp.* Cramped.
cras[S], *a.* Crass.
crasht[P&S], *pp.* Crashed.
crawld[P&S], *pp.* Crawled.
creakt[P&S], *pp.* Creaked.
creamd[P&S], *pp.* Creamed.
creast[P&S], *pp.* Creased.
cre-a'tiv[P&S], *a.* Creative.
cre-a'tiv-ly[S], *adv.* Creatively.
cre-a'tiv-ness[S], *n.* Creativeness
cre'den-civ[S], *a.* Credencive.
cre-den'civ-ness[S], *n.* Credenciveness.
cred'i-bl[P], *a.* Credible.
cred'i-ta-bl[P], *a.* Creditable.
cred'i-ta-bl-ness[P], *n.* Creditableness.
cred'i-tiv[S], *a.* Creditive.
cred'u-lus[S], *a.* Credulous.
cres[S], *n.* Cress.
crev'is[S], *v.* & *n.* Crevice.
crev'ist[S], *pp.* Creviced.
cribd[S], *pp.* Cribbed.
crim'i-na-tiv[S], *a.* Criminative.
crim'pl[P], *v.* & *n.* Crimple.
crim'pld[P], *pp.* Crimpled.
crimpt[P&S], *pp.* Crimped.
crim'sond[S], *pp.* Crimsoned.
crin'kl[P], *v.* & *n.* Crinkle.
crin'kld[P], *pp.* Crinkled.
crip'l[P], *v.* & *n.* Cripple.
crip'ld[P], *pp.* Crippled.
crispt[P&S], *pp.* Crisped.
crit'i-cis"a-bl[P], **crit'i-ciz"a-bl**[P], *a.* Criticizable.
crit'i-cize[P&S], *vt.* & *vi.* Criticise.
cro[S], *v.* & *n.* Crow.
croakt[P&S], *pp.* Croaked.
crocht[P], *a.* Crotched.
crockt[S], *pp.* Crocked.
croed[S], *pp.* Crowed.
croes[S], *v.* & *n.* Crows.
crome[S], *n.* Chrome.
cro-mat'ic[S], *a.* Chromatic.
cro'mo[S], *n.* Chromo.
cron'ic[S], *a.* Chronic.
cron'i-cle[S], *v.* & *n.* Chronicle.
cro-nol'o-gy[S], *n.* Chronology.
crook'ed[P], *a.* Crooked.
crookt[P&S], *pp.* Crooked.
croond[S], *pp.* Crooned.
cropt[S], *pp.* Cropped.
cros[S], *v.*, *a.* & *n.* Cross.
crost[P&S], *pa.* Crossed.
crotcht[S], *a.* Crotched.
croucht[P&S], *pp.* Crouched.
crowd[S], *pp.* Crowed.
crownd[S], *pa.* Crowned.
cru[S], *n.* Crew.
cruch[P], *v.* & *n.* Crutch.
crucht[P&S], *a.* Crutched.
cru'ci-bl[P], *n.* Crucible.
crum[P&S], *v.* & *n.* Crumb.
crum'bl[P], *vt.* & *vi.* Crumble.
crum'bld[P], *pp.* Crumbled.
crumd[P&S], *pp.* Crumbed.
crum'pl[P], *vt.* & *vi.* Crumple.
crum'pld[P], *pp.* Crumpled.
cruncht[S], *pp.* Crunched.
crusht[P&S], *pp.* Crushed.
crutcht[S], *a.* Crutched.
crys'tal-lin[S], *a.* & *n.* Crystalline.
crys'tal-lis"a-bl[P], **crys'tal-liz"a-bl**[S], *a.* Crystallizable.
cubd[S], *pp.* Cubbed.
cudg'eld[S], *pp.* Cudgeled, cudgelled.
cue[P&S], *n.* Queue.
cuf[P&S], *v.* & *n.* Cuff.
cuft[P&S], *pp.* Cuffed.
cul[S], *v.* & *n.* Cull.
culd[P&S], *pp.* Culled.
cul'or[P], *v.* & *n.* Color.
cul'or-a-bl[P], *a.* Colorable.

cul'ord[P], *pa.* Colored.
cul'pa-bl[P], *a.* Culpable.
cul'pa-bl-ness[P], *n.* Culpableness.
cul'ti-vat"a-bl[P], *a.* Cultivatable.
cul'ti-va-bl[P], *a.* Cultivable.
cul'tur-a-bl[P], *a.* Culturable.
cum, cums[P], *vi.* & *vt.* Come, comes.
cum'berd[P&S], *pp.* Cumbered.
cum'ber-sum[P&S], *a.* Cumbersome.
cum'fit[P], *n.* Comfit.
cum'fort[P], *v.* & *n.* Comfort.
cum'fort-a-bl[P], *a.* Comfortable.
cum'fort-er[P], *n.* Comforter.
cum'ing[P], *pa.* & *n.* Coming.
cum'li-ness[P], *n.* Comeliness.
cum'ly[P], *a.* Comely.
cum-pan'ion[P], *v.* & *n.* Companion.
cum-pan'ion-a-bl[P], *a.* Companionable.
cum-pan'ion-ship[P], *n.* Companionship.
cum'pa-ny[P], *v.* & *n.* Company.
cum'pass[P], *v.* & *n.* Compass.
cu'mu-la-tiv[P&S], *a.* Cumulative.
cu'mu-la-tiv-ly[S], *adv.* Cumulatively.
cu'mu-la-tiv-ness[S], *n.* Cumulativeness.
cun'try[P&S], *a.* & *n.* Country.
cup'l[P], *v.* & *n.* Couple.
cup'ld[P], *pa.* Coupled.
cup'ler[P], *n.* Coupler.
cup'let[P], *n.* Couplet.
cup'ling[P], *n.* Coupling.
cupt[P&S], *pp.* Cupped.
cur'a-bl[P], *a.* Curable.
cur'age[P], *n.* Courage.
cu-ra'geous[P], *a.* Courageous
cur'a-tiv[P&S], *a.* Curative.
cur'a-tiv-ly[S], *adv.* Curatively.
cur'a-tiv-ness[S], *n.* Curativeness.
curb'a-bl[P], *a.* Curbable.
curbd[P&S], *pp.* Curbed.
curld[P&S], *pp.* Curled.
curs'ed[P], *a.* Cursed.
cur'siv[P&S], *a.* & *n.* Cursive.
cur'siv-ly[S], *adv.* Cursively.
cur'siv-ness[S], *n.* Cursiveness.
curst[P&S], *pp.* Cursed.
curs'ta-bl[P], *n.* Curstable.
cur-taild'[S], *pp.* Curtailed.
cur'taind[S], *pp.* Curtained.
cur'te-ous[P], *a.* Courteous.
cur'te-san[P], *n.* Courtesan.
curte'sy[P&S], *v.* & *n.* Courtesy.
cur'te-us[S], *a.* Courteous.
curv[P&S], *v.*, *a.* & *n.* Curve.
cur'va-tiv[S], *a.* Curvative.
curvd[P&S], *pp.* Curved.
cur'vet-ing[P], *pres. p.* Curvetting.
cush'iond[S], *pp.* Cushioned.
cus'tom-a-bl-ness[P], *n.* Customableness.
cu-ta'ne-us[S], *a.* Cutaneous.
cu'ti-cl[P], *n.* Cuticle.
cut'las[S], *n.* Cutlass.
cut'l-fish[P], *n.* Cuttlefish.
cuv'e-nant[P], *v.* & *n.* Covenant.
cuv'er[P], *v.* & *n.* Cover.
cuv'erd[P&S], *pp.* Covered.
cuv'er-ing[P], *n.* Covering.
cuv'er-let[P], *n.* Coverlet.
cuv'ert[P], *a.* & *n.* Covert.
cuv'er-ture[P], *n.* Coverture.
cuv'et[P], *vt.* & *vi.* Covet.
cuv'et-ous[P], *a.* Covetous.
cuv'ey[P], *n.* Covey.
cuz'en[P], *vt.* & *vi.* Cozen.
cuz'en-age[P], *n.* Cozenage.
cuz'in[P], *n.* Cousin.
cy"clo-pe'di-a[S], *n.* Cyclopædia.
cy'prest[S], *a.* Cypressed.

D

-d[P&S], *suffix.* -ed.
dabd[P&S], *pp.* Dabbed.
dab'l[P], *vt.* & *vi.* Dabble.
dab'ld[P], *pp.* Dabbled.
dac'tyl[P&S], *n.* Dactyle.
dag'l[P], *vt.* & *vi.* Daggle.
dag'ld[P], *pp.* Daggled.
dam'age-a-bl[P], *a.* Damageable.
dam'age-a-bl-ness[P], *n.* Damageableness.
dam'askt[S], *a.* Damasked.
damd[P&S], *pa.* Damned.
dam'na-bl[P], *a.* Damnable.
dam'na-bl-ness[P], *n.* Damnableness.
dam-nif'i-ca-bl[P], *a.* Damnificable.
damp'end[S], *pp.* Dampened.
dampt[P&S], *pp.* Damped.
dan'dl[P], *vt.* Dandle.
dan'dld[P], *pp.* Dandled.
dan'drif[P], **dan'druf**[P], *n.* Dandriff, dandruff.
dan'gl[P], *vt.* & *vi.* Dangle.
dan'gld[P], *pp.* Dangled.
danst[S], *pp.* Danced.
dap'l[P], *v.* & *a.* Dapple.
dap'ld[P], *pp.* Dappled.
dapt[S], *pp.* Dapped.
dark'end[P&S], *pp.* Darkened.
dark'sum[P&S], *a.* Darksome.
darnd[P&S], *pp.* Darned.
dasht[P&S], *pp.* Dashed.
dat'a-bl, **date'a-bl**[P], *a.* Datable, dateable.
da'tiv[P&S], *a.* & *n.* Dative.
da'tiv-ly[S], *adv.* Datively.
daubd[P&S], *pp.* Daubed.
dau'fin[P], *n.* Dauphin.
dau'ter[S], *n.* Daughter.
dawnd[P&S], *pp.* Dawned.
daz'l[P], *vt.* & *vi.* Dazzle.
daz'ld[P], *pp.* Dazzled.
deaf. See DEF.
de-bard'[P&S], *pp.* Debarred.
de-barkt'[P], *pp.* Debarked.
de-bat'a-bl, **de-bate'a-bl**[P], *a.* Debatable, debateable.
de-baucht'[P&S], *pa.* Debauched.
de-bil'i-ta"tiv[S], *a.* Debilitative.
dec'a-log[P&S], *n.* Decalogue.
de-campt'[P&S], *pp.* Decamped.
de-cay'a-bl[P], *a.* Decayable.
de-cayd'[P&S], *pp.* Decayed.
de-ceast'[P&S], *pp.* Deceased.
de-ceiv'[P], *vt.* & *vi.* Deceive.
de-ceiv'a-bl[P], *a.* Deceivable.
de-ceiv'a-bl-ness[P], *n.* Deceivableness.
de-ceivd'[P&S], *pp.* Deceived.
de-cep'tiv[P&S], *a.* Deceptive.
de-cep'tiv-ly[S], *adv.* Deceptively.
de-cep'tiv-ness[P], *n.* Deceptiveness.
de-cid'a-bl[P], *a.* Decidable.
de-ci'fer[P&S], *vt.* Decipher.
de-ci'ferd[P&S], *pp.* Deciphered.
de-ci'fer-a-bl[P], *a.* Decipherable.
de-ci'siv[P&S], *a.* Decisive.
de-ci'siv-ly[S], *adv.* Decisively.
de-ci'siv-ness[S], *n.* Decisiveness.
deckd[P], *pp.* Decked.
deckt[S], *a.* Decked.
de-claimd'[P&S], *pp.* Declaimed.
de-clar'a-bl[P], *a.* Declarable.
de-clar'a-tiv[P&S], *a.* & *n.* Declarative.
de-clar'a-tiv-ly[S], *adv.* Declaratively.
de-clin'a-bl[P], *a.* Declinable.
de-coct'i-bl[P], *a.* Decoctible.
de-coc'tiv[S], *a.* Decoctive.
de"com-pos'a-bl[P], *a.* Decomposable.
de"com-pound'a-bl[P], *a.* Decompoundable.
de"con-ges'tiv[S], *a.* Decongestive.
dec'o-ra"tiv[P&S], *a.* Decorative.

de-coyd'[P&S], *pp.* Decoyed.
de-creast'[P&S], *pp.* Decreased.
de-cul'or[P], *vt.* Decolor.
de-cul'or-ize[P], *vt.* Decolorize.
de"cre-a'tiv[S], *a.* Decreative.
de-cree'a-bl[P], *a.* Decreeable.
de-cre'tiv[S], *a.* Decretive.
de-cre'tiv-ly[S], *adv.* Decretively.
de-cur'siv[P&S], *a.* Decursive.
ded[P&S], *a.* Dead.
ded'en[S], *vt.* Deaden.
ded'end[P&S], *pp.* Deadened.
ded'en-ing[P&S], *n.* Deadening.
ded'hed"[S], *v.* & *n.* Deadhead.
ded'ly[P&S], *a.* Deadly.
de-cus'sa-tiv[S], *a.* Decussative.
ded'i-ca-tiv[S], *a.* Dedicative.
de-duc'i-bl[P], *a.* Deducible.
de-duc'i-bl-ness[P], *n.* Deducibleness.
de-du'civ[S], *a.* Deducive.
de-duc'tiv[P&S], *a.* Deductive.
de-duc'tiv-ly[S], *adv.* Deductively.
deemd[P&S], *pp.* Deemed.
deep'end[P&S], *pp.* Deepened
def[P&S], *a.* Deaf.
de-fea'si-bl[P], *a.* Defeasible.
de-fea'si-bl-ness[P], *n.* Defeasibleness.
de-fect'i-bl[P], *a.* Defectible.
de-fec'tiv[P&S], *a.* & *n.* Defective.
def'en[S], *vt.* Deafen.
def'end[P&S], *pp.* Deafened.
de-fend'a-bl[P], *a.* Defendable.
def'en-ing[P&S], *pa.* Deafening.
de-fense'[P&S], *n.* Defense, defence.
de-fen'si-bl[P], *a.* Defensible.
de-fen'si-bl-ness[P], *n.* Defensibleness.
de-fen'siv[P&S], *a.* & *n.* Defensive.
de-ferd'[S], *pp.* Deferred.
de-fin'a-bl[P], *a.* Definable.
def'i-nit[P&S], *a.* Definite.
de-fin'i-tiv[P&S], *a.* & *n.* Definitive.
de-fin'i-tiv-ly[S], *adv.* Definitively.
de-fin'i-tiv-ness[S], *n.* Definitiveness.
def'i-nit-ly[S], *adv.* Definitely.
def'i-nit-ness[S], *n.* Definiteness.
def'la-gra-bl[P], *a.* Deflagrable.
de-flect'i-bl[P], *a.* Deflectible.
de-flec'tiv[S], *a.* Deflective.
def'ness[P&S], *n.* Deafness.
de-form'a-bl[P], *a.* Deformable.
de-form'a-tiv[S], *a.* Deformative.
de-formd'[P&S], *pa.* Deformed.
de-frayd'[P&S], *pp.* Defrayed.
de-gen'er-a-tiv[S], *a.* Degenerative.
de-glu'ti-bl[P], *a.* Deglutible.
de-glu'ti-tiv[S], *a.* Deglutitive.
de-gres'siv[S], *a.* Degressive.
de-hor'ta-tiv[S], *a.* Dehortative.
dein[S], *v.* Deign.
deind[S], *pp.* Deigned.
de-jec'til[S], *a.* Dejectile.
del[P&S], *n.* Dell.
de-lay'a-bl[P], *a.* Delayable.
de-layd'[S], *pp.* Delayed.
del'e-bl[P], **del'i-bl**[P], *a.* Deleble, delible.
de-lec'ta-bl[P], *a.* Delectable.
de-lec'ta-bl-ness[P], *n.* Delectableness.
del'e-ga-bl[P], *a.* Delegable.
de-le'tiv[S], *a.* Deletive.
de-lib'er-a-tiv[P&S], *a.* Deliberative.
de-lib'er-a-tiv-ly[S], *adv.* Deliberatively.
de-lib'er-a-tiv-ness[S], *n.* Deliberativeness.
de-lim'i-ta-tiv[S], *a.* Delimitative.
de-lin'e-a-bl[P], *a.* Delineable.
de-lin'e-a-tiv[S], *a.* Delineative.
de-lite'[P], *v.* & *n.* Delight.
de-lit'ed[P], *pa.* Delighted.
de-liv'erd[P&S], *pp.* Delivered
delt[P&S], *pp.* Dealt.
de-lud'a-bl[P], *a.* Deludable.
de-lu'siv[P&S], *a.* Delusive.
delv[S], *v.* & *n.* Delve.
delvd[S], *pp.* Delved.

dem'a-gog[P&S], *n.* Demagogue.
de-mand'a-bl[P], *a.* Demandable.
de-meand'[P&S], *pp.* Demeaned.
de-mean'or[P&S], *n.* Demeanor.
de-mene'[P], *n.* Demesne.
de-men'ta-tiv[S], *a.* Dementative.
de-merst'[S], *a.* Demersed.
de-mis'a-bl[P], *a.* Demisable.
de-mis'siv[S], *a.* Demissive.
dem"o-crat"i-fi'a-bl[P], *a.* Democratifiable.
de-mol'isht[P&S], *pp.* Demolished.
de'mon-is"a-bl[P], **de'mon-iz"a-bl**[P], *a.* Demonisable, demonizable.
de-mon'stra-bl[P], *a.* Demonstrable.
de-mon'stra-bl-ness[P], *n.* Demonstrableness.
de-mon'stra-tiv[P&S], *a.* & *n.* Demonstrative.
de-mon'stra-tiv-ly[S], *adv.* Demonstratively.
de-mon'stra-tiv-ness[S], *n.* Demonstrativeness.
de-mount'a-bl[P], *a.* Demountable.
de-murd'[S], *pp.* Demurred.
de-mur'a-bl[P], *a.* Demurrable.
dend[S], *pp.* Denned.
de-ni'a-bl[P], *a.* Deniable.
de-nom'i-na-bl[P], *a.* Denominable.
de-nom'i-na-tiv[P&S], *a.* & *n.* Denominative.
de-not'a-bl[P], *a.* Denotable.
de-no'ta-tiv[S], *a.* Denotative.
de-no'ta-tiv-ly[S], *adv.* Denotatively.
de-no'tiv[S], *a.* Denotive.
de-nounst'[S], *pp.* Denounced.
den'ti-fris[S], *n.* Dentifrice.
de-nu'da-tiv[S], *a.* Denudative.
de-nu'mer-a-bl[P], *a.* Denumerable.
de-nun'ci-a-bl[P], *a.* Denunciable.
de-nun'ci-a-tiv[S], *a.* Denunciative.
de-pend'a-bl[P], *a.* Dependable.
de-pend'a-bl-ness[P], *n.* Dependableness.
de-ple'tiv[S], *a.* & *n.* Depletive.
de-plor'a-bl[P], *a.* Deplorable.
de-plor'a-bl-ness[P], *n.* Deplorableness.
de-ployd'[P&S], *pp.* Deployed.
de-pos'a-bl[P], *a.* Deposable.
de-pos'it[S], *v.* & *n.* Deposit.
de-pos'i-tiv[S], *a.* Depositive.
dep're-ca-bl[P], *a.* Deprecable.
dep're-ca-tiv[S], *a.* Deprecative.
dep're-ca-tiv-ly[S], *adv.* Deprecatively.
de-pre'ci-a-tiv[S], *a.* Depreciative.
de-pre'ci-a-tiv-ly[S], *adv.* Depreciatively.
dep're-da-bl[P], *a.* Depredable.
de-pres'si-bl[P], *a.* Depressible.
de-pres'siv[P&S], *a.* Depressive.
de-prest'[P&S], *pa.* Depressed.
de-priv'a-bl[P], *a.* Deprivable.
de-priv'a-tiv[S], *a.* Deprivative.
dep'u-ra-tiv[S], *a.* & *n.* Depurative.
dep'u-ta-bl[P], *a.* Deputable.
dep'u-ta-tiv[S], *a.* Deputative.
de-raild'[S], *pp.* Derailed.
de-range'a-bl[P], *a.* Derangeable.
de-ris'i-bl[P], *a.* Derisible.
de-ri'siv[P&S], *a.* Derisive.
de-ri'siv-ly[S], *adv.* Derisively.
de-ri'siv-ness[S], *n.* Derisiveness.
de-riv'a-bl[P], *a.* Derivable.
de-riv'a-tiv[P&S], *a.* & *n.* Derivative.
de-riv'a-tiv-ly[S], *adv.* Derivatively.
de-riv'a-tiv-ness[S], *n.* Derivativeness.
de-rog'a-tiv[S], *a.* Derogative.
de-rog'a-tiv-ly[S], *adv.* Derogatively.
der'ric[S], *n.* Derrick.
derth[P&S], *n.* Dearth.
de-scend'a-bl[P], **de-scend'i-bl**[P], *a.* Descendable, descendible.
de-scen'siv[S], *a.* Descensive.
de-scrib'a-bl[P], *a.* Describable.
de-scrip'tiv[P&S], *a.* Descriptive.
de-serv'[P&S], *vt.* & *vi.* Deserve.

de-servd'[S], *pp.* Deserved.
de-sid'er-a-bl[P], *a.* Desiderable.
de-sid'er-a-tiv[S], *a.* & *n.* Desiderative.
de-sign'a-bl[P], *a.* Designable (capable of being designed).
des'ig-na-bl[P], *a.* Designable (capable of being designated).
des'ig-na-tiv[S], *a.* Designative.
de-signd'[P&S], *pa.* Designed.
de-sir'a-bl[P], *a.* Desirable.
de-sir'a-bl-ness[P], *n.* Desirableness.
de-sis'tiv[S], *a.* Desistive.
des'o-la-tiv[S], *a.* Desolative.
des-pach'[P], *v.* & *n.* Despatch.
de-spair'a-bl[P], *a.* Despairable.
de-spaird'[P&S], *pp.* Despaired.
des'pi-ca-bl[P], *a.* Despicable.
des'pi-ca-bl-ness[P], *n.* Despicableness.
de-spis'a-bl[P], *a.* Despisable.
de-spoild'[P&S], *pp.* Despoiled.
de-squam'a-tiv[S], *a.* Desquamative.
des'tin[S], *vt.* Destine.
des'tind[S], *pp.* Destined.
de-stroy'a-bl[P], *a.* Destroyable.
de-stroyd'[P&S], *pp.* Destroyed.
de-struc'ti-bl[P], *a.* Destructible.
de-struc'ti-bl-ness[P], *n.* Destructibleness.
de-struc'tiv[P&S], *a.* & *n.* Destructive.
de-struc'tiv-ly[S], *adv.* Destructively.
de-struc'tiv-ness[S], *n.* Destructiveness.
det[P&S], *n.* Debt.
de-tach'a-bl[P], *a.* Detachable.
de-tacht'[P&S], *pp.* Detached.
de-taild'[P&S], *pa.* Detailed.
de-taind'[P&S], *pp.* Detained.
de-tect'a-[or i-]bl[P], *a.* Detectable, detectible.
de-tec'tiv[P&S], *a.* & *n.* Detective.
de-ten'tiv[S], *a.* Detentive.
de-terd'[S], *pp.* Deterred.
de-ter'gi-bl[P], *a.* Detergible.
de-te'ri-o-ra"tiv[S], *a.* Deteriorative.
de-ter'min[P&S], *vt.* & *vi.* Determine.
de-ter'mi-na-bl[P], *a.* Determinable.
de-ter'mi-na-bl-ness[P], *n.* Determinableness.
de-ter'mi-na-tiv[S], *a.* & *n.* Determinative.
de-ter'mi-na-tiv-ly[S], *adv.* Determinatively.
de-ter'mi-na-tiv-ness[S], *n.* Determinativeness.
de-ter'mind[P&S], *pa.* Determined.
de-ter'siv[P&S], *a.* & *n.* Detersive.
de-test'a-bl[P], *a.* Detestable.
deth[P&S], *n.* Death.
deth'ly[S], *a.* & *adv.* Deathly.
det'o-na-bl[P], *a.* Detonable.
det'o-na-tiv[S], *a.* Detonative.
de-trac'tiv[S], *a.* Detractive.
de-tru'siv[S], *a.* Detrusive.
det'ter[P], *n.* Debtor.
det'tor[S], *n.* Debtor.
de-vel'op[P&S], *vt.* & *vi.* Develope.
de-vel'op-a-bl[P], *a.* Developable.
de-vel'opt[P&S], *pa.* Developed.
de'vi-a"tiv[S], *a.* Deviative.
dev'ild[S], *pp.* Deviled.
de'vi-us[S], *a.* Devious.
de-viz'a-bl[P], *a.* Devisable.
de-vize'[P], *vt.* & *vi.* Devise.
de-volv'[P&S], *vt.* & *vi.* Devolve.
de-volvd'[P&S], *pp.* Devolved.
de-vor'a-tiv[S], *a.* Devorative.
de-vour'a-bl[P], *a.* Devourable.
de-vourd'[S], *pp.* Devoured.
dewd[P&S], *pp.* Dewed.
di-af'a-nus[S], *a.* Diaphanous.
di-af'a-nous[P], *a.* Diaphanous.
di"a-fo-ret'ic[P], *a.* & *n.* Diaphoretic.
di'a-fram[P&S], *n.* Diaphragm.
di'a-framd[S], *pp.* Diaphragmed.
di'a-graf[P], *n.* Diagraph.
di'a-gramd[S], *pp.* Diagramed.

di'ald[P&S], *pp.* Dialed, dialled.
di'al-ing[P], *n.* Dialling.
di'al-ist[P], *n.* Diallist.
di'a-log[P&S], *v.* & *n.* Dialogue.
di'a-logd[S], *pp.* Dialogued.
di'a-lys"a-bl[P], **di'a-lyz"a-bl**[P], *a.* Dialysable, dialyzable
di"a-re'a[S], *n.* Diarrhea.
dib'l[P], *v.* & *n.* Dibble.
dib'ld[P], *pp.* Dibbled.
di-cef'a-lous[P], *a.* Dicephalous.
dich[P], *v.* & *n.* Ditch.
dicht[P], *pp.* Ditched.
dick'erd[S], *pp.* Dickered.
dic-ta'tiv[S], *a.* Dictative.
di-dac'tiv[S], *a.* Didactive.
did'l[P], *vt.* Diddle.
did'ld[P], *pp.* Diddled.
di-er'e-sis[S], *n.* Diæresis.
dif'ferd[S], *pp.* Differed.
dif"fer-en'ti-a-bl[P], *a.* Differentiable.
dif'fi-cil[S], *a.* Difficile.
dif'fi-cil-ness[S], *n.* Difficileness.
dif-frac'tiv[S], *a.* Diffractive.
dif-frac'tiv-ly[S], *adv.* Diffractively
dif-fran'gi-bl[P], *a.* Diffrangible.
dif-fu'siv[P&S], *a.* Diffusive.
dif-fuze'[P], *vt.* & *vi.* Diffuse.
dif-fuz'i-bl[P], *a.* Diffusible.
dif-the'ri-a[P], *n.* Diphtheria.
dif'thong[P], *n.* Diphthong.
digd[S], *pp.* Digged.
di-gest'i-bl[P], *a.* Digestible.
di-gest'i-bl-ness[P], *n.* Digestibleness.
di-ges'tiv[S], *a.* & *n.* Digestive.
di-ges'tiv-ly[S], *adv.* Digestively.
dig'ga-bl[P], *a.* Diggable.
di'graf[P], *a.* & *n.* Digraph.
di-gres'siv[P&S], *a.* Digressive.
di-gres'siv-ly[S], *adv.* Digressively.
di-gres'siv-ness[S], *n.* Digressiveness.
di-grest'[S], *pp.* Digressed.
dike[S], *v.* & *n.* Dyke.
dil[P&S], *v.* & *n.* Dill.

di-lat'a-bl[P], *a.* Dilatable.
di-lat'a-bl-ness[P], *n.* Dilatableness.
di-la'tiv[S], *a.* Dilative.
di-lu'tiv[S], *a.* Dilutive.
dimd[P&S], *pp.* Dimmed.
di-men'siv[S], *a.* Dimensive.
di-men'siv-ly[S], *adv.* Dimensively.
di-men'siv-ness[S], *n.* Dimensiveness.
d-min'ish-a-bl[P], *a.* Diminishable.
di-min'isht[P&S], *pa.* Diminished.
di-min'u-tiv[P&S], *a.* & *n.* Diminutive.
di-min'u-tiv-ly[S], *adv.* Diminutively.
di-min'u-tiv-ness[S], *n.* Diminutiveness.
di'morf[P], *n.* Dimorph.
dim'pl[P], *v.* & *n.* Dimple.
dim'pld[P], *pp.* Dimpled.
dind[P&S], *pp.* Dinned.
dingd[S], *pp.* Dinged.
din'gl[P], *v.* & *n.* Dingle.
din'gld[P], *pp.* Dingled.
dipt[P&S], *pp.* Dipped.
di-rect'a-bl[P], *a.* Directable.
di-rec'tiv[P&S], *a.* & *n.* Directive.
di-rec'tiv-ly[S], *adv.* Directively.
di-rec'tiv-ness[S], *n.* Directiveness.
dir'i-gi-bl[P], *a.* & *n.* Dirigible.
dis-a'bl[P], *vt.* Disable.
dis-a'bld[P], *pp.* Disabled.
dis"a-buze'[P], *vt.* Disabuse.
dis"af-fir'ma-tiv[S], *a.* Disaffirmative.
dis"a-gree'a-bl[P], *a.* Disagreeable.
dis"a-gree'a-bl-ness[P], *n.* Disagreeableness.
dis"al-low'a-bl[P], *a.* Disallowable.
dis"al-low'a-bl-ness[P], *n.* Disallowableness.
dis"ap-peard'[P&S], *pp.* Disappeared.
dis-ap'pro-ba-tiv[S], *a.* Disapprobative.
dis-armd'[S], *pa.* Disarmed.
dis"ar-rayd'[P&S], *pp.* Disarrayed.
dis"as-sim'i-la-tiv[S], *a.* Disassimilative.

dis"a-vow'a-bl[P], *a.* Disavowable.
dis"a-vowd'[P&S], *pp.* Disavowed.
dis"be-liev'[P], *vt.* & *vi.* Disbelieve.
dis"be-lievd'[P], *pp.* Disbelieved.
dis-bow'eld[P&S], *pp.* Disboweled.
dis-bur'dend[P], *pp.* Disburdened.
dis-burs'a-bl[P], *a.* Disbursable.
dis-burst'[P&S], *pp.* Disbursed.
dis-cern'i-bl[P], *a.* Discernible.
dis-cern'i-bl-ness[P], *n.* Discernibleness.
dis-cernd'[P&S], *pp.* Discerned.
dis-cerp'i-bl[P], *a.* Discerpible.
dis-cerp'ti-bl[P], *a.* Discerptible.
dis-cerp'tiv[S], *a.* Discerptive.
dis-ci'pl[P], *v.* & *n.* Disciple.
dis'ci-plin[P&S], *v.* & *n.* Discipline.
dis'ci-plin-a-bl[P], *a.* Disciplinable.
dis'ci-plin-a"tiv[S], *a.* Disciplinative.
dis'ci-plind[S], *pp.* Disciplined.
dis-claimd'[P&S], *pp.* Disclaimed.
dis-clo'siv[S], *a.* Disclosive.
dis-cloze'[P], *vt.* & *vi.* Disclose.
dis-clo'zure, *n.* Disclosure.
dis-col'ord[S], *pa.* Discolored.
dis"com-mend'a-bl[P], *a.* Discommendable.
dis"com-mend'a-bl-ness[P], *n.* Discommendableness.
dis"con-du'civ[S], *a.* Disconducive.
dis"con-form'a-bl[P], *a.* Disconformable.
dis"con-nec'tiv[S], *a.* Disconnective.
dis"con-nec'tiv-ness[S], *n.* Disconnectiveness.
dis"con-ten'tiv[S], *a.* Discontentive.
dis"con-tin'u-a-bl[P], *a.* Discontinuable.
dis-cord'a-bl[P], *a.* Discordable.
dis-count'a-bl[P], *a.* Discountable.
dis-cour'siv[S], *a.* Discoursive.
dis-courst'[S], *pp.* Discoursed.
dis-cov'erd[S], *pp.* Discovered. See also DISCUVER.

dis-cred'it-a-bl[P], *a.* Discreditable.
dis-cre'tiv[S], *a.* Discretive.
dis-cre'tiv-ly[S], *adv.* Discretively.
dis-cre'tiv-ness[S], *n.* Discretiveness.
dis-crim'i-na-bl[P], *a.* Discriminable.
dis-crim'i-na-tiv[P&S], *a.* Discriminative.
dis-crim'i-na-tiv-ly[S], *adv.* Discriminatively.
dis-cul'or[P], *vt.* Discolor.
dis-cul'ord[P], *pa.* Discolored.
dis-cum'fit[P], *vt.* Discomfit.
dis-cum'fi-ture[P], *n.* Discomfiture.
dis-cum'fort[P], *v.* & *n.* Discomfort.
dis-cur'age[P], *vt.* Discourage.
dis-cur'age-a-bl[P], *a.* Discourageable.
dis-cur'age-ment[P], *n.* Discouragement.
dis-cur'siv[P&S], *a.* Discursive.
dis-cur'siv-ly[S], *adv.* Discursively.
dis-cur'siv-ness[S], *n.* Discursiveness.
dis-cur'te-ous[P&S], *a.* Discourteous.
dis-cur'te-sy[S], *n.* Discourtesy.
dis-cuss'a-[or **i-**]**bl**[P], *a.* Discussable.
dis-cus'siv[P&S], *a.* Discussive.
dis-cust'[P&S], *pp.* Discussed.
dis-cuv'er[P], *vt.* & *vi.* Discover.
dis-cuv'er-a-bl[P], *a.* Discoverable.
dis-cuv'erd[P], *pp.* Discovered.
dis-cuv'er-y[P], *n.* Discovery.
dis-dain'a-bl[P], *a.* Disdainable.
dis-daind'[P], *pp.* Disdained.
dis"em-barkt'[P&S], *pp.* Disembarked.
dis"em-bar'rast[P&S], *pp.* Disembarrassed.
dis"em-bow'eld[P&S], *pp.* Disemboweled.
dis"en-tan'gl[P], *vt.* Disentangle.
dis-en-tan'gld[P], *pp.* Disentangled.
dis"es-teemd'[P], *pp.* Disesteemed.
dis-fa'vor[P&S], *v.* & *n.* Disfavour.
dis-fa'vord[P&S], *pp.* Disfavored, disfavoured.
dis-grun'tl[P], *vt.* Disgruntle.

dis-guize′[P], *v.* & *n.* Disguise.
dis-hart′en[P&S], *vt.* Dishearten.
dis-hart′end[P&S], *pp.* Disheartened.
di-shev′eld[P&S], *pa.* Dishevelled.
dis-hon′or[S], *v.* & *n.* Dishonor.
dis-hon′or-a-bl[P], *a.* Dishonorable.
dis-hon′or-a-bl-ness[P], *n.* Dishonorableness.
dis-hon′ord[P&S], *pp.* Dishonored.
disht[P&S], *pp.* Dished.
dis″il-lu′siv[S], *a.* Disillusive.
dis″im-ag′in[S], *vt.* Disimagine.
dis-in′te-gra-bl[P], *a.* Disintegrable.
dis-in′te-gra-tiv[S], *a.* Disintegrative.
dis″in-terd′[P&S], *pp.* Disinterred.
dis″in-volv′[S], *vt.* Disinvolve.
dis-joind′[S], *pp.* Disjoined.
dis-junc′tiv[P&S], *a.* & *n.* Disjunctive.
dis-lik′a-bl, dis-like′a-bl[P], *a.* Dislikable, dislikeable.
dis′lo-ca-bl[P], *a.* Dislocable.
dis-man′tl[P], *vt.* Dismantle.
dis-man′tld[P], *pp.* Dismantled.
dis-mayd′[S], *pp.* Dismayed.
dis-mem′berd[P&S], *a.* Dismembered.
dis-miss′i-bl[P], *a.* Dismissible.
dis-mis′siv[P&S], *a.* Dismissive.
dis-mist′[P&S], *pp.* Dismissed.
dis-mount′a-bl[P], *a.* Dismountable.
dis″o-beyd′[S], *pp.* Disobeyed.
dis-or′derd[S], *pa.* Disordered.
dis-own′a-bl[P], *a.* Disownable.
dis-ownd′[S], *pp.* Disowned.
dis-pach′[P], *v.* & *n.* Dispatch.
dis-pan′siv[S], *a.* Dispansive.
dis-par′age-a-bl[P], *a.* Disparageable.
dis-patch′[S], *v.* & *n.* Dispatch, despatch.
dis-patcht′[S], *pp.* Dispatched, despatched.
dis-peld′[P&S], *pp.* Dispelled.
dis-pen′sa-bl[P], *a.* Dispensable.
dis-pen′sa-bl-ness[P], *n.* Dispensableness.
dis-pen′sa-tiv[P&S], *a.* Dispensative.
dis-pen′sa-tiv-ly[S], *adv.* Dispensatively.
dis-penst′[P&S], *pp.* Dispensed.
dis-per′siv[P&S], *a.* Dispersive.
dis-perst′[S], *pa.* Dispersed.
dis-place′a-bl[P], *a.* Displaceable.
dis-playd′[P&S], *pa.* Displayed.
dis-ple′zur-a-bl[P], *a.* Displeasurable.
dis-ple′zure[P], *v.* & *n.* Displeasure.
dis-plo′siv†[P], *a.* Displosive.
dis-pos′a-bl[P], *a.* Disposable.
dis-pos′a-bl-ness[P], *n.* Disposableness.
dis-pos′i-tiv[S], *a.* Dispositive.
dis-pos′i-tiv-ly[S], *adv.* Dispositively.
dis″pos-sest′[P&S], *pp.* Dispossessed.
dis-prais′a-bl[P], *a.* Dispraisable.
dis-pro′ba-tiv[S], *a.* Disprobative.
dis″pro-por′tion-a-bl[P], *a.* Disproportionable.
dis″pro-por′tion-a-bl-ness[P], *n.* Disproportionableness.
dis-prov′a-bl[P], *a.* Disprovable.
dis-pun′ish-a-bl[P], *a.* Dispunishable.
dis′pu-ta-bl[P], *a.* Disputable.
dis′pu-ta-bl-ness[P], *n.* Disputableness.
dis-pu′ta-tiv[P&S], *a.* Disputative.
dis-qui′e-tiv[P&S], *a.* Disquietive.
dis-quis′i-tiv[P&S], *a.* Disquisitive.
dis-quis′i-tiv-ly[S], *adv.* Disquisitively.
dis″re-gard′a-bl[P], *a.* Disregardable.
dis-rep′u-ta-bl[P], *a.* Disreputable.
dis″re-spect′a-bl[P], *a.* Disrespectable.
dis-rup′tiv[P&S], *a.* Disruptive.
dis-rup′tiv-ly[S], *adv.* Disruptively.
dis-rup′tiv-ness[S], *n.* Disruptiveness.
dis-sect′i-bl[P], *a.* Dissectible.
dis-sec′tiv[P&S], *a.* Dissective.
dis-seizd′[S], *pp.* Disseized.
dis-sem′bl[P], *vt.* & *vi.* Dissemble.
dis-sem′bld[P], *pp.* Dissembled.
dis-sem′i-na-tiv[S], *a.* Disseminative.

dis'ser-ta-tiv[s], *a.* Dissertative.
dis-serv'[p&s], *vt.* Disserve.
dis-ser'vice-a-bl[p], *a.* Disserviceable.
dis-ser'vice-a-bl-ness[p], *n.* Disserviceableness.
dis-ser'vis[s], *n.* Disservice.
dis-sim'u-la-tiv[s], *a.* Dissimulative.
dis'si-pa-bl[p], *a.* Dissipable.
dis'si-pa-tiv[s], *a.* Dissipative.
dis-so'cia-bl[p], *a.* Dissociable.
dis-so'cia-bl-ness[p], *n.* Dissociableness.
dis-so'cia-tiv[p&s], *a.* Dissociative.
dis'so-lu-bl[p], *a.* Dissoluble.
dis'so-lu-bl-ness[p], *n.* Dissolubleness.
dis'so-lu-tiv[s], *a.* Dissolutive.
dis-solv'[p&s], *vt.* & *vi.* Dissolve.
dis-solv'a[or -i]**-bl**[p], *a.* Dissolvable, dissolvible.
dis-solv'a-bl-ness[p], *n.* Dissolvableness.
dis-solvd'[p&s], *pp.* Dissolved.
dis-sua'siv[p&s], *a.* & *n.* Dissuasive.
dis-syl'la-bl[p], *n.* Dissyllable.
dis'taf[p&s], *n.* Distaff.
dis-taind'[p], *pp.* Distained.
dis'tanst[s], *pp.* Distanced.
dis-tem'perd[p&s], *pp.* Distempered.
dis-ten'si-bl[p], *a.* Distensible.
dis-ten'siv[s], *a.* Distensive.
dis'tic[s], *n.* Distich.
dis-til'[p&s], *vt.* & *vi.* Distill.
dis-tild'[p&s], *pa.* Distilled.
dis-tinc'tiv[p&s], *a.* & *n.* Distinctive.
dis-tinc'tiv-ly[s], *adv.* Distinctively.
dis-tinc'tiv-ness[s], *n.* Distinctiveness.
dis-tin'guish-a-bl[p], *a.* Distinguishable.
dis-tin'guish-a-bl-ness[p], *n.* Distinguishableness.
dis-tin'guisht[p&s], *pa.* Distinguished.
dis-tor'tiv[s], *a.* Distortive.
dis-tract'i-bl[p], *a.* Distractible.
dis-trac'til[s], *a.* Distractile.
dis-trac'tiv[p&s], *a.* Distractive.
dis-trac'tiv-ly[s], *adv.* Distractively.
dis-train'a-bl[p], *a.* Distrainable.
dis-traind'[p&s], *pp.* Distrained.
dis-traut'[s], *a.* Distraught.
dis-trest'[p&s], *pp.* Distressed.
dis-trib'u-ta-bl[p], *a.* Distributable.
dis-trib'u-tiv[p&s], *a.* & *n.* Distributive.
dis-trib'u-tiv-ly[s], *adv.* Distributively.
dis-trib'u-tiv-ness[s], *n.* Distributiveness.
dis-turb'a-tiv[s], *a.* Disturbative.
dis-turbd'[p&s], *pp.* Disturbed.
dis-uze'[p], *vt.* Disuse.
ditcht[s], *pp.* Ditched.
di-ver'si-fi"a-bl[p], *a.* Diversifiable.
di-vert'i-bl[p], *a.* Divertible.
di-ver'tiv[s], *a.* Divertive.
di-vest'i-bl[p], *a.* Divestible.
di-vest'i-tiv[s], *a.* Divestitive.
di-vid'a-bl[p], *a.* Dividable.
di-vid'a-bl-ness[p], *n.* Dividableness.
di-vin'a-bl[p], *a.* Divinable.
di-vis'i-bl[p], *a.* Divisible.
di-vis'i-bl-ness[p], *n.* Divisibleness.
di-vi'siv[s], *a.* Divisive.
di-vi'siv-ly[s], *adv.* Divisively.
di-vi'siv-ness[s], *n.* Divisiveness.
di-vorce'a-bl, di-vorc'i-bl[p], *a.* Divorceable, divorcible.
di-vor'civ[s], *a.* Divorcive.
diz'end[s], *pp.* Dizened.
do[s], *n.* Doe.
do'a-bl[p], *a.* Doable.
doc'i-bl[p], *a.* Docible.
doc'il[p&s], *a.* Docile.
dockt[p&s], *pp.* Docked.
doc'tord[s], *pp.* Doctored.
doc'trin[p&s], *n.* Doctrine.
dod'derd[s], *a.* Doddered.
do"dec-a-syl'la-bl[p], *n.* Dodecasyllable.

dof[P&S], *vt.* & *vi.* Doff.
doft[P&S], *pp.* Doffed.
dogd[S], *pp.* Dogged.
dol[P&S], *n.* Doll.
dole'sum[S], *a.* Dolesome.
dol'fin[P&S], *n.* Dolphin.
dol"i-cho-ce-fal'ic[P], *a.* Dolichocephalic.
do'lor[S], *n.* Dolour.
dom'a-bl†[P], *a.* Domable.
do-mes'ti-ca-bl[P], *a.* Domesticable.
do-mes'ti-ca-tiv[S], *a.* Domesticative.
dom'i-cil[P&S], *v.* & *n.* Domicile.
dom'i-cild[P&S], *pp.* Domiciled.
dom'i-na-tiv[S], *a.* Dominative.
dom"i-neerd'[S], *pp.* Domineered.
do'na-bl[P], *a.* Donable.
don'a-tiv[P&S], *a.* & *n.* Donative.
dond[S], *pp.* Donned.
don'ky[S], *n.* Donkey.
doomd[S], *pp.* Doomed.
dor'mi-tiv[S], *a.* & *n.* Dormitive.
doubt'a-bl[P], *a.* Doubtable.
dout[P&S], *v.* & *n.* Doubt.
dout'ed[S], *pp.* Doubted.
dout'ful[P&S], *a.* Doubtful.
dout'less[S], *a.* & *adv.* Doubtless.
dow'a-bl[P], *a.* Dowable.
dow'erd[P&S], *a.* Dowered.
downd[S], *pp.* Downed.
drab'l[P], *vt.* & *vi.* Drabble.
drab'ld[P], *pp.* Drabbled.
draf[P], *n.* Draff.
draft[P&S], *v.* & *n.* Draught.
drafts'man[S], *n.* Draughtsman.
draft'y[S], *a.* Draughty.
dragd[P&S], *pp.* Dragged.
drag'l[P], *vt.* & *vi.* Draggle.
drag'ld[P], *pp.* Draggled.
dra-goond'[P&S], *pp.* Dragooned.
draind[S], *pp.* Drained.
dram[S], *v.* & *n.* Drachm.
dram'a-tiz"a-bl[P], *a.* Dramatizable.
dram'a-tize[S], *vt.* & *vi.* Dramatise.
drawld[S], *pp.* Drawled.
dread'a-bl[P], *a.* Dreadable.
dreamd[P&S], *pp.* Dreamed.
dred[P&S], *v.*, *a.* & *n.* Dread.
dred'ful[P], *a.* Dreadful.
dredgd[P&S], *pp.* Dredged.
dremt[P&S], *pp.* Dreamt.
drencht[P&S], *pp.* Drenched.
dres[S], *v.* & *n.* Dress.
drest[P&S], *pp.* Dressed.
drib'l[P], *v.* & *n.* Dribble.
drib'ld[P], *pp.* Dribbled.
drib'let[P], *n.* Dribblet.
dril[P&S], *v.* & *n.* Drill.
drild[P&S], *pp.* Drilled.
drink'a-bl[P], *a.* & *n.* Drinkable.
drink'a-bl-ness[P], *n.* Drinkableness.
dript[P&S], *pp.* Dripped.
driv'eld[S], *pp.* Driveled, drivelled.
drivn[P], *pp.* Driven.
driz'l[P], *v.* & *n.* Drizzle.
driz'ld[P], *pp.* Drizzled.
droopt[S], *pp.* Drooped.
dropt[P&S], *pp.* Dropped.
dros[S], *n.* Dross.
drout[S], *n.* Drought.
drownd[P&S], *pp.* Drowned.
dru[S], *imp.* Drew.
drubd[S], *pp.* Drubbed.
drugd[P&S], *pp.* Drugged.
drumd[P&S], *pp.* Drummed.
drum'hed"[S], *n.* Drumhead.
dubd[S], *pp.* Dubbed.
du'bi-ta-bl[P], *a.* Dubitable.
du'bi-ta-tiv[S], *a.* Dubitative.
du'bi-ta-tiv-ly[S], *adv.* Dubitatively.
dub'l[P], *v.*, *a.* & *n.* Double.
dub'ld[P], *pp.* Doubled.
dub'let[P], *n.* Doublet.
dub'ling[P], *n.* Doubling.
dub-loon'[P], *n.* Doubloon.
dub'ly[P], *adv.* Doubly.
duckt[P&S], *pp.* Ducked.
duc'ti-bl[P], *a.* Ductible.

duc'til[P&S], *a.* Ductile.
duc'til-ly[S], *adv.* Ductilely.
duc'til-ness[S], *n.* Ductileness.
du'el-ist[P], *n.* Duellist.
duf[S], *n.* Duff.
dul[P&S], *v.* & *a.* Dull.
duld[P&S], *pp.* Dulled.
dul'ness[S], *n.* Dullness.
dum[P&S], *v.* & *a.* Dumb.
dumpt[S], *pp.* Dumped.
dund[S], *pp.* Dunned.
dup'a-bl, dupe'a-bl[P], *a.* Dupable, dupeable.
du'pli-ca-bl[P], *a.* Duplicable.
du'pli-ca-tiv[S], *a.* Duplicative.
du'ra-bl[P], *a.* Durable.
du'ra-bl-ness[P], *n.* Durableness.
du'ra-tiv[S], *a.* Durative.
du'ti-a-bl[P], *a.* Dutiable.
duv[P], *n.* Dove.
duv'tail"[P], *v.* & *n.* Dovetail.
duv'taild"[P], *a.* Dovetailed.
duz'en[P], *n.* Dozen.
dwarft[P&S], *pp.* Dwarfed.
dwel[P&S], *vi.* Dwell.
dweld[P&S], **dwelt**[S], *pp.* Dwelled.
dwin'dl[P], *vt.* & *vi.* Dwindle.
dwin'dld[P], *pp.* Dwindled.

E

ea'gl[P], *n.* Eagle.
eard[P&S], *a.* Eared.
eat'a-bl[P], *a.* & *n.* Eatable.
eat'a-bl-ness[P], *n.* Eatableness.
eat'n[P], *pp.* Eaten.
eb[P&S], *v.* & *n.* Ebb.
ebd[P&S], *pp.* Ebbed.
ech[P], *vt.* & *vi.* Etch.
e-chit'e-nin[S], *n.* Echitenine.
echt[P], *pp.* Etched.
e-clips'[P], *v.* & *n.* Eclipse.
e-clips'a-bl[P], *a.* Eclipsable.
e-clipst'[P&S], *pp.* Eclipsed.
ec'log[P&S], *n.* Eclogue.
ec'o[S], *v.* & *n.* Echo.
ec"u-men'i-cal[S], *a.* Ecumenical.
edgd[P&S], *a.* Edged.
ed'i-bl[P], *a.* & *n.* Edible.
ed'i-bl-ness[P], *n.* Edibleness.
ed'i-fis[S], *n.* Edifice.
e'dile[S], *n.* Ædile.
ed'u-ca-bl[P], *a.* Educable.
ed'u-cat"a-bl[P], *a.* Educatable.
ed'u-ca"tiv[S], *a.* Educative.
e-duc'i-bl[P], *a.* Educible.
e-duc'tiv[S], *a.* Eductive.
e-fem'e-ra[P], *n.* Ephemera.
e-fem'e-ral[P], *a.* Ephemeral.
ef'fa-bl[P], *a.* Effable.
ef-face'a-bl[P], *a.* Effaceable.
ef-fa'civ[S], *a.* Effacive.
ef-fec'ti-bl[P], *a.* Effectible.
ef-fec'tiv[P&S], *a.* & *n.* Effective.
ef-fec'tu-al[P], *a.* Effectual.
ef"fer-vesc'i-bl[P], *a.* Effervescible.
ef"fer-ves'civ[S], *a.* Effervescive.
ef-frunt'er-y[P], *n.* Effrontery.
ef-fu'siv[P&S], *a.* Effusive.
ef-fuze'[P], *vt.* & *vi.* Effuse.
eg[P&S], *v.* & *n.* Egg.
egd[P&S], *pp.* Egged.
e'gis[S], *n.* Ægis.
e-jac'u-la-tiv[S], *a.* Ejaculative.
e-ject'a-bl[P], *a.* Ejectable.
e-jec'tiv[S], *a.* Ejective.
el[S], *n.* Ell.
e-lab'o-ra-tiv[S], *a.* Elaborative.
e-laps'[P], *vi.* Elapse.
e-lapst'[P&S], *pp.* Elapsed.
e-la'tiv[S], *a.* Elative.
el'bowd[S], *a.* Elbowed.
e-lect'a-bl[P], *a.* Electable.
e-lec"tion-eerd'[S], *pp.* Electioneered.
e-lec'tiv[P&S], *a.* & *n.* Elective.

e-lec'tiv-ly[s], *adv.* Electively.
e-lec'tiv-ness[s], *n.* Electiveness.
e-lec'tri-fi"a-bl[p], *a.* Electrifiable.
e-lec'trize[p], *vt.* Electrise.
e-lec'tro-lyz"a-bl[p], *a.* Electrolyzable.
e-lec'tro-mo"tiv[s], *a.* & *n.* Electromotive.
e-lec"tro-neg'a-tiv[s], *a.* & *n.* Electronegative.
e-lec"tro-neg'a-tiv-ly[s], *adv.* Electronegatively.
e-lec"tro-pos'i-tiv[s], *a.* & *n.* Electropositive.
el'e-fant[p&s], *n.* Elephant.
el'i-gi-bl[p], *a.* Eligible.
el'i-gi-bl-ness[p], *n.* Eligibleness.
e-lim'i-na-tiv[s], *a.* Eliminative.
el-lips'[p], *n.* Ellipse.
e-lon'ga-tiv[s], *a.* Elongative.
e-lu'ci-da-tiv[s], *a.* Elucidative.
e-lud'i-bl[p], *a.* Eludible.
e-lu'siv[p&s], *a.* Elusive.
e-lu'siv-ly[s], *adv.* Elusively.
e-lu'siv-ness[s], *n.* Elusiveness.
em'a-na-tiv[s], *a.* Emanative.
e-man'ci-pa-tiv[s], *a.* Emancipative.
e-mas'cu-la-tiv[s], *a.* Emasculative.
em-bankt'[s], *pp.* Embanked.
em-barkt'[p&s], *pp.* Embarked.
em-bar'rast[p&s], *pp.* Embarrassed.
em-bel'lisht[p&s], *pp.* Embellished.
em-bez'l[p], *vt.* Embezzle.
em-bez'ld[p], *pp.* Embezzled.
em-bit'terd[s], *pp.* Embittered.
em-bold'end[s], *pp.* Emboldened.
em-bost'[p&s], *pa.* Embossed.
em-bow'eld[p], *pp.* Emboweled, embowelled.
em-bow'erd[p&s], *pp.* Embowered.
em-brace'a-bl[p], *a.* Embraceable.
em-bra'civ[s], *a.* Embracive.
em-bran'gl[p], *vt.* Embrangle.
em-bran'gld[p], *pp.* Embrangled.
em-broi'derd[p&s], *pp.* Embroidered.
em-broild'[p&s], *pp.* Embroiled.
e-mend'a-bl[p], *a.* Emendable.
em'fa-sis[p&s], *n.* Emphasis.
em'fa-size[p], *vt.* Emphasize.
em-fat'ic[p&s], *a.* Emphatic.
e-mis'si-bl[p], *a.* Emissible.
e-mis'siv[s], *a.* Emissive.
e-mit'ta-bl[p], *a.* Emittable.
e-mo'tiv[s], *a.* Emotive.
e-mo'tiv-ly[s], *adv.* Emotively.
e-mo'tiv-ness[s], *n.* Emotiveness.
em-ploy'a-bl[p], *a.* Employable.
em-ployd'[p&s], *pp.* Employed.
em-pow'erd[s], *pp.* Empowered.
em-pur'pl[p], *vt.* Empurple.
em'u-la-bl[p], *a.* Emulable.
em'u-la-tiv[s], *a.* Emulative.
em'u-la-tiv-ly[s], *adv.* Emulatively.
e-mul'siv[p&s], *a.* Emulsive.
en-a'bl[p], *vt.* Enable.
en-act'a-bl[p], *a.* Enactable.
en-ac'tiv[p&s], *a.* Enactive.
en-am'eld[p&s], *pp.* Enameled, enamelled.
en-am'or[s], *vt.* Enamour.
en-am'ord[s], *pp.* Enamored.
en-campt'[p&s], *pp.* Encamped.
en-cir'cl[p], *vt.* Encircle.
en-cir'cld[p], *pp.* Encircled.
en-cloze'[p], *vt.* Enclose.
en-clo'zure[p], *n.* Enclosure.
en-com'past[p&s], *pp.* Encompassed.
en-coun'terd[p&s], *pp.* Encountered.
en-croacht'[p&s], *pp.* Encroached.
en-cum'berd[p&s], *pp.* Encumbered.
en-cum'pas[p], *vt.* Encompass.
en-cur'age[p], *vt.* Encourage.
en-cy"clo-pe'di-a[s], *n.* Encyclopædia.
end'a-bl[p], *a.* Endable.
en-dan'gerd[s], *pp.* Endangered.
en-deard'[p&s], *pp.* Endeared.
en-dev'or[p&s], *v.* & *n.* Endeavor.
en-dev'ord[p&s], *pp.* Endeavored.

en-dorst'[S], *a.* Endorsed.
en-dowd'[P&S], *pp.* Endowed.
en-dur'a-bl[P], *a.* Endurable.
en-dur'a-bl-ness[P], *n.* Endurableness.
en'er-va"tiv[S], *a.* Enervative.
en-fee'bl[P], *vt.* Enfeeble.
en-fee'bld[P], *pp.* Enfeebled
en-fef'[P], *vt.* Enfeoff.
en-feft'[P], *pp.* Enfeoffed.
en-force'a-bl, en-forc'i-bl[P], *a.* Enforceable, enforcible.
en-forst'[S], *pp.* Enforced.
en-gen'derd[P], *pp.* Engendered.
en'gin[P&S], *v.* & *n.* Engine.
en"gi-neerd'[S], *pp.* Engineered.
en'gin-ry[P], *n.* Enginery.
en-gir'dl[P], *vt.* Engirdle.
En'glish-a-bl[P], *a.* Englishable.
en-graind'[P&S], *pp.* Engrained.
en-grost', *pp.* Engrossed.
en-gulft'[P&S], *pp.* Engulfed.
en-han'siv, en-han'civ[S], *a.* Enhansive, enhancive.
en-hanst'[S], *pp.* Enhanced.
en-joind'[S], *pp.* Enjoined.
en-joy'a-bl[P], *a.* Enjoyable.
en-joy'a-bl-ness[P], *n.* Enjoyableness.
en-joyd'[P&S], *pp.* Enjoyed.
en-kin'dl[P], *vt.* Enkindle.
en-large'a-bl[P], *a.* Enlargeable.
en-large'a-bl-ness[P], *n.* Enlargeableness.
en-light'end[S], *pp.* Enlightened.
en-li'vend[S], *pp.* Enlivened.
e-nor'mus[S], *a.* Enormous.
e-nounst'[S], *pp.* Enounced.
en-rav'isht[P], *pp.* Enravished.
en-richt'[P&S], *pp.* Enriched.
en-rol'[P], *vt.* Enroll.
en-rold'[P&S], *pp.* Enrolled.
en-san'guin[P&S], *vt.* Ensanguine.
en-seald'[P], *pp.* Ensealed.
en-tail'a-bl[P], *a.* Entailable.
en-taild'[P&S], *pp.* Entailed.
en-tan'gl[P], *vt.* Entangle.
en-tan'gld[P], *a.* Entangled.
en'ter-a-bl[P], *a.* Enterable.
en'terd[P&S], *pp.* Entered.
en'ter-prize[S], *v.* & *n.* Enterprise.
en'ter-prized[S], *pp.* Enterprised.
en'ter-priz"ing[S], *pres. p.* Enterprising.
en"ter-tain'a-bl[P], *a.* Entertainable.
en"ter-taind'[P&S], *pp.* Entertained.
en-thrald'[S], *pp.* Enthralled.
en-tice'a-bl[P], *a.* Enticeable.
en'ti-ta-tiv[S], *a.* Entitative.
en'ti-ta-tiv-ly[S], *adv.* Entitatively.
en-transe'[P], *vt.* Entrance.
en-trans'ing[P], *pres. p.* Entrancing.
en-transt'[P&S], *pp.* Entranced.
en-trapt'[P&S], *pp.* Entrapped.
en-treat'a-bl[P], *a.* Entreatable.
en-treat'a-bl-ness[P], *n.* Entreatableness.
en-treat'iv[S], *a.* Entreative.
e-nuf'[P&S], *a., n., adv.* & *interj.* Enough.
e-nu'mer-a-bl[P], *a.* Enumerable.
e-nu'mer-a-tiv[S], *a.* Enumerative.
e-nun'ci-a-bl[P], *a.* Enunciable.
e-nun'ci-a-tiv[P&S], *a.* Enunciative.
en-vel'op[S], *v.* & *n.* Envelope.
en-vel'opt[P&S], *pp.* Enveloped.
en-ven'omd[P&S], *pa.* Envenomed.
en'vi-a-bl[P], *a.* Enviable.
en'vi-a-bl-ness[P], *n.* Enviableness.
en-vi'rond[S], *pp.* Environed.
en'vi-us[S], *a.* Envious.
E-o'li-an[S], *a.* & *n.* Æolian.
e'on[S], *n.* Æon.
ep'au-let[P&S], *n.* Epaulette.
ep'i-graf[P], *n.* Epigraph.
ep'i-log[P&S], *n.* Epilogue.
e-pif'a-ny[P], *n.* Epiphany.
e-pis'co-pa-bl[P], *a.* Episcopable.
ep'i-taf[P], *v.* & *n.* Epitaph.
ep'oc[S], *n.* Epoch.
ep'o-nym[S], *n.* Eponyme.

e'qua-bl[P], *a.* Equable.
e'qua-bl-ness[P], *n.* Equableness.
e'quald[P&S], *pp.* Equalled.
e-quipt'[P&S], *pp.* Equipped.
eq'ui-ta-bl[P], *a.* Equitable.
er[P&S], *vi.* Err.
e'ra[S], *n.* Era.
e-rad'i-ca-bl[P], *a.* Eradicable.
e-rad'i-ca-tiv[S], *a.* Eradicative.
e-ras'a-[or **-i-**]**bl**[P], *a.* Erasable.
e-ra'siv[S], *a.* Erasive.
erd[P&S], *pp.* Erred.
e-rect'a-bl[P], *a.* Erectable.
e-rec'til[S], *a.* Erectile.
e-rec'tiv[S], *a.* Erective.
erl[P], *n.* Earl.
er'ly[P], *a.* & *adv.* Early.
er'min[P&S], *v.* & *n.* Ermine.
er'i-gi-bl[P], *a.* Erigible.
ern[P], *vt.* Earn.
ernd[P], *pp.* Earned.
er'nest[P], *a.* & *n.* Earnest.
ern'ings[P], *n. pl.* Earnings.
e-ro'siv[P&S], *a.* Erosive.
erth[P], *v.* & *n.* Earth.
erth'en[P], *v.* & *a.* Earthen.
erth'ling[P], *n.* Earthling.
erth'ly[P], *a.* Earthly.
e-rup'tiv[P&S], *a.* & *n.* Eruptive.
es-cap'a-bl[P], *a.* Escapable.
es"ca-tol'o-gy[S], *n.* Eschatology.
es-chewd'[P&S], *pp.* Eschewed.
es-cheat'a-bl[P], *a.* Escheatable.
e-sof'a-gus[S], *n.* Esophagus.
es-tab'lisht[P&S], *pp.* Established.
es-thet'ic[S], *a.* & *n.* Æsthetic.
es-thet'ics[S], *n.* Æsthetics.
es'ti-ma-bl[P], *a.* Estimable.
es'tiv[S], *n.* Estive.
es'ti-vate[S], *vi.* Æstivate.
etcht[S], *pp.* Etched.
e'ther[S], *n.* Æther.
e"ti-ol'o-gy[S], *n.* Ætiology.
et'i-quet"[S], *n.* Etiquette.
eu'fe-mism[P], *n.* Euphemism.
eu"fe-mis'tic[P], *a.* Euphemistic.
eu-fon'ic[P], *a.* Euphonic.
eu-fo'ni-ous[P], *a.* Euphonious.
eu'fo-ny[P], *n.* Euphony.
eu'fu-ism[P], *n.* Euphuism.
e-vac'u-a-tiv[S], *a.* Evacuative.
e-vad'a-bl, e-vad'i-bl[P], *a.* Evadable, evadible.
e-vag'i-na-bl[P], *a.* Evaginable.
e-val'u-a-bl[P], *a.* Evaluable.
e-vap'o-ra-bl[P], *a.* Evaporable.
e-vap'o-ra-tiv[S], *a.* Evaporative.
e-va'siv[P&S], *a.* & *n.* Evasive.
e-va'siv-ly[S], *adv.* Evasively.
e-va'siv-ness[S], *n.* Evasiveness.
e'vend[S], *pp.* Evened.
e-ver'si-bl[P], *a.* Eversible.
ev'i-den-civ[S], *a.* Evidencive.
ev'i-denst[S], *pp.* Evidenced.
e-vinc'i-bl[P], *a.* Evincible.
e-vin'civ[P&S], *a.* Evincive.
e-vinst'[S], *pp.* Evinced.
ev'i-ta-bl[P], *a.* Evitable.
ev'o-ca-bl[P], *a.* Evocable.
e-vo'ça-tiv[S], *a.* Evocative.
ev'o-lu"tiv[S], *a.* Evolutive.
e-volv'[P&S], *vt.* & *vi.* Evolve.
e-volvd'[P&S], *pp.* Evolved.
e-vol'va-bl[P], *a.* Evolvable.
e-vul'siv[S], *a.* Evulsive.
ex-act'a-bl[P], *a.* Exactable.
ex-ac'tiv[S], *a.* Exactive.
ex-ag'ger-a-tiv[S], *a.* Exaggerative.
ex-ag'ger-a-tiv-ly[S], *adv.* Exaggeratively.
ex-alt'a-tiv[S], *a.* Exaltative.
ex-am'in[P&S], *vt.* Examine.
ex-am'i-na-bl[P], *a.* Examinable.
ex-am'i-na-tiv[S], *a.* Examinative.
ex-am'ind[P&S], *pp.* Examined.
ex-am'pl[P], *n.* Example.
ex-as'per-a-tiv[S], *a.* Exasperative.
ex-cede'[S], *vt.* & *vi.* Exceed.

ex-celd′^{s}, *pp.* Excelled.
ex-cep′tion-a-bl^{p}, *a.* Exceptionable.
ex-cep′tion-a-bl-ness^{p}, *n.* Exceptionableness.
ex-cep′tiv^{s}, *a.* Exceptive.
ex-cerp′tiv^{s}, *a.* Excerptive.
ex-ces′siv$^{p\&s}$, *a.* Excessive.
ex-change′a-bl^{p}, *a.* Exchangeable.
ex-cis′a-bl^{p}, *a.* Excisable.
ex-cit′a-bl^{p}, *a.* Excitable.
ex-cit′a-bl-ness^{p}, *n.* Excitableness.
ex-ci′ta-tiv^{s}, *a.* Excitative.
ex-ci′tiv^{s}, *a.* Excitive.
ex-clam′a-tiv^{s}, *a.* Exclamative.
ex-clam′a-tiv-ly^{s}, *adv.* Exclamatively.
ex-clu′siv$^{p\&s}$, *a.* & *n.* Exclusive.
ex-clu′siv-ly^{s}, *adv.* Exclusively.
ex-clu′siv-ness^{s}, *n.* Exclusiveness.
ex-cog′i-ta-bl^{p}, *a.* Excogitable.
ex-cog′i-ta-tiv^{s}, *a.* Excogitative.
ex″com-mu′ni-ca-bl^{p}, *a.* Excommunicable.
ex″com-mu′ni-ca-tiv^{s}, *a.* Excommunicative.
ex-cor′i-a-bl^{p}, *a.* Excoriable.
ex″cre-men′tiv^{s}, *a.* Excrementive.
ex-cre′tiv$^{p\&s}$, *a.* Excretive.
ex-cru′ci-a-bl^{p}, *a.* Excruciable.
ex-cul′pa-tiv^{s}, *a.* Exculpative.
ex-cur′siv$^{p\&s}$, *a.* Excursive.
ex-curvd′^{s}, *a.* Excurved.
ex-cu′sa-tiv^{s}, *a.* Excusative.
ex-cuz′a-bl^{p}, *a.* Excusable.
ex-cuz′a-bl-ness^{p}, *n.* Excusableness.
ex-cuze′^{p}, *vt.* Excuse.
ex′e-cra-bl^{p}, *a.* Execrable.
ex′e-cra-bl-ness^{p}, *n.* Execrableness.
ex′e-cra-tiv^{s}, *a.* Execrative.
ex′e-cra-tiv-ly^{s}, *adv.* Execratively.
ex-ec′u-tiv$^{p\&s}$, *a.* & *n.* Executive.
ex-ec′u-tiv-ly^{s}, *adv.* Executively.
ex-em′pli-fi-ca-tiv^{s}, *a.* Exemplificative.
ex-em′pli-fi″a-bl^{p}, *a.* Exemplifiable.
ex-empt′i-bl^{p}, *a.* Exemptible.
ex-emp′tiv^{s}, *a.* Exemptive.
ex′er-cis″a[or **-i-**]**bl**^{p}, *a.* Exercisable, exercisible.
ex′er-cize^{p}, *v.* & *n.* Exercise.
ex-ert′iv^{s}, *a.* Exertive.
ex-ha′la-bl^{p}, *a.* Exhalable.
ex-haust′i-bl^{p}, *a.* Exhaustible.
ex-haus′tiv^{s}, *a.* Exhaustive.
ex-haus′tiv-ly^{s}, *adv.* Exhaustively.
ex-haus′tiv-ness^{s}, *n.* Exhaustiveness.
ex-hib′i-ta-bl^{p}, *a.* Exhibitable.
ex-hib′i-tiv^{s}, *a.* Exhibitive.
ex-hib′i-tiv-ly^{s}, *adv.* Exhibitively.
ex-hil′a-ra-tiv^{s}, *a.* Exhilarative.
ex-hort′a-tiv^{s}, *a.* Exhortative.
ex-hort′a-tiv-ly^{s}, *adv.* Exhortatively.
ex′i-gi-bl^{p}, *a.* Exigible.
ex-ist′i-bl^{p}, *a.* Existible.
ex′o-ra-bl^{p}, *a.* Exorable.
ex′o-ra-bl-ness^{p}, *n.* Exorableness.
ex′or-cize$^{p\&s}$, *vt.* & *vi.* Exorcise.
ex-pan′si-bl^{p}, *a.* Expansible.
ex-pan′si-bl-ness^{p}, *n.* Expansibleness.
ex-pan′sil^{s}, *a.* Expansile.
ex-pan′siv$^{p\&s}$, *a.* Expansive.
ex-pan′siv-ly^{s}, *adv.* Expansively.
ex-pan′siv-ness^{s}, *n.* Expansiveness.
ex-pa′ti-a-tiv^{s}, *a.* Expatiative.
ex-pect′a-bl^{p}, *a.* Expectable.
ex-pec′ta-tiv^{s}, *a.* Expectative.
ex-pec′tiv^{s}, *a.* Expective.
ex-ped′i-tiv†^{s}, *a.* Expeditive.
ex-peld′$^{p\&s}$, *pp.* Expelled.
ex-pel′la-bl^{p}, *a.* Expellable.
ex-pend′a-bl^{p}, *a.* Expendable.
ex-pen′siv$^{p\&s}$, *a.* Expensive.
ex-pen′siv-ly^{s}, *adv.* Expensively.
ex-pen′siv-ness^{s}, *n.* Expensiveness.
ex-per″i-men′ta-tiv^{s}, *a.* Experimentative.
ex-pe′ri-enst^{s}, *pp.* Experienced.

ex'pi-a-bl[p], *a.* Expiable.
ex'pi-a"tiv[s], *a.* Expiative.
ex-pir'a-bl[p], *a.* Expirable.
ex-plain'a-bl[p], *a.* Explainable.
ex-plaind'[p&s], *pp.* Explained.
ex-plan'a-tiv[s], *a.* Explanative.
ex'ple-tiv[p&s], *a.* & *n.* Expletive.
ex'pli-ca-bl[p], *a.* Explicable.
ex'pli-ca-bl-ness[p], *n.* Explicableness.
ex'pli-ca-tiv[p&s], *a.* Explicative.
ex-ploit'a-bl[p], *a.* Exploitable.
ex-ploit'a-tiv[s], *a.* Exploitative.
ex-plor'a-bl[p], *a.* Explorable.
ex-plor'a-tiv[s], *a.* Explorative.
ex-plo'si-bl[p], *a.* Explosible.
ex-plo'siv[p&s], *a.* & *n.* Explosive.
ex-po'ni-bl[p], *a.* Exponible.
ex-port'a-bl[p], *a.* Exportable.
ex-pos'i-tiv[s], *a.* Expositive.
ex-pos'tu-la-tiv[s], *a.* Expostulative.
ex-press'i-bl[p], *a.* Expressible.
ex-pres'siv[p&s], *a.* Expressive.
ex-pres'siv-ly[s], *adv.* Expressively.
ex-pres'siv-ness[s], *n.* Expressiveness.
ex-prest'[p&s], *pp.* Expressed.
ex-pro'bra-tiv[s], *a.* Exprobrative.
ex-pug'na-bl[p], *a.* Expugnable.
ex-pul'siv[p&s], *a.* Expulsive.
ex-pul'siv-ness[s], *n.* Expulsiveness.
ex-pulst'[s], *pp.* Expulsed.
ex-punge'a-bl[p], *a.* Expungeable.
ex'qui-sit[p&s], *a.* & *n.* Exquisite.
ex'qui-sit-ly[s], *adv.* Exquisitely.
ex'qui-sit-ness[s], *n.* Exquisiteness.
ex-quis'i-tiv[s], *a.* Exquisitive.
ex-quis'i-tiv-ly[s], *adv.* Exquisitively.
ex-quis'i-tiv-ness[s], *n.* Exquisitiveness.
ex-sic'ca-tiv[s], *a.* & *n.* Exsiccative.
ex-tend'i-bl[p], *a.* Extendible.
ex-ten'si-bl[p], *a.* Extensible.
ex-ten'si-bl-ness[p], *n.* Extensibleness.
ex-ten'sil[s], *a.* Extensile.
ex-ten'siv[p&s], *a.* Extensive.
ex-ten'siv-ly[s], *adv.* Extensively.
ex-ten'siv-ness[s], *n.* Extensiveness.
ex-ten'u-a-tiv[s], *a.* Extenuative.
ex-ter'mi-na-bl[p], *a.* Exterminable.
ex-ter'mi-na-tiv[s], *a.* & *n.* Exterminative.
ex-tinc'tiv[s], *a.* Extinctive.
ex-tin'guish-a-bl[p], *a.* Extinguishable.
ex-tin'guish-a-bl-ness[p], *n.* Extinguishableness.
ex-tin'guisht[p&s], *pp.* Extinguished.
ex-tir'pa-bl[p], *a.* Extirpable.
ex-tir'pa-tiv[s], *a.* Extirpative.
ex-told'[p&s], *pp.* Extolled.
ex-tor'siv[s], *a.* Extorsive.
ex-tor'siv-ly[s], *adv.* Extorsively.
ex-tract'a-[or **-i-**]**bl**[p], *a.* Extractable, extractible.
ex-trac'tiv[p&s], *a.* & *n.* Extractive.
ex"tra-dit'a-bl[p], *a.* Extraditable.
ex'tri-ca-bl[p], *a.* Extricable.
ex-tro'i-tiv[s], *a.* Extroitive.
ex-tru'siv[s], *a.* Extrusive.
ex-u'da-tiv[s], *a.* Exudative.
ex-ul'cer-a-tiv[s], *a.* Exulcerative.
ex-u'vi-a-bl[p], *a.* Exuviable.
ey[p], *v.* & *n.* Eye.
eye'a-bl[p], *a.* Eyeable.

F

f[p]. Ph.
fab'ri-ca"tiv[s], *a.* Fabricative.
face'a-bl[p], *a.* Faceable.
fac'il[s], *a.* Facile.
fa-cil'i-ta"tiv[s], *a.* Facilitative.
fac'ti-tiv[p&s], *a.* & *n.* Factitive.
fac'tord[s], *pa.* Factored.
fac'ul-ta-tiv[s], *a.* Facultative.
fad'a-bl, fade'a-bl[p], *a.* Fadable, fadeable.

fa'e-ton[P], *n.* Phaeton.
fagd[P&S], *pp.* Fagged.
fag'ot[S], *v.* & *n.* Faggot.
faild[P&S], *pp.* Failed.
fal"an-ste'ri-an[P], *a.* Phalansterian.
fal'an-ste-ry[P], *n.* Phalanstery.
fa'lanx[P], *n.* Phalanx.
fal'li-bl[P], *a.* Fallible.
fal'li-bl-ness[P], *n.* Fallibleness.
fal'lowd[S], *pp.* Fallowed.
fal'si-fi"a-bl[P], *a.* Falsifiable.
fal'terd[P&S], *pp.* Faltered.
fam'in[P&S], *n.* Famine.
fam'isht[P&S], *pp.* Famished.
fa'mus[S], *a.* Famous.
fand[S], *pp.* Fanned.
fan'tasm[P&S], *n.* Phantasm.
fan-tas"ma-go'ri-a[P&S], *n.* Phantasmagoria.
fan-tas'tic[S], *a.* & *n.* Phantastic.
fan'ta-sy[S], *n.* Phantasy.
fan'tom[P&S], *n.* Phantom.
fare'wel'[P], *a.*, *n.* & *interj.* Farewell.
far'ma-cy[P&S], *n.* Pharmacy.
farmd[P&S], *pp.* Farmed.
far'ynx[P], *n.* Pharynx.
fas'ci-cl[P], *n.* Fascicle.
fase[P], *n.* Phase.
fash'ion-a-bl[P], *a.* & *n.* Fashionable.
fash'ion-a-bl-ness[P], *n.* Fashionableness.
fash'iond[P&S], *pp.* Fashioned.
fast'end[P&S], *pp.* Fastened.
fa'therd[P&S], *pp.* Fathered.
fath'om-a-bl[P], *a.* Fathomable.
fath'omd[P&S], *pp.* Fathomed.
fat'i-ga-bl[P], *a.* Fatigable.
fat'i-ga-bl-ness[P], *n.* Fatigableness.
fat'ta-bl[P], *a.* Fattable.
fat'tend[P&S], *pp.* Fattened.
fa'vor[P&S], *v.* & *n.* Favour.
fa'vor-a-bl[P], *a.* Favorable.
fa'vor-a-bl-ness[P], *n.* Favorableness.
fa'vord[P&S], *a.* Favored.
fa'vor-it[P&S], *a.* & *n.* Favorite.
fawnd[P&S], *pp.* Fawned.
fear'a-bl[P], *a.* Fearable.
feard[P&S], *pp.* Feared.
fea'si-bl[P], *a.* Feasible.
fea'si-bl-ness[P], *n.* Feasibleness.
feb'ril[P&S], **-rile**[S], *a.* Febrile.
fech[P], *v.* & *n.* Fetch.
fecht[P], *pp.* Fetched.
fed'er-a-tiv[P&S], *a.* Federative.
fee'a-bl[P], *a.* Feeable.
fee'bl[P], *a.* Feeble.
feignd[S], *pp.* Feigned.
fein[P&S], *vt.* & *vi.* Feign.
feind[P], *pp.* Feigned.
fel[S], *v.*, *a.* & *n.* Fell.
feld[S], *pp.* Felled.
fel'lo[S], *a.* & *n.* Fellow.
fel'loes[S], *n. pl.* Fellows.
fe-lo'ni-us[S], *a.* Felonious.
fem'i-nin[P&S], **-nine**[S], *a.* Feminine.
fe'nix[P&S], *n.* Phenix.
fe-nom'e-nal[P], *a.* Phenomenal.
fe-nom'e-non[P], *n.* Phenomenon.
fense[P], *v.* & *n.* Fence.
fenc'i-bl[P], *a.* & *n.* Fencible.
fend'a-bl[P], *a.* Fendable.
fen'siv[S], *a.* Fensive.
fenst[S], *pp.* Fenced.
fer-ment'a-[or **-i-**]**bl**[P], *a.* Fermentable, fermentible.
fer-men'ta-tiv[P&S], *a.* Fermentative.
fer-men'ta-tiv-ly[S], *adv.* Fermentatively.
fer-men'ta-tiv-ness[S], *n.* Fermentativeness.
fer"men-tes'ci-bl[P], *a.* Fermentescible.
fer-men'tiv[S], *a.* Fermentive.
fer'til, -tile[P&S], *a.* Fertile.
fer'til-ly[S], *adv.* Fertilely.
fer'til-ness[S], *n.* Fertileness.
fer'ti-liz"a-bl[P], *a.* Fertilizable.
fer'vor[S], *n.* Fervour.

fes'ant[s], *n.* Pheasant.
fes'terd[s], *pp.* Festered.
fes'tiv[r&s], *a.* Festive.
fes'tiv-ly[s], *adv.* Festively.
fes-toond'[s], *a.* Festooned.
fetcht[s], *pp.* Fetched.
feth'er[r&s], *v.* & *n.* Feather.
feth'erd[r&s], *a.* Feathered.
feth'er-y[r&s], *a.* Feathery.
fet'terd[s], *a.* Fettered.
fe'verd[r&s], *pa.* Fevered.
fez'ant[r], *n.* Pheasant.
fi'al, vi'al[r], *n.* Phial, vial.
fibd[s], *pp.* Fibbed.
fi'ber[r&s], *n.* Fibre.
fi'berd[r&s], *a.* Fibered.
fi'brin[r], *n.* Fibrine.
fick'l[r], *v.* & *a.* Fickle.
fic'til[s], *a.* & *n.* Fictile.
fic'til-ness[s], *n.* Fictileness.
fic'tiv[s], *a.* Fictive.
fic'tiv-ly[s], *adv.* Fictively.
fid'l[r], *v.* & *n.* Fiddle.
fid'ld[r], *pp.* Fiddled.
fidg'et-ing[r], *pres. p.* Fidgetting.
fierse[r], *a.* Fierce.
figd[s], *pp.* & *a.* Figged.
fight'a-bl[r], *a.* Fightable.
fig'ur-a-bl[r], *a.* Figurable.
fig'ur-a-tiv[s], *a.* Figurative.
fil[r&s], *v.* & *n.* Fill.
fi-lan'der[r], *vi.* Philander.
fil"an-throp'ic[r], *a.* Philanthropic.
fi-lan'thro-pist[r], *n.* Philanthropist.
fi-lan'thro-py[r], *n.* Philanthropy.
filcht[r&s], *pp.* Filched.
fild[r&s], *pp.* Filled.
fil"har-mon'ic[r], *a.* Philharmonic.
fil'i-bus"terd[s], *pp.* Filibustered.
fill'a-bl[r], *a.* Fillable.
fi-lip'pic[r], *n.* Philippic.
fil'ipt[r], *pp.* Filliped.
fil'lipt[s], *pp.* Filliped.
filmd[s], *pp.* Filmed.

fi-lol'o-ger[r&s], *n.* Philologer.
fil"o-log'i-cal[r&s], *a.* Philological.
fi-lol'o-gist[r&s], *n.* Philologist.
fi-lol'o-gy[r&s], *n.* Philology.
fil'o-mel[r], *n.* Philomel.
fil"o-pe'na[r], *n.* Philopena.
fi-los'o-fer[r], *n.* Philosopher.
fil"o-sof'ic[r], *a.* Philosophic.
fi-los'o-fize[r&s], *vt.* & *vi.* Philosophize.
fi-los'o-fy[r&s], *n.* Philosophy.
fil'terd[r&s], *pp.* Filtered.
fin'a-bl[r], *a.* Finable.
fin'ger-a-bl[r], *a.* Fingerable.
fin'gerd[r&s], *pa.* Fingered.
fin'isht[r&s], *pa.* Finished.
fish'a-bl[r], *a.* Fishable.
fisht[r&s], *pp.* Fished.
fis'sil[r&s], **-sile**[s], *a.* Fissile.
fis'siv[s], *a.* Fissive.
fit'ta-bl[r], *a.* Fittable.
fix'a-bl[r], *a.* Fixable.
fix'a-tiv[s], *a.* & *n.* Fixative.
fixt[r&s], *pa.* Fixed.
fiz[r], *v.* & *n.* Fizz.
fizd[r&s], *pp.* Fizzed.
fiz'l[r], *v.* & *n.* Fizzle.
fiz'ld[r], *pp.* Fizzled.
flagd[r&s], *pp.* Flagged.
flag'el-la-tiv[s], *a.* Flagellative.
flaild[s], *pp.* Flailed.
flankt[s], *a.* Flanked.
flan'neld[s], *a.* Flanneled.
flapt[r&s], *pp.* Flapped.
flasht[r&s], *pp.* Flashed.
flat'tend[r&s], *pp.* Flattened.
flat'ter-a-bl[r], *a.* Flatterable.
flat'terd[r&s], *pp.* Flattered.
fla'vor[r&s], *v.* & *n.* Flavour.
fla'vord[r&s], *a.* Flavored, flavoured.
flawd[r&s], *pp.* Flawed.
flaxt[s], *pp.* Flaxed.
flayd[s], *pp.* Flayed.
fle-bot'o-my[r], *n.* Phlebotomy.
fleckt[s], *pa.* Flecked.

fledgd[P&S], *pp.* Fledged.
fleerd[P], *pp.* Fleered.
flegm[P], *n.* Phlegm.
fleg-mat'ic[P], *a.* Phlegmatic.
flem[S], *n.* Phlegm.
flesht[P], *pp.* Fleshed.
flex'i-bl[P], *a.* Flexible.
flex'i-bl-ness[P], *n.* Flexibleness.
flex'il[P&S], *a.* Flexile.
flex'iv†[S], *a.* Flexive.
flext[S], *a.* Flexed.
flick'erd[S], *pp.* Flickered.
flickt[S], *pp.* Flicked.
flincht[P&S], *pp.* Flinched.
flipt[S], *pp.* Flipped.
flirt'a-bl[P], *a.* Flirtable.
flit'terd[S], *pp.* Flittered.
flo[1S], *n.* Floe.
flo[2S], *v.* & *n.* Flow.
float'a-bl[P], *a.* Floatable.
flockt[S], *pp.* Flocked.
floed[S], *pp.* Flowed.
floes[S], *n. pl.* Flows.
flogd[P&S], *pp.* Flogged.
flog'ga-bl[P], *a.* Floggable.
floord[P&S], *pp.* Floored.
flopt[S], *pp.* Flopped.
flos[S], *n.* Floss.
flot'ta-bl[P], *a.* Flottable.
floun'derd[P&S], *pp.* Floundered.
flounst[S], *pp.* Flounced.
flourd[S], *pp.* Floured.
flour'isht[S], *pp.* Flourished.
flowd[S], *pp.* Flowed.
flow'erd[S], *pp.* Flowered.
flox[P&S], *n.* Phlox.
flu[S], *v.* & *n.* Flue.
flu[S], *imp.* Flew.
fluc'tu-a-bl[P], *a.* Fluctuable.
flur'ish[P], *v.* & *n.* Flourish.
flur'isht[P], *pp.* Flourished.
flusht[P&S], *pp.* Flushed.
flus'terd[P&S], *pp.* Flustered.
flut'ter-a-bl[P], *a.* Flutterable.
flut'terd[P&S], *pp.* Fluttered.
flux'i-bl[P], *a.* Fluxible.
flux'i-bl-ness[P], *n.* Fluxibleness.
fluxt[P&S], *pp.* Fluxed.
fly'a-bl[P], *a.* Flyable.
fo[S], *n.* Foe.
foald[P&S], *pp.* Foaled.
foamd[P&S], *pp.* Foamed.
fobd[P&S], *pp.* Fobbed.
fo'cust[P&S], *pp.* Focused.
fod'derd[S], *pp.* Foddered.
fœ'nix[P], *n.* Phœnix, phenix.
fogd[S], *pp.* Fogged.
foi'bl[P], *n.* Foible.
foild[P&S], *a.* Foiled.
fol'li-cl[P], *n.* Follicle.
fol'loed[S], *pp.* Followed.
fol'lowd[P&S], *pp.* Followed.
fon'dl[P], *vt.* & *vi.* Fondle.
fon'dld[P], *pp.* Fondled.
fo-net'ic[P&S], *a.* & *n.* Phonetic.
fo'net-ist[P], *n.* Phonetist.
fon'ic[P], *a.* Phonic.
fo'no-graf[P&S], *v.* & *n.* Phonograph.
fo-nog'ra-fer[P&S], *n.* Phonographer.
fo″no-graf'ic[P&S], *a.* Phonographic.
fo-nog'ra-fy[P&S], *n.* Phonography.
fo″no-log'ic[P], *a.* Phonologic.
fo-nol'o-gist[P], *n.* Phonologist.
fo-nol'o-gy[P], *n.* Phonology.
fo'no-type[P], *n.* Phonotype.
foold[P&S], *pp.* Fooled.
for-bad'[P], *vt.* Forbade.
for-bear'a-bl[P], *a.* Forbearable.
for-bid'a-bl[P], *a.* Forbidable.
for-bid'n[P], *pa.* Forbidden.
for'ci-bl[P], *a.* Forcible.
for'ci-bl-ness[P], *n.* Forcibleness.
ford'a-bl[P], *a.* Fordable.
ford'a-bl-ness[P], *n.* Fordableness.
fore-gon'[P], *pa.* Foregone.
fore'hed[S], *n.* Forehead.
for'en[P&S], *a.* Foreign.
for'en-er[P&S], *n.* Foreigner.

fore-know'a-bl[P], *a.* foreknowable.
fore-see'a-bl[P], *a.* Foreseeable.
fore-warnd'[S], *pp.* Forewarned.
for'feit-a-bl[P], *a.* Forfeitable.
for'fit[S], *v.* & *n.* Forfeit.
forge'a-bl[P], *a.* Forgeable.
for-get'a-bl, for-get'ta-bl[P], *a.* Forgetable, forgettable.
for-get'a-[or **ta-**]**bl-ness**[P], *n.* Forgetableness, forgettableness.
for'ge-tiv[S], *a.* Forgetive.
for-giv'[P&S], *vt.* & *vi.* Forgive.
for-giv'a-bl[P], *a.* Forgivable.
for-giv'ness[P], *n.* Forgiveness.
for-gon'[P], *pp.* Forgone.
for'hed[P], *n.* Forehead.
forkt[S], *a.* Forked.
form'a-bl[P], *a.* Formable.
form'a-tiv[P&S], *a.* & *n.* Formative.
formd[P&S], *pa.* Formed.
for'mi-da-bl[P], *a.* Formidable.
for'mi-da-bl-ness[P], *n.* Formidableness.
forst[S], *pp.* Forced.
fort'a-lis[S], *n.* Fortalice.
for'ti-fi"a-bl[P], *a.* Fortifiable.
fos'fate[P], *n.* Phosphate.
fos-for'ic[P], *a.* Phosphoric.
fos'for-us[P&S], *n.* Phosphorus.
foss[P], *n.* Fosse.
fos'terd[P&S], *pp.* Fostered.
fo'to-graf[P&S], *v.* & *n.* Photograph.
fo-tog'ra-fer[P&S], *n.* Photographer.
fo"to-graf'ic[P&S], *a* Photographic.
fo'to-graft[P&S], *pp.* Photographed.
fo-tog'ra-fy[P&S], *n.* Photography.
fo-tom'e-ter[P], *n.* Photometer.
fo-tom'e-try[P], *n.* Photometry.
fo'to-sphere[S], *n.* Photosphere.
fo'to-type[P], *n.* Phototype.
fould[P&S], *pp.* Fouled.
foun'derd[P&S], *pp.* Foundered.
foxt[P&S], *pa.* Foxed.
frac'ta-bl[P], *n.* Fractable.
frac'til[S], *a.* Fractile.
frag'il[P&S], *a.* Fragile.
frag'il-ly[S], *adv.* Fragilely.
fram'a-bl[P], *a.* Framable.
fram'a-bl-ness[P], *n.* Framableness.
fran'gi-bl[P], *a.* Frangible.
fran'gi-bl-ness[P], *n.* Frangibleness.
frank'a-bl[P], *a.* Frankable.
frankt[S], *pp.* Franked.
frase[P&S], *v.* & *n.* Phrase.
fra"se-ol'o-gy[P&S], *n.* Phraseology.
fraut[S], *pa.* Fraught.
frayd[S], *pp.* Frayed.
fraz'l[P], *v.* & *n.* Frazzle.
fraz'ld[P], *pp.* Frazzled.
freakt[S], *pp.* Freaked.
freck'l[P], *v.* & *n.* Freckle.
freck'ld[P], *pa.* Freckled.
freez[P], *vt.* & *vi.* Freeze.
frend[P], *n.* Friend.
fre-nol'o-gist[P], *n.* Phrenologist.
fre-nol'o-gy[P&S], *n.* Phrenology.
fren'zy[P], *v.* & *n.* Phrensy.
frencht[S], *a.* Frenched.
fre-quent'a-bl[P], *a.* Frequentable.
fre-quen'ta-tiv[S], *a.* & *n.* Frequentative.
fresh'end[P&S], *pp.* Freshened.
fri'a-bl[P], *a.* Friable.
fri'a-bl-ness[P], *n.* Friableness.
frib'l[P], *v., a.* & *n.* Fribble.
frib'ld[P], *pp.* Fribbled.
fric'a-tiv[S], *a.* & *n.* Fricative.
fric'tion-a-bl[P], *a.* Frictionable.
friez[P], *v.* & *n.* Frieze.
fright'en-a-bl[P], *a.* Frightenable.
fright'end[P&S], *pp.* Frightened.
fril[P&S], *v.* & *n.* Frill.
frild[P&S], *pp.* Frilled.
friskt[P&S], *pp.* Frisked.
frit'terd[P&S], *pp.* Frittered.
friv'o-lus[S], *a.* Frivolous.
friz[P], *v.* & *n.* Frizz.
frizd[P&S], *pp.* Frizzed.

friz'l[P], *v.* & *n.* Frizzle.
friz'ld[P], *pp.* Frizzled.
frockt[S], *pp.* Frocked.
frol'ickt[P], *pp.* Frolicked.
frol'ic-sum[P&S], *a.* Frolicsome.
frol'ict[S], *pp.* Frolicked.
frotht[S], *pp.* Frothed.
frownd[P&S], *pp.* Frowned.
fruc'ti-fi"a-bl[P], *a.* Fructifiable.
fruc'ti-fi-ca-tiv[S], *a.* Fructificative.
fru-giv'o-rus[S], *a.* Frugivorous.
fru'i-tiv[S], *a.* Fruitive.
frunt[P], *v.*, *a.* & *n.* Front.
frus'tra-bl[P], *a.* Frustrable.
frus'tra-tiv[S], *a.* Frustrative.
fud'l[P], *vt.* & *vi.* Fuddle.
fud'ld[P], *pp.* Fuddled.
fu'eld[S], *pp.* Fueled.
fu'ga-tiv[S], *a.* Fugative.
fu'gi-tiv[P&S], *a.* & *n.* Fugitive.
fu'gi-tiv-ly[S], *adv.* Fugitively.
fu'gi-tiv-ness[S], *n.* Fugitiveness.
ful[P&S], *v.*, *a.*, *n.* & *adv.* Full.
fuld[P&S], *pp.* Fulled.
ful-fil'[P&S], *vt.* Fulfill.
ful-fild'[P&S], *pp.* Fulfilled.
ful'min[S], *vt.* & *vi.* Fulmine.
ful'ness[S], *n.* Fullness.
ful'sum[P&S], *a.* Fulsome.
fum'bl[P], *v.* & *n.* Fumble.
fum'bld[P], *pp.* Fumbled.
fund'a-bl[P], *a.* Fundable.
fun'gi-bl[P], *a.* & *n.* Fungible.
fun'neld[S], *pp.* Funneled.
fur'bish-a-bl[P], *a.* Furbishable.
fur'bisht[P&S], *pp.* Furbished.
furd[S], *pp.* & *a.* Furred.
furld[P&S], *pp.* Furled.
fur'lo[P&S], *v.* & *n.* Furlough.
fur'loed[P&S], *pp.* Furloughed.
fur'nish-a-bl[P], *a.* Furnishable.
fur'nisht[P&S], *pa.* Furnished.
fur'ro[S], *v.* & *n.* Furrow.
fur'roed[S], *a.* Furrowed.
fur'therd[P&S], *pp.* Furthered.
fur'tiv[P&S], *a.* Furtive.
fur'tiv-ly[S], Furtively.
fur'tiv-ness[S], *n.* Furtiveness.
furz[P], *v.* & *n.* Furze.
fus[S], *v.* & *n.* Fuss.
fus'cus[S], *a.* Fuscous.
fust[P&S], *pp.* Fussed.
fu'til[P&S], **fu'tile**[P], *a.* Futile.
fu'til-ly[S], *adv.* Futilely.
fu'til-ness[S], *n.* Futileness.
fuz[P], *n.* Fuzz.
fuze[P], *v.* & *n.* Fuse.
fu'zi-bl[P], *a.* Fusible.
fu'zi-bl-ness[P], *n.* Fusibleness.
fu'zion[P], *n.* Fusion.
fy-lac'ter-y[P], *n.* Phylactery.
fys'ic[P&S], *v.* & *n.* Physic.
fys'i-cal[P], *a.* Physical.
fy-si'cian[P&S], *n.* Physician.
fys'i-cist[P], *n.* Physicist.
fys'ickt[P], *pp.* Physicked.
fys'ics[P&S], *n.* Physics.
fys"i-og'no-mist[P], *n.* Physiognomist.
fys"i-og'no-my[P], *n.* Physiognomy.
fys"i-o-log'ic[P], *a.* Physiologic.
fys"i-ol'o-gist[P], *n.* Physiologist.
fys"i-ol'o-gy[P&S], *n.* Physiology.
fy-tog'ra-fy[P], *n.* Phytography.
fy-tol'o-gy[P], *n.* Phytology.

G

gabd[P&S], *pp.* Gabbed.
gab'l[P], *v.* & *n.* Gabble.
gab'ld[P], *pp.* Gabbled.
gaf[P&S], *v.* & *n.* Gaff.
gaf'l[P], *n.* Gaffle.
gagd[P&S], *pp.* Gagged.
gage'a-bl[P], *a.* Gageable.
gag'l[P], *v.* & *n.* Gaggle.

gag'ld[P], *pp.* Gaggled.
gain'a-bl[P], *a.* Gainable.
gaind[P&S], *pp.* Gained.
gai'terd[S], *pp.* Gaitered.
ga-lag'in, ga-lag'i-nin[S], *a.* & *n.* Galagine, galaginine.
gal'an-tin[S], *n.* Galantine.
gald[S], *pa.* Galled.
galld[P], *pa.* Galled.
gal'lopt[S], *pp.* Galloped.
gal'ly[S], *n.* Galley.
gam'bl[P], *v.* & *n.* Gamble.
gam'bld[P], *pp.* Gambled.
gamd[S], *pp.* Gammed.
game'sum[P&S], *a.* Gamesome.
gam'mond[S], *pp.* Gammoned.
gang[P], *n.* Gangue.
gang'a-bl[P], *a.* Gangable.
gapt[S], *pp.* Gapped.
gar"an-tee'[P], *v.* & *n.* Guarantee.
gar'an-ty[P], *v.* & *n.* Guaranty.
garbd[S], *pp.* Garbed.
gar'bl[P], *v.* & *n.* Garble.
gar'bld[P], *pp.* Garbled.
gard[P&S], *v.* & *n.* Guard.
gar'den-a-bl[P], *a.* Gardenable.
gar'dend[P&S], *pp.* Gardened.
gar'di-an[P&S], *a.* & *n.* Guardian.
gar'gl[P], *v.* & *n.* Gargle.
gar'gld[P], *pp.* Gargled.
gar'nerd[P&S], *pp.* Garnered.
gar'nisht[S], *a.* Garnished.
gar'ri-sond[S], *a.* Garrisoned.
gar'terd[S], *pp.* Gartered.
gasht[P&S], *pp.* Gashed.
gas'i-fi"a-bl[P], *a.* Gasifiable.
gaspt[P&S], *pp.* Gasped.
gast[S], *pp.* Gassed.
gast'li-ness[P], *n.* Ghastliness.
gast'ly[P&S], *a.* & *adv.* Ghastly.
gath'er-a-bl[P], *a.* Gatherable.
gath'erd[S], *pp.* Gathered.
gauz[P], *n.* Gauze.
gav'eld[S], *pp.* Gaveled, gavelled.
ga-zel'[P], *n.* Gazelle.
ga-zet'[P], *v.* & *n.* Gazette.
geard[S], *pp.* Geared.
gel'a-bl[P], *a.* Gelable.
gel'a-tin[P], *n.* Gelatine.
ge-lat"i-niz'a-bl[P], *a.* Gelatinizable.
geld'a-bl[P], *a.* Geldable.
gem'i-na-tiv[S], *a.* & *n.* Geminative.
gen'der-a-bl[P], *a.* Genderable.
gen'derd[P&S], *pp.* Gendered.
gen'er-a-bl[P], *a.* Generable.
gen'er-a-bl-ness[P], *n.* Generableness.
gen'er-ald[S], *pp.* Generaled, generalled.
gen'er-al-iz"[or **-is"**]**a-bl**[P], *a.* Generalizable, generalisable.
gen'er-a-tiv[S], *a.* Generative.
gen'i-tiv[P&S], *a.* & *n.* Genitive.
gen'tl[P], *v.*, *a.* & *n.* Gentle.
gen'tld[P], *pp.* Gentled.
gen'tl-man[P], *n.* Gentleman.
gen'u-in[P&S], *a.* Genuine.
gen'u-in-ly[S], *adv.* Genuinely.
gen'u-in-ness[S], *n.* Genuineness.
ge-og'ra-fer[P], *n.* Geographer.
ge"o-graf'ic, -i-cal[P], *a.* Geographic, geographical.
ge-og'ra-fy[P&S], *n.* Geography.
ger'mi-na-bl[P], *a.* Germinable.
ger'mi-na-tiv[S], *a.* Germinative.
ger'mi-na-tiv-ly[S], *adv.* Germinatively.
ge-run'div[S], *n.* Gerundive.
ge-run'div-ly[S], *adv.* Gerundively.
gess[P], *v.* & *n.* Guess.
gest[P], *pp.* Guessed.
gest[P], *n.* Guest.
ges'ta-tiv[S], *a.* Gestative.
ges-tic'u-la"tiv[S], *a.* Gesticulative.
ges-tic'u-la-tiv-ly[S], *adv.* Gesticulatively.
get-at'a-bl[P], *a.* Getatable.
get-at'a-bl-ness[P], *n.* Getatableness.
Ghib'el-lin[S], *a.* & *n.* Ghibelline.

gibd[s], *a.* Gibbed.
gib'berd[s], *pp.* Gibbered.
gigd[s], *pp.* Gigged.
gig'l[p], *v.* & *n.* Giggle. —
gig'ld[p], *pp.* Giggled.
gig'ni-tiv[s], *a.* Gignitive.
gil[p&s], *v.* & *n.* Gill.
gild[s], *pp.* Gilled.
gild[p], *n.* Guild.
gilt[p], *n.* Guilt.
gilt'y[p], *a.* Guilty.
gind[s], *pp.* Ginned.
gin'gerd[s], *pp.* Gingered.
gir'dl[p], *v.* & *n.* Girdle.
gir'dld[p], *pp.* Girdled.
girtht[s], *pp.* Girthed.
giv[p&s], *vt.* & *vi.* Give.
give'a-bl[p], *a.* Giveable.
giv'n[p], *pa.* Given.
glad'dend[s], *pp.* Gladdened.
glad'sum[p&s], *a.* Gladsome.
glam'or[s], *vt.* Glamour.
glam'ord[s], *pp.* Glamoured.
glanst[s], *pp.* Glanced.
glas[s], *v.* & *n.* Glass.
glast[s], *pp.* Glassed.
gleamd[p&s], *pp.* Gleamed.
gleand[p&s], *pp.* Gleaned.
glibd[s], *pp.* Glibbed.
glim'merd[s], *pp.* Glimmered.
glimps[p], *v.* & *n.* Glimpse.
glimpst[p&s], *pp.* Glimpsed.
glis'tend[s], *pp.* Glistened.
glis'terd[p&s], *pp.* Glistered.
glit'terd[p&s], *pp.* Glittered.
glo[s], *v.* & *n.* Glow.
gloed[s], *pp.* Glowed.
gloes[s], *3d pers. sing. pres. ind.* Glows.
gloomd[p&s], *pp.* Gloomed.
glo'ri-us[s], *a.* Glorious.
glos'so-graf[p], *n.* Glossograph.
glos-sog'ra-fer[p], *n.* Glossographer.
glos-sog'ra-fy[p], *n.* Glossography.
glost[s], *pp.* Glossed.
glowd[s], *pp.* Glowed.
glow'erd[s], *pp.* Glowered.
glu[s], *v.* & *n.* Glue.
glyc'er-in[p], *n.* Glycerine.
glyf[p], *n.* Glyph.
glyf'o-graf[p], *v.* & *n.* Glyphograph.
glyf-og'ra-fy[p], *n.* Glyphography.
glyp'to-graf[p], *n.* Glyptograph.
gnarld[p&s], *a.* Gnarled.
gnasht[s], *pp.* Gnashed.
gnaw'a-bl[s], *a.* Gnawable.
gnawd[p&s], *pp.* Gnawed.
go"a-hed'i-tiv[s], *a.* Goaheaditive.
go"a-hed'a-[or **-i-**]**tiv-ness**[s], *n.* Go-aheadativeness, goaheaditiveness.
gob'l[p], *v.* & *n.* Gobble.
gob'ld[p], *pp.* Gobbled.
God'hed[p&s], *n.* Godhead.
go'fer[s], *n.* Gopher.
gof'ferd[s], *pp.* Goffered.
gog'l[p], *v.* & *n.* Goggle.
gog'ld[p], *pp.* Goggled.
goi'ter[p], *n.* Goitre.
goi'terd[s], *a.* Goitered.
golft[s], *pp.* Golfed.
gon[p&s], *pa.* Gone.
good"=by'[p], *a.*, *n.* & *interj.* Good=bye.
gost[p&s], *n.* Ghost.
gost'ly[s], *a.* Ghostly.
gos'sipt[s], *pp.* Gossiped.
got'n[p], *pp.* Gotten.
gownd[s], *pp.* Gowned.
grabd[p&s], *pp.* Grabbed.
grab'l[p], *vt.* & *vi.* Grabble.
grab'ld[p], *pp.* Grabbled.
grac'il[s], *a.* Gracile.
graf[p], *v.* & *n.* Graff.
graf[p], *n.* Graph.
graf'ic[p&s], *a.* Graphic.
graind[p&s], *pp.* Grained.
gral'lin[s], *a.* & *n.* Gralline.
gram"i-niv'o-rus[s], *a.* Graminivorous.
gram'ma-log[s], *n.* Grammalogue.
gran'it[p&s], *n.* Granite.

grant'a-bl[P], *a.* Grantable.
gran'u-la-tiv[S], *a.* Granulative.
gras[S], *v.* & *n.* Grass.
grasp'a-bl[P], *a.* Graspable.
graspt[P&S], *pp.* Grasped.
grav"i-per-cep'tiv[S], *a.* Gravipercep-tive.
grav"i-sen'si-tiv[S], *a.* Gravisensitive.
grav'i-ta-tiv[S], *a.* Gravitative.
greaz[P&S], **grease**[P], *vt.* Grease.
greazd[P], **greast**[P&S], *pp.* Greased.
green'a-bl[P], *a.* Greenable.
grib'l[P], *n.* Gribble.
grid'l[P], *v.* & *n.* Griddle.
grid'ld[P], *pp.* Griddled.
grid'i"rond[S], *pp.* Gridironed.
griev[P], *vt.* & *vi.* Grieve.
grievd[P&S], *pp.* Grieved.
griev'us[S], *a.* Grievous.
gril[P&S], *v.* & *n.* Grill.
grild[P], *pp.* Grilled.
grind[S], *pp.* Grinned.
gript[P&S], *pp.* Gripped.
griz'l[P], *v.* & *n.* Grizzle.
griz'ld[P], *a.* Grizzled.
gro[S], *vt.* & *vi.* Grow.
groes[S], *3d per. sing. pres. indic.* Grows.
groand[S], *pp.* Groaned.
grogd[S], *pp.* Grogged.
groind[S], *a.* Groined.
groomd[P&S], *pp.* Groomed.
groov[P], *v.* & *n.* Groove.
groovd[P&S], *pa.* Grooved.
gros[S], *a.* & *n.* Gross.
groupt[P&S], *pp.* Grouped.
grov'eld[P&S], *pp.* Groveled.
growld[P&S], *pp.* Growled.
gru[S], *imp.* Grew.
grubd[P&S], *pp.* Grubbed.
grudgd[P&S], *pp.* Grudged.
gruf[P&S], *a.* Gruff.
grum'bl[P], *v.* & *n.* Grumble.
grum'bld[P], *pp.* Grumbled.
guard'a-bl[P], *a.* Guardable.
guize[P], *v.* & *n.* Guise.
gul[S], *v.* & *n.* Gull.
gulft[P&S], *pp.* Gulfed.
gul'li-[or -la-]bl[P], *a.* Gullible, gullable.
gulpt[P&S], *pp.* Gulped.
gur'gl[P], *v.* & *n.* Gurgle.
gur'gld[P], *pp.* Gurgled.
gusht[P&S], *pp.* Gushed.
guv'ern[P], *vt.* & *vi.* Govern.
guv'ern-a-bl[P], *a.* Governable.
guv'ernd[P], *pp.* Governed.
guv'er-ness[P], *n.* Governess.
guv'ern-ing[P], *pa.* Governing.
guv'ern-ment[P], *n.* Government.
guv'er-nor[P], *n.* Governor.
gus'ta-tiv[S], *a.* Gustative.
gus'ta-tiv-ness[S], *n.* Gustativeness.
gut'ta-bl[P], *a.* Guttable.
gut'terd[S], *pp.* Guttered.
guz'l[P], *v.* & *n.* Guzzle.
guz'ld[P], *pp.* Guzzled.

H

hab'it-a-bl[P], *a.* Habitable.
hab'it-a-bl-ness[P], *n.* Habitableness.
hab'i-ta-tiv[S], *a.* Habitative.
hach[P], *v.* & *n.* Hatch.
hach'ment[P], *n.* Hatchment.
hack'l[P], *v.* & *n.* Hackle.
hack'ld[P], *pp.* Hackled.
hack'ny[S], *v., a.* & *n.* Hackney.
had'doc[S], *n.* Haddock.
hackt[P&S], *pp.* Hacked.
hag'l[P], *v.* & *n.* Haggle.
hag'ld[P], *pp.* Haggled.
haild[P&S], *pp.* Hailed.
hal'lo[S], *v.* Hallow.
hal'loes[S], *3d per. sing. pres. ind.* Hallows.

hal'lowd[P], *pp.* Hallowed.
hal'terd[P&S], *pp.* Haltered.
halv[P], *vt.* Halve.
halvd[P&S], *pp.* Halved.
ham'bl[P], *vt.* & *vi.* Hamble.
ham'moc[S], *n.* Hammock.
ham'perd[P&S], *pp.* Hampered.
hand'cuf″[P], *v.* & *n.* Handcuff.
hand'cuft″[P&S], *pp.* Handcuffed.
hand'i-capt[S], *pp.* Handicapped.
han'dl[P], *v.* & *n.* Handle.
han'dld[P], *pp.* Handled.
hand'sum[P&S], *a.* Handsome.
hangd[P&S], *pp.* Hanged.
hang'a-bl[P], *a.* Hangable.
han'kerd[S], *pp.* Hankered.
hapd[P], *pp.* Happed.
hap'pend[P&S], *pp.* Happened.
hapt[S], *pp.* Happed.
ha-rang'[P&S], *v.* & *n.* Harangue.
ha-rangd'[P&S], *pp.* Harangued.
har'ast[P&S], *pp.* Harassed.
har'bor[P], *v.* & *n.* Harbour.
har'bord[P&S], *pp.* Harbored, harboured.
hard'end[S], *pp.* Hardened.
hark'en[P&S], *vt.* & *vi.* Hearken.
hark'end[P&S], *pp.* Hearkened.
harkt[P&S], *pp.* Harked.
harmd[P&S], *pp.* Harmed.
har-mo'ni-us[S], *a.* Harmonious.
har'nest[P&S], *a.* Harnessed.
har-poond'[S], *pp.* Harpooned.
harpt[P&S], *pp.* Harped.
har'rowd[P&S], *pp.* Harrowed.
hart[P&S], *v.* & *n.* Heart.
hart'en[S], *vt.* Hearten.
harth[P&S], *n.* Hearth.
hart'y[P&S], *a.* & *n.* Hearty.
hasht[P&S], *pp.* Hashed.
haspt[S], *pp.* Hasped.
has'soc[S], *n.* Hassock.
hast'end[S], *pp.* Hastened.
hat'a-bl, hate'a-bl[P], *a.* Hatable, hateable.
hatch'ett-in[S], *n.* Hatchettine.
hatcht[P&S], *pp.* Hatched.
hauld[P&S], *pp.* Hauled.
hau'ty[P&S], *a.* Haughty.
hav[P&S], *vt.* & *vi.* Have.
hav'oc[P], *v.* & *n.* Havock.
hav'ockt[P], *pp.* Havocked.
hawd[S], *pp.* Hawed.
hawkt[P&S], *pp.* Hawked.
hayd[S], *pp.* Hayed.
haz'ard-a-bl[P], *a.* Hazardable.
heald[P&S], *pp.* Healed.
heapt[P&S], *pp.* Heaped.
heav[P], *v.* & *n.* Heave.
heavd[P&S], *pa.* Heaved.
heavs[P], *n.* Heaves.
hec'tord[S], *pp.* Hectored.
hed[P&S], *v.*, *a.* & *n.* Head.
hed'ake″[P&S], *n.* Headache.
hedgd[P&S], *pp.* Hedged.
hed'land″[P&S], *n.* Headland.
hed'long″[P&S], *a.* & *adv.* Headlong.
heeld[P&S], *a.* Heeled.
hef'er[P], *n.* Heifer.
height'end[P], *pp.* Heightened.
hel[P&S], *n.* Hell.
helmd[S], *pp.* Helmed.
help'a-bl[P], *a.* Helpable.
helpt[P&S], *pp.* Helped.
helth[P&S], *n.* Health.
helth'ful[S], *a.* Healthful.
helth'y[P&S], *a.* Healthy.
helv[P&S], *v.* & *n.* Helve.
helvd[S], *pp.* Helved.
hemd[S], *pp.* Hemmed.
hem'i-sfere[S], *n.* Hemisphere.
hem'i-stic[S], *n.* Hemistich.
hem'loc[S], *n.* Hemlock.
hem'or-age[S], *n.* Hemorrhage.
hense[P], *adv.* Hence.
her-biv'o-rus[S], *a.* Herbivorous.
herd[P], *pp.* Heard.
he-red'i-ta-tiv[S], *a.* Hereditative.
her'i-ot-a-bl[P], *a.* Heriotable.

her'i-ta-bl[P], *a.* Heritable.
her-maf'ro-dite[P], *a.* & *n.* Hermaphrodite.
her'o-in[S], *n.* Heroine.
herse[P], *n.* Hearse.
herst[P], *pp.* Hearsed.
hes'i-ta-tiv[S], *a.* Hesitative.
hes'i-ta-tiv-ly[S], *adv.* Hesitatively.
heth'er[P&S], *n.* Heather.
hev'en[P&S], *v.* & *n.* Heaven.
hev'y[P&S], *a.* & *n.* Heavy.
hic'cof, hic'cup[P], *v.* & *n.* Hiccough, hiccup.
hic'coft[P], **hic'cupt**[P&S], *pp.* Hiccoughed, hiccuped.
hich[P], *v.* & *n.* Hitch.
hid'e-us[S], *a.* Hideous.
hid'n[P], *pa.* Hidden.
hi'er-o-glyf[S], *n.* Hieroglyph.
hil[P&S], *v.* & *n.* Hill.
hild[P&S], *a.* Hilled.
hil'loc[S], *n.* Hillock.
hin'derd[P&S], *pp.* Hindered.
hipt[P&S], *pp.* & *a.* Hipped.
hir'cin[S], *a.* Hircine.
his[S], *v.* & *n.* Hiss.
hist[P&S], *pp.* Hissed.
hitcht[S], *pp.* Hitched.
ho[S], *v.* & *n.* Hoe.
hob'l[P], *v.* & *n.* Hobble.
hock[P], *vt.* Hough.
hogd[S], *pa.* Hogged.
hole[P], *a.* & *n.* Whole.
hole'ly[P], *adv.* Wholly.
hole'sale[P], *a.* & *n.* Wholesale.
hole'sum[P], *a.* Wholesome.
hol'lo[S], *v.*, *a.* & *n.* Hollow.
hol'loed[S]; *pp.* Hollowed.
hol″o-crys'tal-lin[S], *a.* Holocrystalline.
hol″o-hy'a-lin[S], *a.* Holohyaline.
hol'sterd[S], *a.* Holstered.
hom'age-a-bl[P], *a.* Homageable.
home'sted[P&S], *v.* & *n.* Homestead.
hom'i-nin[S], *a.* Hominine.
ho″mo-cin-chon'i-cin[S], *n.* Homocinchonicine.
ho″mo-cin-chon'i-din[S], *n.* Homocinchonidine.
ho″mo-cin'cho-nin[S], *n.* Homocinchonine.
hom'o-fone[S], *n.* Homophone.
ho'mo-graf[S], *n.* Homograph.
hon'or[P], *v.* & *n.* Honour.
hon'or-a-bl[P], *a.* & *n.* Honorable, honourable.
hon'or-a-bl-ness[P], *n.* Honorableness.
hon'ord[P&S], *pp.* Honored, honoured.
hon'y[S], *v.*, *a.* & *n.* Honey.
hood'winkt[P&S], *pp.* Hoodwinked.
hooft[P&S], *pp.* & *a.* Hoofed.
hookt[P&S], *pa.* Hooked.
hoop'ing-cof″[P], *n.* Hooping-cough.
hoopt[P&S], *pp.* Hooped.
hopt[P], *pp.* Hopped.
hornd[P&S], *a.* Horned.
ho-rog'ra-fy[P], *n.* Horography.
hor'o-log[P], *n.* Horologue.
hor'ri-bl[P], *a.* Horrible.
hor'ri-bl-ness[S], *n.* Horribleness.
horst[P&S], *pp.* Horsed.
hor'ta-tiv[P&S], *a.* Hortative.
hor'ta-tiv-ly[S], *adv.* Hortatively.
hos'pi-ta-bl[P], *a.* Hospitable.
hos'pi-ta-bl-ness[P], *n.* Hospitableness.
hos'til[S], *a.* & *n.* Hostile.
houz[P], *vt.* & *vi.* House.
houzd[P], *pp.* & *a.* Housed.
houz'ing[P], *n.* Housing.
hov'eld[S], *pp.* Hoveled, hovelled.
hov'erd[S], *pp.* Hovered.
howld[P&S], *pp.* Howled.
huch[P], *v.* & *n.* Hutch.
hucht[P], *pp.* Hutched.
hud'l[P], *v.* & *n.* Huddle.
huf[P&S], *v.*, *a.* & *n.* Huff.

huft[P&S], *pp.* Huffed.
hugd[P&S], *pp.* Hugged.
hul[S], *v.* & *n.* Hull.
huld[S], *pp.* Hulled.
hulkt[S], *pp.* Hulked.
hum'bl[P], *v.* & *a.* Humble.
hum'bld[P], *pp.* Humbled.
humd[S], *imp.* & *pp.* Hummed.
hu-mil'i-a"tiv[S], *a.* Humiliative.
hum'moc[S], *v.* & *n.* Hummock.
hu'mor[P], *v.* & *n.* Humour.
hu'mord[P&S], *pa.* Humored, humoured.
humpt[P&S], *a.* Humped.
huncht[S], *pp.* Hunched.
hun'ey[P], *v.*, *a.* & *n.* Honey.
hun'eyd[P], *a.* Honeyed.
hun'ied[P], *a.* Honied.
hunt'a-bl[P], *a.* Huntable.
hurld[S], *pp.* Hurled.
hur-rahd'[S], *pp.* Hurrahed.
hus'band-a-bl[P], *a.* Husbandable.
husht[P], *pp.* Hushed.
huskt[S], *a.* Husked.
hus'tl[P], *v.* & *n.* Hustle.
hus'tld[P], *pp.* Hustled.
hutcht[S], *a.* Hutched.
hy"a-cin'thin[S], *a.* Hyacinthine.
hy'a-lin[S], *a.* & *n.* Hyaline.
hy'brid-is"a-bl[P], *a.* Hybridisable.
hy'brid-iz"a-[or **-is"a-**]**bl**[P], *a.* Hybridizable, hybridisable.
hy'dra-zin[S], *n.* Hydrazine.
hy"dro-cou'ma-rin[S], *n.* Hydrocoumarine.
hy"dro-cy'a-nid[S], *n.* Hydrocyanide.
hy"dro-fo'bi-a[P], *n.* Hydrophobia.
hy-drog'ra-fy[P], *n.* Hydrography.
hy"dro-pic'a-lin[S], *n.* Hydropicaline.
hy'e-nin[S], *a.* Hyenine.
hy'fen[P&S], *v.* & *n.* Hyphen.
hy'fend[P], *pp.* Hyphened.
hy'phend[S], *pp.* Hyphened.
hyp'no-tiz"[or **-tis"**]**a-bl**[P], *a.* Hypnotizable, hypnotisable.
hyp'o-crit[P&S], *n.* Hypocrite.

I

ich[P], *v.* & *n.* Itch.
icht[P], *pp.* Itched.
i'ci-cl[P], *n.* Icicle.
i-de'a-tiv[S], *a.* Ideative.
i-den'ti-fi"a-bl[P], *a.* Identifiable.
id"i-o-re-pul'siv[S], *a.* Idiorepulsive.
ig-nit'i-[or **a-**]**bl**[S], *a.* Ignitible, ignitable.
ig-no'bl[P], *a.* Ignoble.
ig-no'bl-ness[P], *n.* Ignobleness.
ig-nor'a-bl[P], *a.* Ignorable.
il[P], *a.*, *n.* & *adv.* Ill.
i'land[P&S], *v.* & *n.* Island.
ile[P&S], *v.* & *n.* Isle.
i'let[P&S], *n.* Islet.
il'la-tiv[P&S], *a.* Illative.
il-land'a-bl[P], *a.* Illandable.
il-leg'i-bl[P], *a.* Illegible.
il-leg'i-bl-ness[P], *n.* Illegibleness.
il-lev'i-a-bl[P], *a.* Illeviable.
il-lim'i-ta-bl[P], *a.* & *n.* Illimitable.
il-lim'i-ta-bl-ness[P], *n.* Illimitableness.
il-lo'ca-bl[P], *a.* Illocable.
il-lu'mi-na-tiv[S], *a.* Illuminative.
il-lu'min[S], *vt.* Illumine.
il-lu'sion-a-bl[P], *a.* Illusionable.
il-lu'siv[P&S], *a.* Illusive.
il-lu'siv-ly[S], *adv.* Illusively.
il-lu'siv-ness[S], *n.* Illusiveness.
il-lus'tra-bl[P], *a.* Illustrable.
il-lus'tra-ta-bl[P], *a.* Illustratable.
il-lus'tra-tiv[P&S], *a.* Illustrative.
il-lus'tri-us[S], *a.* Illustrious.
il'ness[P], *n.* Illness.
im'age-a-bl[P], *a.* Imageable.

im-ag'in[P&S], *vt. & vi.* Imagine.
im-ag'i-na-bl[P], *a.* Imaginable.
im-ag'i-na-bl-ness[P], *n.* Imaginableness.
im-ag'i-na-tiv[P&S], *a.* Imaginative.
im-ag'i-na-tiv-ly[S], *adv.* Imaginatively.
im-ag'i-na-tiv-ness[S], *n.* Imaginativeness.
im-ag'ind[P&S], *pp.* Imagined.
im'be-cil[P&S], *a. & n.* Imbecile.
im-bit'terd†[P], *pa.* Imbittered.
im'bri-ca-tiv[S], *a.* Imbricative.
im-brownd'†[P], *pa.* Imbrowned.
im-bru'[S], *vt.* Imbrue.
im'i-ta-bl[P], *a.* Imitable.
im'i-ta-bl-ness[P], *n.* Imitableness.
im'i-ta-tiv[P&S], *a.* Imitative.
im'i-ta-tiv-ly[S], *adv.* Imitatively.
im'i-ta-tiv-ness[S], *n.* Imitativeness.
im-mal'le-a-bl[P], *a.* Immalleable.
im-man'a-cl[P], *vt.* Immanacle.
im-med'i-ca-bl[P], *a.* Immedicable.
im-mem'o-ra-bl[P], *a.* Immemorable.
im-men'sur-a-bl[P], *a.* Immensurable.
im-me'zur-a-bl[P], *a.* Immeasurable.
im-mis'ci-bl[P], *a.* Immiscible.
im-mit'i-ga-bl[P], *a.* Immitigable.
im-mix'a-bl[P], *a.* Immixable.
im-mor'tal-iz"a-bl[P], *a.* Immortalizable.
im-mo'tiv[S], *a.* Immotive.
im-mov'a-bl[P], *a. & n.* Immovable.
im-mov'a-bl-ness[P], *n.* Immovableness.
im-mu'ta-bl[P], *a.* Immutable.
im-mu'ta-bl-ness[P], *n.* Immutableness.
im-pair'a-bl[P], *a.* Impairable.
im-paird'[P&S], *pp.* Impaired.
im-pal'pa-bl[P], *a.* Impalpable.
im-part'i-bl[P], *a.* Impartible.
im"par-tic'i-pa-bl[P], *a.* Imparticipable.
im-par'tiv[S], *a.* Impartive.
im-pass'a-bl[P], *a.* Impassable.
im-pass'a-bl-ness[P], *n.* Impassableness.
im-pas'si-bl[P], *a.* Impassible.
im-pas'si-bl-ness[P], *n.* Impassibleness.
im-pas'siond[S], *a.* Impassioned.
im-pas'siv[P&S], *a.* Impassive.
im-pas'siv-ly[S], *adv.* Impassively.
im-pas'siv-ness[S], *n.* Impassiveness.
im-pay'a-bl[P], *a.* Impayable.
im-peach'a-bl[P], *a.* Impeachable.
im-peacht'[S], *pp.* Impeached.
im-pec'ca-bl[P], *a.* Impeccable.
im-peld'[P&S], *pp.* Impelled.
im-pen'e-tra-bl[P], *a.* Impenetrable.
im-pen'e-tra-bl-ness[P], *n.* Impenetrableness.
im-pen'e-tra-tiv[S], *a.* Impenetrative.
im-per'a-tiv[P&S], *a. & n.* Imperative.
im-per'a-tiv-ly[S], *adv.* Imperatively.
im-per'a-tiv-ness[S], *n.* Imperativeness.
im"per-ceiv'a-bl[P], *a.* Imperceivable.
im"per-cep'ti-bl[P], *a. & n.* Imperceptible.
im"per-cep'ti-bl-ness[P], *n.* Imperceptibleness.
im"per-cep'tiv[S], *a.* Imperceptive.
im"per-fec'ti-bl[P], *a.* Imperfectible.
im"per-fec'tiv[S], *a.* Imperfective.
im-per'fo-ra-bl[P], *a.* Imperforable.
im"per-form'a-bl[P], *a.* Imperformable.
im-per'ild[P&S], *pp.* Imperilled.
im-per'ish-a-bl[P], *a.* Imperishable.
im-per'ish-a-bl-ness[P], *n.* Imperishableness.
im-pe'ri-us[S], *a.* Imperious.
im-per'me-a-bl[P], *a.* Impermeable.
im-per'me-a-bl-ness[P], *n.* Impermeableness.
im"per-mis'si-bl[P], *a.* Impermissible.

im-per'son-a-tiv[s], *a.* Impersonative.
im"per-scrip'ti-bl[p], *a.* Imperscriptible.
im"per-spir'a-bl[p], *a.* Imperspirable.
im"per-suad'a-bl[p], *a.* Impersuadable.
im"per-suad'a-bl-ness[p], *n.* Impersuadableness.
im"per-sua'si-bl[p], *a.* Impersuasible.
im"per-tran'si-bl[p], *a.* Impertransible.
im"per-turb'a-bl[p], *a.* Imperturbable.
im"per-turb'a-bl-ness[p], *n.* Imperturbableness.
im"per-vert'i-bl[p], *a.* Impervertible.
im-per'vi-a-bl[p], *a.* Imperviable.
im"per'vi-a-bl-ness[p], *n.* Imperviableness.
im'pe-tra-bl[p], *a.* Impetrable.
im'pe-tra-tiv[s], *a.* Impetrative.
im-pla'ca-bl[p], *a.* Implacable.
im-pla'ca-bl-ness[s], *n.* Implacableness.
im-plau'si-bl[p], *a.* Implausible.
im-plau'si-bl-ness[p], *n.* Implausibleness.
im-plead'a-bl[p], *a.* Impleadable.
im-pli'a-bl[p], *a.* Impliable.
im'pli-ca-tiv[s], *a.* Implicative.
im-plo'siv[s], *a.* & *n.* Implosive.
im-po'lar-iz"a-bl[p], *a.* Impolarizable.
im-pon'der-a-bl[p], *a.* & *n.* Imponderable.
im-pon'der-a-bl-ness[p], *n.* Imponderableness.
im-pos'a-bl[p], *a.* Imposable.
im-pos'i-tiv[s], *a.* Impositive.
im-pos'si-bl[p], *a.* & *n.* Impossible.
im-po'ta-bl[p], *a.* Impotable.
im-pov'er-isht[p&s], *pp.* Impoverished.
im-prac'ti-ca-bl[p], *a.* Impracticable.
im-prac'ti-ca-bl-ness[p], *n.* Impracticableness.
im-preg'na-bl[p], *a.* Impregnable.
im-preg'na-bl-ness[p], *n.* Impregnableness.
im-preg'na-tiv[s], *a.* Impregnative.
im"pre-scrib'a-bl[p], *a.* Imprescribable.
im"pre-scrip'ti-bl[p], *a.* Imprescriptible.
im-press'i-bl[p], *a.* Impressible.
im-press'i-bl-ness[p], *n.* Impressibleness.
im-pres'sion-a-bl[p], *a.* Impressionable.
im-pres'sion-a-bl-ness[p], *n.* Impressionableness.
im-pres'siv[p&s], *a.* Impressive.
im-pres'siv-ly[s], *adv.* Impressively.
im-pres'siv-ness[s], *n.* Impressiveness.
im-prest'[p&s], *pp.* Impressed.
im"pre-vent'a-bl[p], *a.* Impreventable.
im"pre-vis'i-bl[p], *a.* Imprevisible.
im-prim'i-tiv[s], *a.* Imprimitive.
im-pris'ond[s], *pp.* Imprisoned.
im-prob'a-bl[p], *a.* Improbable.
im-prob'a-bl-ness[p], *n.* Improbableness.
im-prob'a-tiv[s], *a.* Improbative.
im"pro-duc'i-bl[p], *a.* Improducible.
im"pro-gres'siv[s], *a.* Improgressive.
im"pro-gres'siv-ly[s], *adv.* Improgressively.
im-prov'a-bl[p], *a.* Improvable.
im-prov'a-bl-ness[p], *n.* Improvableness.
im-pug'na-bl[p], *a.* Impugnable.
im-pul'siv[p&s], *a.* Impulsive.
im-put'a-bl[p], *a.* Imputable.
im-put'a-bl-ness[p], *n.* Imputableness.
im-pu'ta-tiv[s], *a.* Imputative.
im-pu'ta-tiv-ly[p], *adv.* Imputatively.
im"pu-tres'ci-bl[p], *a.* Imputrescible.
in[p], *n.* Inn.

in"ac-cep'ta-bl[P], *a.* Inacceptable.
in"ac-ces'si-bl[P], *a.* Inaccessible.
in"ac-ces'si-bl-ness[P], *n.* Inaccessibleness.
in-ac'tiv[P&S], *a.* Inactive.
in-ac'tiv-ly[S], *adv.* Inactively.
in-ac'tiv-ness[S], *n.* Inactiveness.
in"a-dapt'a-bl[P], *a.* Inadaptable.
in"a-dap'tiv[P&S], *a.* Inadaptive.
in-ad'e-qua-tiv[S], *a.* Inadequative.
in"ad-he'siv[P&S], *a.* Inadhesive.
in"ad-mis'si-bl[P], *a.* Inadmissible.
in"ad-vis'a-bl[P], *a.* Inadvisable.
in-af'fa-bl[P], *a.* Inaffable.
in"ag-gres'siv[P&S], *a.* Inaggressive.
in-a'lien-a-bl[P], *a.* Inalienable.
in-a'lien-a-bl-ness[P], *n.* Inalienableness.
in-al'ter-a-bl[P], *a.* Inalterable.
in-al'ter-a-bl-ness[P], *n.* Inalterableness.
in"a-mis'si-bl[P], *a.* Inamissible.
in"a-mis'si-bl-ness[P], *n.* Inamissibleness.
in"a-mov'a-bl[P], *a.* Inamovable.
in"ap-peal'a-bl[P], *a.* Inappealable.
in"ap-peas'a-bl[P], *a.* Inappeasable.
in"ap-pel'la-bl[P], *a.* Inappellable.
in-ap'pe-ti-bl[P], *a.* Inappetible.
in-ap'pli-ca-bl[P], *a.* Inapplicable.
in-ap'pli-ca-bl-ness[P], *n.* Inapplicableness.
in-ap'po-sit[S], *a.* Inapposite.
in"ap-pre'ci-a-bl[P], *a.* Inappreciable.
in"ap-pre'ci-a-tiv[P&S], *a.* Inappreciative.
in"ap-pre'ci-a-tiv-ly[S], *adv.* Inappreciatively.
in"ap-pre'ci-a-tiv-ness[S], *n.* Inappreciativeness.
in-ap"pre-hen'si-bl[P], *a.* Inapprehensible.
in-ap"pre-hen'siv[P&S], *a.* Inapprehensive.
in-ap"pre-hen'siv-ness[S], *n.* Inapprehensiveness.
in"ap-proach'a-bl[P], *a.* Inapproachable.
in"ap-pro'pri-a-bl[P], *a.* Inappropriable.
in-ar'a-bl[P], *a.* Inarable.
in"as-sim'i-la-bl[P], *a.* Inassimilable.
in"at-tack'a-bl[P], *a.* Inattackable.
in"at-ten'tiv[P&S], *a.* Inattentive.
in-au'di-bl[P], *a.* Inaudible.
in-au'di-bl-ness[P], *n.* Inaudibleness.
in-au'gu-ra-tiv[S], *a.* Inaugurative.
in"au-thor'i-ta-tiv[P&S], *a.* Inauthoritative.
in"a-vail'a-bl[P], *a.* Inavailable.
in"a-vert'i-bl[P], *a.* Inavertible.
in"a-void'a-bl[P], *a.* Inavoidable.
in-cal'cu-la-bl[P], *a.* Incalculable.
in-cal'cu-la-bl-ness[P], *n.* Incalculableness.
in-ca'pa-bl[P], *a.* & *n.* Incapable.
in-car'na-din[S], *v.* & *a.* Incarnadine.
in-car'na-tiv[S], *a.* & *n.* Incarnative.
in-cen'siv[S], *a.* Incensive.
in-censt'[P&S], *pp.* Incensed.
in-cen'sur-a-bl[P], *a.* Incensurable.
in-cen'tiv[P&S], *a.* & *n.* Incentive.
in-cen'tiv-ly[S], *adv.* Incentively.
in-cep'tiv[P&S], *a.* & *n.* Inceptive.
in-ces'sa-bl[P], *a.* Incessable.
in-cho'a-tiv[S], *a.* & *n.* Inchoative.
incht[S], *a.* Inched.
in-cin'er-a-bl[P], *a.* Incinerable.
in-ci'siv[S], *a.* Incisive.
in-cit'a-bl[P], *a.* Incitable.
in-ci'ta-tiv[S], *a.* Incitative.
in-ci'tiv[S], *a.* Incitive.
in-clin'a-bl[P], *a.* Inclinable.
in-clin'a-bl-ness[P], *n.* Inclinableness.
in-cloze'[P], *vt.* Inclose.
in-clud'i-bl[P], *a.* Includible.
in-clu'siv[P&S], *a.* & *n.* Inclusive.
in-clu'siv-ly[S], *adv.* Inclusively.

in″co-ag′u-la-bl[P], *a.* Incoagulable.
in″co-erc′i-bl[P], *a.* Incoercible.
in-cog′i-ta-bl[S], *a.* Incogitable.
in-cog′i-ta-tiv[S], *a.* Incogitative.
in-cog′ni-tiv[S], *a.* Incognitive.
in-cog′ni-za-bl[P], *a.* Incognizable.
in″cog-nos′ci-bl[P], *a.* Incognoscible.
in″co-he′siv[S], *a.* Incohesive.
in″com-bus′ti-bl[P], *a.* & *n.* Incombustible.
in″com-bus′ti-bl-ness[P], *n.* Incombustibleness.
in″com-men′su-ra-bl[P], *a.* & *n.* Incommensurable.
in″com-men′su-ra-bl-ness[P], *n.* Incommensurableness.
in″com-mis′ci-bl[P], *a.* Incommiscible.
in″com-mu′ni-ca-bl[P], *a.* Incommunicable.
in″com-mu′ni-ca-bl-ness[P], *n.* Incommunicableness.
in″com-mu′ni-ca-tiv[S], *a.* Incommunicative.
in″com-mut′a-bl[P], *a.* Incommutable.
in-com′pa-ra-bl[P], *a.* & *n.* Incomparable.
in″com′pa-ra-bl-ness[P], *n.* Incomparableness.
in″com-pat′i-bl[P], *a.* Incompatible.
in″com-pat′i-bl-ness[P], *n.* Incompatibleness.
in″com-pen′sa-bl[P], *a.* Incompensable.
in″com-plet′a-bl[P], *a.* Incompletable.
in″com-pos′it[S], *a.* Incomposite.
in″com-pos′si-bl[P], *a.* Incompossible.
in-com″pre-hen′si-bl[P], *a.* & *n.* Incomprehensible.
in-com″pre-hen′si-bl-ness[P], *n.* Incomprehensibleness.
in-com″pre-hen′siv[S], *a.* Incomprehensive.
in″com-press′i-bl[P], *a.* Incompressible.
in″com-press′i-bl-ness[P], *n.* Incompressibleness.
in″com-put′a-bl[P], *a.* Incomputable.
in″con-ceiv′a-bl[P], *a.* Inconceivable.
in″con-ceiv′a-bl-ness[P], *n.* Inconceivableness.
in″con-clu′siv[S], *a.* Inconclusive.
in″con-clu′siv-ly[S], *adv.* Inconclusively.
in″con-clu′siv-ness[S], *n.* Inconclusiveness.
in″con-dens′a-[or **i-**]**bl**[P], *a.* Incondensable.
in″con-du′civ[P&S], *a.* Inconducive.
in″con-fut′a-bl[P], *a.* Inconfutable.
in″con-geal′a-bl[P], *a.* Incongealable.
in″con-join′a-bl[P], *a.* Inconjoinable.
in″con-sec′u-tiv[P&S], *a.* Inconsecutive.
in″con-sid′er-a-bl[P], *a.* Inconsiderable.
in″con-sid′er-a-bl-ness[P], *n.* Inconsiderableness.
in″con-sol′a-bl[P], *a.* Inconsolable.
in″con-sol′a-bl-ness[P], *n.* Inconsolableness.
in″con-stru′a-bl[P], *a.* Inconstruable.
in″con-struct′i-bl[P], *a.* Inconstructible.
in″con-sult′a-bl[P], *a.* Inconsultable.
in″con-sum′a-bl[P], *a.* Inconsumable.
in″con-tam′i-na-bl[P], *a.* Incontaminable.
in″con-temp′ti-bl[P], *a.* Incontemptible.
in″con-test′a-bl[P], *a.* Incontestable.
in″con-test′a-bl-ness[P], *n.* Incontestableness.
in″con-trac′til[P&S], *a.* Incontractile.
in″con-trol′la-bl[P], *a.* Incontrollable.
in-con″tro-vert′i-bl[P], *a.* Incontrovertible.
in-con″tro-vert′i-bl-ness[P], *n.* Incontrovertibleness.

in″con-vers′a-blʳ, *a.* Inconversable.
in″con-vert′i-blʳ, *a.* Inconvertible.
in″con-vert′i-bl-nessʳ, *n.* Inconvertibleness.
in″con-vin′ci-blʳ, *a.* Inconvincible.
in-co″pre-sent′a-blʳ, *a.* Incopresentable.
in-cor′po-ra-blʳ, *a.* Incorporable.
in-cor′po-ra-tivˢ, *a.* Incorporative.
in-cor′ri-gi-blʳ, *a.* & *n.* Incorrigible.
in″cor-rod′i-blʳ, *a.* Incorrodible.
in″cor-ro′si-blʳ, *a.* Incorrosible.
in″cor-rupt′i-blʳ, *a.* Incorruptible.
In″cor-rupt′i-blʳ, *n.* Incorruptible.
in″cor-rupt′i-bl-nessʳ, *n.* Incorruptibleness.
in-cras′sa-tivˢ, *a.* & *n.* Incrassative.
in-creas′a-blʳ, *a.* Increasable.
in-creas′a-bl-nessʳ, *n.* Increasableness.
in-creast′ʳ&ˢ, *pp.* Increased.
in″cre-a′tivˢ, *a.* Increative.
in-cred′i-blʳ, *a.* Incredible.
in-cred′i-bl-nessʳ, *n.* Incredibleness.
in-crus′tivˢ, *a.* Incrustive.
in-crys′tal-liz″[or **-lis″**]**a-bl**ʳ, *a.* Incrystallizable.
in′cu-ba-tivˢ, *a.* Incubative.
in-cul′pa-blʳ, *a.* Inculpable.
in-cul′pa-bl-nessʳ, *n.* Inculpableness.
in-cul′pa-tivˢ, *a.* Inculpative.
in-cur′a-blʳ, *a.* & *n.* Incurable.
in-cur′a-bl-nessʳ, *n.* Incurableness.
in-curd′ʳ&ˢ, *pp.* Incurred.
in-cur′sivˢ, *a.* Incursive.
indʳ, *pp.* Inned.
in″de-ci′fer-a-blʳ, *a.* Indecipherable.
in″de-ci′fer-a-bl-nessʳ, *n.* Indecipherableness.
in-dec′i-ma-blʳ, *a.* Indecimable.
in″de-ci′sivˢ, *a.* Indecisive.
in″de-ci′siv-lyˢ, *adv.* Indecisively.
in″de-ci′siv-nessˢ, *n.* Indecisiveness.
in″de-clin′a-blʳ, *a.* & *n.* Indeclinable.
in″de-clin′a-bl-nessˢ, *n.* Indeclinableness.
in-de″com-po′ni-blʳ, *a.* Indecomponible.
in-de″com-pos′a-blʳ, *a.* Indecomposable.
in-de″com-pos′a-bl-nessʳ, *n.* Indecomposableness.
in″de-fat′i-ga-blʳ, *a.* Indefatigable.
in″de-fat′i-ga-bl-nessʳ, *n.* Indefatigableness.
in″de-fea′si-blʳ, *a.* Indefeasible.
in″de-fea′si-bl-nessʳ, *n.* Indefeasibleness.
in″de-fec′ti-blʳ, *a.* Indefectible.
in″de-fec′tivˢ, *a.* Indefective.
in″de-fen′si-blʳ, *a.* Indefensible.
in″de-fen′si-bl-nessʳ, *n.* Indefensibleness.
in″de-fin′a-blʳ, *a.* Indefinable.
in″de-fin′a-bl-nessʳ, *n.* Indefinableness.
in-def′i-nitˢ, *a.* Indefinite.
in″de-fin′i-tivʳ&ˢ, *a.* Indefinitive.
in″de-fin′i-tiv-lyˢ, *adv.* Indefinitively.
in″de-fin′i-tiv-nessˢ, *n.* Indefinitiveness.
in″de-flect′i-blʳ, *a.* Indeflectible.
in″de-form′a-blʳ, *a.* Indeformable.
in″de-lec′ta-blʳ, *a.* Indelectable.
in-del′i-blʳ, *a.* Indelible.
in-del′i-bl-nessʳ, *n.* Indelibleness.
in″de-mon′stra-blʳ, *a.* Indemonstrable.
in″de-mon′stra-bl-nessʳ, *n.* Indemonstrableness.
in″de-pend′a-blʳ, *a.* Independable.
in-dep′re-ca-blʳ, *a.* Indeprecable.
in″de-priv′a-blʳ, *a.* Indeprivable.
in″de-scrib′a-blʳ, *a.* Indescribable.
in″de-scrib′a-bl-nessʳ, *n.* Indescribableness.
in″de-scrip′tivˢ, *a.* Indescriptive.

in″de-sir′a-bl[P], *a.* Indesirable.
in″de-struc′ti-bl[P], *a.* Indestructible.
in″de-struc′ti-bl-ness[P], *n.* Indestructibleness.
in″de-tect′a-[or **i-**]**bl**[P], *a.* Indetectable, indetectible.
in″de-ter′mi-na-bl[P], *a.* Indeterminable.
in″de-ter′mi-na-bl-ness[P], *n.* Indeterminableness.
in″de-ter′mi-na-tive[S], *a.* Indeterminative.
in″de-ter′mind[S], *pa.* Indetermined.
in-det′ted[S], *pa.* Indebted.
in′dext[P&S], *pp.* Indexed.
in-dic′a-tiv[P&S], *a.* & *n.* Indicative.
in-dic′a-tiv-ly[S], *adv.* Indicatively.
in-dic′tiv[S], *a.* Indictive.
in″dif-fu′si-bl[P], *a.* Indiffusible.
in″di-gest′i-bl[P], *a.* Indigestible.
in″di-gest′i-bl-ness[P], *n.* Indigestibleness.
in″di-ges′tiv[S], *a.* Indigestive.
in″di-men′si-bl[P], *a.* Indimensible.
in″di-min′ish-a-bl[P], *a.* Indiminishable.
in″dis-cern′i-bl[P], *a.* Indiscernible.
in″dis-cern′i-bl-ness[P], *n.* Indiscernibleness.
in-dis′ci-plin-a-bl[P], *a.* Indisciplinable.
in-dis′ci-plin[S], *n.* Indiscipline.
in″dis-crim′i-na-tiv[S], *a.* Indiscriminative.
in″dis-crim′i-na-tiv-ly[S], *adv.* Indiscriminatively.
in″dis-cuv′er-a-bl[P], *a.* Indiscoverable.
in″dis-cuss′a-[or **i-**]**bl**[P], *a.* Indiscussable, indiscussible.
in″dis-pen′sa-bl[P], *a.* & *n.* Indispensable.
in″dis-pen′sa-bl-ness[P], *n.* Indispensableness.

in-dis′put-a-bl[P], *a.* Indisputable.
in-dis′put-a-bl-ness[P], *n.* Indisputableness.
in-dis′si-pa-bl[P], *a.* Indissipable.
in-dis′so-lu-bl[P], *a.* Indissoluble.
in-dis′so-lu-bl-ness[P], *n.* Indissolubleness.
in″dis-solv′a-bl[P], *a.* Indissolvable.
in″dis-solv′a-bl-ness[P], *n.* Indissolvableness.
in″dis-tinc′tiv[S], *a.* Indistinctive.
in″dis-tinc′tiv-ly[S], *adv.* Indistinctively.
in″dis-tinc′tiv-ness[S], *n.* Indistinctiveness.
in″dis-tin′guish-a-bl[P], *a.* Indistinguishable.
in″dis-tin′guish-a-bl-ness[P], *n.* Indistinguishableness.
in″dis-trib′u-ta-bl[P], *a.* Indistributable.
in″di-vert′i-bl[P], *a.* Indivertible.
in″di-vid′a-bl[P], *a.* Individable.
in″di-vis′i-bl[P], *a.* & *n.* Indivisible.
in″di-vis′i-bl-ness[P], *n.* Indivisibleness.
in-doc′i-bl[P], *a.* Indocible.
in-doc′i-bl-ness[P], *n.* Indocibleness.
in-doc′il[S], *a.* Indocile.
in-dom′i-ta-bl[P], *a.* Indomitable.
in-dom′i-ta-bl-ness[P], *n.* Indomitableness.
in-dors′a-bl[P], *a.* Indorsable.
in-dorst′[P&S], *pp.* Indorsed.
in-du′bi-ta-bl[P], *a.* & *n.* Indubitable.
in-du′bi-ta-bl-ness[P], *n.* Indubitableness.
in-du′bi-ta-tiv-ly[S], *adv.* Indubitatively.
in-duc′i-bl[P], *a.* Inducible.
in-du′civ[S], *a.* Inducive.
in-duc′til[P&S], *a.* Inductile.
in-duc′tiv[S], *a.* Inductive.
in-duc′tiv-ly[S], *adv.* Inductively.

in-duc'tiv-ness[s], *n.* Inductiveness.
in-dulge'a-bl[r], *a.* Indulgeable.
in-dur'a-bl[r], *a.* Indurable.
in-dus'tri-us[s], *a.* Industrious.
in-du'tiv[s], *a.* Indutive.
in-ed'i-bl[r], *a.* Inedible.
in-ed'u-ca-bl[r], *a.* Ineducable.
in-ef'fa-bl[r], *a.* & *n.* Ineffable.
in-ef'fa-bl-ness[r], *n.* Ineffableness.
in"ef-face'a-bl[r], *a.* Ineffaceable.
in"ef-fec'ti-bl[r], *a.* Ineffectible.
in"ef-fec'tiv[s], *a.* Ineffective.
in"ef-fec'tiv-ly[s], *adv.* Ineffectively.
in"ef-fec'tiv-ness[s], *n.* Ineffectiveness.
in-el'i-gi-bl[r], *a.* Ineligible.
in-el'i-gi-bl-ness[r], *n.* Ineligibleness.
in"e-lim'i-na-bl[r], *a.* Ineliminable.
in"e-luc'ta-bl[r], *a.* Ineluctable.
in"e-lud'i-bl[r], *a.*Ineludible.
in-e'qua-bl[r], *a.* Inequable.
in-eq'ui-ta-bl[r], *a.* Inequitable.
in"e-rad'i-ca-bl[r], *a.* Ineradicable.
in"e-ras'a-[or **i-**]**bl**[r], *a.* Inerasable, inerasible.
in-er'ra-bl[r], *a.* Inerrable.
in-er'ra-bl-ness[r], *n.* Inerrableness.
in"es-cap'a-bl[r], *a.* Inescapable.
in-es'ti-ma-bl[r], *a.* Inestimable.
in-es'ti-ma-bl-ness[r], *n.* Inestimableness.
in"e-vap'o-ra-bl[r], *a.* Inevaporable.
in"e-va'si-bl[r], *a.* Inevasible.
in-ev'i-ta-bl[r], *a.* Inevitable.
in-ev'i-ta-bl-ness[r], *n.* Inevitableness.
in"ex-cit'a-bl[r], *a.* Inexcitable.
in"ex-clu'siv-ly[r&s], *adv.* Inexclusively.
in-ex"com-mu'ni-ca-bl[r], *a.* Incommunicable.
in"ex-cus'a-bl[r], *a.* Inexcusable.
in"ex-cus'a-bl-ness[r], *n.* Inexcusableness.
in-ex'e-cra-bl[r], *a.* Inexecrable.
in-ex'e-cut-a-bl[r], *a.* Inexecutable.
in"ex-ha'la-bl[r], *a.* Inexhalable.
in"ex-haust'i-bl[r], *a.* Inexhaustible.
in"ex-haust'i-bl-ness[r], *n.* Inexhaustibleness.
in"ex-haus'tiv[s], *a.* Inexhaustive.
in-ex'i-gi-bl[r], *a.* Inexigible.
in-ex'o-ra-bl[r], *a.* Inexorable.
in-ex'o-ra-bl-ness[r], *n.* Inexorableness.
in"ex-pan'si-bl[r], *a.* Inexpansible.
in"ex-pan'siv[r&s], *a.* Inexpansive.
in"ex-pen'siv[s], *a.* Inexpensive.
in-ex'pi-a-bl[r], *a.* Inexpiable.
in-ex'pi-a-bl-ness[r], *n.* Inexpiableness.
in"ex-plain'a-bl[r], *a.* Inexplainable.
in-ex'pli-ca-bl[r], *a.* Inexplicable.
in-ex'pli-ca-bl-ness[r], *n.* Inexplicableness.
in"ex-plor'a-bl[r], *a.* Inexplorable.
in"ex-press'i-bl[r], *a.* Inexpressible.
in"ex-press'i-bl-ness[r], *n.* Inexpressibleness.
in"ex-pres'siv[s], *a.* Inexpressive.
in"ex-pug'na-bl[r], *a.* Inexpugnable.
in"ex-pug'na-bl-ness[r], *n.* Inexpugnableness.
in"ex-punge'a-bl[r], *a.* Inexpungeable.
in"ex-ten'si-bl[r], *a.* Inextensible.
in"ex-ten'siv[s], *a.* Inextensive.
in"ex-ter'mi-na-bl[r], *a.* Inexterminable.
in"ex-tin'guish-a-bl[r], *a.* Inextinguishable.
in"ex-tir'pa-bl[r], *a.* Inextirpable.
in-ex'tri-ca-bl[r], *a.* Inextricable.
in-ex'tri-ca-bl-ness[r], *n.* Inextricableness.
in-fal'li-bl[r], *a.* Infallible.
in-fal'li-bl-ness[r], *n.* Infallibleness.
in'fa-mus[s], *a.* Infamous.
in'fan-til[s], *a.* Infantile.
in'fan-tin[s], *a.* Infantine.

in-fat'i-ga-bl[P], *a.* Infatigable.
in-fea'si-bl[P], *a.* Infeasible.
in-fea'si-bl-ness[P], *n.* Infeasibleness.
in-fect'i-bl[P], *a.* Infectible.
in-fec'tiv[S], *a.* Infective.
in-fec'tiv-ly[S], *adv.* Infectively.
in-fec'tiv-ness[S], *n.* Infectiveness.
in-fem'i-nin[P&S], *a.* Infeminine.
in-fer'a-bl[P], *a.* Inferable.
in-ferd'[P&S], *pp.* Inferred.
in-fer'ri-bl[P], *a.* Inferrible.
in-fer'til[S], *a.* Infertile.
in'fi-nit[P&S], *a.* & *n.* Infinite.
in-fin'i-tiv[S], *a.* & *n.* Infinitive.
in-fin'i-tiv-ly[S], *adv.* Infinitively.
in-fixt'[P&S], *pp.* Infixed.
in-flam'ma-bl[P], *a.* & *n.* Inflammable.
in-flam'ma-bl-ness[P], *n.* Inflammableness.
in-flam'ma-tiv[S], *a.* Inflammative.
in-flat'a-bl[P], *a.* Inflatable.
in-fla'til[S], *a.* Inflatile.
in-flec'tiv[P&S], *a.* Inflective.
in-fledgd'[P&S], *pa.* Infledged.
in-flex'i-bl[P], *a.* Inflexible.
in-flex'i-bl-ness[P], *n.* Inflexibleness.
in-flex'iv[P&S], *a.* Inflexive.
in-flext'[S], *a.* Inflexed.
in-flic'ta-bl[P], *a.* Inflictable.
in-flic'tiv[S], *a.* Inflictive.
in'flu-en-civ[S], *a.* Influencive.
in'flu-enst[S], *pp.* Influenced.
in-flux'i-bl[P], *a.* Influxible.
in-flux'iv[S], *a.* Influxive.
in-flux'iv-ly[S], *adv.* Influxively.
in-form'a-bl[P], *a.* Informable.
in-form'a-tiv[S], *a.* Informative.
in-form'a-tiv-ly[S], *adv.* Informatively.
in-formd'[P&S], *a.* Informed.
in-fract'i-bl[P], *a.* Infractible.
in-fran'gi-bl[P], *a.* Infrangible.
in-fran'gi-bl-ness[P], *n.* Infrangibleness.
in-frus'tra-bl[P], *a.* Infrustrable.
in-fus'i-bl[P], *a.* Infusible.
in-fus'i-bl-ness[P], *n.* Infusibleness.
in-fu'siv[S], *a.* Infusive.
in-fuze'[P], *vt.* & *vi.* Infuse.
in-gen'er-a-bl[P], *a.* Ingenerable.
in-ges'tiv[S], *a.* Ingestive.
in'graind[S], *pp.* Ingrained.
in-gus'ta[or -ti-]bl[P], *a.* Ingustable, ingustible.
in-hab'i-ta-bl[P], *a.* Inhabitable.
in-hab'i-ta"tiv[S], *a.* Inhabitative.
in-hab'i-ta"tiv-ness[S], *n.* Inhabitativeness.
in-hab'i-tiv-ness[S], *n.* Inhabitiveness.
in-her'i-ta-bl[P], *a.* Inheritable.
in-her'i-ta-bl-ness[P], *n.* Inheritableness.
in-he'siv-ly[S], *adv.* Inhesively.
in-hos'pi-ta-bl[P], *a.* Inhospitable.
in-hos'pi-ta-bl-ness[P], *n.* Inhospitableness.
in"im-ag'i-na-bl[P], *a.* Inimaginable.
in-im'i-ta-bl[P], *a.* Inimitable.
in-im'i-ta-bl-ness[P], *n.* Inimitableness.
in-ir'ri-ta-bl[P], *a.* Inirritable.
in-ir'ri-ta"tiv[P&S], *a.* Inirritative.
in-i'tiald[S], *pp.* Initialed, initialled.
in-i'ti-a-tiv[S], *a.* & *n.* Initiative.
in-ju'di-ca-bl[P], *a.* Injudicable.
in-jus'ti-fi"a-bl[P], *a.* Injustifiable.
in-jus'tis[S], *n.* Injustice.
inkt[P&S], *pp.* Inked.
in-nas'ci-bl[P], *a.* Innascible.
in-na'tiv[S], *a.* Innative.
in-nav'i-ga-bl[P], *a.* Innavigable.
in-nav'i-ga-bl-ness[P], *n.* Innavigableness.
in-nom'i-na-bl[P], *a.* Innominable.
in'no-va"tiv[S], *a.* Innovative.
in-nu'mer-a-bl[P], *a.* Innumerable.
in-nu'mer-a-bl-ness[P], *n.* Innumerableness.

in″ob-serv′a-bl[P], *a.* Inobservable.
in″ob-tain′a-bl[P], *a.* Inobtainable.
in″ob-tru′siv[P&S], *a.* Inobtrusive.
in″ob-tru′siv-ly[S], *adv.* Inobtrusively.
in″ob-tru′siv-ness[S], *n.* Inobtrusiveness.
in-oc′u-la-bl[P], *a.* Inoculable.
in″of-fen′siv[S], *a.* Inoffensive.
in″of-fen′siv-ly[S], *adv.* Inoffensively.
in″of-fen′siv-ness[S], *n.* Inoffensiveness.
in-op′er-a-bl[P], *a.* Inoperable.
in-op′er-a-tiv[S], *a.* Inoperative.
in″op-pres′siv[P&S], *a.* Inoppressive.
in″os-ten′si-bl[P], *a.* Inostensible.
in-ox′i-da-bl[P], *a.* Inoxidable.
in-quench′a-bl[P], *a.* Inquenchable.
in′qui-lin[S], *a.* Inquiline.
in-quir′a-bl[P], *a.* Inquirable.
in-quis′i-tiv[P&S], *a.* Inquisitive.
in-quis′i-tiv-ly[S], *adv.* Inquisitively.
in-quis′i-tiv-ness[S], *n.* Inquisitiveness.
in-salv′a-bl[P], *a.* Insalvable.
in-san′a-bl[P], *a.* Insanable.
in-san′a-bl-ness[P], *n.* Insanableness.
in-sa′ti-a-bl[P], *a.* Insatiable.
in-sa′ti-a-bl-ness[P], *n.* Insatiableness.
in-scrib′a-bl[P], *a.* Inscribable.
in-scrib′a-bl-ness[P], *n.* Inscribableness.
in-scrip′ti-bl[P], *a.* Inscriptible.
in-scrip′tiv[S], *a.* Inscriptive.
in-scrip′tiv-ly[S], *adv.* Inscriptively.
in-scru′ta-bl[P], *a.* Inscrutable.
in-scru′ta-bl-ness[P], *n.* Inscrutableness.
in-sec′a-bl[P], *a.* Insecable.
in′sec-til[S], *a.* Insectile.
in″se-nes′ci-bl[P], *a.* Insenescible.
in-sen′si-bl[P], *a.* Insensible.
in-sen′si-bl-ness[P], *n.* Insensibleness.
in-sen′si-tiv[P&S], *a.* Insensitive.
in-sen′si-tiv-ness[S], *n.* Insensitiveness.
in-sep′a-ra-bl[P], *a.* & *n.* Inseparable.
in-sep′a-ra-bl-ness[P], *n.* Inseparableness.
in-ser′tiv[S], *a.* Insertive.
in-sev′er-a-bl[P], *a.* Inseverable.
in-sin′u-a-tiv[S], *a.* Insinuative.
in-so′cia-bl[P], *a.* Insociable.
in-so′cia-bl-ness[P], *n.* Insociableness.
in-sol′u-bl[P], *a.* & *n.* Insoluble.
in-sol′u-bl-ness[P], *n.* Insolubleness.
in-solv′a-bl[P], *a.* Insolvable.
in-spect′a-bl[P], *a.* Inspectable.
in-spec′tiv[S], *a.* Inspective.
in-spir′a-bl[P], *a.* Inspirable.
in-spir′a-tiv[S], *a.* Inspirative.
in-stald′[S], *pp.* Installed.
in-staild′[P], *pp.* Installed.
in′stanst[S], *pp.* Instanced.
in-sted′[P&S], **in sted**[S], *adv.* Instead.
in-stil′[S], *vt.* Instill.
in-stild′[S], *pp.* Instilled.
in-stinc′tiv[P&S], *a.* Instinctive.
in-stinc′tiv-ly[S], *adv.* Instinctively.
in′sti-tu″tiv[S], *a.* Institutive.
in′sti-tu″tiv-ly[S], *adv.* Institutively.
in-struct′i-bl[P], *a.* Instructible.
in-struc′tiv[P&S], *a.* Instructive.
in-struc′tiv-ly[S], *adv.* Instructively.
in-struc′tiv-ness[S], *n.* Instructiveness.
in″sub-du′a-bl[P], *a.* Insubduable.
in″sub-mer′gi-bl[P], *a.* Insubmergible.
in″sub-mers′i-bl[P], *a.* Insubmersible.
in″sub-mis′siv[P&S], *a.* Insubmissive.
in″sub-vert′i-bl[P], *a.* Insubvertible.
in-suf′fer-a-bl[P], *a.* Insufferable.
in-suf′fer-a-bl-ness[P], *n.* Insufferableness.
in-su′per-a-bl[P], *a.* Insuperable.
in-su′per-a-bl-ness[P], *n.* Insuperableness.
in″sup-port′a-bl[P], *a.* Insupportable.

in″sup-port′a-bl-ness^{p}, *n.* Insupportableness.
in″sup-pos′a-bl^{p}, *a.* Insupposable.
in″sup-press′i-bl^{p}, *a.* Insuppressible.
in″sup-pres′siv^{s}, *a.* Insuppressive.
in-sur′a-bl^{p}, *a.* Insurable.
in″sur-mount′a-bl^{p}, *a.* Insurmountable.
in″sur-mount′a-bl-ness^{p}, *n.* Insurmountableness.
in″sur-pass′a-bl^{p}, *a.* Insurpassable.
in″sus-cep′ti-bl^{p}, *a.* Insusceptible.
in″sus-cep′tiv^{s}, *a.* Insusceptive.
in-tac′til$^{p\&s}$, *a.* Intactile.
in-tan′gi-bl^{p}, *a.* Intangible.
in-tan′gi-bl-ness^{p}, *n.* Intangibleness.
in′te-gra-bl^{p}, *a.* Integrable.
in′te-gra″tiv^{s}, *a.* Integrative.
in-teg′ri-tiv^{s}, *a.* Integritive.
in″tel-lec′ti-bl^{p}, *a.* Intellectible.
in″tel-lec′tiv^{s}, *a.* Intellective.
in″tel-lec′tiv-ly^{s}, *adv.* Intellectively.
in-tel′li-gi-bl^{p}, *a.* & *n.* Intelligible.
in-tel′li-gi-bl-ness^{p}, *n.* Intelligibleness.
in-tem′per-a-bl^{p}, *a.* Intemperable.
in-ten′sa-tiv^{s}, *a.* Intensative.
in-ten′si-tiv^{s}, *a.* Intensitive.
in-ten′siv^{s}, *a.* & *n.* Intensive.
in-ten′siv-ly^{s}, *adv.* Intensively.
in-ten′siv-ness^{s}, *n.* Intensiveness.
in-ten′tiv†^{s}, *a.* Intentive.
in″ter-ac′tiv^{s}, *a.* Interactive.
in″ter-ad′di-tiv^{s}, *a.* Interadditive.
in-ter′ca-la″tiv^{s}, *a.* Intercalative.
in″ter-cep′tiv^{s}, *a.* Interceptive.
in″ter-change′a-bl^{p}, *a.* Interchangeable.
in″ter-change′a-bl-ness^{p}, *n.* Interchangeableness.
in″ter-com-mu′ni-ca-bl^{p}, *a.* Intercommunicable.
in″ter-com-mu′ni-ca-tiv^{s}, *a.* Intercommunicative.
in″ter-com′pa-ra-bl^{p}, *a.* Intercomparable.
in″ter-con-vert′i-bl^{p}, *a.* Interconvertible.
in-terd′^{s}, *pp.* Interred.
in″ter-de-riv′a-tiv^{s}, *n.* Interderivative.
in″ter-de-struc′tiv-ness^{s}, *n.* Interdestructiveness.
in″ter-dic′tiv^{s}, *a.* Interdictive.
in″ter-jec′tiv^{s}, *a.* Interjective.
in″ter-jec′tiv-ly^{s}, *adv.* Interjectively.
in″ter-leav′^{p}, *vt.* Interleave.
in″ter-leavd′^{p}, *pp.* Interleaved.
in″ter-linkt′$^{p\&s}$, *pp.* Interlinked.
in′ter-lockt^{s}, *pp.* Interlocked.
in″ter-loc′u-tiv^{s}, *a.* Interlocutive.
in″ter-mar′riage-a-bl^{p}, *a.* Intermarriageable.
in″ter-med′l^{p}, *vi.* Intermeddle.
in-ter′mi-na-bl^{p}, *a.* & *n.* Interminable.
in″ter-mis′siv^{s}, *a.* Intermissive.
in-ternd′^{s}, *pp.* Interned.
in″ter-ne′cin^{s}, *a.* Internecine.
in″ter-ne′civ^{s}, *a.* Internecive.
in″ter-pen′e-tra-bl^{p}, *a.* Interpenetrable.
in″ter-pen′e-tra-tiv^{s}, *a.* Interpenetrative.
in″ter-pen′e-tra-tiv-ly^{s}, *adv.* Interpenetratively.
in-ter′po-la-bl^{p}, *a.* Interpolable.
in-ter′po-la-tiv^{s}, *a.* Interpolative.
in-ter′po-la-tiv-ly^{s}, *adv.* Interpolatively.
in″ter-pos′i-tiv^{s}, *a.* Interpositive.
in-ter′pret-a-bl^{p}, *a.* Interpretable.
in-ter′pret-a-bl-ness^{p}, *n.* Interpretableness.
in-ter′pre-ta-tiv^{s}, *a.* Interpretative.
in-ter′pre-tiv^{s}, *a.* Interpretive.
in-ter′pre-tiv-ly^{s}, *adv.* Interpretively.

in-ter'ro-ga-bl^{r}, *a.* Interrogable.
in"ter-rog'a-tiv$^{r\&s}$, *a.* & *n.* Interrogative.
in"ter-rup'tiv^{s}, *a.* Interruptive.
in"ter-rup'tiv-ly^{s}, *adv.* Interruptively.
in"ter-sperst'$^{r\&s}$, *pp.* Interspersed.
in'ter-stis^{s}, *n.* Interstice.
in"ter-sub-jec'tiv^{s}, *a.* Intersubjective.
in"ter-sus-cep'tiv^{s}, *a.* Intersusceptive.
in"ter-veind'^{s}, *a.* Interveined.
in"ter-ven'tiv^{s}, *a.* Interventive.
in'ter-viewd^{s}, *pp.* Interviewed.
in"ter-vis'i-bl^{r}, *a.* Intervisible.
in"ter-volv'^{s}, *v.* & *n.* Intervolve.
in"ter-volvd'^{s}, *pp.* Intervolved.
in-tes'ta-bl^{r}, *a.* Intestable.
in-tes'tin$^{r\&s}$, *a.* & *n.* Intestine.
in-tim'i-da-tiv^{s}, *a.* Intimidative.
in-tol'er-a-bl^{r}, *a.* & *adv.* Intolerable.
in-tol'er-a-bl-ness^{r}, *n.* Intolerableness.
in-ton'a-bl^{r}, *a.* Intonable.
in-tox'i-ca-bl^{r}, *a.* Intoxicable.
in-tox'i-ca"tiv^{s}, *a.* Intoxicative.
in"tra-cli-tel'lin^{s}, *a.* Intraclitelline.
in-trac'ta-bl^{r}, *a.* & *n.* Intractable.
in-trac'ta-bl-ness^{r}, *n.* Intractableness.
in-trac'til^{s}, *a.* Intractile.
in"trans-fer'a-bl^{r}, *a.* Intransferable.
in"trans-form'a-bl^{r}, *a.* Intransformable.
in"trans-fu'si-[or **-a-**]**bl**^{r}, *a.* Intransfusible, intransfusable.
in"trans-gress'i-bl^{r}, *a.* Intransgressible.
in-tran'sit-a-bl^{r}, *a.* Intransitable.
in-tran'si-tiv^{s}, *a.* & *n.* Intransitive.
in-tran'si-tiv-ly^{s}, *adv.* Intransitively.
in-tran'si-tiv-ness^{s}, *n.* Intransitiveness.
in"trans-lat'a-bl^{r}, *a.* Intranslatable.
in"trans-mis'si-bl^{r}, *a.* Intransmissible.
in"trans-mut'a-bl^{r}, *a.* Intransmutable.
in-trencht'^{s}, *pp.* Intrenched.
in"tro-cep'tiv^{s}, *a.* Introceptive.
in"tro-con-vert'i-bl^{r}, *a.* Introconvertible.
in"tro-duc'i-bl^{r}; *a.* Introducible.
in"tro-duc'tion^{r}, *n.* Introduction.
in"tro-duc'tiv^{s}, *a.* Introductive.
in"tro-duc'tiv-ly^{s}, *adv.* Introductively.
in"tro-mis'si-bl^{r}, *a.* Intromissible.
in"tro-mis'siv^{s}, *a.* Intromissive.
in"tro-pul'sive^{s}, *a.* Intropulsive.
in"tro-spec'tiv^{s}, *a.* Introspective.
in"tro-spec'tiv-ly^{s}, *adv.* Introspectively.
in"tro-spec'tiv-ness^{s}, *n.* Introspectiveness.
in"tro-ver'si-bl^{r}, *a.* Introversible.
in"tro-ver'siv^{s}, *a.* Introversive.
in"tro-ver'tiv^{s}, *a.* Introvertive.
in-tru'siv$^{r\&s}$, *a.* & *n.* Intrusive.
in-tru'siv-ly^{s}, *adv.* Intrusively.
in-tru'siv-ness^{s}, *n.* Intrusiveness.
in-tu'i-tiv^{s}, *a.* Intuitive.
in-tu'i-tiv-ly^{s}, *adv.* Intuitively.
in-tu'i-tiv-ness^{s}, *n.* Intuitiveness.
in"tus-sus-cep'tiv^{s}, *a.* Intussusceptive.
in-un'da-bl^{r}, *a.* Inundable.
in-urnd'$^{r\&s}$, *pp.* Inurned.
in-vad'a-bl^{r}, *a.* Invadable.
in-vag'i-na-bl^{r}, *a.* Invaginable.
in-val'u-a-bl^{r}, *a.* Invaluable.
in-val'u-a-bl-ness^{r}, *n.* Invaluableness.
in-va'ri-a-bl^{r}, *a.* & *n.* Invariable.
in-va'ri-a-bl-ness^{r}, *n.* Invariableness.
in-va'siv^{s}, *a.* Invasive.

in-vec′tiv[P&S], *a.* & *n.* Invective.
in-vec′tiv-ness[S], *n.* Invectiveness.
in-veighd′[S], *pp.* Inveighed.
in-vend′i-bl[P], *a.* Invendible.
in-vend′i-bl-ness[P], *n.* Invendibleness.
in-vent′i-[or **-a-**]**bl**[P], *a.* Inventible.
in-vent′i-bl-ness[P], *n.* Inventibleness.
in-ven′tiv[P&S], *a.* Inventive.
in-vers′a-bl[P], *a.* Inversable.
in-ver′sa-til[S], *a.* Inversatile.
in-ver′siv[S], *a.* Inversive.
in-verst′[S], *pp.* Inversed.
in-vert′i-bl[P], *a.* Invertible.
in-ver′tiv[S], *a.* Invertive.
in-vest′a-bl[P], *a.* Investable.
in-ves′ti-ga-bl[P], *a.* Investigable.
in-ves′ti-ga″tiv[S], *a.* Investigative.
in-ves′ti-tiv[S], *a.* Investitive.
in-vid′i-us[S], *a.* Invidious.
in-vig′o-ra″tiv[S], *a.* Invigorative.
in-vig′o-ra″tiv-ly[S], *adv.* Invigoratively.
in-vin′ci-bl[P], *a.* & *n.* Invincible.
in-vin′ci-bl-ness[P], *n.* Invincibleness.
in-vi′o-la-bl[P], *a.* Inviolable.
in-vi′o-la-bl-ness[P], *n.* Inviolableness.
in-vir′il[S], *a.* Invirile.
in-vis′i-bl[P], *a.* & *n.* Invisible.
in-vis′i-bl-ness[P], *n.* Invisibleness.
in-vit′a-bl[P], *a.* Invitable.
in-vit′ri-fi″a-bl[P], *a.* Invitrifiable.
in-vo′ca-bl[P], *a.* Invocable.
in-voc′a-tiv[S], *a.* Invocative.
in-vol′a-til[P&S], *a.* Involatile.
in′vo-lu″tiv[S], *a.* Involutive.
in-volv′[P&S], *vt.* Involve.
in-volvd′[P&S], *pp.* Involved.
in-vul′ner-a-bl[P], *a.* Invulnerable.
in-vul′ner-a-bl-ness[P], *n.* Invulnerableness.
in-weav′[P], *vt.* Inweave.
in-wrapt′[P&S], *pp.* Inwrapped.
i′o-din[P], **i′o-dine**[P], *n.* Iodine.
i′on-iz″a-bl[P], *a.* Ionizable.
i-ras′ci-bl[P], *a.* Irascible.
i-ras′ci-bl-ness[P], *n.* Irascibleness.
ir′i-din[S], *a.* Iridine.
ir″i-dos′min[S], *n.* Iridosmine.
i′rist[S], *a.* Irised.
irk′sum[P&S], *a.* Irksome.
irkt[S], *pp.* Irked.
i′rond[S], *pp.* Ironed.
ir-ra′di-a″tiv[S], *a.* & *n.* Irradiative.
ir-rad′i-ca-bl[P], *a.* Irradicable.
ir-rar′e-fi″a-bl[P], *a.* Irrarefiable.
ir-ra′tion-a-bl[P], *a.* Irrationable.
ir-re′al-iz″a-bl[P], *a.* Irrealizable.
ir″re-but′ta-bl[P], *a.* Irrebuttable.
ir″re-cep′tiv[S], *a.* Irreceptive.
ir″re-claim′a-bl[P], *a.* Irreclaimable.
ir″re-claim′a-bl-ness[P], *n.* Irreclaimableness.
ir-rec′og-niz″a-bl[P], *a.* Irrecognizable.
ir-rec′on-cil″a-bl[P], *a.* & *n.* Irreconcilable.
ir-rec′on-cil″a-bl-ness[P], *n.* Irreconcilableness.
ir″re-cov′er-a-bl[P], *a.* Irrecoverable.
ir″re-cov′er-a-bl-ness[P], *n.* Irrecoverableness.
ir″re-cu′sa-bl[P], *a.* Irrecusable.
ir″re-deem′a-bl[P], *a.* Irredeemable.
ir″re-deem′a-bl-ness[P], *n.* Irredeemableness.
ir″re-dres′si-bl[P], *a.* Irredressible.
ir″re-duc′i-bl[P], *a.* Irreducible.
ir″re-duc′i-bl-ness[P], *n.* Irreducibleness.
ir″re-duc′ti-bl[P], *a.* Irreductible.
ir″re-flec′tiv[S], *a.* Irreflective.
ir″re-flec′tiv-ly[S], *adv.* Irreflectively.
ir″re-flec′tiv-ness[S], *n.* Irreflectiveness.
ir″re-flex′iv[S], *a.* Irreflexive.
ir″re-form′a-bl[P], *a.* Irreformable.
ir-ref′ra-ga-bl[P], *a.* Irrefragable.

ir-ref'ra-ga-bl-ness^{p}, *n.* Irrefragableness.
ir"re-fran'gi-bl^{p}, *a.* Irrefrangible.
ir"re-fran'gi-bl-ness^{p}, *n.* Irrefrangibleness.
ir"re-fus'a-bl^{p}, *a.* Irrefusable.
ir"re-fut'a-bl^{p}, *a.* Irrefutable.
ir"re-fut'a-bl-ness^{p}, *n.* Irrefutableness.
ir-rel'a-tiv^{s}, *a.* & *n.* Irrelative.
ir-rel'a-tiv-ly^{s}, *adv.* Irrelatively.
ir-rel'a-tiv-ness^{s}, *n.* Irrelativeness.
ir"re-liev'a-bl^{p}, *a.* Irrelievable.
ir-re'me-a-bl^{p}, *a.* Irremeable.
ir"re-me'di-a-bl^{p}, *a.* Irremediable.
ir"re-me'di-a-bl-ness^{p}, *n.* Irremediableness.
ir"re-mem'ber-a-bl^{p}, *a.* Irrememberable.
ir"re-mis'si-bl^{p}, *a.* Irremissible.
ir"re-mis'siv^{s}, *a.* Irremissive.
ir"re-mov'a-bl^{p}, *a.* Irremovable.
ir"re-mov'a-bl-ness^{p}, *n.* Irremovableness.
ir"re-mu'ner-a-bl^{p}, *a.* Irremunerable.
ir"ren'der-a-bl^{p}, *a.* Irrenderable.
ir"re-new'a-bl^{p}, *a.* Irrenewable.
ir"re-nun'ci-a-bl^{p}, *a.* Irrenunciable.
ir-rep'a-ra-bl^{p}, *a.* Irreparable.
ir-rep'a-ra-bl-ness^{p}, *n.* Irreparableness.
ir"re-peal'a-bl^{p}, *a.* Irrepealable.
ir"re-peal'a-bl-ness^{p}, *n.* Irrepealableness.
ir"re-place'a-bl^{p}, *a.* Irreplaceable.
ir"re-plev'i-a-bl^{p}, *a.* Irrepleviable.
ir"re-plev'i-sa-bl^{p}, *a.* Irreplevisable.
ir"re-port'a-bl^{p}, *a.* Irreportable.
ir-rep"re-hen'si-bl^{p}, *a.* Irreprehensible.
ir-rep"re-hen'si-bl-ness^{p}, *n.* Irreprehensibleness.
ir-rep"re-sent'a-bl^{p}, *a.* Irrepresentable.
ir"re-pres'si-bl^{p}, *a.* Irrepressible.
ir"re-pres'si-bl-ness^{p}, *n.* Irrepressibleness.
ir"re-pres'siv^{s}, *a.* Irrepressive.
ir"re-proach'a-bl^{p}, *a.* Irreproachable.
ir"re-proach'a-bl-ness^{p}, *n.* Irreproachableness.
ir-re"pro-duc'i-bl^{p}, *a.* Irreproducible.
ir-re"pro-duc'tiv^{s}, *a.* Irreproductive.
ir"re-prov'a-bl^{p}, *a.* Irreprovable.
ir"re-sis'ti-bl^{p}, *a.* Irresistible.
ir"re-sis'ti-bl-ness^{p}, *n.* Irresistibleness.
ir-res'o-lu-bl^{p}, *a.* Irresoluble.
ir"re-solv'a-bl^{p}, *a.* Irresolvable.
ir"re-solv'a-bl-ness^{p}, *n.* Irresolvableness.
ir"re-solvd'^{s}, *a.* Irresolved.
ir"re-spect'a-bl^{p}, *a.* Irrespectable.
ir"re-spec'tiv^{s}, *a.* Irrespective.
ir"re-spir'a-bl^{p}, *a.* Irrespirable.
ir"re-spon'si-bl^{p}, *a.* Irresponsible.
ir"re-spon'si-bl-ness^{p}, *n.* Irresponsibleness.
ir"re-spon'siv^{s}, *a.* Irresponsive.
ir"re-strain'a-bl^{p}, *a.* Irrestrainable.
ir"re-stric'tiv^{s}, *a.* Irrestrictive.
ir"re-sul'tiv^{s}, *a.* Irresultive.
ir"re-sus'ci-ta-bl^{p}, *a.* Irresuscitable.
ir"re-ten'tiv^{s}, *a.* Irretentive.
ir"re-trace'a-bl^{p}, *a.* Irretraceable.
ir"re-trac'til^{s}, *a.* Irretractile.
ir"re-triev'a-bl^{p}, *a.* Irretrievable.
ir"re-triev'a-bl-ness^{p}, *n.* Irretrievableness.
ir"re-veal'a-bl^{p}, *a.* Irrevealable.
ir"re-vers'i-bl^{p}, *a.* Irreversible.
ir"re-vers'i-bl-ness^{p}, *n.* Irreversibleness.
ir"re-vert'i-bl^{p}, *a.* Irrevertible.
ir"re-vis'a-bl^{p}, *a.* Irrevisable.
ir"rev'o-ca-bl^{p}, *a.* Irrevocable.

ir″rev′o-ca-bl-ness[P], *n.* Irrevocableness.
ir′ri-ga-bl[P], *a.* Irrigable.
ir′ri-ga″tiv[S], *a.* Irrigative.
ir′ri-ta-bl[P], *a.* Irritable.
ir′ri-ta-bl-ness[P], *n.* Irritableness.
ir′ri-ta″tiv[P&S], *a.* Irritative.
ir-rupt′i-bl[P], *a.* Irruptible.
ir-rup′tiv[S], *a.* Irruptive.
-is[S]. -ice, -ise (unstrest).
i″so-ag-glu′ti-na-tiv[S], *a.* Isoagglutinative.
is′o-la-bl[P], *a.* Isolable.
is′o-la″tiv[S], *a.* Isolative.
is′su-a-bl[P], *a.* Issuable.
-it. -ite (unstrest).
itcht[S], *pp.* Itched.
i′temd[S], *pp.* Itemed.
it′er-a″tiv[P&S], *a.* & *n.* Iterative.
it′er-a″tiv-ly[S], *adv.* Iteratively.
it′er-a″tiv-ness[S], *n.* Iterativeness.
i-thag′in[S], *n.* Ithagine.
-itly. -itely.
-itness[S]. -iteness.
-iv[S]. -ive (unstrest).
-ivly[S]. -ively.
-ivness[S]. -iveness.
i′vo-rin[S], *a.* Ivorine.
-ize[S], *verb suffix.* -ise.

J

jab′berd[P&S], *pp.* Jabbered.
jabd[S], *pp.* Jabbed.
jackt[S], *pp.* Jacked.
jagd[S], *pp.* Jagged.
jail[P], *v.* & *n.* Gaol.
jaild[P&S], *pp.* Jailed.
jamd[P&S], *pp.* Jammed.
jam′bo-rin[S], *n.* Jamborine.
jam′bo-sin[S], *n.* Jambosine.
ja-pand′[S], *pa.* Japanned.
jard[P&S], *pp.* Jarred.
jar′gond[S], *pp.* Jargoned.
jas′min[P&S], *n.* Jasmine.
jaun′dis[S], *v.* & *n.* Jaundice.
jaun′dist[S], *pa.* Jaundiced.
jawd[S], *a.* Jawed.
jeerd[P&S], *pp.* Jeered.
jel′ous[P&S], *v.* & *a.* Jealous.
jel′ous-y[P&S], *n.* Jealousy.
jel′us[S], *v.* & *a.* Jealous.
jep′ard[P], *vt.* Jeopard.
jep′ard-y[P], *n.* Jeopardy
jerkt[P&S], *pp.* Jerked.
jer′sy[S], *n.* Jersey.
jes′sa-min[P&S], *n.* Jessamine.
jest[S], *pa.* Jessed.
jew′eld[S], *pp.* Jeweled, jewelled.
jibd[P&S], *pp.* Jibbed.
jigd[S], *pp.* Jigged.
jig′gerd[P], *a.* Jiggered.
jobd[S], *pp.* Jobbed.
jock′y[S], *v.* & *n.* Jockey.
jogd[S], *pp.* Jogged.
jog′l[P], *v.* & *n.* Joggle.
jog′ld[P], *pp.* Joggled.
joind[P&S], *pp.* Joined.
jold[S], *pp.* Jolled.
jolt′erd[S], *pp.* Joltered.
jos′tl[P], *vt.* & *vi.* Jostle.
jos′tld[P], *pp.* Jostled.
joyd[S], *pp.* Joyed.
joy′us[S], *a.* Joyous.
judge′a-bl[P], *a.* Judgeable.
judg′ment[S], *n.* Judgement.
ju-di-ca-bl[P], *a.* Judicable.
ju′di-ca″tiv[P&S], *a.* Judicative.
jugd[S], *pp.* Jugged.
jug′l[P], *v.* & *n.* Juggle.
jug′ld[P], *pp.* Juggled.
jum′bl[P], *v.* & *n.* Jumble.
jum′bld[P], *pp.* Jumbled.
jumpt[S], *pa.* Jumped.

jun'gl[F], *n.* Jungle.
ju"ris-dic'tiv[S], *a.* Jurisdictive.
jur'nal[F&S], *v.* & *n.* Journal.
jur'nal-ism[F], *n.* journalism.
jur'nal-ist[F], *n.* Journalist.
jur'ney[F], *v.* & *n.* Journey.
jur'neyd[F], *pp.* Journeyed.
jur'ny[S], *v.* & *n.* Journey.
jus'siv[S], *a.* & *n.* Jussive.
just[F&S], *v.* & *n.* Joust.
jus-ti'ci-a-bl[F], *a.* Justiciable.
jus'ti-fi"a-bl[F], *a.* Justifiable.
jus'ti-fi"a-bl-ness[F], *n.* Justifiableness.
jus-tif'i-ca-tiv[S], *a.* Justificative.
jus'tis[S], *n.* Justice.
ju've-nil[F&S], **ju've-nile**[F], *a.* & *n.* Juvenile.
ju've-nil-ly[S], *adv.* Juvenilely.
ju've-nil-ness[S], *n.* Juvenileness.
jux"ta-pos'i-tiv[S], *a.* & *n.* Juxtapositive.

K

kang[F], *n.* Kangue.
keeld[S], *pp.* Keeled.
keel'hauld[F&S], *pp.* Keelhauled.
keend[S], *pp.* Keened.
keep'a-bl[F], *a.* Keepable.
keevd[S], *pp.* Keeved.
kend[S], *pp.* Kenned.
ken'neld[S], *pp.* Kenneled, kennelled.
kernd[S], *a.* Kerned.
ker'neld[S], *pp.* Kerneled, kernelled.
ker'sy[S], *a.* & *n.* Kersey.
ket'l[F], *n.* Kettle.
key[F], *n.* Quay.
keyd[S], *a.* Keyed.
kich'en[F], *n.* Kitchen.
kickt[S], *pp.* Kicked.
kid'napt[F&S], *pp.* Kidnapped.
kid'ny[S], *n.* Kidney.
kil[F&S], *v.* & *n.* Kill.
kild[F], *pp.* Killed.
kil'a-bl[F], *a.* Killable.
kin'dl[F], *vt.* Kindle.
kin'dld[F], *pp.* Kindled.
kin'e-neg"a-tiv[S], *a.* Kinenegative.
kis[S], *v.* & *n.* Kiss.
kiss'a-bl[F], *a.* Kissable.
kiss'a-bl-ness[F], *n.* Kissableness.
kist[F&S], *pp.* Kissed.
knackt[S], *pp.* Knacked.
knagd[S], *pp.* Knagged.
knapt[S], *pp.* Knapped.
knead'a-bl[F], *a.* Kneadable.
kneeld[S], *pp.* Kneeled.
knel[F], *v.* & *n.* Knell.
kneld[S], *pp.* Knelled.
knit'ta-bl[F], *a.* Knittable.
kno[S], *vt.* & *vi.* Know.
knobd[S], *a.* Knobbed.
knockt[S], *pp.* Knocked.
knold[S], *pp.* Knolled.
knowl'edge-a-bl[F], *a.* Knowledgable.
knowl'edge-a-bl-ness[F], *n.* Knowledgeableness.
knuck'l[F], *v.* & *n.* Knuckle.
knuck'ld[F], *pp.* Knuckled.

L

la'beld[S], *pp.* Labeled, labelled.
la'bor[F], *v.* & *n.* Labour.
la'bord[F&S], *a.* Labored, laboured.
lab"y-rin'thin[S], *a.* Labyrinthine.
lac'er-a-tiv[S], *a.* Lacerative.
la-cer'tin[S], *a.* Lacertine.
lach[F], *v.* & *n.* Latch.
lacht[F], *pp.* Latched.

lackt[P&S], *pp.* Lacked.
lack'y[S], *v.* & *n.* Lackey.
lac'ri-ma-bl[P], **lach'ry-ma-bl**[P], **lac'-ry-ma-bl**[P], *a.* Lacrimable, lachrymable, lacrymable.
lac'ri-mal[S], *a.* Lacrymal, lachrymal.
lac'ta-rin[S], *n.* Lactarine.
la-cus'trin[S], *a.* Lacustrine.
lad'derd[S], *a.* Laddered.
laf[P&S], *v.* & *n.* Laugh.
laf'a-bl[P], *a.* Laughable.
laff'ing[S], *ppr.* & *verbal n.* Laughing.
laft[P], *pp.* Laughed.
laf'ter[P&S], *n.* Laughter.
lagd[S], *pp.* Lagged.
lam[P&S], *v.* & *n.* Lamb.
lam'ba-tiv[S], *n.* Lambative.
lamd[S], *pp.* Lambed.
lamd[S], *pp.* Lammed.
lam'en-ta-bl[P], *a.* Lamentable.
lam'en-ta-bl-ness[P], *n.* Lamentableness.
lam'i-na-bl[P], *a.* Laminable.
lam-poond'[S], *pp.* Lampooned.
lam'pro-tin[S], *a.* & *n.* Lamprotine.
lam'pry[S], *n.* Lamprey.
lampt[S], *pp.* Lamped.
lam'py-rin[S], *a.* & *n.* Lampyrine.
lancht[P], *pp.* Lanched.
lan'guisht[P&S], *pp.* Languished.
lan'in[S], *a.* & *n.* Lanine.
lanst[S], *pp.* Lanced.
lan'ternd[S], *pp.* Lanterned.
la-peld'[S], *pp.* Lapelled.
laps[P&S], *v.* & *n.* Lapse.
laps'a-bl[P], **laps'i-bl**[P], *a.* Lapsable, lapsible.
lapst[P&S], *a.* Lapsed.
lapt[S], *pp.* Lapped.
lar'i-din[S], *a.* Laridine.
larkt[S], *pp.* Larked.
las[S], *n.* Lass.
lasht[P&S], *pp.* Lashed.
latcht[S], *pp.* Latched.
lath'erd[P&S], *pp.* Lathered.
latht[S], *pp.* Lathed.
Lat'ind[S]. *pp.* Latined.
lat"i-pen'nin[S], *a.* Latipennine.
lat'tis[S], *v.* & *n.* Lattice.
lat'tist[S], *pp.* Latticed.
laud'a-bl[P], *a.* Laudable.
laud'a-bl-ness[P], *n.* Laudableness.
laud'a-tiv[S], *a.* Laudative.
launcht[P&S], *pa.* Launched.
laun'derd[S], *pp.* Laundered.
lau'reld[S], *a.* Laureled, laurelled.
lav'en-derd[S], *pp.* Lavendered.
lav'en-tin[S], *n.* Laventine.
lav'isht[S], *pp.* Lavished.
lawnd[S], *pa.* Lawned.
lax'a-tiv[P&S], *a.* & *n.* Laxative.
lax'a-tiv-ness[S], *n.* Laxativeness.
leacht[S], *pp.* Leached.
lead'a-bl[P], *a.* Leadable.
lead'a-bl-ness[P], *n.* Leadableness.
leaft[S], *a.* Leafed.
leag[P&S], *v.* & *n.* League.
leagd[S], *pp.* Leagued.
lea'ger[S], *n.* Leaguer.
lea'gerd[S], *pp.* Leaguered.
leakt[P&S], *pp.* Leaked.
leand, lent[P&S], *pp.* Leaned, leant.
leapt[P], **lept**[P&S], *pp.* Leaped, leapt.
learn'a-bl[P], *a.* Learnable.
leas'a-bl[P], *a.* Leasable.
leasht[S], *pp.* Leashed.
least[P&S], *pp.* Leased.
leav[P], *v.* & *n.* Leave.
leavd[S], *a.* Leaved.
lec"a-no'rin[S], *a.* Lecanorine.
le-cid'e-in[S], *a.* Lecideine.
led[P&S], *v.* & *n.* Lead.
led[P], *pp.* Led.
led'en[P&S], *v.* & *a.* Leaden.
leerd[P&S], *pp.* Leered.
leg'a-bl[P], *a.* Legable.
le'gal-ize, *vt.* Legalise.
leg'a-tin[S], *a.* Legatine.

leg'a-tiv^{s}, *a.* Legative.
legd^{s}, *a.* Legged.
leg'i-bl^{p}, *a.* Legible.
leg'i-bl-ness^{p}, *n.* Legibleness.
leg'is-la"tiv$^{p\&s}$, *a.* & *n.* Legislative.
leg'is-la"tiv-ly^{s}, *adv.* Legislatively.
length'end^{s}, *pp.* Lengthened.
len'i-tiv$^{p\&s}$, *a.* & *n.* Lenitive.
le'o-nin^{s}, *a.* & *n.* Leonine.
le'o-nin-ly^{s}, *adv.* Leoninely.
lep'ard^{p}, *n.* Leopard.
lep'o-rin^{s}, *a.* & *n.* Leporine.
lep"to-pod'i-in^{s}, *a.* & *n.* Leptopodiine.
lep'to-rhin^{s}, *a.* Leptorhine.
lep"to-staph'y-lin^{s}, *a.* Leptostaphyline.
lern^{p}, *vt.* & *vi.* Learn.
lernd^{p}, **lernt**^{p}, *pp.* Learned, learnt.
lern'ed^{p}, *pa.* Learned.
lern'ing^{p}, *n.* Learning.
les^{s}, *a.*, *n.* & *adv.* Less.
less'end$^{p\&s}$, *pp.* Lessened.
les'sond^{s}, *pp.* Lessoned.
leth'er$^{p\&s}$, *v.* & *n.* Leather.
leth'erd^{s}, *a.* Leathered.
leth'ern$^{p\&s}$, *a.* Leathern.
let'ta-bl^{p}, *a.* Lettable.
let'terd^{s}, *a.* Lettered.
let'tis^{s}, *n.* Lettuce.
leu-cis'cin^{s}, *a.* & *n.* Leuciscine.
Le-vant'in^{s}, *a.* & *n.* Levantine.
lev'eld$^{p\&s}$, *pp.* Leveled, levelled.
lev'el-ing^{p}, *n.* Levelling.
lev'en$^{p\&s}$, *v.* & *n.* Leaven.
lev'end^{p}, *pa.* Leavened.
lev'erd^{s}, *pp.* Levered.
lev'i-a-bl^{p}, *a.* Leviable.
lev"i-ga-bl^{p}, *a.* Levigable.
lev'i-ta"tiv^{s}, *a.* Levitative.
lex"i-cog'ra-fer^{p}, *n.* Lexicographer.
lex"i-cog'ra-fy^{p}, *n.* Lexicography.
li'a-bl^{p}, *a.* Liable.
li'a-bl-ness^{p}, *a.* Liableness.
li'beld$^{p\&s}$, *pp.* Libeled, libelled.
li-bel'lu-lin^{s}, *a.* Libelluline.
Lib'er-al=Con-ser'va-tiv^{s}, *n.* Liberal=Conservative.
lib'er-a-tiv^{s}, *a.* Liberative.
lib'er-tin$^{p\&s}$, **-tine**$^{p\&s}$, *a.* & *n.* Libertine.
li'cens-a-bl^{p}, *a.* Licensable.
li'cense^{s}, *v.* & *n.* Licence.
li'censt$^{p\&s}$, *pa.* Licensed.
li'chend^{s}, *pp.* Lichened.
lickt$^{p\&s}$, *pp.* Licked.
lic'o-ris^{s}, *n.* Licorice.
lift'a-bl^{p}, *a.* Liftable.
light'a-bl^{p}, *a.* Lightable.
light'end$^{p\&s}$, *pp.* Lightened.
light'erd^{s}, *pp.* Lightered.
light'sum^{s}, *a.* Lightsome.
lik'a-bl^{p}, **like'a-bl**^{p}, *a.* Likable, likeable.
lik'a-bl-ness^{p}, **like'a-bl-ness**^{p}, *n.* Likableness, likeableness.
lik'end^{s}, *pp.* Likened.
lim$^{p\&s}$, *v.* & *n.* Limb.
lim'berd^{s}, *pp.* Limbered.
limb^{s}, *a.* Limbed.
lim'it-a-bl^{p}, *a.* Limitable.
lim'it-a-bl-ness^{p}, *n.* Limitableness.
lim'i-ta"tiv^{s}, *a.* Limitative.
lim'i-tiv^{s}, *a.* Limitive.
limpt$^{p\&s}$, *pp.* Limped.
lin'a-bl^{p}, **line'a-bl**^{p}, *a.* Linable, lineable.
lin'gerd^{s}, *pp.* Lingered.
lin-guat'u-lin^{s}, *a.* & *n.* Linguatuline.
lin'sy=wool'sy^{s}, *n.* Linsey=woolsey.
lin'teld^{s}, *pp.* Linteled, lintelled.
li-ot'ri-chin^{s}, *a.* & *n.* Liotrichine.
lipt$^{p\&s}$, *a.* Lipped.
liq"ue-fac'tiv^{s}, *a.* Liquefactive.
liq'ue-fi"a-bl^{p}, *a.* Liquefiable.
liq'uid-a-bl^{p}, *a.* Liquidable.
lispt$^{p\&s}$, *pp.* Lisped.
list'a-bl^{p}, *a.* Listable.

lis'tendP&S, *pp.* Listened.
lis'ter-inS, *a.* Listerine.
li'terS, *n.* Litre.
lith'a-gogP, *a.* & *n.* Lithagogue.
lith'o-grafP, *v.* & *n.* Lithograph.
lith'o-graftP, *pp.* Lithographed.
lith-og'ra-ferP, *n.* Lithographer.
lith-og'ra-fyP, *n.* Lithography.
lit'i-ga-blP, *a.* Litigable.
lit'lP, *a.* & *n.* Little.
lit'terdS, *pp.* Littered.
livP&S, *vt.* & *vi.* Live.
liv'a-blP, **live'a-bl**P, *a.* Livable, liveable.
liv'a-bl-nessP, *n.* Livableness.
livdP&S, *a.* Lived.
liv'endS, *pp.* Livened.
liv'erdS, *a.* Livered.
liv'longP, *a.* Livelong.
loS, *v.*, *a.* & *n.* Low.
loaftS, *pp.* Loafed.
loamdS, *pp.* Loamed.
loan'a-blP, *a.* Loanable.
loandS, *pp.* Loaned.
loathdS, *pp.* Loathed.
loath'sumP&S, *a.* Loathsome.
lobdS, *pp.* Lobbed.
lo"bo-don'tinS, *a.* Lobodontine.
lo'ca-blP, *a.* Locable.
lo'cal-iz"a-blP, *a.* Localizable.
loc'a-tivS, *a.* & *n.* Locative.
lock'a-blP, *a.* Lockable.
locktS, *pp.* Locked.
lo"co-de-scrip'tivS, *a.* Locodescriptive.
lo"co-mo'bilS, *n.* Locomobile.
lo"co-mo'tivS, *a.* & *n.* Locomotive.
lo"co-mo'tiv-nessS, *n.* Locomotiveness.
loctP, *pp.* Locked.
loc"u-ple'ta-tivS, *a.* Locupletative.
lodge'a-blP, *a.* Lodgeable.
lodg'mentS, *n.* Lodgement.
logdS, *pp.* & *pa.* Logged.
loi'terdP&S, *pp.* Loitered.
loldS, *pp.* Lolled.
lo'ma-tinS, *a.* Lomatine.
lone'sumS, *a.* Lonesome.
longdS, *pp.* Longed.
lon"ge-pen'ninS, *a.* Longipennine.
long'sumS, *a.* Longsome.
looktP&S, *pp.* Looked.
loomdP&S, *a.* Loomed.
looptP&S, *pp.* Looped.
loos'endP&S, *pp.* Loosened.
loostP&S, *pp.* Loosed.
loptP&S, *pp.* Lopped.
lo"phi-o-don'tinS, *a.* Lophiodontine.
losS, *n.* Loss.
los'a-blP, **lose'a-bl**P, *a.* Losable, loseable.
lo'so-fanP&S, *n.* Losophan.
lo-tof'a-gusS, *a.* Lotophagous.
love, lovable, etc. See LUV.
lowdS, *pp.* Lowed.
low'er-a-blP, *a.* Lowerable.
low'erdS, *pp.* Lowered.
lu'bri-ca"tivS, *a.* Lubricative.
lu'ci-blP, *a.* Lucible.
lu'cra-tivP&S, *a.* Lucrative.
lu'cra-tiv-lyS, *adv.* Lucratively.
lu'cra-tiv-nessS, *n.* Lucrativeness.
lufP&S, *v.* & *n.* Luff.
luftP&S, *pp.* Luffed.
lugdS, *pp.* Lugged.
lulP, *v.* & *n.* Lull.
luldP&S, *pp.* Lulled.
lum'berdS, *pp.* Lumbered.
lum'bri-cinS, *a.* Lumbricine.
lu'minS, *n.* Lumine.
lu'mi-nusS, *a.* Luminous.
lumptP&S, pp. Lumped.
lunchtS, *pp.* Lunched.
lu'pinS, *a.* & *n.* Lupine.
lurchtS, *pp.* Lurched.
lurktS, *pp.* Lurked.
lus'terP, *v.* & *n.* Lustre.
lus'terdS, *pp.* Lustered, lustred.

lus'tra-tiv[s], *a.* Lustrative.
lu'trin[s], *a.* & *n.* Lutrine.
luv[p], *v.* & *n.* Love.
luv'a-bl[p], *a.* Lovable.
luvd[p], *pp.* Loved.
luv'ly[p], *a.* & *adv.* Lovely.
ly"co-don'tin[s], *a.* & *n.* Lycodontine.
lymf[p&s], *n.* Lymph.
lym-fat'ic[p&s], *a.* & *n.* Lymphatic.
lyncht[p&s], *pp.* Lynched.

M

mach[p], *v.* & *n.* Match.
macht[p], *pp.* Matched.
mac"ro-glos'sin[s], *a.* & *n.* Macroglossine.
mac"ro-phyl'lin[s], *a.* Macrophylline.
mac"ro-pin[s], *a.* Macropine.
ma-crop'o-din[s], *a.* & *n.* Macropodine.
mac'ro-rhin[s], **mac'ror-rhin**[s], *a.* Macrorhine, macrorrhine.
mad'dend[s], *pp.* Maddened.
mad'derd[s], *pp.* Maddered.
mag'is-tra-tiv[s], *a.* Magistrative.
mag'ne-tin[s], *n.* Magnetine.
mag'net-iz"[or **-is"**]**a-bl**[p], *a.* Magnetizable, magnetisable.
mag"net-o-mo'tiv[s], *a.* Magnetomotive.
mag'ni-fi"a-bl[p], *a.* Magnifiable.
mag-nif'i-ca-tiv[s], *a.* & *n.* Magnificative.
maild[p&s], *pp.* Mailed.
maimd[p&s], *pp.* Maimed.
main-tain'a-bl[p], *a.* Maintainable.
main-tain'a-bl-ness[p], *n.* Maintainableness.
main-taind'[p&s], *pp.* Maintained.
maiz[p], *n.* Maize.
mak'a-bl[p], *a.* Makable.
mal"a-co-no'tin, *a.* & *n.* Malaconotine.
mal"a-co-scol'i-cin[s], *a.* Malacoscolicine.
ma-la'ri-us[s], *a.* Malarious.
mald[s], *pp.* Malled.
ma-lignd'[s], *pp.* Maligned.
ma-lin'gerd[s], *pp.* Malingered.
mal'is[s], *n.* Malice.
malld[p], *pp.* Malled.
mal'le-a-bl[p], *a.* Malleable.
mal'le-a-bl-ness[p], *n.* Malleableness.
ma-ma'[s], *n.* Mamma.
mam'moc[s], *n.* Mammock.
man'a-cl[p], *v.* & *n.* Manacle.
mand[s], *pp.* Manned.
man'age-a-bl[p], *a.* Manageable.
man'age-a-bl-ness[p], *n.* Manageableness.
man'ci-pa-bl[p], *a.* Mancipable.
man'ci-pa-tiv[s], *a.* Mancipative.
man'da-tiv[s], *a.* Mandative.
man'du-ca-bl[p], *a.* Manducable.
ma-neu'ver[p&s], *v.* & *n.* Manœuvre.
ma-neu'verd[p&s], *pp.* Maneuvered, manœuvred.
man'gl[p], *v.* & *n.* Mangle.
man-gld[p], *vt.* Mangled.
man'i-fest"a-[or **i-**]**bl**[p], *a.* Manifestable, manifestible.
man"i-fes'ta-tiv[s], *a.* Manifestative.
man'i-fes-tiv[s], *a.* Manifestive.
ma-nip'u-la-bl[p], *a.* Manipulable.
ma-nip'u-la"tiv[s], *a.* Manipulative.
man'nerd[s], *a.* Mannered.
man"u-duc'tiv[s], *a.* Manuductive.
man"u-fac'tur-a-bl[p], *a.* Manufacturable.
man"u-mis'siv[s], *a.* Manumissive.
man'u-mo"tiv[s], *a.* Manumotive.
ma-nur'a-bl[p], *a.* Manurable.
mapt[s], *pp.* Mapped.
marcht[p&s], *pp.* Marched.

mard[S], *pp.* Marred.
mar'gind[S], *a.* Margined.
markt[P&S], *pa.* Marked.
mar'ket-a-bl[P], *a.* Marketable.
marld[S], *pp.* Marled.
mar'lin[S], *v.* & *n.* Marline.
ma-roond'[S], *pp.* Marooned.
mar'riage-a-bl[P], *a.* Marriageable.
mar'riage-a-bl-ness[P], *n.* Marriageableness.
mar'shald[S], *pp.* Marshaled, marshalled.
mar'tyrd[S], *pp.* Martyred.
mar'veld[P&S], *pp.* Marveled, marvelled.
mar'vel-ous[P], *a.* Marvellous.
mas[S], *v.* & *n.* Mass.
mas'cu-lin[P&S], **-ine**[S], *a.* & *n.* Masculine.
masht[S], *pp.* Mashed.
maskt[P&S], *pa.* Masked.
mas'siv[P&S], *a.* Massive.
mas'siv-ly[S], *adv.* Massively.
mas'siv-ness[S], *n.* Massiveness.
mast[S], *pp.* Massed.
mas'terd[P&S], *pp.* Mastered.
mas'ti-ca-bl[P], *a.* Masticable.
mas'tif[S], *n.* Mastiff.
mas"to-don'tin[S], *a.* & *n.* Mastodontine.
match'a-bl[P], *a.* Matchable.
match'a-bl-ness[P], *n.* Matchableness.
matcht[S], *pp.* Matched.
ma-te'ri-al-ize[P&S], *vt.* & *vi.* Materialise.
ma'tris[S], *n.* Matrice.
mat'terd[S], *pp.* Mattered.
mat'toc[S], *n.* Mattock.
mat'u-ra"tiv[S], *a.* & *n.* Maturative.
ma-tur'a-bl[P], *a.* Maturable.
mauld[S], *pp.* Mauled.
maun'derd[S], *pp.* Maundered.
max-il"lo-pal'a-tin[S], *a.* & *n.* Maxillopalatine.
mea'ger[P&S], *a.* Meagre.
meal'a-bl[P], *a.* Mealable.
me-an'derd[S], *pp.* Meandered.
me-an'drin[S], *a.* Meandrine, mæandrine.
mea'sls[P], *n.* Measles.
me-can'ic[S], *a.* & *n.* Mechanic.
med'ald[S], *pp.* Medaled.
med'dle-sum[S], *a.* Meddlesome.
me"di-as'tin[S], *n.* Mediastine.
me'di-a"tiv[S], *a.* Mediative.
med'i-ca-bl[P], *a.* Medicable.
med'i-ca"tiv[S], *a.* Medicative.
med'i-cin[P&S], *n.* Medicine.
med'i-cind[S], *pp.* Medicined.
me"di-e'val[S], *a.* & *n.* Mediæval.
me"di-o-pal'a-tin[S], *a.* Mediopalatine.
me"di-o-pon'tin[S], *a.* Mediopontine.
med'i-ta"tiv[P&S], *a.* Meditative.
med'i-ta"tiv-ly[S], *adv.* Meditatively.
med'i-ta"tiv-ness[S], *n.* Meditativeness.
med'l[P], *vi.* Meddle.
med'ld[P], *pp.* Meddled.
med'l-sum[P], *a.* Meddlesome.
med'ly[S], *a.* & *n.* Medley.
med'ow[P&S], *n.* Meadow.
me-fit'ic[P&S], *a.* Mephitic.
me-fi'tis[P], *n.* Mephitis.
me-gac'er-o-tin[S], *a.* Megacerotine.
meg"a-der'min[S], *a.* & *n.* Megadermine.
meg"a-lo'pin[S], *a.* Megalopine.
meg"a-lo'tin[S], *a.* & *n.* Megalotine.
me-gap'ter-in[S], *a.* & *n.* Megapterine.
meg"a-the'ri-in[S], *a.* & *n.* Megatheriine.
mel'an-col-y[P&S], *a.* & *n.* Melancholy.
mel"e-ag'rin[S], *a.* & *n.* Meleagrine.
me'lio-ra-tiv[S], *a.* Meliorative.
me-liph'a-gin[S], *a.* & *n.* Meliphagine.
mel"li-su'gin[S], *a.* & *n.* Mellisugine.
mel-liv'o-rin[S], *a.* & *n.* Mellivorine.
mel'lo[S], *v.* & *a.* Mellow.

mel'lowd[S], *pp.* Mellowed.
mel″o-lon'thin[S], *a.* & *n.* Melolonthine.
melt'a-bl[P], *a.* Meltable.
mem'o-ra-bl[P], *a.* Memorable.
mem'o-ra-bl-ness[P], *n.* Memorableness.
mem'o-ra-tiv[S], *a.* Memorative.
me-mo'ri-al-ize[P&S], *vt.* Memorialise.
mem'o-riz″a-bl[P], *a.* Memorizable.
men'ace-a-bl[P], *a.* Menaceable.
mend'a-bl[P], *a.* Mendable.
men″i-sper'min[S], *n.* Menispermine.
men'su-ra-bl[P], *a.* Mensurable.
men'su-ra-bl-ness[P], *n.* Mensurableness.
men'su-ra″tiv[S], *a.* Mensurative.
ment[P&S], *pp.* Meant.
men'tion-a-bl[P], *a.* Mentionable.
men'tiond[S], *pp.* Mentioned.
meph'i-tin[S], *a.* & *n.* Mephitine.
mer'a-lin[S], *n.* Meraline.
mer'can-til[P&S], **-ile**[P&S], *a.* Mercantile.
mer'chan-dis″[or **-diz″**]**a-bl**[P], *a.* Merchandisable, merchandizable.
mer'chan-dize[P], *v.* & *n.* Merchandise.
mer'chant-a-bl[P], *a.* Merchantable.
mer'chant-a-bl-ness[P], *n.* Merchantableness.
mer'gin[S], *a.* & *n.* Mergine.
me'ro-pin[S], *a.* & *n.* Meropine.
mer'u-lin[S], *a.* Meruline.
mes[S], *v.* & *n.* Mess.
mesht[P&S], *pa.* Meshed.
mes'mer-iz″a-bl[P], *a.* Mesmerizable.
mes'o-rhin[S], *a.* Mesorhine.
mes″o-taph'y-lin[S], *a.* Mesotaphyline.
mest[P&S], *pp.* Messed.
mes'ure[S], *v.* & *n.* Measure.
me-tab'o-liz″a-bl[P], *a.* Metabolizable.
met″a-fys'ics[P], *n.* Metaphysics.
met'ald[S], *a.* Metaled, metalled.
met'al-in[S], *n.* Metaline.
met'al-lin[S], *a.* Metalline.
met″a-mor'fose[P], *vt.* Metamorphose.
met″a-mor'fo-sis[P&S], *n.* Metamorphosis.
me'ter[P&S], *v.* & *n.* Metre.
me'terd[S], *pp.* Metered.
met'l[P], *n.* Mettle.
met'ld[P], *a.* Mettled.
met'l-sum[P], *a.* Mettlesome.
met'tle-sum[S], *a.* Mettlesome.
mewd[S], *pp.* Mewed.
mewld[P&S], *pp.* Mewled.
me'zu-ra-bl[P], *a.* Measurable.
me'zure[P], *v.* & *n.* Measure.
me'zured[P], *pa.* Measured.
mi″cro-phyl'lin[S], *a.* Microphylline.
mi-crop'o-din[S], *a.* & *n.* Micropodine.
mi″cro-spor'in[S], *a.* Microsporine.
mid'l[P], *v., a.* & *n.* Middle.
mid'ling[P], *a.* Middling.
mid'rif[S], *n.* Midriff.
mif[S], *v., a.* & *n.* Miff.
mift[S], *pp.* Miffed.
mi'gra-tiv[S], *a.* Migrative.
mil[P&S], *v.* & *n.* Mill.
mild[P&S], **mild**[P], *a.* Milled.
mil'dewd[P&S], *pp.* Mildewed.
mil'i-o-lin[S], *a.* & *n.* Milioline.
milkt[S], *pp.* Milked.
mil'le-por″in[S], *a.* Milleporine.
mim'ickt[P], *pp.* Mimicked.
mim'ict[S], *pp.* Mimicked.
mim'in[S], *a.* & *n.* Mimine.
min'a-bl[P], **mine'a-bl**[P], *a.* Minable, mineable.
min'er-al-iz″[or **-is″**]**a-bl**[P], *a.* Mineralizable, mineralisable.
min'gl[P], *vt.* & *vi.* Mingle.
min'gld[P], *pp.* Mingled.
min'gle-a-bl[P], *a.* Mingleable.
min'isht[S], *pp.* Minished.
minst[S], *pp.* Minced.

min'is-terd[s], *pp.* Ministered.
min'is-tra"tiv[s], *a.* Ministrative.
mir'a-cl[p], *v.* & *n.* Miracle.
mir'rord[s], *pp.* Mirrored.
mis[s], *v.* & *n.* Miss.
mis"ap-pre'ci-a-tiv[s], *a.* Misappreciative.
mis-ap"pre-hen'siv[s], *a.* Misapprehensive.
mis"be-cum'[p], *vt.* Misbecome.
mis'chief-a-bl[p], *a.* Mischiefable.
mis'chie-vus[s], *a.* Mischievous.
mis"con-stru'a-bl[p], *a.* Misconstruable.
mis"con-struc'tiv[s], *a.* Misconstructive.
mis"cre-a'tiv[s], *a.* Miscreative.
mis'er-a-bl[p], *a.* Miserable.
mis'er-a-bl-ness[p], *n.* Miserableness.
mis-giv'[p&s], *vt.* & *vi.* Misgive.
mis"in-tel'li-gi-bl[p], *a.* Misintelligible.
mis"in-ter'pret-a-bl[p], *a.* Misinterpretable.
mis-lead'a-bl[p], *a.* Misleadable.
mis-man'age-a-bl[p], *a.* Mismanageable.
mis'o-log[p], *n.* Misologue.
mis-rep"re-sen'ta-tiv[s], *a.* & *n.* Misrepresentative.
mis'si-bl[p], *a.* Missible.
mis'sil[p&s], **-ile**[s], *a.* & *n.* Missile.
mis'siv[p&s], *a.* & *n.* Missive.
mist[s], *pp.* Missed.
mis-tak'a-bl[p], *a.* Mistakable.
mis'tl-toe[p], *n.* Mistletoe.
mis-un"der-stand'a-bl[p], *a.* Misunderstandable.
mis-uze'[p], *vt.* Misuse.
mi'ter[p], *v.* & *n.* Mitre.
mi'terd[s], *pp.* Mitered.
mit'i-ga-bl[p], *a.* Mitigable.
mit'i-ga"tiv, *a.* & *n.* Mitigative.
mit'tend[s], *pp.* Mittened.
mix'a-bl[p], **mix'i-bl**[p], *a.* Mixable, mixible.
mixt[s], *pp.* & *pa.* Mixed.
mo[s], *v.* & *n.* Mow.
moand[s], *pp.* Moaned.
mobd[s], *pp.* Mobbed.
mo'bil[s], **-ile**[s], *a.* Mobile.
mock'a-bl[p], *a.* Mockable.
mockt[p&s], *pp.* Mocked.
mod'eld[s], *pp.* Modeled, modelled.
mod'i-fi"a-bl[p], *a.* Modifiable.
mod'i-fi"a-bl-ness[p], *n.* Modifiableness.
mod'i-fi-ca"tiv[s], *n.* Modificative.
mod'u-la-tiv[s], *a.* Modulative.
moed[s], *pp.* Mowed.
Mo-gun'tin[s], *a.* Moguntine.
moild[s], *pp.* Moiled.
mois'tend[s], *pp.* Moistened.
mold[s], *v.* & *n.* Mould.
mold'a-bl[p], **mould'a-bl**[p], *a.* Moldable, mouldable.
mold'[or **mould'**]**a-bl-ness**[p], *n.* Moldableness, mouldableness.
mold'er[s], *v.* & *n.* Moulder.
mold'erd[s], *pp.* Moldered.
mold'ing[s], *n.* Moulding.
mold'y[s], *a.* Mouldy.
mo'lin[s], *a.* & *n.* Moline.
mol'li-fi"a-bl[p], *a.* Mollifiable.
mol'lin[s], *n.* Molline.
mo-los'sin[s], *a.* & *n.* Molossine.
molt[s], *v.* & *n.* Moult.
mon'arc[s], *v.*, *a.* & *n.* Monarch.
mon'eyd[s], *a.* Moneyed.
mon'isht[s], *pp.* Monished.
mon'i-tiv[p&s], *a.* Monitive.
mon'ky[s], *v.* & *n.* Monkey.
mon"o-cer'a-tin[s], *a.* Monoceratine.
mon'o-crome[s], *n.* Monochrome.
mon'o-graf[p], *v.* & *n.* Monograph.
mon'o-log[p&s], *n.* Monologue.
mon"o-phyl'lin[s], *a.* Monophylline.
mon'o-rhin[s], **mon'or-rhin**[s], *a.* & *n.* Monorhine, monorrhine.
mon'o-stic[s], *n.* Monostich.

mon'o-syl''la-bl[p], *v.* & *n.* Monosyllable.
mon-tic'o-lin[s], *a.* Monticoline.
mon'y[s], *v.* & *n.* Money.
moond[s], *a.* Mooned.
moord[p&s], *pp.* Moored.
mopt[s], *pp.* Mopped.
mor'al-ize[s], *vt.* & *vi.* Moralise.
mor'fi-a[s], *n.* Morphia.
mor-fol'o-gy[s], *n.* Morphology.
mor'mo-pin[s], *a.* & *n.* Mormopine.
mor'tard[s], *a.* Mortared.
mort'gage-a-bl[p], *a.* Mortgageable.
mor'tis[s], *v.* & *n.* Mortise.
mor'tist[s], *pp.* Mortised.
mos[s], *v.* & *n.* Moss.
most[p&s], *pp.* Mossed.
mo''ta-cil'lin[s], *n.* Motacilline.
moth'erd[s], *a.* Mothered.
mo'til[s], **-ile**[s], *a.* & *n.* Motile.
mo'tiond[s], *pp.* Motioned.
mo'tiv[p&s], *v.*, *a.* & *n.* Motive.
mo'tivd[s], *pp.* Motived.
mot'ly[s], *a.* & *n.* Motley.
mo'tord[s], *pp.* Motored.
mournd[s], *pp.* Mourned.
mouth'a-bl[p], *a.* Mouthable.
mouthd[s], *pa.* Mouthed.
mouz[p], *vt.* & *vi.* Mouse.
mouz'er[p], *n.* Mouser.
mov'a-bl[p], **move'a-bl**[p], *a.* & *n.* Movable, moveable.
mov'a-bl-ness[p], *n.* Movableness.
mowd[p&s], *pp.* Mowed.
mud'l[p], *v.* & *n.* Muddle.
muf[p&s], *v.* & *n.* Muff.
muf'l[p], *v.* & *n.* Muffle.
muf'ld[p], *pp.* Muffled.
muft[p&s], *pp.* Muffed.
mugd[s], *pp.* Mugged.
mul[s], *v.* & *n.* Mull.
mulcht[p&s], *pp.* Mulched.
mulct'a-bl[p], *a.* Mulctable.
muld[s], *pp.* Mulled.
mul'len[s], *n.* Mullein.
mul'liond[s], *a.* Mullioned.
mul''ti-cau'lin[s], *a.* Multicauline.
mul''ti-fa'ri-us[s], *a.* Multifarious.
mul'ti-pli''a-bl[p], *a.* Multipliable.
mul'ti-pli''a-bl-ness[p], *n.* Multipliableness.
mul'ti-pli-ca-bl[p], *a.* Multiplicable.
mul'ti-pli-ca''tiv[s], *a.* & *n.* Multiplicative.
mul'ti-pli-ca''tiv-ly[s], *adv.* Multiplicatively.
mum'bl[p], *v.* & *n.* Mumble.
mum'bld[p], *pp.* Mumbled.
muncht[p&s], *pp.* Munched.
mun-dif'i-ca-tiv[s], *a.* Mundificative.
mun'ey[p], *v.* & *n.* Money.
munk[p], *n.* Monk.
mun'key[p], *v.* & *n.* Monkey.
munk'ish[p], *a.* Monkish.
mur'derd[p&s], *pp.* Murdered.
mur'murd[p&s], *pp.* Murmured.
mur'rin[s], **mur'rhin**[s], *a.* Murrine, murrhine.
mus[s], *v.* & *n.* Muss.
mus'ca-din[s], *n.* Muscadine.
mus'car-din[s], *n.* Muscardine.
mus-cic'a-pin[s], *a.* & *n.* Muscicapine.
mus-cic'o-lin[s], *a.* Muscicoline.
mus'cl[p], *n.* Muscle.
must[s], *pp.* Mussed.
mus'te-lin[s], *a.* & *n.* Musteline.
mus'terd[s], *pp.* Mustered.
mu'ta-bl[p], *a.* Mutable.
mu'ta-bl-ness[p], *n.* Mutableness.
mu'ta-tiv[s], *a.* Mutative.
mu'tiv[s], *a.* Mutive.
mut'terd[s], *pp.* Muttered.
muz'l, *v.* & *n.* Muzzle.
muz'ld[p], *pp.* Muzzled.
my''a-des'tin[s], *a.* & *n.* Myadestine.
my-ce'tin[s], *a.* & *n.* Mycetine.
my''i-a-des'tin[s], *a.* & *n.* Myiadestine.
my''i-ag'rin[s], *a.* & *n.* Myiagrine.

myl″i-ob′a-tin[s], *a.* & *n.* Myliobatine.
my-og′a-lin[s], *a.* & *n.* Myogaline.
myr″me-co′bi-in[s], *a.* & *n.* Myrmecobiine.
myr″me-coph′a-gin[s], *a.* & *n.* Myrmecophagine.
myr′mi-cin[s], *a.* Myrmicine.
myr′tl[r], *n.* Myrtle.
mys′ta-cin[s], *a.* Mystacine.
mys-tac′o-pin[s], *a.* & *n.* Mystacopine.
my-zom′e-lin[s], *a.* & *n.* Myzomeline.

N

nabd[r&s], *pp.* Nabbed.
nack[s], *v.* & *n.* Knack.
nag[s], *vt.* & *vi.* Knag.
nagd[s], *pp.* Nagged.
naild[r&s], *pp.* Nailed.
nam′a-bl[r], **name′a-bl**[r], *a.* Namable, nameable.
nan′din[s], *n.* Nandine.
nap[s], *vt.* & *vi.* Knap.
nap′sac[s], *n.* Knapsack.
napt[s], *pp.* Napped.
naptha, naftha[r], *n.* Naphtha.
nar-cis′sin[s], *a.* Narcissine.
narl[s], *v.* & *n.* Gnarl.
narld[s], *a.* Gnarled.
narl′y[s], *a.* Gnarly.
nar-rat′a-bl[r], *a.* Narratable.
nar′ra-tiv[r&s], *a.* & *n.* Narrative.
nar′ra-tiv-ly[s], *adv.* Narratively.
nar′rowd[r&s], *pp.* Narrowed.
nash[s], *vt.* & *vi.* Gnash.
na″so-pal′a-tin[s], *a.* Nasopalatine.
nat[s], *n.* Gnat.
nave[s], *n.* Knave.
na′tiv[r&s], *a.* & *n.* Native.
na′tiv-ly[s], *adv.* Natively.
na′tiv-ness[s], *n.* Nativeness.
nat′u-ra-bl[r], *a.* Naturable.
nat′u-ral-ize[s], *vt.* & *vi.* Naturalise.
nau′se-a-tiv[s], *a.* Nauseative.
nav′i-ga-bl[r], *a.* Navigable.
nav′i-ga-bl-ness[r], *n.* Navigableness.
naw[s], *vt.* & *vi.* Gnaw.
nead[s], *vt.* Knead.
neapt[s], *a.* Neaped.
neard[r&s], *pp.* Neared.
ne-ces′si-ta″tiv[s], *a.* Necessitative.
neckt[s], *a.* Necked.
nec′tar-in[s], *a.* & *n.* Nectarine.
nee[s], *v.* & *n.* Knee.
nee′dl[r], *v.* & *n.* Needle.
neel[s], *vi.* Kneel.
neel′ing[s], *pres. p.* Kneeling.
nef′ew[r], *n.* Nephew.
ne-frit′ic[r], *a.* Nephritic.
neg′a-tiv[r&s], *v.*, *a.* & *n.* Negative.
neg′a-tivd[s], *pp.* Negatived.
neg′a-tiv-ly[s], *adv.* Negatively.
neg′a-tiv-ness[s], *n.* Negativeness.
neg-lect′a- or **i-bl**[r], *a.* Neglectable, neglectible.
neg′lige-a-bl[r], *a.* Negligeable.
neg′li-gi-bl[r], *a.* Negligible.
neg′li-gi-bl-ness[r], *n.* Negligibleness.
ne-go′ti-a-bl[r], *a.* Negotiable.
neigh′bor[s], *v.*, *a.* & *n.* Neighbor, neighbour.
neigh′bord[s], *pp.* Neighbored.
neighd[s], *pp.* Neighed.
neis[s], *n.* Gneiss.
nel[s], *v.* & *n.* Knell.
nelt[s], *imp.* & *pp.* Knelt.
nem′a-lin[s], *a.* Nemaline.
nem″a-to-scol′i-cin[s], *a.* Nematoscolicine.
ne-mer′tin[s], *a.* & *n.* Nemertine.
nem″o-rhæ′din[s], *a.* Nemorbædine.
nem″o-ric′o-lin[s], *a.* Nemoricoline.
ne″o-mor′phin[s], *a.* & *n.* Neomorphine.

nerv[p&s], *v.* & *n.* Nerve.
nervd[p&s], *pp.* & *a.* Nerved.
ner′vin[s], *a.* & *n.* Nervine.
nes′tl[p], *vt.* & *vi.* Nestle.
nes′tld[p], *pp.* Nestled.
net[s], *a.* Nett.
net′tl[p], *v.* & *n.* Nettle.
neu′tral-ize[p&s], *vt.* Neutralise.
nev′ew[p], *n.* Nephew.
new″fan′gld[p], *a.* Newfangled.
new″=fash′iond[p], *a.* New=fashioned.
nex′i-bl[p], *a.* Nexible.
nibd[s], *pp.* Nibbed.
nib′l[p], *v.* & *n.* Nibble.
nib′ld[p], *pp.* Nibbled.
nick′eld[s], *pp.* & *a.* Nickeled, nickelled.
nickt[p&s], *pp.* Nicked.
nick′name″a-bl[p], *a.* Nicknameable.
nic′nac[s], *n.* Knickknack.
ni-cot′i-din[s], *n.* Nicotidine.
nife[s], *v.* & *n.* Knife.
nigd[s], *a.* Nigged.
nig′l[p], *v.* & *n.* Niggle.
nig′ld[p], *pp.* Niggled.
nimd[s], *a.* Nimbed.
nim′bl[p], *v.* & *a.* Nimble.
nim′bl-ness[p], *n.* Nimbleness.
nip′l[p], *v.* & *n.* Nipple.
nip′ld[p], *pp.* Nippled.
nipt[s], *pp.* Nipped.
nit[s], *vt.* & *vi.* Knit.
ni′ter[p&s], *v.* & *n.* Nitre.
ni-tram′i-din[s], *n.* Nitramidine.
ni′tra-tin[s], *n.* Nitratine.
ni′tri-fi″a-bl[p], *a.* Nitrifiable.
nit′ting[s], *n.* Knitting.
nob[s], *v.* & *n.* Knob.
nobd[s], *pp.* Nobbed.
noch[p], *v.* & *n.* Notch.
nocht[p], *pp.* Notched.
nock[s], *v.* & *n.* Knock.
nock′er[s], *n.* Knocker.
nock′ing[s], *n.* Knocking.
noc-til′i-o-nin[s], *n.* Noctilionine.
nod′l, *v.* & *n.* Noddle.
no″do-sa′rin[s], *a.* & *n.* Nodosarine.
noi′sum[s], *a.* Noisome.
noll[s], *v.* & *n.* Knoll.
nome[s], *n.* Gnome.
no′men-cla″tiv[s], *a.* Nomenclative.
no′mic[s], *a.* Gnomic.
nom′i-na-bl[p], *a.* Nominable.
nom′i-na-tiv[p&s], *a.* & *n.* Nominative.
nom′i-na-tiv-ly[s], *adv.* Nominatively.
no′mon[s], *n.* Gnomon.
non″=a-mal′ga-ma-bl[p], *a.* Non=amalgamable.
non″=ap-por′tion-a-bl[p], *a.* Non=apportionable.
non″=ap-pos′a-bl[p], *a.* Non=apposable.
non″=ar′bi-tra-bl[p], *a.* Non=arbitrable.
non″=as-sess′a-bl[p], *a.* Non=assessable.
non″=co-ag′u-la-bl[p], *a.* Non=coagulable.
non″=co-er′civ[p&s], *a.* Non=coercive.
non″=cog′ni-tiv[s], *a.* Non=cognitive.
non″=col-lap′si-[or a-]bl[p], *a.* Non=collapsible, non=collapsable.
non″=com-men′su-ra-bl[p], *a.* Non=commensurable.
non″=com′mon-a-bl[p], *a.* Non=commonable.
non″=com-mu′ta-tiv[s], *a.* Non=commutative.
non″=com-pet′i-tiv[p&s], *a.* Non=competitive.
non″=con-dens′i-bl[p], *a.* Non=condensible.
non″=con-duc′tiv[s], *a.* Non=conductive.
non″=con-no′ta-tiv[s], *a.* Non=connotative.
non″=con-sec′u-tiv[p&s], *a.* Non=consecutive.
non″=con-ser′va-tiv[p&s], *a.* Non=conservative.

non″=con-struc′tivP&S, *a.* Non=constructive.

non″=cor-ro′di-blP, *a.* Non=corrodible.

non=cor-ros′ivP&S, *a.* Non=corrosive.

non″=crys′tal-lin, -ineS, *a.* Non=crystalline.

non″=cu′mu-la-tivP&S, *a.* Non=cumulative.

non″=del′e-ga-blP, *a.* Non=delegable.

non″=de-prest′P&S, *a.* Non=depressed.

non″=de-squam′a-tivS, *a.* Non=desquamative.

non″=de-vel′op-a-blP, *a.* Non=developable.

non″=di-lat′a-blP, *a.* Non=dilatable.

non″=du′ti-a-blP, *a.* Non=dutiable.

non″=eat′a-blP, *a.* Non=eatable.

non″=ed′i-blP, *a.* Non=edible.

non″=ef-fec′tivP&S, *a.* Non=effective.

non″=em-fat′icP, *a.* Non=emphatic.

non-en′ti-ta″tivS, *a.* Nonentitative.

non-en′ti-tivS, *a.* Nonentitive.

non″=ex-com-mu′ni-ca-blP, *a.* Non=excommunicable.

non″=ex-cu′za-blP, *a.* Non=excusable.

non″=ex-ec′u-tivP&S, *a.* Non=executive.

non″=ex-pan′sivP&S, *a.* Non=expansive.

non″=ex-pan′siv-lyS, *adv.* Non=expansively.

non″=ex-plo′sivP&S, *a.* Non=explosive.

non″=ex-ten′silS, *a.* Non=extensile.

non″=ex-ten′sivP&S, *a.* Non=extensive.

non=feb′rilP&S, **non=feb′rile**S, *a.* Non=febrile.

non=fe-nom′e-nalP, *a.* Non=phenomenal.

non=fer-ment′a-[or **i-**]**bl**P, *a.* Non=fermentable, non=fermentible.

non=fis′silP&S, **non=fis′sile**S, *a.* Non=fissile.

non=fo-net′icP, *a.* Non=phonetic.

non=for′feit-a-blP, *a.* Non=forfeitable.

non=freez′a-blP, *a.* Non=freezable.

non=fund′a-blP, *a.* Non=fundable.

non=fun′gi-blP, *a.* & *n.* Non=fungible.

non=hos′til, -ileS, *a.* Non=hostile.

non=ig-nit′i-[or **a-**]**bl**P, *a.* Non=ignitible, non=ignitable.

non=im′i-ta-tivP&S, *a.* Non=imitative.

non″=in-duc′tivS, *a.* Non=inductive.

non=in-flam′ma-blP, *a.* Non=inflammable.

non=in′te-gra-blP, *a.* Non=integrable.

non=ir′ri-ga-blP, *a.* Non=irrigable.

non=ir′ri-ta-blP, *a.* Non=irritable.

non=mag′ne-tiz″[or **-is″**]**a-bl**P, *a.* Non=magnetizable, non=magnetisable.

non=mar′riage-a-blP, *a.* Non=marriageable.

non=mis′ci-blP, *a.* Non=miscible.

non=mo′bil, -ileS, *a.* Non=mobile.

non=na′tivP&S, *a.* Non=native.

non=nav′i-ga-blP, *a.* Non=navigable.

non=ne-go′ti-a-blP, *a.* Non=negotiable.

non=nu′tri-tivP&S, *a.* Non=nutritive.

non=os′cinS, *a.* & *n.* Non=oscine.

non=pas′ser-inS, *a.* & *n.* Non=passerine.

non=peakt′S, *a.* Non=peaked.

non=per′me-a-blP, *a.* Non=permeable.

non′plustS, *pp.* Nonplused, nonplussed.

non=po′lar-iz″[or **-is″**]**a-bl**P, *a.* Non=polarizable, non=polarisable.

non=pos′i-tivP&S, *a.* Non=positive.

non=pre-hen′silP&S, **non=pre-hen′sile**S, *a.* Non=prehensile.

non=prim′i-tivP&S, *a.* Non=primitive.

non=prin′ci-pldP, *pa.* Non=principled.

non=prob′a-blP, *a.* Non=probable.

non=pro-duc′tivP&S, *a.* non=productive.

non=pro-duc'tiv-ness[P&S], *n.* Non=productiveness.
non=pro-fest'[P&S], *pa.* Non=professed.
non=pro-gres'siv[P&S], *a.* Non=progressive.
non=pro-trac'til[S], *a.* Non=protractile.
non=pu-tres'ci-bl[P], *a.* Non=putrescible.
non=re-ceit'[P], *n.* Non=receipt.
non=rel'a-tiv[P&S], *a.* & *n.* Non=relative.
non=re-pay'a-bl[P], *a.* Non=repayable.
non=rep"re-sen'ta-tiv[P&S], *a.* Non=representative.
non=re"pro-duc'tiv[P&S], *a.* Non=reproductive.
non=re-spect'a-bl[P], *a.* Non=respectable.
non=re-spir a-bl[P], *a.* Non=respirable.
non=re-trac'til, -ile[S], *a.* Non=retractile.
non=re-turn'a-bl[P], *a.* Non=returnable.
non=re-ver'si-bl[P], *a.* Non=reversible.
non=sac'cha-rin, -ine[S], *a.* Non=saccharine.
non=sen'si-bl[P], *a.* Non=sensible.
non=sen'si-tiv[P&S], *a.* Non=sensitive.
non"=sub-mis'siv[P&S], *a.* Non=submissive.
noost[S], *pp.* Noosed.
nop[S], *n.* Knop.
nor'den-skiöl-din[S], *n.* Nordenskiöldine.
nor'ma-tiv[S], *a.* Normative.
nor'ma-tiv-ly[S], *adv.* Normatively.
nos'tic[S], *a.* & *n.* Gnostic.
not[S], *v.* & *n.* Knot.
no'ta-bl[P], *a.* & *n.* Notable.
no'ta-bl-ness[P], *n.* Notableness.
notcht[S], *a.* Notched.
no'tice-a-bl[P], *a.* Noticeable.
no'ti-fi"a-bl[P], *a.* Notifiable.
no'tis[S], *v.* & *n.* Notice.
no'tist[S], *pp.* Noticed.
nour'isht[S], *pp.* Nourished.
not'ting[S], *n.* Knotting.
no-va'tiv[S], *a.* Novative.
nov'is[S], *a.* & *n.* Novice.
noz'l[P], *v.* & *n.* Nozzle.
nu'bil[P&S], **-ile**[S], *a.* Nubile.
nuck'le[S], *v.* & *n.* Knuckle.
nu'cle-o-lin[S], *n.* Nucleoline.
nul[P&S], *v.*, *a.* & *n.* Null.
nuld[S], *pp.* Nulled.
num[S], *v.* & *a.* Numb.
num'berd[S], *pp.* Numbered.
numd[S], *pp.* Numbed.
nu-me'ni-in[S], *a.* & *n.* Numeniine.
nu'mer-a-bl[P], *a.* Numerable.
nu'mer-a-bl-ness[P], *n.* Numerableness.
nu'mer-a"tiv[S], *a.* & *n.* Numerative.
num'skul"[P], *n.* Numskull.
nun'ci-a"tiv[S], *a.* Nunciative.
nun'cu-pa"tiv[S], *a.* Nuncupative.
nund[S], *pp.* Nunned.
nur'ish[P], *vt.* & *vi.* Nourish.
nur'ish-a-bl[P], *a.* Nourishable.
nur'isht[P], *pp.* Nourished.
nurl[S], *v.* & *n.* Knurl.
nurld[S], *a.* Knurld.
nurst[S], *pp.* Nursed.
nu'tri-tiv[P&S], *a.* & *n.* Nutritive.
nuz'l[P], *v.* & *n.* Nuzzle.
nyc'ta-gin[S], *n.* Nyctagine.
nyc-tib'i-in[S], *a.* & *n.* Nyctibiine.
nyc"ti-ce'bin[S], *a.* & *n.* Nycticebine.
nyc"ti-or'ni-thin[S], *a.* & *n.* Nyctiornithine.
nyc"ti-pith'e-cin[S], *a.* & *n.* Nyctipithecine.
nymf[P&S], *n.* Nymph.

O

oard$^{P\&S}$, *a.* Oared.
o-bey'a-bl^{P}, *a.* Obeyable.
o-beyd'^{S}, *pp.* Obeyed.
ob-ject'a-bl^{P}, *a.* Objectable.
ob-jec'ta-tiv^{S}, *a.* Objectative.
ob-jec'tion-a-bl^{P}, *a.* Objectionable.
ob-jec'tiv$^{P\&S}$, *a.* & *n.* Objective.
ob-jec'tiv-ly^{S}, *adv.* Objectively.
ob-jur'ga-tiv^{S}, *a.* Objurgative.
ob-jur'ga-tiv-ly^{S}, *adv.* Objurgatively.
ob'li-ga-bl^{P}, *a.* Obligable.
ob'li-ga"tiv^{S}, *a.* Obligative.
ob'li-ga"tiv-ness^{S}, *n.* Obligativeness.
ob-lit'er-a"tiv^{S}, *a.* Obliterative.
ob-serv'$^{P\&S}$, *vt.* & *vi.* Observe.
ob-serv'a-bl^{P}, *a.* Observable.
ob-serv'a-bl-ness^{P}, *n.* Observableness.
ob-ser'va-tiv^{S}, *a.* Observative.
ob-servd'$^{P\&S}$, *pp.* Observed.
ob-ses'siv^{S}, *a.* Obsessive.
ob-sest'^{S}, *pp.* Obsessed.
ob'sta-cl^{P}, *a.* & *n.* Obstacle.
ob-struc'tiv^{S}, *a.* & *n.* Obstructive.
ob-struc'tiv-ly^{S}, *adv.* Obstructively.
ob-struc'tiv-ness^{S}, *n.* Obstructiveness.
ob-tain'a-bl^{P}, *a.* Obtainable.
ob-taind'$^{P\&S}$, *pp.* Obtained.
ob-tru'siv$^{P\&S}$, *a.* Obtrusive.
ob-tru'siv-ly^{S}, *adv.* Obtrusively.
ob-tru'siv-ness^{S}, *n.* Obtrusiveness.
ob'vo-lu"tiv^{S}, *a.* Obvolutive.
oc-ca'sion-a-bl^{P}, *a.* Occasionable.
oc-ca'siond^{S}, *pp.* Occasioned.
oc-clu'siv^{S}, *a.* Occlusive.
oc'cu-pa"tiv^{S}, *a.* Occupative.
oc'cu-pi"a-bl^{P}, *a.* Occupiable.
oc-curd'$^{P\&S}$, *pp.* Occurred.
o"ce-an'i-tin^{S}, *a.* & *n.* Oceanitine.
o-cher^{S}, *v.*, *a.* & *n.* Ochre.
oc"to-co-ral'lin^{S}, *a.* & *n.* Octocoralline.
oc"to-don'tin^{S}, *a.* & *n.* Octodontine.
oc"to-syl'la-bl^{P}, *a.* Octosyllable.
od$^{P\&S}$, *a.* & *n.* Odd.
od'a-cin^{S}, *a.* & *n.* Odacine.
o'di-us^{S}, *a.* Odious.
o"don-toph'o-rin^{S}, *a.* Odontophorine.
o'dor^{S}, *n.* Odor, odour.
o'dor-us^{S}, *a.* Odorous.
of'fend'a-bl^{P}, *a.* Offendable.
of-fense'$^{P\&S}$, *n.* Offence.
of-fen'siv$^{P\&S}$, *a.* & *n.* Offensive.
of-fen'siv-ly^{S}, *adv.* Offensively.
of-fen'siv-ness^{S}, *n.* Offensiveness.
of'fer-a-bl^{P}, *a.* Offerable.
of'ferd$^{P\&S}$, *pp.* Offered.
of'fis^{S}, *n.* Office.
o-fid'i-an^{P}, *a.* & *n.* Ophidian.
of-thal'mi-a^{P}, *n.* Ophthalmia.
of-thal'mic^{P}, *a.* Ophthalmic.
of-thal'my^{P}, *n.* Ophthalmy.
o'ger$^{P\&S}$, *n.* Ogre.
oild^{S}, *pp.* Oiled.
old'=fash"ion-a-bl^{P}, *a.* Old=fashionable.
ol-fact'i-[or a-]bl^{P}, *a.* Olfactible, olfactable.
ol-fac'tiv^{S}, *a.* Olfactive.
ol'i-go-syl"la-bl^{P}, *n.* Oligosyllable.
ol'iv$^{P\&S}$, *a.* & *n.* Olive.
ol'iv-ness^{S}, *n.* Oliveness.
om'ber^{S}, *n.* Ombre.
om'e-let^{S}, *n.* Omelette.
o'mend^{S}, *a.* Omened.
o-mis'si-bl^{P}, *a.* Omissible.
o-mis'siv^{S}, *a.* Omissive.
om"ni-rep"re-sen'ta-tiv^{S}, *a.* Omnirepresentative.
om"ni-rep"re-sen'ta-tiv-ness^{S}, *n.* Omnirepresentativeness.

om″ni-spec′tiv[s], *a.* Omnispective.
om′pha-cin[s], *a.* Omphacine.
onse[s], *a., n. & adv.* Once.
ooz[p], *v. & n.* Ooze.
oozd[p&s], *pp.* Oozed.
o′pal-in[s], *a. & n.* Opaline.
o′pen-a-bl[p], *a.* Openable.
o′pend[p&s], *pp.* Opened.
op′er-at″a-bl[p], *a.* Operatable.
op′er-a″tiv[s], *a. & n.* Operative.
op′er-a″tiv-ly[s], *adv.* Operatively.
op′er-a″tiv-ness[s], *n.* Operativeness.
o-pin′i-a″tiv[s], *a.* Opiniative.
o-pin′ion-a-bl[p], *a.* Opinionable.
o-pin′ion-a″tiv[s], *a.* Opinionative.
o-pin′ion-a″tiv-ly[s], *adv.* Opinionatively.
o-pin′ion-a″tiv-ness[s], *n.* Opinionativeness.
op″is-thoc′o-min[s], *n.* Opisthocomine.
op-pos′a-bl[p], *a.* Opposable.
op′po-sit[p&s], *a. & n.* Opposite.
op-pos′i-tiv[s], *a.* Oppositive.
op-pos′i-tiv-ly[s], *adv.* Oppositively.
op-pos′i-tiv-ness[s], *n.* Oppositiveness.
op′po-sit-ly[s], *adv.* Oppositely.
op′po-sit-ness[s], *n.* Oppositeness.
op-pres′siv[p&s], *a.* Oppressive.
op-pres′siv-ly[s], *adv.* Oppressively.
op-pres′siv-ness[s], *n.* Oppressiveness.
op-prest′[p&s], *a.* Oppressed.
op′ta-tiv[p&s], *a. & n.* Optative.
op′ta-tiv-ly[s], *adv.* Optatively.
or′a-cl[p], *n.* Oracle.
orbd[p&s], *pa.* Orbed.
or-dain′a-bl[p], *a.* Ordainable.
or-daind′[s], *pp.* Ordained.
or′der-a-bl[p], *a.* Orderable.
or′derd[p&s], *pp.* Ordered.
or′di-na″tiv[s], *n.* Ordinative.
o-rec′tiv[s], *a.* Orective.
o″re-o-pha′sin[s], *a. & n.* Oreophasine.
o″re-ot′ra-gin[s], *a.* Oreotragine.
or′fan[p&s], *v., a. & n.* Orphan.
or′gan-iz″[or **-is″**]**a-bl**[p], *a.* Organizable, organisable.
or′gan-ize[p], *vt. & vi.* Organise.
or′gan-zin[s], *v. & n.* Organzine.
or′i-fis[s], *n.* Orifice.
o-rig′i-na-bl[p], *a.* Originable.
o-rig′i-na-tiv[s], *a.* Originative.
o-rig′i-na-tiv-ly[s], *adv.* Originatively.
or″na-men′ta-tiv[s], *a.* Ornamentative.
or′phand[s], *pp.* Orphaned.
or′tho-graf[p], *n.* Orthograph.
or-thog′ra-fer[p], *n.* Orthographer.
or″tho-graf′ic[p], *a.* Orthographic.
or-thog′ra-fy[p], *n.* Orthography.
or″tho-pe′dic[s], *a.* Orthopædic.
or′tiv[s], *a.* Ortive.
os′cil-la″tiv[s], *a.* Oscillative.
os′cil-la″tiv-ly[s], *adv.* Oscillatively.
os′cin[s], *a. & n.* Oscine.
os-ten′si-bl[p], *a.* Ostensible.
os-ten′si-bl-ness[p], *n.* Ostensibleness.
os-ten′siv[s], *a.* Ostensive.
os-ten′siv-ly[s], *adv.* Ostensively.
os′tra-cin[s], *a. & n.* Ostracine.
os′tra-ciz″a-bl[p], *a.* Ostracizable.
os′tra-cize[p&s], *vt.* Ostracise.
o-tar′i-in[s], **o′ta-rin**[s], *a.* Otariine, otarine.
our-selvs′[s], *pron. pl.* Ourselves.
out-liv′[p], *vt. & vi.* Outlive.
out-spred′[p&s], *vt. & vi.* Outspread.
out-strech′[p], *vt.* Outstretch.
out-strecht′[p&s], *pp.* Outstretched.
out-stript′[s], *pp.* Outstripped.
out-walkt′[p&s], *pp.* Outwalked.
ov′end[s], *a.* Ovened.
o″ver-aw′[p], *vt.* Overawe.
o″ver-awd′[p&s], *pp.* Overawed.
o″ver-com′a-bl[p], *a.* Overcomable.
o′ver-hed″[s], *a. & adv.* Overhead.
o″ver-lapt′[s], *pp.* Overlapped.
o′ver-leapt″[s], *pp.* Overleaped.

o″ver-lookt′[S], *pp.* Overlooked.
o″ver-past′[P&S], *pp.* Overpassed.
o″ver-spred′[P&S], *vt.* Overspread.
o″ver-straind′[S], *pp.* Overstrained.
o″ver-turn′a-bl[P], *a.* Overturnable.
o″ver-whelmd′[S], *pp.* Overwhelmed.
o″vi-bo′vin[S], *a.* & *n.* Ovibovine.
o′vil[S], *a.* Ovile.
o′vin[S], *a.* Ovine.
o′vu-lin[S], *a.* Ovuline.
ow[P], *vt.* & *vi.* Owe.
owd[P&S], *pp.* Owed.
ownd[P&S], *pp.* Owned.
ox′id[P], *n.* Oxide.
ox′i-da-bl[P], *a.* Oxidable.
ox′i-da″tiv[S], *a.* Oxidative.
ox′i-diz″[or **-dis″**]**a-bl[P],** *a.* Oxidizable, oxidisable.
ox′y-gen-iz″[or **-is″**]**a-bl[P],** *a.* Oxygenizable, oxygenisable.
ox″y-sul′fid[S], *n.* Oxysulfide.

P

pa′ca-bl[P], *a.* Pacable.
pach[P], *v.* & *n.* Patch.
pach′a-bl[P], *a.* Patchable.
pacht[P], *pp.* Patched.
pach″y-ceph′a-lin[S], *a.* & *n.* Pachycephaline.
pac″i-fi′a-bl[P], *a.* Pacifiable.
pack′a-bl[P], *a.* Packable.
packt[P&S], *pp.* Packed.
pack′thred″[P&S], *n.* Packthread.
pad′doc[S], *v.* & *n.* Paddock.
pad′l[S], *v.* & *n.* Paddle.
pad′ld[P], *pp.* Paddled.
pad′lockt[P&S], *pp.* Padlocked.
paind[P&S], *pa.* Pained.
paird[P&S], *pa.* Paired.
pal′at-a-bl[P], *a.* Palatable.
pal′at-a-bl-ness[P], *n.* Palatableness.
pal′a-tin[P&S], -ine[P], *a.* & *n.* Palatine.
pald[S], *pp.* Palled.
pa″le-og′ra-fy[P], *n.* Paleography.
pa″le-o-lith′ic[S], *a.* & *n.* Palæolithic.
pa″le-on-tol′o-gy[S], *n.* Palæontology.
Pa″le-o-zo′ic[S], *a.* & *n.* Palæozoic.
palld[P], *pp.* Palled.
pal′li-a-tiv[P&S], *a.* & *n.* Palliative.
pal′li-a-tiv-ly[S], *adv.* Palliatively.
palmd[P&S], *a.* Palmed.
pal′pa-bl[P], *a.* Palpable.
pal′pa-bl-ness[P], *n.* Palpableness.
pal′pa-cl[P], *n.* Palpacle.
pal′terd[P&S], *pp.* Paltered.
pal′u-din[S], *a.* Paludine.
pa-lus′trin[S], *a.* Palustrine.
pam′flet[P&S], *n.* Pamphlet.
pam′perd[P&S], *pp.* Pampered.
pand[S], *pp.* Panned.
pan′co-lin[S], *n.* Pancoline.
pan′derd[P&S], *pp.* Pandered.
pan′eld[P&S], *pp.* Paneled, panelled.
pan′i-cl[P], *n.* Panicle.
pan′i-cld[P], *a.* Panicled.
pan′ther-in[S], *a.* Pantherine.
pan′to-graf[P], *n.* Pantograph.
pa′pa-bl[P], *a.* Papable.
pa′perd[P&S], *pp.* Papered.
papt[S], *pp.* Papped.
par′a-bl[P], *v.* & *n.* Parable.
par″a-cal′ca-rin[S], *a.* Paracalcarine.
par″a-fer-na′li-a[P], *n. pl.* Paraphernalia.
par′af-fin[S], *v.* & *n.* Paraffine.
par′a-fras″a-bl[P], *a.* Paraphrasable.
par′a-frase[P&S], *v.* & *n.* Paraphrase.
par′a-frast[P], *n.* Paraphrast.
par′a-gond[S], *pp.* Paragoned.
par′a-graf[P&S], *v.* & *n.* Paragraph.
par′a-graf-er[S], *n.* Paragrapher.
par′a-graft[P&S], *pp.* Paragraphed.
par′al-lel″a-bl[P], *a.* Parallelable.

par'a-leld[P&S], *pp.* Paralleled, parallelled.
par'a-lyze[S], *vt.* Paralyse.
par"a-naph'tha-lin[S], *n.* Paranaphthaline.
par'a-nymf[P], *n.* Paranymph.
pa-ras'ti-cin[S], *a.* & *n.* Parasticine.
par'boild[P&S], *pp.* Parboiled.
par'celd[P&S], *pp.* Parceled, parcelled.
parcht[P&S], *pp.* Parched.
pard'in[S], *a.* Pardine.
par'don-a-bl[P], *a.* Pardonable.
par'don-a-bl-ness[P], *n.* Pardonableness.
par'dond[P&S], *pp.* Pardoned.
parkes'in[S], *n.* Parkesine.
parkt[S], *pp.* Parked.
par'la-ment[P], *n.* Parliament.
par'leyd[P&S], *pp.* Parleyed.
par'lor[S], *n.* Parlor, parlour.
par'ly[S], *v.* & *n.* Parley.
par'o-di-a-bl[P], *a.* Parodiable.
pars'a-bl[P], *a.* Parsable.
par"si-mo'ni-us[S], *a.* Parsimonious.
pars'ly[S], *n.* Parsley.
par'sond[S], *a.* Parsoned.
parst[P&S], *pp.* Parsed.
part'i-[or **a-**]**bl**[P], *a.* Partible, partable.
par-tak'a-bl[P], *a.* Partakable.
par"the-no-gen'i-tiv[S], *a.* Parthenogenitive.
par-tic'i-pa-bl[P], *a.* Participable.
par-tic'i-pa"tiv[S], *a.* Participative.
par-tic'i-pa"tiv-ly[S], *adv.* Participatively.
par'ti-ci-pl[P], *n.* Participle.
par'ti-cl[P], *n.* Particle.
par-ti'tiond[S], *pp.* Partitioned.
par'ti-tiv[P&S], *a.* & *n.* Partitive.
par'ti-tiv-ly[S], *adv.* Partitively.
par'ti-zan[S], *a.* & *n.* Partisan.
part'nerd[S], *pp.* Partnered.
par-tu'ri-tiv[S], *a.* Parturitive.
pas[S], *v.* & *n.* Pass.
pas'ci-bl[P], *a.* Pascible.
pass'a-bl[P], *a.* Passable.
pass'a-bl-ness[P], *n.* Passableness.
pas'ser-in[S], *a.* & *n.* Passerine.
pas'si-bl[P], *a.* Passible.
pas'si-bl-ness[P], *n.* Passibleness.
pas'siv[P&S], *a.* & *n.* Passive.
pas'siv-ly[S], *adv.* Passively.
pas'siv-ness[S], *n.* Passiveness.
past[P&S], *pp.* Passed.
pas'tur-a-bl[P], *a.* Pasturable.
patcht[S], *pp.* Patched.
pat'ent-a-bl[P], *a.* Patentable.
pa-trold'[P&S], *pp.* Patrolled.
pat'ro-niz"[or **-nis"**]**a-bl**[P], *a.* Patronizable.
pat'ron-ize[S], *vt.* Patronise.
pat'ta-bl[P], *a.* Pattable.
pat'terd[S], *pp.* Pattered.
pat'tern-a-bl[P], *a.* Patternable.
pat'ternd[P&S], *pp.* Patterned.
Paul'in[S], *a.* Pauline.
pa-vil'iond[P&S], *pp.* Pavilioned.
pawd[P&S], *a.* Pawed.
pawn'a-bl[P], *a.* Pawnable.
pawnd[P&S], *pp.* Pawned.
pay'a-bl[P], *a.* Payable.
peace'a-bl[P], *a.* Peaceable.
peace'a-bl-ness[P], *n.* Peaceableness.
peacht[P&S], *pp.* Peached.
peakt[S], *a.* Peaked.
peald[P&S], *pp.* Pealed.
peas[P], *n. sing.* & *pl.* Pease.
peb'l[P], *v.* & *n.* Pebble.
peb'rin[S], *n.* Pebrine.
pec'ca-bl[P], *a.* Peccable.
peckt[P&S], *pp.* Pecked.
ped'l[P], *vt.* & *vi.* Peddle.
ped'ld[P], *pp.* Peddled.
ped'ler[P], *n.* Peddler.
ped'a-gog[P&S], *v.* & *n.* Pedagogue.
pe-dic'u-lin[S], *a.* Pediculine.
ped'o-mo"tiv[S], *n.* Pedomotive.
pe"do-bap'tist[S], *n.* Pædobaptist.

pe-dun'cl[P], *n.* Peduncle.
peeld[P&S], *a.* Peeled.
peept[P&S], *pp.* Peeped.
peerd[P&S], *pp.* Peered.
pegd[P&S], *a.* Pegged.
pe'jo-ra"tiv[S], *a.* Pejorative.
pe'jo-ra"tiv-ly[S], *adv.* Pejoratively.
pel[P], *n.* Pell.
pel'li-cl[P], *n.* Pellicle.
pel"-mel'[P], *adv.* Pell-mell.
pel-tig'er-in[S], *a.* Peltigerine.
pen'cild[P&S], *a.* Pencilled, penciled.
pend[P&S], *pp.* Penned.
pen-den'tiv[S], *n.* Pendentive.
pen'di-cl[P], *n.* Pendicle.
pen'du-lin[S], *a.* & *n.* Penduline.
pe-ner'o-plin[S], *a.* Peneropline.
pen'e-tra-bl[P], *a.* Penetrable.
pen'e-tra-bl-ness[P], *n.* Penetrableness.
pen'e-tra"tiv[P&S], *a.* Penetrative.
pen'e-tra"tiv-ly[S], *adv.* Penetratively.
pen'e-tra"tiv-ness[S], *n.* Penetrativeness.
pense[P], *n. pl.* Pence.
pen-sic'u-la-tiv[S], *a.* Pensiculative.
pen'sil[P&S], **-sile**[P&S], *a.* Pensile.
pen'sion-a-bl[P], *a.* Pensionable.
pen'siond[P&S], *pp.* Pensioned.
pen'siv[P&S], *a.* Pensive.
pen-tac'tin[S], *n.* Pentactine.
pe'ple[P], *v.* & *n.* People.
pep'perd[P&S], *pp.* Peppered.
per-ceiv'[P], *vt.* Perceive.
per-ceiv'a-bl[P], *a.* Perceivable.
per-ceivd'[P&S], *pp.* Perceived.
per-cen'til[S], *a.* Percentile.
per-cep'ti-bl[P], *a.* Perceptible.
per-cep'ti-bl-ness[P], *n.* Perceptibleness.
per-cep'tiv[P&S], *a.* Perceptive.
per-cep'tiv-ly[S], *adv.* Perceptively.
per-cep'tiv-ness[S], *n.* Perceptiveness.
percht[P&S], *a.* Perched.
per'co-la"tiv[S], *a.* Percolative.
per-cus'siv[S], *a.* & *n.* Percussive.
per-cus'siv-ly[S], *adv.* Percussively.
per-cus'siv-ness[S], *n.* Percussiveness.
per-cust'[S], *pp.* Percussed.
per'du-ra-bl[P], *a.* Perdurable.
per'du-ra-bl-ness[P], *n.* Perdurableness.
per'e-grin[S], *a.* Peregrine.
per-fect'i-bl[P], *a.* Perfectible.
per-fec'tiv[P&S], *a.* Perfective.
per-fec'tiv-ly[S], *adv.* Perfectively.
per-fec'tiv-ness[S], *n.* Perfectiveness.
per'fo-ra-bl[P], *a.* Perforable.
per'fo-ra"tiv[P&S], *a.* Perforative.
per-form'a-bl[P], *a.* Performable.
per-formd'[P&S], *pp.* Performed.
per-fu'siv[S], *a.* Perfusive.
pe-rif'er-y[P&S], *n.* Periphery.
per'i-frase[P], *vt.* & *vi.* Periphrase.
per"i-fras'tic[P], *a.* Periphrastic.
per"i-gour'din[S], *n.* Perigourdine.
per"i-jour'din[S], *n.* Perijourdine.
per'ild[P&S], *pp.* Perilled, periled.
per'i-og[P&S], *n.* Periogue.
per'ish-a-bl[P], *a.* Perishable.
per'ish-a-bl-ness[P], *n.* Perishableness.
per'isht[P&S], *pa.* Perished.
per"i-u'ter-in[S], *a.* Periuterine.
per'i-wigd[P&S], *pp.* Periwigged.
per'i-win"kl[P], *n.* Periwinkle.
perkt[P&S], *pp.* Perked.
perl[P], *v.*, *a.* & *n.* Pearl.
per'lin[S], *a.* Perline.
per'me-a-bl[P], *a.* Permeable.
per'me-a-bl-ness[P], *n.* Permeableness.
per'me-a-tiv[S], *a.* Permeative.
per-mis'ci-bl[P], *a.* Permiscible.
per-mis'si-bl[P], *a.* Permissible.
per-mis'si-bl-ness[P], *n.* Permissibleness.
per-mis'siv[P&S], *a.* Permissive.
per-mis'siv-ly[S], *adv.* Permissively.

per-mis'siv-ness[s], *n.* Permissiveness.
per-mut'a-bl[p], *a.* Permutable.
per-mut'a-bl-ness[p], *n.* Permutableness.
per'nin[s], *a.* Pernine.
per-ox'i-diz"a-bl[p], *a.* Peroxidizable.
per'pe-tra-bl[p], *a.* Perpetrable.
per-pet'u-a-bl[p], *a.* Perpetuable.
per-plex'a-bl[p], *a.* Perplexable.
per-plext'[p&s], *pa.* Perplexed.
per'qui-sit[p&s], *n.* Perquisite.
per'ro-tin[s], *n.* Perrotine.
per'se-cu"tiv[s], *a.* Persecutive.
per'se-cu"tiv-ness[s], *n.* Persecutiveness.
per-sis'tiv[s], *a.* Persistive.
per-sis'tiv-ly[s], *adv.* Persistively.
per-sis'tiv-ness[s], *n.* Persistiveness.
per'son-a-bl[p], *a.* Personable.
per'son-a-bl-ness[p], *n.* Personableness.
per'son-a-tiv[s], *a.* Personative.
per-son'i-fi"a-bl[p], *a.* Personifiable.
per-son'i-fi-ca"tiv[s], *a.* Personificative.
per-spec'tiv[p&s], *a.* & *n.* Perspective.
per-spec'tiv-ly[s], *adv.* Perspectively.
per-spir'a-bl[p], *a.* Perspirable.
per-suad'a-bl[p], *a.* Persuadable.
per-suad'a-bl-ness[p], *n.* Persuadableness.
per-sua'si-bl[p], *a.* Persuasible.
per-sua'si-bl-ness[p], *n.* Persuasibleness.
per-sua'siv[p&s], *a.* & *n.* Persuasive.
per-sua'siv-ly[s], *adv.* Persuasively.
per-sua'siv-ness[s], *n.* Persuasiveness.
per-taind'[p&s], *pp.* Pertained.
per-turb'a-bl[p], *a.* Perturbable.
per-turbd'[p&s], *pp.* Perturbed.
per-va'siv[p&s], *a.* Pervasive.
per-va'siv-ly[s], *adv.* Pervasively.
per-ver'siv[p&s], *a.* Perversive.
per-vert'i-bl[p], *a.* Pervertible.
per-ver'tiv[s], *a.* Pervertive.
pes'ant[s], *a.* & *n.* Peasant.
pes'terd[p&s], *pp.* Pestered.
pes'tl[p], *v.* & *n.* Pestle.
pet'ald[s], *pp.* Petaled.
pe-ti'tiond[p&s], *pp.* Petitioned.
pet"ri-fac'tiv[p&s], *a.* Petrifactive.
pet'ri-fi"a-bl[p], *a.* Petrifiable.
Pe'trin[s], *a.* Petrine.
pet'ty[p], *a.* Petit.
pez'ant[p], *a.* & *n.* Peasant.
pez'ant-ry[p], *n.* Peasantry.
phac"o-che'[or **chœ'**]**rin**[s], *a.* Phacocherin, phacochœrin.
phæ"o-cys'tin[s], *a.* Phæocystine.
phas-cog'a-lin[s], *a.* & *n.* Phascogaline.
phas"co-larc'tin[s], *a.* & *n.* Phascolarctine.
pha'si-a-nin[s], *a.* & *n.* Phasianine.
phe'nix[s], *n.* Phœnix.
phe"no-crys'tal-lin[s], *a.* Phenocrystalline.
phe-nom'e-non[s], *n.* Phenomenon.
phe"no-saf'ri-nin[s], *n.* Phenosafrinine.
Phi-lis'tin[s], *a.* & *n.* Philistine.
phil"o-gen'i-tiv[s], *a.* Philogenitive.
phil"o-pro-gen'i-tiv[s], *a.* Philoprogenitive.
phil"o-pro-gen'i-tiv-ness[s], *n.* Philoprogenitiveness.
phœ"ni-coph'a-lin[s], *a.* & *n.* Phœnicophaline.
phœ"ni-coph'i-lin[s], *a.* & *n.* Phœnicophiline.
phyl'lo-rhin[s], **phyl"lo-rhi'nin**[s], *a.* & *n.* Phyllorhine, phyllorhinine.
phyl-los'co-pin[s], *a.* Phylloscopine.
phyl"lo-stom'a-tin[s], *a.* & *n.* Phyllostomatine.
phyl-los'to-min[s], *a.* & *n.* Phyllostomine.
pich[p], *v.* & *n.* Pitch.
pich'er[p], *n.* Pitcher.

picht$^{P\&S}$, *pa.* Pitched.
pich′y^{P}, *a.* Pitchy.
pick′a-bl^{P}, *a.* Pickable.
pick′l^{P}, *v.* & *n.* Pickle.
pick′ld^{P}, *pp.* Pickled.
pickt$^{P\&S}$, *pa.* Picked.
pic′nict$^{P\&S}$, *pp.* Picnicked.
pic″ro-car′min^{S}, *n.* Picrocarmine.
pic′tur-a-bl^{P}, *a.* Picturable.
pic′tur-a-bl-ness^{P}, *n.* Picturableness.
pi-er′i-din^{S}, *a.* Pieridine.
pierst^{S}, *pp.* Pierced.
pigd^{S}, *pp.* Pigged.
pig′my^{S}, *a.* & *n.* Pygmy.
pig′no-ra″tiv^{S}, *a.* Pignorative.
pil$^{P\&S}$, *v.* & *n.* Pill.
pild^{S}, *pp.* Pilled.
pil′ferd$^{P\&S}$, *pp.* Pilfered.
pil′grimd^{S}, *pp.* Pilgrimed.
pi′lin^{S}, *a.* Piline.
pil′lage-a-bl^{P}, *a.* Pillageable.
pil′lard^{S}, *a.* Pillared.
pil′lo^{S}, *v.* & *n.* Pillow.
pil′lowd$^{P\&S}$, *pp.* Pillowed.
pi-mel′o-din^{S}, *a.* & *n.* Pimelodine.
pim′pl^{P}, *n.* Pimple.
pim′pld^{P}, *a.* Pimpled.
pimpt$^{P\&S}$, *pp.* Pimped.
pincht$^{P\&S}$, *pa.* Pinched.
pind$^{P\&S}$, *pp.* Pinned.
pi-nic′o-lin^{S}, *a.* Pinicoline.
pin′iond$^{P\&S}$, *a.* Pinioned.
pinkt$^{P\&S}$, *pa.* Pinked.
pin′na-cl^{P}, *v.* & *n.* Pinnacle.
pin′na-cld^{P}, *pp.* Pinnacled.
pin′tl^{P}, *n.* Pintle.
pi″o-neerd′$^{P\&S}$, *pp.* Pioneered.
pipt^{S}, *a.* Pipped.
pisht$^{P\&S}$, *pp.* Pished.
pis′told^{S}, *pp.* Pistoled, pistolled.
pitcht^{S}, *pa.* Pitched.
pitht^{S}, *pp.* Pithed.
pit′i-a-bl^{P}, *a.* Pitiable.
pit′i-a-bl-ness^{P}, *n.* Pitiableness.
pla′ca-bl^{P}, *a.* Placable.
pla′ca-bl-ness^{P}, *n.* Placableness.
plaind$^{P\&S}$, *pp.* Plained.
plain′tif$^{P\&S}$, *n.* Plaintiff.
plain′tiv$^{P\&S}$, *a.* Plaintive.
pland$^{P\&S}$, *pp.* Planned.
plan′isht^{S}, *pp.* Planished.
plankt$^{P\&S}$, *pp.* Planked.
plasht$^{P\&S}$, *pp.* Plashed.
plas′terd$^{P\&S}$, *pp.* Plastered.
plat″y-phyl′lin^{S}, *a.* Platyphylline.
plat′y-rhin^{S}, *a.* Platyrhine.
plau′si-bl^{P}, *a.* Plausible.
plau′si-bl-ness^{P}, *n.* Plausibleness.
plau′siv$^{P\&S}$, *a.* Plausive.
play′a-bl^{P}, *a.* Playable.
playd$^{P\&S}$, *pp.* Played.
pleacht^{S}, *pp.* Pleached.
plead′a-bl^{P}, *a.* Pleadable.
plea′sur-a-bl^{P}, *a.* Pleasurable.
plea′sur-a-bl-ness^{P}, *n.* Pleasurableness.
plec′o-tin^{S}, *a.* & *n.* Plecotine.
pledge′a-bl^{P}, *a.* Pledgeable.
pledgd$^{P\&S}$, *pp.* Pledged.
plen′isht^{S}, *pp.* Plenished.
plen′te-us^{S}, *a.* Plenteous.
ples′ant^{S}, *a.* Pleasant.
ple′sure^{S}, *v.* & *n.* Pleasure.
plez′ant^{P}, *a.* Pleasant.
ple′zur-a-bl^{P}, *a.* Pleasurable.
ple′zure^{P}, *v.* & *n.* Pleasure.
pli′a-bl^{P}, *a.* Pliable.
pli′a-bl-ness^{P}, *n.* Pliableness.
plic′a-tiv^{S}, *a.* Plicative.
plo′siv^{S}, *n.* Plosive.
plow$^{P\&S}$, *v.* & *n.* Plough.
plow′a-bl^{P}, *a.* Plowable.
plowd$^{P\&S}$, *pp.* Plowed.
pluckt$^{P\&S}$, *pa.* Plucked.
plugd$^{P\&S}$, *pp.* Plugged.
plum^{P}, *v.*, *a.*, *n.* & *adv.* Plumb.
plumd$^{P\&S}$, *pp.* Plumbed.
plum′mer^{P}, *n.* Plumber.

plum'ming[P], *n.* Plumbing.
plum'-line"[P], *v.* & *n.* Plumb-line.
plumpt[P&S], *pp.* Plumped.
plun'der-a-bl[P], *a.* Plunderable.
plun'derd[P&S], *pp.* Plundered.
plu'ra-tiv[S], *a.* Plurative.
pluv'er[P], *n.* Plover.
plu'vi-a-lin[S], *a.* Pluvialine.
poacht[P&S], *pp.* Poached.
po-da'ger-in[S], *a.* Podagerine.
poi'sond[P&S], *pa.* Poisoned.
pold[S], *pa.* Polled.
pol"i-op'to-lin[S], *a.* & *n.* Polioptoline.
pol'ish-a-bl[P], *a.* Polishable.
pol'isht[P&S], *pa.* Polished.
poll'a-bl[P], *a.* Pollable.
pol'loc[S], *n.* Pollock.
po-lyb'o-rin[S], *a.* & *n.* Polyborine.
pol'y-graf[P], *n.* Polygraph.
po-lyg'ra-fy[P], *n.* Polygraphy.
pol'yp[S], *n.* Polype.
pol'y-pid[S], *n.* Polypide.
pol'y-syl"la-bl[P], *n.* Polysyllable.
pom'a-rin[S], *a.* Pomarine.
po-mat'o-rhin[S], *a.* Pomatorhine.
Pomp'tin[S], *a.* Pomptine.
pon'der-a-bl[P], *a.* & *n.* Ponderable.
pon'der-a-bl-ness[P], *n.* Ponderableness.
pon'derd[P&S], *pp.* Pondered.
pon"der-o-mo'tiv[S], *a.* Ponderomotive.
pon'tif[P&S], *n.* Pontiff.
Pon'tin[S], *a.* Pontine.
pon-toond'[S], *pp.* Pontooned.
poo'dl[P], *n.* Poodle.
poold[S], *pp.* Pooled.
pop'lard[S], *a.* Poplared.
popt[P&S], *pp.* Popped.
por'cin[S], *a.* Porcine.
por"fy-rit'ic[P], *a.* Porphyritic.
por'fy-ry[P&S], *n.* Porphyry.
port'a-bl[P], *a.* Portable.
port'a-bl-ness[P], *n.* Portableness.
por'tald[S], *a.* Portaled.
por'ta-til[S], *a.* Portatile.
por'ta-tiv[S], *a.* Portative.
por'tion-a-bl[P], *a.* Portionable.
por'tiond[P&S], *pp.* Portioned.
por-trayd'[P&S], *pp.* Portrayed.
po'rus[S], *a.* Porous.
pos'i-tiv[P&S], *a.* & *n.* Positive.
pos'i-tiv-ly[S], *adv.* Positively.
pos'i-tiv-ness[S], *n.* Positiveness.
pos-ses'siv[P&S], *a.* & *n.* Possessive.
pos-ses'siv-ly[S], *adv.* Possessively.
pos-ses'sive-ness[P], *n.* Possessiveness.
pos-sest'[P&S], *pa.* Possessed.
pos'si-bl[P], *a.* & *n.* Possible.
pos'si-bl-ness[P], *n.* Possibleness.
post'a-bl[P], *a.* Postable.
post-gen'er-a-tiv[S], *a.* Postgenerative.
post-mu'ta-tiv[S], *a.* Postmutative.
post-op'er-a-tiv[S], *a.* Postoperative.
post-pal'a-tin[S], *a.* & *n.* Postpalatine.
post-pon'a-bl[P], *a.* Postponable.
post-pon'til[S], *a.* Postpontile.
post-pos'i-tiv[S], *a.* & *n.* Postpositive.
po'ta-bl[P], *a.* & *n.* Potable.
po'ta-bl-ness[P], *n.* Potableness.
pot'l[P], *n.* Pottle.
pot'terd[S], *pp.* Pottered.
poucht[P&S], *a.* Pouched.
poul'tis[S], *v.* & *n.* Poultice.
poul'tist[S], *pp.* Poulticed.
pounst[S], *pp.* Pounced.
pourd[P&S], *pp.* Poured.
pow'der-a-bl[P], *a.* Powderable.
pow'derd[P&S], *pa.* Powdered.
pow'erd[S], *pp.* Powered.
prac'ti-ca-bl[P], *a.* Practicable.
prac'ti-ca-bl-ness[P], *n.* Practicableness.
prac'tis[P&S], *v.* & *n.* Practise, practice.
prac'tist[P&S], *pa.* Practised, practiced.
prac'tiv[S], *a.* Practive.
prankt[P&S], *a.* Pranked.

pranst[S], *pp.* Pranced.
prat'l[P], *v.* & *n.* Prattle.
prat'ld[P], *pp.* Prattled.
prat'ler[P], *n.* Prattler.
prayd[P&S], *pp.* Prayed.
preach'a-bl[P], *a.* Preachable.
preacht[P&S], *pp.* Preached.
pre-al'la-bl[P], *a.* Preallable.
pre'am-bl[P], *v.* & *n.* Preamble.
prec'a-tiv[P&S], *a.* Precative.
pre-cep'tiv[P&S], *a.* Preceptive.
pre-cep'tiv-ly[S], *adv.* Preceptively.
pre-cinc'tiv[S], *a.* Precinctive.
prec'i-pis[S], *n.* Precipice.
pre-cip'i-ta-bl[P], *a.* Precipitable.
pre-cip'i-ta"tiv[S], *a.* Precipitative.
pre-ci'siv[S], *a.* Precisive.
pre-clu'siv[P&S], *a.* Preclusive.
pre-clu'siv-ly[S], *adv.* Preclusively.
pre-cog'ni-tiv[S], *a.* Precognitive.
pre"con-ceiv'[P], *vt.* Preconceive.
pre-cur'siv[P&S], *a.* Precursive.
pre-des'tin[P&S], *vt.* Predestine.
pre-des'tind[P&S], *pp.* Predestined.
pre"de-ter'min[P&S], *vt.* & *vi.* Predetermine.
pre"de-ter'mi-na-bl[P], *a.* Predeterminable.
pre"de-ter'mi-na"tiv[S], *a.* Predeterminative.
pre"de-ter'mind[P&S], *pp.* Predetermined.
pred'i-ca-bl[P], *a.* & *n.* Predicable.
pred'i-ca"tiv[S], *a.* Predicative.
pred'i-ca"tiv-ly[S], *adv.* Predicatively.
pre-dict'a-bl[P], *a.* Predictable.
pre-dic'tiv[S], *a.* Predictive.
pre-dic'tiv-ly[S], *adv.* Predictively.
pre-dic'tiv-ness[S], *n.* Predictiveness.
pre-empt'i-bl[P], *a.* Preemptible.
pre-emp'tiv[S], *a.* Preemptive.
preend[P&S], *pp.* Preened.
pre"es-tab'lisht[P&S], *pp.* Preestablished.
pref'er-a-bl[P], *a.* & *n.* Preferable.
pref'er-a-bl-ness[P], *n.* Preferableness.
pre-ferd'[P&S], *pa.* Preferred.
pre-fig'ur-a-tiv[P&S], *a.* Prefigurative.
pre-fixt'[P&S], *pp.* Prefixed.
pre-form'a-tiv[S], *a.* & *n.* Preformative.
preg'na-bl[P], *a.* Pregnable.
pre-hen'si-bl[P], *a.* Prehensible.
pre-hen'sil[P&S], **-ile**[S], *a.* Prehensile.
pre-hen'siv[S], *a.* Prehensive.
pre-hen'siv-ness[S], *n.* Prehensiveness.
prej'u-dis[S], *v.* & *n.* Prejudice.
prej'u-dist[S], *pa.* Prejudiced.
pre-lu'siv[P&S], *a.* Prelusive.
pre-lu'siv-ly[S], *adv.* Prelusively.
pre-med'i-ta"tiv[S], *a.* Premeditative.
prem'is[P&S], *n.* Premise, premiss.
pre-mize'[P], *vt.* & *vi.* Premise.
pre-mizd'[P], *pp.* Premised.
pre-mu'ta-tiv[S], *a.* Premutative.
pre-no'men[S], *n.* Prænomen.
pren'tis[S], *n.* Prentice.
pren'tist[S], *pp.* Prenticed.
pre"or-daind'[P&S], *pp.* Preordained.
prep'a-ra-bl[P], *a.* Preparable.
pre-par'a-tiv[P&S], *a.* & *n.* Preparative.
pre-par'a-tiv-ly[S], *adv.* Preparatively.
pre"per-cep'tiv[S], *a.* Preperceptive.
pre-pon'til[S], *a.* Prepontile.
pre-pos'i-tiv[P&S], *a.* & *n.* Prepositive.
pre-pos'i-tiv-ly[S], *adv.* Prepositively.
pre"pos-sest'[P&S], *pp.* Prepossessed.
pre-req'ui-sit[P&S], *a.* & *n.* Prerequisite.
pre-rog'a-tiv[P&S], *a.* & *n.* Prerogative.
pres[S], *v.* & *n.* Press.
pre-scrip'ti-bl[P], *a.* Prescriptible.
pre-scrip'tiv[P&S], *a.* Prescriptive.
pre-scrip'tiv-ly[S], *adv.* Prescriptively.
pre-scrip'tiv-ness[S], *n.* Prescriptiveness.
pre-sent'a-bl[P], *a.* Presentable.
pre-sen'ta-tiv[S], *a.* Presentative.

pre-sen'ta-tiv-ness[s], *n.* Presentativeness.
pre-sen'tiv[s], *a.* & *n.* Presentive.
pre-sen'tiv-ly[s], *adv.* Presentively.
pre-sen'tiv-ness[s], *n.* Presentiveness.
pre-serv'[p&s], *vt.* & *vi.* Preserve.
pre-serv'a-bl[p], *a.* Preservable.
pre-ser'va-tiv[p&s], *a.* & *n.* Preservative.
pre-servd'[p&s], *pp.* Preserved.
press'a-bl[p], *a.* Pressable.
prest[p&s], *pp.* Pressed.
pre-sum'a-bl[p], *a.* Presumable.
pre-sump'tiv[p&s], *a.* Presumptive.
pre-sump'tiv-ly[s], *adv.* Presumptively.
pre-tense'[p&s], *n.* Pretence.
pre-tenst'[s], *pp.* Pretensed.
pre-ten'siv[s], *a.* Pretensive.
pre-ten'ta-tiv[s], *a.* Pretentative.
pret'er-it[p&s], *a.* & *n.* Preterite.
pre-ter'i-tiv[s], *a.* Preteritive.
pre"ter-mit'[s], *vt.* Prætermit.
pre"ter-sea'son-a-bl[p], *a.* Preterseasonable.
pre-vaild'[p&s], *pp.* Prevailed.
pre-vent'a-bl[p], *a.* Preventable.
pre-vent'a-tiv[s], *a.* & *n.* Preventative.
pre-ven'tiv[p&s], *a.* & *n.* Preventive.
pre-ven'tiv-ly[s], *adv.* Preventively.
pre-ven'tiv-ness[s], *n.* Preventiveness.
pre-vis'iv[s], *a.* Previsive.
preyd[p&s], *pp.* Preyed.
prick'l[p], *v.* & *n.* Prickle.
prickt[p&s], *pa.* Pricked.
prigd[s], *pp.* Prigged.
primd[s], *pp.* Primmed.
pri-me'val[s], *a.* Primæval.
pri'min[s], *n.* Primine.
prim'i-tiv[p&s], *a.* & *n.* Primitive.
prim'i-tiv-ly[s], *adv.* Primitively.
prim'i-tiv-ness[s], *n.* Primitiveness.
pri"mo-gen'i-tiv[s], *a.* Primogenitive.
prin-cip'i-a-tiv[s], *a.* Principiative.
prin'ci-pl[p], *v.* & *n.* Principle.
prin'ci-pld[p], *pp.* Principled.
prinkt[p&s], *pp.* Prinked.
print'a-bl[p], *a.* Printable.
pri"o-no-don'tin[s], *a.* Prionodontine.
pri-on'o-pin[s], *a.* & *n.* Prionopine.
pris'ma-tin[s], *a.* Prismatine.
pris'ond[p&s], *pp.* Prisoned.
pris'tin[p&s], **-ine**[p&s], *a.* Pristine.
priv'a-tiv[p&s], *a.* & *n.* Privative.
priv'a-tiv-ly[s], *adv.* Privatively.
priv'a-tiv-ness[s], *n.* Privativeness.
priz'a-bl[p], **prize'a-bl**[p], *a.* Prizable, prizeable.
prob'a-bl[p], *a.* Probable.
pro'ba-tiv[p&s], *a.* Probative.
pro'ba-tiv-ly[s], *adv.* Probatively.
pro-cede'[s], *vi.* Proceed.
pro-ces'siv[s], *a.* Processive.
pro'cre-a"tiv[p&s], *a.* Procreative.
pro'cre-a"tiv-ness[s], *n.* Procreativeness.
pro-cur'a-bl[p], *a.* Procurable.
pro-cur'siv[s], *a.* Procursive.
pro-duc'i-bl[p], *a.* Producible.
pro-duct'i-bl[p], *a.* Productible.
pro-duc'til[s], *a.* Productile.
pro-duc'tiv[p&s], *a.* Productive.
pro-duc'tiv-ly[s], *adv.* Productively.
pro-duc'tiv-ness[p&s], *n.* Productiveness.
prof'a-na-bl[p], *a.* Profanable.
prof'e-cy[p], *n.* Prophecy.
pro-fest'[p&s], *pa.* Professed.
prof'e-sy[p], *vt.* & *vi.* Prophesy.
prof'et[p&s], *n.* Prophet.
prof'et-ess[p], *n.* Prophetess.
pro-fet'ic[p&s], *a.* Prophetic.
prof'ferd[p&s], *pp.* Proffered.
prof'i-ta-bl[p], *a.* Profitable.
prof'i-ta-bl-ness[p], *n.* Profitableness.
pro"fy-lac'tic[p], *a.* & *n.* Prophylactic.
progd[s], *pp.* Progged.
pro-gen'i-tiv-ness[s], *n.* Progenitiveness.

prog-nos'ti-ca-bl[r], *a.* Prognosticable.
prog-nos'ti-ca"tiv[s], *a.* Prognosticative.
pro'gram[s], *n.* Programme.
pro-gres'siv[r&s], *a.* Progressive.
pro-gres'siv-ly[s], *adv.* Progressively.
pro-gres'siv-ness[s], *n.* Progressiveness.
pro-grest'[r&s], *pp.* Progressed.
pro-hib'i-tiv[r&s], *a.* Prohibitive.
pro-hib'i-tiv-ly[s], *adv.* Prohibitively.
pro-ject'a-bl[r], *a.* Projectable.
pro-jec'til[r&s], **-ile**[s], *a.* & *n.* Projectile.
pro-jec'tiv[s], *a.* Projective.
pro'log[r&s], *v.* & *n.* Prologue.
pro-long'a-bl[r], *a.* Prolongable.
pro-longd'[r&s], *pp.* Prolonged.
prom'is[r&s], *v.* & *n.* Promise.
prom'ist[r&s], *pp.* Promised.
pro-mis'siv[s], *a.* Promissive.
pro-mo'tiv[r&s], *a.* Promotive.
promp'tiv[s], *a.* Promptive.
prongd[s], *pp.* Pronged.
pro-nounce'a-bl[r], *a.* Pronounceable.
pro-nounst'[s], *pp.* Pronounced.
pro-nun'ci-a-bl[r], *a.* Pronunciable.
pro-nun'ci-a-tiv[s], *a.* Pronunciative.
prop'a-ga-bl[r], *a.* Propagable.
prop'a-ga-bl-ness[r], *n.* Propagableness.
pro-pal'a-nin[s], *n.* Propalanine.
pro-peld'[r&s], *pp.* Propelled.
pro-pel'la-bl[r], *a.* Propellable.
pro-pi'ti-a-bl[r], *a.* Propitiable.
pro-por'tion-a-bl[r], *a.* Proportionable.
pro-por'tion-a-bl-ness[r], *n.* Proportionableness.
pro-por'tiond[r&s] *pp.* Proportioned.
pro-pos'a-bl[r], *a.* Proposable.
propt[r&s], *pp.* Propped.
pro-pul'siv[r&s], *a.* Propulsive.
pro-rat'a-bl[r], *a.* Proratable.
pro-scol'e-cin[s], *a.* Proscolecine.
pro-scrib'a-bl[r], *a.* Proscribable.
pro-scrip'tiv[r&s], *a.* Proscriptive.
pro-scrip'tiv-ly[s], *adv.* Proscriptively.
pro-scrip'tiv-ness[s], *n.* Proscriptiveness.
pros'e-cut"a-bl[r], *a.* Prosecutable.
Pros'er-pin[s], *n.* Proserpine.
pro-spec'tiv[r&s], *a.* & *n.* Prospective.
pro-spec'tiv-ly[s], *adv.* Prospectively.
pro-spec'tiv-ness[s], *n.* Prospectiveness.
pros'perd[r&s], *pp.* Prospered.
prot-am'phi-rin[s], *n.* Protamphirine.
pro-tec'tiv[r&s], *a.* & *n.* Protective.
pro-tec'tiv-ly[s], *adv.* Protectively.
pro-tec'tiv-ness[s], *n.* Protectiveness.
pro-ten'siv[s], *a.* Protensive.
pro-test'a-bl[r], *a.* Protestable.
pro-trac'til[s], *a.* Protractile.
pro-trac'tiv[r&s], *a.* Protractive.
pro-trud'a-bl[r], *a.* Protrudable.
pro-tru'si-bl[r], *a.* Protrusible.
pro-tru'sil[s], *a.* Protrusile.
pro-tru'siv[r&s], *a.* Protrusive.
pro-tru'siv-ly[s], *adv.* Protrusively.
pro-tru'siv-ness[s], *n.* Protrusiveness.
prov'a-bl[r], *a.* Provable.
prov'a-bl-ness[r], *n.* Provableness.
pro-vid'a-bl[r], *a.* Providable.
pro-vi'siond[s], *pp.* Provisioned.
pro-voc'a-tiv[r&s], *a.* & *n.* Provocative.
pro-voc'a-tiv-ly[s], *adv.* Provocatively.
pro-voc'a-tiv-ness[s], *n.* Provocativeness.
pro-vok'a-bl[r], *a.* Provokable.
prowld[r&s], *pp.* Prowled.
prun'a-bl[r], *a.* Prunable.
psam'mo-phin[s], *a.* & *n.* Psammophine.
pseu-dos'ci-nin[s], *a.* Pseudoscinine.
pseu"do-sto'min[s], *a.* Pseudostomine.
psit'ta-cin[s], *a.* & *n.* Psittacine.
psit"ta-co-ful'vin[s], *n.* Psittacofulvine.

psit-tac′u-lin[s], *a.* & *n.* Psittaculine.

pter″y-go-pal′a-tin[s], *a.* Pterygopalatine.

ptil″o-no-ryn′chin[s], *a.* & *n.* Ptilonorynchine.

pub′lish-a-bl[p], *a.* Publishable.

pub′lisht[p&s], *pp.* Published.

puck′erd[p&s], *pp.* Puckered.

pud′l[p], *v.* & *n.* Puddle.

pud′ld[p], *pp.* Puddled.

pud′ling[p], *n.* Puddling.

pu′er-il[p&s], **-ile**[p&s], *a.* Puerile.

pu′er-il-ness[s], *n.* Puerileness.

puf[p], *v.* & *n.* Puff.

puft[p&s], *pa.* Puffed.

pugd[s], *vt.* Pugged.

pul[p&s], *v.* & *n.* Pull.

puld[p&s], *pp.* Pulled.

pu′li-cin[s], *a.* Pulicine.

pul-las′trin[s], *a.* Pullastrine.

pul′lu-la″tiv[s], *a.* Pullulative.

pul′lu-la″tiv-ly[s], *adv.* Pullulatively.

pul′ly[s], *n.* Pulley.

pul′sa-til[p&s], *a.* Pulsatile.

pul′sa-tiv[p&s], *a.* Pulsative.

pul′sa-tiv-ly[s], *adv.* Pulsatively.

pulst[p&s], *pp.* Pulsed.

pul′ver-a-bl[p], *a.* Pulverable.

pul′ver-iz″[or **-is″**]**a-bl**[p], *a.* Pulverizable, pulverisable.

pum′is[s], *v.* & *n.* Pumice.

pum′mel[p], *v.* & *n.* Pommel.

pum′meld[p], *pp.* Pommeled.

pumpt[p&s], *pp.* Pumped.

puncht[p&s], *pp.* Punched.

punc′tu-a-tiv[s], *a.* Punctuative.

pund[p&s], *pp.* Punned.

pun′ish-a-bl[p], *a.* Punishable.

pun′ish-a-bl-ness[p], *n.* Punishableness.

pun′isht[p&s], *pp.* Punished.

pu′ni-tiv[p&s], *a.* Punitive.

pu′ni-tiv-ly[s], *adv.* Punitively.

pu′ni-tiv-ness[s], *n.* Punitiveness.

pun′na-bl[p], *a.* Punnable.

pupt[s], *pp.* Pupped.

pur[p&s], *v.* & *n.* Purr.

pur′chas-a-bl[p], *a.* Purchasable.

pur′chast[s], *pp.* Purchased.

purd[p&s], *pp.* Purred.

pur′ga-tiv[p&s], *a.* & *n.* Purgative.

pur′ga-tiv-ly[s], *adv.* Purgatively.

purge′a-bl[p], *a.* Purgeable.

pu′ri-fi-ca″tiv[s], *a.* Purificative.

purld[p&s], *pp.* Purled.

pur′lin[p], *n.* Purline.

pur-loind′[p&s], *pp.* Purloined.

pur′pl[p], *v., a.* & *n.* Purple.

pur′pld[p], *pp.* Purpled.

pur′po-siv[s], *a.* Purposive.

pur′po-siv-ly[s], *adv.* Purposively.

pur′po-siv-ness[s], *n.* Purposiveness.

pur′post[s], *pp.* Purposed.

purst[p&s], *pp.* Pursed.

pur-su′a-bl[p], *a.* Pursuable.

pur-veyd′[p&s], *pp.* Purveyed.

pus[s], *n.* Puss.

pusht[p&s], *pp.* Pushed.

pu′ta-tiv[p&s], *a.* Putative.

pu″tre-fac′tiv[p&s], *a.* Putrefactive.

pu″tre-fac′tiv-ness[s], *n.* Putrefactiveness.

pu′tre-fi″a-bl[p], *a.* Putrefiable.

pu-tres′ci-bl[p], *a.* Putrescible.

put′terd[p&s], *pp.* Puttered.

put′toc[s], *n.* Puttock.

puz′l[p], *v.* & *n.* Puzzle.

puz′ld[p], *pp.* Puzzled.

pyc″no-no′tin[s], *a.* & *n.* Pycnonotine.

py-ral′li-din[s], *a.* & *n.* Pyrallidine.

pyr″rho-cor′a-cin[s], *a.* & *n.* Pyrrhocoracine.

pyr′rhu-lin[s], *a.* & *n.* Pyrrhuline.

pyr′u-lin[s], *a.* Pyruline.

Q

quackt[P&S], *pp.* Quacked.
quad'ra-bl[P], *a.* Quadrable.
quad"ri-de-riv'a-tiv[S], *n.* Quadriderivative.
quad'ri-syl"la-bl[P], *n.* Quadrisyllable.
quad"ri-vol'tin[S], *a.* & *n.* Quadrivoltine.
quad'ru-pl[P], *v.*, *a.* & *n.* Quadruple.
quaf[P], *v.* & *n.* Quaff.
quaft[P&S], *pp.* Quaffed.
quaild[P&S], *pp.* Quailed.
qual'i-fi"a-bl[P], *a.* Qualifiable.
qual'i-fi-ca"tiv[S], *a.* & *n.* Qualificative.
qual'i-ta"tiv[P&S], *a.* Qualitative.
qual'i-ta"tiv-ly[S], *adv.* Qualitatively.
quan'ti-fi"a-bl[P], *a.* Quantifiable.
quan'ti-ta"tiv[P&S], *a.* & *n.* Quantitative.
quan'ti-ta"tiv-ly[S], *adv.* Quantitatively.
quan'ti-ta"tiv-ness[S], *n.* Quantitativeness.
quar'an-tin"a-bl[P], *a.* Quarantinable.
quar'reld[P&S], *pp.* Quarreled, quarrelled.
quar'rel-sum[P&S], *a.* Quarrelsome.
quar'ri-a-bl[P], *a.* Quarriable.
quar'terd[S], *a.* Quartered.
quar-tet'[S], *n.* Quartette.
qua'verd[S], *pp.* Quavered.
queend[S], *pp.* Queened.
queerd[S], *pp.* Queered.
quel[P], *vt.* Quell.
queld[P&S], *pp.* Quelled.
quench'a-bl[P], *a.* Quenchable.
quencht[P&S], *pp.* Quenched.
quer'cin[S], *a.* Quercine.
ques'i-tiv[S], *a.* Quesitive.
ques'tion-a-bl[P], *a.* Questionable.
ques'tion-a-bl-ness[P], *n.* Questionableness.
ques'tiond[S], *pp.* Questioned.
ques'tor[S], *n.* Quæstor.
queue. See CUE.
quib'l[P], *v.* & *n.* Quibble.
quib'ld[P] *pp.* Quibbled.
quick'end[P&S], *pp.* Quickened.
quickt[S], *pp.* Quicked.
quid'da-tiv[S], *a.* Quiddative.
quid'di-ta"tiv[S], *a.* Quidditative.
quid'l[P], *v.* & *n.* Quiddle.
qui'e-tiv[S], *a.* & *n.* Quietive.
quil[P&S], *v.* & *n.* Quill.
quild[S], *a.* Quilled.
quin'i-bl[P], *vi.* & *n.* Quinible.
quin"que-loc'u-lin[S], *a.* Quinqueloculine.
quin-tet'[S], *n.* Quintette.
quin'tin[S], *n.* Quintine.
quipt[S], *pp.* Quipped.
quire[S], *v.* & *n.* Choir.
quis'ca-lin[S], *a.* & *n.* Quiscaline.
quiv'erd[P&S], *a.* Quivered.
quiz'za-bl[P], *a.* Quizzable, quizzible.
quot'a-bl[P], *a.* Quotable.
quot'a-bl-ness[P], *n.* Quotableness.
quo'ta-tiv[S], *a.* Quotative.

R

rack[S], *n.* Wrack.
rackt[P&S], *pp.* Racked.
ra'di-a-bl[P], *a.* Radiable.
ra'di-a"tiv[S], *a.* Radiative.
ra"di-o-ac'tiv[S], *a.* Radioactive.
raf'l[P], *v.* & *n.* Raffle.
raf'ld[P], *pp.* Raffled.
ragd[S], *pp.* Ragged.

rai'bl[P], *vt.* & *vi.* Raible.
raild[P&S], *pp.* Railed.
rain'bowd"[S], *a.* Rainbowed.
raind[P&S], *pp.* Rained.
rais'a-bl[P], *a.* Raisable.
raith[S], *n.* Wraith.
raiz[P], *v.* & *n.* Raise.
raizd[P], *a.* & *pp.* Raised.
ral'lin[S], *a.* Ralline.
ram'bl[P], *v.* & *n.* Ramble.
ram'bld[P], *pp.* Rambled.
ramd[P&S], *pp.* Rammed.
rampt[P&S], *pp.* Ramped.
ran'cor[P&S], *n.* Rancour.
ran'ger-in[S], *a.* Rangerine.
ran-gif'er-in[S], *a.* Rangiferine.
ran'gle[S], *v.* & *n.* Wrangle.
ra'nin[S], *a.* Ranine.
ran'kl[P], *vi.* Rankle.
ran'kld[P], *pp.* Rankled.
rankt[P&S], *pp.* Ranked.
ran'sackt[P&S], *pp.* Ransacked.
ran'som-a-bl[P], *a.* Ransomable.
ran'somd[P&S], *pp.* Ransomed.
rap[S], *v.* & *n.* Wrap.
rap'in[P&S], **-ine**[S], *n.* Rapine.
rap'so-dy[S], *n.* Rhapsody.
rapt[P&S], *pp.* Rapped.
rar"e-fac'tiv[S], *a.* Rarefactive.
rar'e-fi"a-bl[P], *a.* Rarefiable.
rasht[S], *pp.* Rashed.
raspt[P&S], *pa.* Rasped.
rat'a-bl[P], **rate'a-bl**[P], *a.* Ratable, rateable.
rath[S], *n.* Wrath.
ra"ti-oc'i-na"tiv[S], *a.* Ratiocinative.
ra'tion-a-bl[P], *a.* Rationable.
ra"tion-al-iz'[or **-is'**]**a-bl**[P], *a.* Rationalizable, rationalisable.
ra'tiond[S], *pp.* Rationed.
rat'l[P], *v.* & *n.* Rattle.
rat'ld[P], *pp.* Rattled.
rav'eld[P&S], *pp.* Raveled, ravelled.
rav'el-ing[P], *n.* Ravelling.
rav'end[P&S], *pp.* Ravened.
rav'e-nus[S], *a.* Ravenous.
rav'isht[P&S], *pp.* Ravished.
rayd[S], *pp.* Rayed.
raze[S], *vt.* & *vi.* Rase.
ra'zor-a-bl[P], *a.* Razorable.
reacht[S], *pp.* Reached.
re-ac'tiv[S], *a.* & *n.* Reactive.
re-ac'tiv-ly[S], *adv.* Reactively.
re-ac'tiv-ness[S], *n.* Reactiveness.
read'a-bl[P], *a.* Readable.
read'a-bl-ness[P], *n.* Readableness.
reak[S], *vt.* Wreak.
re'al-iz"a-bl[P], *a.* Realizable.
reamd[S], *pp.* Reamed.
reap'a-bl[P], *a.* Reapable.
reapt[P&S], *pp.* Reaped.
reard[P&S], *pp.* Reared.
rea'son-a-bl[P], *a.* Reasonable.
rea'son-a-bl-ness[P], *n.* Reasonableness.
rea'sond[P&S], *pa.* Reasoned.
reath[S], *n.* Wreath.
reathe[S], *vt.* & *vi.* Wreathe.
re-beld'[P&S], *pp.* Rebelled.
re-bel'lius[S], *a.* Rebellious.
re-bound'a-bl[P], *a.* Reboundable.
re-buft'[S], *pp.* Rebuffed.
re-buk'a-bl[P], *a.* Rebukable.
re-but'ta-bl[P], *a.* Rebuttable.
re-cald'[S], *pp.* Recalled.
re-call'a-bl[P], *a.* Recallable.
re"ca-pit'u-la"tiv[S], *a.* Recapitulative.
re-ceipt'a-bl[P], *a.* Receiptable.
re-ceit'[P], *v.* & *n.* Receipt.
re-ceiv'[P], *vt.* & *vi.* Receive.
re-ceiv'a-bl[P], *a.* Receivable.
re-ceivd'[P&S], *pp.* Received.
re-cep'ti-bl[P], *a.* Receptible.
re-cep'tiv[P&S], *a.* Receptive.
re-cep'tiv-ly[S], *adv.* Receptively.
re-cep'tiv-ness[S], *n.* Receptiveness.
re-ces'siv[S], *a.* & *n.* Recessive.

re-ces′siv-ly[s], *adv.* Recessively.
re-cest′[s], *a.* Recessed.
re-cip′ro-ca-bl[p], *a.* Reciprocable.
re-cip′ro-can-tiv[s], *a.* Reciprocantive.
re-cip′ro-ca″tiv[s], *a.* Reciprocative.
rec″i-ta-tiv′[s], *n.* Recitative.
rec″i-ta-tiv′ly[s], *adv.* Recitatively.
reck[s], *v.* & *n.* Wreck.
reck′on-a-bl[p], *a.* Reckonable.
reck′ond[s], *pp.* Reckoned.
reckt[s], *pp.* Recked.
re-claim′a-bl[p], *a.* Reclaimable.
re-claim′a-bl-ness[p], *n.* Reclaimableness.
re-claimd′[s], *pp.* Reclaimed.
re-clin′a-bl[p], *a.* Reclinable.
re-clu′siv[s], *a.* Reclusive.
re-clu′siv-ness[s], *n.* Reclusiveness.
re-cog′ni-tiv[s], *a.* Recognitive.
rec′og-niz″[or **-nis″**]**a-bl**[p], *a.* Recognizable, recognisable.
rec′og-nize[s], *vt.* & *vi.* Recognise.
re-coild′[p&s], *pp.* Recoiled.
rec″ol-lec′tiv[s], *a.* Recollective.
rec″ol-lec′tiv-ly[s], *adv.* Recollectively.
rec″ol-lec′tiv-ness[s], *n.* Recollectiveness.
rec″om-mend′a-bl[p], *a.* Recommendable.
rec″om-mend′a-bl-ness[p], *n.* Recommendableness.
rec′om-penst[s], *pp.* Recompensed.
rec″om-pen′sa-bl[p], *a.* Recompensable.
rec′om-pen″siv[s], *a.* Recompensive.
rec′on-cil″a-bl[p], **rec′on-cile″a-bl**[p], *a.* Reconcilable, reconcileable.
rec′on-cil″a-bl-ness[p], *n.* Reconcilableness.
rec″on-noi′ter[s], *v.* & *n.* Reconnoitre.
rec″on-noi′terd[s], *pp.* Reconnoitered.
re″con-struc′tiv[s], *a.* Reconstructive.
re″con-struc′tiv-ness[s], *n.* Reconstructiveness.
re″con-vert′i-bl[p], *a.* Reconvertible.
re-cord′a-bl[p], *a.* Recordable.
re-cor′da-tiv[s], *a.* Recordative.
re-cov′erd[s], *pp.* Recovered.
rec′re-a″tiv[s], *a.* Recreative.
re-crim′i-na″tiv[s], *a.* Recriminative.
rec′tan-gl[p], *n.* Rectangle.
rec′ti-fi″a-bl[p], *a.* Rectifiable.
rec′ti-fi-ca″tiv[s], *a.* Rectificative.
re-cu′per-a″tiv[s], *a.* Recuperative.
re-cu′per-a″tiv-ness[s], *n.* Recuperativeness.
re-curd′[s], *pp.* Recurred.
re-curv′[s], *vt.* & *vi.* Recurve.
re-curvd′[s], *pp.* Recurved.
re-cu′sa-tiv[s], *a.* Recusative.
re-cuv′er[p], *v.* & *n.* Recover.
re-cuv′er-a-bl[p], *a.* Recoverable.
re-cuv′er-a-bl-ness[p], *n.* Recoverableness.
re-cuv′erd[p], *pp.* Recovered.
red[p&s], *pa.* Read.
red′dend[p&s], *pp.* Reddened.
re-deem′a-bl[p], *a.* Redeemable.
re-deem′a-bl-ness[p], *n.* Redeemableness.
re-deemd′[s], *pp.* Redeemed.
re-demp′ti-bl[p], *a.* Redemptible.
re-demp′tiv[s], *a.* Redemptive.
re-demp′tiv-ly[s], *adv.* Redemptively.
re-demp″tor-is′tin[s], *n.* Redemptoristine.
re-din′te-gra″tiv[s], *a.* Redintegrative.
re-doubt′a-bl-ness[p], *n.* Redoubtableness.
re-dout′[p&s], *n.* Redoubt.
re-dout′a-bl[s], *a.* Redoubtable.
re-dout′ed[s], *pa.* Redoubted.
re-dress′i-bl[p], **re-dress′a-bl**[p], *a.* Redressible, redressable.
re-dres′siv[p&s], *a.* Redressive.
re-drest′[s], *pp.* Redressed.
re-duc′i-bl[p], *a.* Reducible.
re-duc′i-bl-ness[p], *n.* Reducibleness.

re-duc'tiv[P&S], *a.* Reductive.
re-du'pli-ca"tiv[S], *a.* Reduplicative.
re-du'pli-ca"tiv-ly[S], *a.* Reduplicatively.
red'y[P&S], *v., a.* & *n.* Ready.
reeft[P&S], *pp.* Reefed.
reekt[P&S], *pp.* Reeked.
reel'a-bl[P], *a.* Reelable.
reeld[P&S], *pp.* Reeled.
re"en-force'a-bl[P], *a.* Reenforceable.
re"en-[or **-in-**]**forc'i-bl**[P], *a.* Reenforcible, reinforcible.
reevd[S], *pp.* Reeved.
re-fec'tiv[S], *a.* & *n.* Refective.
ref'er-a-bl[P], *a.* Referable.
re-fer'ri-bl[P], *a.* Referrible.
re-ferd'[P&S], *pp.* Referred.
re-flect'i-bl[P], *a.* Reflectible.
re-flec'tiv[P&S], *a.* Reflective.
re-flec'tiv-ly[S], *adv.* Reflectively.
re-flec'tiv-ness[S], *n.* Reflectiveness.
re-flex'i-bl[P], *a.* Reflexible.
re-flex'iv[P&S], *a.* & *n.* Reflexive.
re-flex'iv-ly[S], *adv.* Reflexively.
re-flex'iv-ness[S], *n.* Reflexiveness.
re-form'a-bl[P], *a.* Reformable.
re-form'a-tiv[P&S], *a.* Reformative.
re-formd'[P&S], *pa.* Reformed.
re-fract'a-bl[P], *a.* Refractable.
re-frac'tiv[S], *a.* Refractive.
re-frac'tiv-ness[S], *n.* Refractiveness.
re-fraind'[S], *pp.* Refrained.
re-fran'gi-bl[P], *a.* Refrangible.
re-fran'gi-bl-ness[P], *n.* Refrangibleness.
re-fresht'[P&S], *pp.* Refreshed.
re-frig'er-a"tiv[S], *a.* & *n.* Refrigerative.
re-fut'a-bl[P], *a.* Refutable.
re-fut'a-tiv[S], *a.* Refutative.
re-fuz'a-bl[P], *a.* Refusable.
re-fuz'al[P], *n.* Refusal.
re-fuze'[P], *vt.* & *vi.* Refuse.
re-gain'a-bl[P], *a.* Regainable.
re-gaind'[S], *pp.* Regained.
re-gard'a-bl[P], *a.* Regardable.
re-gen'er-a-bl[P], *a.* Regenerable.
re-gen'er-a"tiv[S], *a.* Regenerative.
re-gen'er-a"tiv-ly[S], *adv.* Regeneratively.
reg'is-ter-a-bl[P], *a.* Registerable.
reg'is-terd[S], *pp.* Registered.
reg'is-tra-bl[P], *a.* Registrable.
reg'na-tiv[S], *a.* Regnative.
re-gres'siv[P&S], *a.* Regressive.
re-gres'siv-ly[S], *adv.* Regressively.
re-gres'siv-ness[S], *n.* Regressiveness.
re-gret'ta-bl[P], *a.* Regrettable.
reg'u-la-bl[P], *a.* Regulable.
reg'u-lat"a-bl[P], *a.* Regulatable.
reg'u-la"tiv[S], *a.* Regulative.
reg'u-la"tiv-ly[S], *adv.* Regulatively.
reg'u-lin[S], *a.* & *n.* Reguline.
re-herse'[P], *vt.* & *vi.* Rehearse.
re-herst'[P], *pp.* Rehearsed.
reignd[S], *pp.* Reigned.
re"im-burs'a-bl[P], *a.* Reimbursable.
re"im-burst'[S], *pp.* Reimbursed.
rein[S], *v.* & *n.* Reign.
reind[P&S], *pp.* Reined.
re-it'er-a"tiv[S], *a.* & *n.* Reiterative.
re-it'er-a"tiv-ly, *adv.* Reiteratively.
re-ject'a-bl[P], *a.* Rejectable.
re-ject'a-bl-ness[P], *n.* Rejectableness.
re-ject'iv[S], *a.* Rejective.
re-joind'[P&S], *pp.* Rejoined.
re-laps'[P], *v.* & *n.* Relapse.
re-laps'a-bl[P], *a.* Relapsable.
re-lapst'[P&S], *pp.* Relapsed.
re-lat'a-bl[P], *a.* Relatable.
rel'a-tiv[P&S], *a.* & *n.* Relative.
rel'a-tiv-ness[S], *n.* Relativeness.
re-lax'a-bl[P], *a.* Relaxable.
re-lax'a-tiv[S], *a.* & *n.* Relaxative.
re-laxt'[P&S], *pp.* Relaxed.
re-layd'[S], *pp.* Relayed.
re-leas'a-bl[P], *a.* Releasable.

re-least′[P&S], *pp.* Released.
rel′e-ga-bl[P], *a.* Relegable.
re-li′a-bl[P], *a.* Reliable.
re-li′a-bl-ness[P], *n.* Reliableness.
re-liev′[P], *vt.* Relieve.
re-liev′a-bl[P], *a.* Relievable.
re-lievd′[P&S], *pp.* Relieved.
re-lin′quisht[P&S], *pp.* Relinquished.
rel′ish-a-bl[P], *a.* Relishable.
rel′isht[P&S], *pp.* Relished.
relm[P&S], *n.* Realm.
re-maind′[P&S], *pp.* Remained.
re-mark′a-bl[P], *a.* Remarkable.
re-mark′a-bl-ness[P], *n.* Remarkableness.
re-markt′[P&S], *pa.* Remarked.
re-mem′ber-a-bl[P], *a.* Rememberable.
re-mem′berd[P&S], *pp.* Remembered.
re-mis′si-bl[P], *a.* Remissible.
re-mis′siv[S], *a.* Remissive.
re-mit′ta-bl[P], *a.* Remittable.
re-mon′stra-tiv-ly[S], *adv.* Remonstratively.
re-mov′a-bl[P], *a.* & *n.* Removable.
re-mov′a-bl-ness[P], *n.* Removableness.
re-mu′ner-a″tiv[P&S], *a.* Remunerative.
ren[S], *n.* Wren.
ren′ard-in[S], *a.* Renardine.
re-nas′ci-bl[P], *a.* Renascible.
rench[S], *v.* & *n.* Wrench.
ren′der-a-bl[P], *a.* Renderable.
ren′derd[P&S], *pp.* Rendered.
rend′i-bl[P], *a.* Rendible.
re-new′a-bl[P], *a.* Renewable.
re-newd′[S], *pp.* Renewed.
re-nounce′a-bl[P], *a.* Renounceable.
re-nounst′[S], *pp.* Renounced.
ren′o-va″tiv[S], *a.* Renovative.
re-nownd′[P&S], *a.* Renowned.
rent′a-bl[P], *a.* Rentable.
re-nun′ci-a″tiv[S], *a.* Renunciative.
re-pair′a-bl[P], *a.* Repairable.
re-paird′[P&S], *pp.* Repaired.
rep′a-ra-bl[P], *a.* Reparable.
re-par′a-tiv[P&S], *a.* Reparative.
re-pass′a-bl[P], *a.* Repassable.
re-pay′a-bl[P], *a.* Repayable.
re-peal′a-bl[P], *a.* Repealable.
re-peal′a-bl-ness[P], *n.* Repealableness.
re-peald′[S], *pp.* Repealed.
re-peat′a-bl[P], *a.* Repeatable.
re-peld′[P&S], *pp.* Repelled.
re″per-cus′siv[S], *a.* & *n.* Repercussive.
re″per-cus′siv-ly[S], *a.* Repercussively.
re″per-cus′siv-ness[S], *n.* Repercussiveness.
re-pet′i-tiv[S], *a.* Repetitive.
re-pet′i-tiv-ness[S], *n.* Repetitiveness.
re-place′a-bl[P], *a.* Replaceable.
re-plant′a-bl[P], *a.* Replantable.
re-plen′isht[P&S], *pp.* Replenished.
re-ple′tiv[S], *a.* Repletive.
re-ple′tiv-ly[S], *adv.* Repletively.
re-plev′ind[S], *pp.* Replevined.
re-plev′i-a-bl[P], *a.* Repleviable.
re-plev′is-a-bl[P], *a.* Replevisable.
rep′li-ca″til[S], *a.* Replicatile.
rep′li-ca″tiv[S], *a.* Replicative.
rep′li-ca″tiv-ly[S], *adv.* Replicatively.
re-port′a-bl[P], *a.* Reportable.
rep″re-hen′si-bl[P], *a.* Reprehensible.
rep″re-hen′si-bl-ness[P], *n.* Reprehensibleness.
rep″re-hen′siv[S], *a.* Reprehensive.
rep″re-hen′siv-ly[S], *adv.* Reprehensively.
rep″re-sent′a-bl[P], *a.* Representable.
rep″re-sen′ta-tiv[P&S], *a.* & *n.* Representative.
rep″re-sen′ta-tiv-ly[S], *adv.* Representatively.
rep″re-sen′ta-tiv-ness[S], *n.* Representativeness.
re-pres′siv[S], *a.* Repressive.

re-pres′siv-ness[S], *n.* Repressiveness.
re-prest′[P&S], *pp.* Repressed.
re-priev′[P], *v.* & *n.* Reprieve.
re-prievd′[P&S], *pp.* Reprieved.
re-proach′a-bl[P], *a.* Reproachable.
re-proach′a-bl-ness[P], *n.* Reproachableness.
re-proacht′[P&S], *pp.* Reproached.
rep′ro-ba″tiv[S], *a.* Reprobative.
rep′ro-ba″tiv-ly[S], *adv.* Reprobatively.
re″pro-duc′i-bl[P], **re″pro-duce′a-bl**[P], *a.* Reproducible, reproduceable.
re″pro-duc′tiv[P&S], *a.* Reproductive.
re″pro-duc′tiv-ly[S], *adv.* Reproductively.
re″pro-duc′tiv-ness[S], *n.* Reproductiveness.
re-prov′a-bl[P], *a.* Reprovable.
rep′til[P&S], **-tile**[S], *n.* Reptile.
re-pub′lisht[P&S], *pp.* Republished.
re-pu′di-a-bl[P], *a.* Repudiable.
re-pu′di-a″tiv[S], *a.* Repudiative.
re-pul′lu-la″tiv[S], *a.* Repullulative.
re-pul′siv[P&S], *a.* Repulsive.
re-pulst′[S], *pp.* Repulsed.
rep′u-ta-bl[P], *a.* Reputable.
rep′u-ta-bl-ness[P], *n.* Reputableness.
re-pu′ta-tiv[S], *a.* Reputative.
re-pu′ta-tiv-ly[S], *adv.* Reputatively.
re-quir′a-bl[P], *a.* Requirable.
req′ui-sit[P&S], *a.* & *n.* Requisite.
req′ui-sit-ness[S], *n.* Requisiteness.
req″ui-si′tiond[S], *pp.* Requisitioned.
re-quit′a-bl[P], *a.* Requitable.
re-scind′a-bl[P], *a.* Rescindable.
re-scis′si-bl[P], *a.* Rescissible.
re-scrip′tiv[S], *a.* Rescriptive.
re-scrip′tiv-ly[S], *adv.* Rescriptively.
res′cu-a-bl[P], *a.* Rescuable.
re-sem′bl[P], *vt.* & *vi.* Resemble.
re-sem′bld[P], *pp.* Resembled.
re-serv′[P&S], *v.* & *n.* Reserve.
re-serv′a-bl[P], *a.* Reservable.
re-ser′va-tiv[S], *a.* Reservative.
re-servd′[P&S], *pp.* & *pa.* Reserved.
re-set′ta-bl[P], *a.* Resettable.
re-signd′[S], *pa.* Resigned.
res′i-nus[S], *a.* Resinous.
re-sist′i-bl[P], *a.* Resistible.
re-sist′i-bl-ness[P], *n.* Resistibleness.
re-sis′tiv[S], *a.* Resistive.
re-sis′tiv-ness[S], *n.* Resistiveness.
res′o-lu-bl[P], *a.* Resoluble.
res′o-lu-bl-ness[P], *n.* Resolubleness.
res′o-lu″tiv[S], *a.* & *n.* Resolutive.
re-solv′[P&S], *v.* & *n.* Resolve.
re-solv′a-bl[P], *a.* Resolvable.
re-solv′a-bl-ness[P], *n.* Resolvableness.
re-solvd′[P&S], *pp.* & *pa.* Resolved.
re-sorp′tiv[S], *a.* Resorptive.
re-spect′a-bl[P], *a.* & *n.* Respectable.
re-spect′a-bl-ness[P], *n.* Respectableness.
re-spec′tiv[P&S], *a.* Respective.
re-spec′tiv-ly[S], *adv.* Respectively.
re-sper′siv[S], *a.* Respersive.
re-spir′a-bl[P], *a.* Respirable.
re-spir′a-bl-ness[P], *n.* Respirableness.
re-spir′a-tiv[S], *a.* Respirative.
res′pit[P&S], **-ite**[S], *v.* & *n.* Respite.
re-spon′si-bl[P], *a.* & *n.* Responsible.
re-spon′si-bl-ness[P], *n.* Responsibleness.
re-spon′siv[P&S], *a.* Responsive.
re-spon′siv-ly[S], *adv.* Responsively.
re-spon′siv-ness[S], *n.* Responsiveness.
rest[S], *v.* & *n.* Wrest.
res′ti-tu″tiv[S], *a.* Restitutive.
res′tiv[P&S], *a.* Restive.
res′tiv-ly[S], *adv.* Restively.
res′tiv-ness[S], *n.* Restiveness.
res′tle[S], *v.* & *n.* Wrestle.
re-stor′a-bl[P], *a.* Restorable.
re-stor′a-tiv[S], *a.* & *n.* Restorative.
re-stor′a-tiv-ly[S], *adv.* Restoratively.
re-strain′a-bl[P], *a.* Restrainable.
re-straind′[P&S], *pp.* Restrained.

re-stric'tiv[P&S], *a.* Restrictive.
re-stric'tiv-ly[S], *adv.* Restrictively.
re-stric'tiv-ness[S], *n.* Restrictiveness.
re-sum'a-bl[P], *a.* Resumable.
re-sump'tiv[S], *a.* Resumptive.
re-sump'tiv-ly[S], *adv.* Resumptively.
res″ur-rec'tiv[S], *a.* Resurrective.
re-sus'ci-ta″tiv[S], *a.* Resuscitative.
re-ta'bl[P], *n.* Retable.
re-taild'[P&S], *pp.* Retailed.
re-tain'a-bl[P], *a.* Retainable.
re-tain'a-bl-ness[P], *n.* Retainableness.
re-taind'[P&S], *pp.* Retained.
re-tal'i-a″tiv[P&S], *a.* Retaliative.
re-tard'a-tiv[S], *a.* Retardative.
retch[S], *n.* Wretch.
retch'ed[S], *a.* Wretched.
retcht[S], *pp.* Retched.
re-ten'tiv[P&S], *a.* Retentive.
re-ten'tiv-ly[S], *adv.* Retentively.
re-ten'tiv-ness[S], *n.* Retentiveness.
ret'o-ric[S], *n.* Rhetoric.
re-tor'tiv[S], *a.* Retortive.
re-toucht'[S], *pp.* Retouched.
re-trace'a-bl[P], *a.* Retraceable.
re-tract'a-bl[P], **re-tract'i-bl**[P], *a.* Retractable, retractible.
re-trac'til[P&S], **-ile**[S], *a.* Retractile.
re-trac'tiv[S], *a.* Retractive.
re-trac'tiv-ly[S], *adv.* Retractively.
re-trac'tiv-ness[S], *n.* Retractiveness.
re-trencht'[P&S], *pp.* Retrenched.
re-trib'u-tiv[P&S], *a.* Retributive.
re-trib'u-tiv-ly[S], *adv.* Retributively.
re-triev'[P], *vt.* & *vi.* Retrieve.
re-triev'a-bl[P], *a.* Retrievable.
re-triev'a-bl-ness[P], *n.* Retrievableness.
re-trievd'[P&S], *pp.* Retrieved.
re″tro-ac'tiv[S], *a.* Retroactive.
re″tro-ac'tiv-ly[S], *adv.* Retroactively.
re″tro-ces'siv[S], *a.* Retrocessive.
re″tro-gen'er-a-tiv[S], *a.* Retrogenerative.
re″tro-gres'siv[S], *a.* Retrogressive.
re″tro-gres'siv-ly[S], *adv.* Retrogressively.
re″tro-pul'siv[S], *a.* Retropulsive.
ret″ro-spec'tiv[P&S], *a.* Retrospective.
re″tro-ten'siv[S], *a.* Retrotensive.
re″tro-ten'siv-ly[S], *adv.* Retrotensively.
re″tro-vac'cin[S], *n.* Retrovaccine.
re-tuch'[P], *vt.* Retouch.
re-tucht'[P], *pp.* Retouched.
re-turn'a-bl[P], *a.* Returnable.
re-turnd'[P&S], *pp.* Returned.
reum[S], *n.* Rheum.
reu'ma-tism[S], *n.* Rheumatism.
re″u-nit'a-bl[P], *a.* Reunitable.
re-vampt'[S], *pp.* Revamped.
re-veal'a-bl[P], *a.* Revealable.
re-veal'a-bl-ness[P], *n.* Revealableness.
re-veald'[S], *pa.* Revealed.
rev'eld[P&S], *pp.* Reveled, revelled.
rev'e-la″tiv[S], *a.* Revelative.
rev'el-ing[P], *n.* Revelling.
re-venge'a-bl[P], *a.* Revengeable.
re-ver'a-bl[P], *a.* Reverable.
re-ver'ber-a-tiv[S], *a.* Reverberative.
re-ver'sa-til[S], *a.* Reversatile.
re-vers'i-bl[P], **re-vers'a-bl**[P], *a.* & *n.* Reversible, reversable.
re-vers'i-bl-ness[P], *n.* Reversibleness.
re-ver'sion-a-bl[P], *a.* Reversionable.
re-ver'siv[S], *a.* Reversive.
re-verst'[P&S], *pa.* Reversed.
re-vert'i-bl[P], *a.* Revertible.
re-ver'tiv-ly[S], *adv.* Revertively.
re-view'a-bl[P], *a.* Reviewable.
re-viewd'[P&S], *pp.* Reviewed.
re-vis'a-bl[P], **re-vis'i-bl**[P], *a.* Revisable, revisible.
re-viv'a-bl[P], *a.* Revivable.
re″vi-vis'ci-bl[P], *a.* Reviviscible.
re-vize'[P], *v.* & *n.* Revise.
rev'o-ca-bl[P], **rev'o-ka-bl**[P], *a.* Revocable, revokable.

rev′o-ca″tiv[s], *a.* Revocative.
rev′o-lu-bl[p], *a.* Revoluble.
rev″o-lu′tiv[s], *a.* Revolutive.
re-volv′[p&s], *vt.* & *vi.* Revolve.
re-volv′a-bl[p], *a.* Revolvable.
re-volvd′[p&s], *pp.* Revolved.
re-vul′siv[p&s], *a.* & *n.* Revulsive.
re-vul′siv-ly[s], *adv.* Revulsively.
re-ward′a-bl[p], *a.* Rewardable.
re-ward′a-bl-ness[p], *n.* Rewardableness.
Rhad″a-man′thin[s], **-tin**[s], *a.* Rhadamanthine, Rhadamantin.
rhi-noc′e-rin[s], *a.* Rhinocerine.
rhi-noc″e-ron′tin[s], *a.* Rhinocerontine.
rhi-nol′o-phin[s], *a.* & *n.* Rhinolophine.
rhi″no-po′ma-tin[s], *a.* Rhinopomatine.
rhyn′cho-pin[s], *a.* & *n.* Rhynchopine.
rhyth-miz′a-bl[p], *a.* Rhythmizable.
rib′bond[s], *pp.* Ribboned.
ribd[s], *pp.* & *pa.* Ribbed.
rid′a-bl[p], **ride′a-bl**[p], *a.* Ridable, rideable.
ri-dic′u-lus[s], *a.* Ridiculous.
rid′l[p], *v.* & *n.* Riddle.
rid′ld[p], *pp.* Riddled.
rid′n[p], *pp.* Ridden.
rif′raf″[p], *n.* Riffraff.
rigd[p&s], *pp.* & *pa.* Rigged.
rig′gle[s], *v.* & *n.* Wriggle.
right[s], *n.* Wright.
right′a-bl[p], *a.* Rightable.
rig′or[p&s], *n.* Rigor, rigour.
rig′or-us[s], *a.* Rigorous.
ril[p&s], *v.* & *n.* Rill.
rild[s], *pp.* Rilled.
rime[p&s], *v.* & *n.* Rhyme.
rim′er[p&s], *n.* Rhymer.
rim′pl[p], *v.* & *n.* Rimple.
ring[s], *vt.* & *vi.* Wring.
ring′a-bl[p], *a.* Ringable.
ringd[s], *pa.* Ringed.
rin′kle[s], *v.* & *n.* Wrinkle.
ri-noc′e-ros[s], *n.* Rhinoceros.
rinst[p&s], *pp.* Rinsed.
rip′end[p&s], *pp.* Ripened.
rip′l[p], *v.* & *n.* Ripple.
rip′ld[p], *pp.* Rippled.
ript[s], *pp.* Ripped.
ris′i-bl[p], *a.* Risible.
ris′i-bl-ness[p], *n.* Risibleness.
riskt[p&s], *pp.* Risked.
rist[s], *n.* Wrist.
rite[s], *v.* & *n.* Write.
rit′er[s], *n.* Writer.
rithe[s], *vt.* & *vi.* Writhe.
rit′ing[s], *n.* Writing.
rit′ten[s], *pp.* Written.
ri′vald[p&s], *pp.* Rivaled, rivalled.
riv′er-in[s], *a.* Riverine.
riv′et-ed[p], *pp.* Rivetted.
riv′n[p], *pa.* Riven.
rize[p], *vt.* & *vi.* Rise.
riz′n[p], *pp.* Risen.
ri′zome[s], *n.* Rhizome.
ro[s], *n.* Roe.
ro[s], *v.* & *n.* Row.
roamd[s], *pp.* Roamed.
roard[p&s], *pp.* Roared.
robd[p&s], *pp.* Robbed.
rockt[p&s], *pp.* Rocked.
ro″do-den′dron[s], *n.* Rhododendron.
roed[s], *a.* Rowed.
roes[s], 3rd per. sing. pres. ind. Rows.
roild[p&s], *pp.* Roiled.
roist′erd[s], *pp.* Roistered.
rold[p&s], *pp.* Rolled.
rol′lu-lin[s], *a.* & *n.* Rolluline.
rom′boid[s], *a.* & *n.* Rhomboid.
rom′bus[s], *n.* Rhombus.
rompt[p&s], *pp.* Romped.
rong[s], *v.*, *a.*, *n.* & *adv.* Wrong.
rooft[p&s], *pp.* Roofed.
roomd[p&s], *a.* Roomed.
rop′a-bl[p], **rope′a-bl**[p], *a.* Ropable, ropeable.

ros'ind[s], *pa.* Rosined.
ro'tat-a-bl[p], *a.* Rotatable
ro'ta-tiv[s], *a.* Rotative.
ro'ta-tiv-ly[s], *adv.* Rotatively.
roth[s], *a.* Wroth.
rot'n[p], *a.* Rotten.
rought[s], *imp.* & *pp.* Wrought.
rout'a-bl[p], *a.* Routable.
rowd[p&s], *pp.* & *a.* Rowed.
roze[p], *imp.* Rose.
ru[s], *v.* & *n.* Rue.
ru'barb[s], *n.* Rhubarb.
rub'berd[s], *pp.* Rubbered.
rubd[s], *pp.* Rubbed.
rud'doc[s], *n.* Ruddock.
Ru-dolph'in[s], *a.* Rudolphine.
ruf[p&s], *v., a.* & *n.* Rough.
ruf[p&s], *v.* & *n.* Ruff.
ruf'en[p], *vt.* & *vi.* Roughen.
ruf'end[p], *pp.* Roughened.
ruf'en-ing[p], *pres. p.* Roughening.
ruff'en[s], *vt.* & *vi.* Roughen.
ruf'fer[s], *a.* & *n.* Rougher.
ruf'l[p], *v.* & *n.* Ruffle.
ruf'ld[p], *a.* Ruffled.
ruft[p&s], *a.* Ruffed.
ru'in-a-bl[p], *a.* Ruinable.
ru'ind[s], *pp.* Ruined.
rul'a-bl[p], *a.* Rulable.
rul'loc[s], *n.* Rullock.
rum'bl[p], *v.* & *n.* Rumble.
rum'bld[p], *pp.* Rumbled.
ru'mi-na"tiv[s], *a.* Ruminative.
ru'mi-na"tiv-ly[s], *adv.* Ruminatively.
ru'mor[s], *v.* & *n.* Rumor, rumour.
ru'mord[s], *pp.* Rumored.
run'dl[p], *n.* Rundle.
rung[s], *imp.* & *pp.* Wrung.
run'na-bl[p], *a.* Runnable.
ru-pes'trin[s], *a.* Rupestrine.
ru"pi-cap'rin[s], *a.* Rupicaprine.
ru-pic'o-lin[s], *a.* Rupicoline.
rup'til[s], *a.* Ruptile.
rup'tiv[s], *a.* Ruptive.
rup'tur-a-bl[p], *a.* Rupturable.
rusht[p&s], *pp.* Rushed.
ru'sin[s], *a.* Rusine.
rus'tl[p], *v.* & *n.* Rustle.
rus'tld[p], *pp.* Rustled.
rythm[s], *n.* Rhythm.

S

sa'ber[p&s], *v.* & *n.* Sabre.
sa'berd[p&s], *pp.* Sabered.
sab'u-lin[s], *a.* Sabuline.
sac'ca-rin[s], *a.* & *n.* Saccharin, saccharine.
sackt[p&s], *pp.* Sacked.
sad'dend[p&s], *pp.* Saddened.
sad'l[p], *v.* & *n.* Saddle.
sad'ld[p], *pp.* & *a.* Saddled.
safe'gard"[s], *v.* & *n.* Safeguard.
saf'fire[p], *n.* Sapphire.
sagd[p&s], *pp.* Sagged.
sag-mat'o-rhin[s], *a.* Sagmatorhine.
sag'van-dit[s], *n.* Sagvandite.
sai'gin[s], *a.* & *n.* Saigine.
sail'a-bl[p], *a.* Sailable.
saild[p&s], *a.* Sailed.
sal'a-bl[p], **sale'a-bl**[p], *a.* Salable, saleable.
sal'a-bl-ness[p], *n.* Salableness.
sal"a-man'drin[s], *a.* & *n.* Salamandrine.
sal'an-gin[s], *n.* Salangine.
sal'i-fi"a-bl[p], *a.* Salifiable.
sal'lo[s], *a.* & *n.* Sallow.
sal'lowd[s], *pp.* Sallowed.
sal-pin"go-staph'y-lin[s], *a.* Salpingostaphyline.
salt"pe'ter[p&s], *n.* Saltpetre.
salv[p&s], *v.* & *n.* Salve.
sal'va-bl[p], *a.* Salvable.
sal'va-bl-ness[p], *n.* Salvableness.

salvd[P&S], *pp.* Salved.
sal've-lin[S], *a.* Salveline.
sam'fire[P], *n.* Samphire.
san'a-bl[P], *a.* Sanable.
san'a-bl-ness[P], *n.* Sanableness.
san'a-tiv[P&S], *a.* Sanative.
sanc'ti-fi"a-bl[P], *a.* Sanctifiable.
sanc'ti-fi"a-bl-ness[P], *n.* Sanctifiableness.
sanc'tion-a-bl[P], *a.* Sanctionable.
sanc'tion-a-tiv[S], *a.* Sanctionative.
sanc'tiond[S], *pp.* Sanctioned.
san'dald[P&S], *a.* Sandaled.
san'guin[P&S], *a.* & *n.* Sanguine.
san'guin-less[P&S], *a.* Sanguineless.
san'guin-ly[P&S], *adv.* Sanguinely.
san'i-din[S], *n.* Sanidine.
sans"cu-lot'tid[S], *n.* Sansculottide.
san'ta-lin[S], *a.* Santaline.
sa-pon'i-fi"a-bl[P], *a.* Saponifiable.
sap'phir-in[S], *a.* & *n.* Sapphirine.
sapt[S], *pp.* Sapped.
sar-cof'a-gus[S], *n.* Sarcophagus.
sar'co-lin[S], *a.* Sarcoline.
sar-din'[P], **-ine'**[P], *n.* Sardine.
sasht[P&S], *pp.* Sashed.
sa'ti-a-bl[P], *a.* Satiable.
sa'ti-a-bl-ness[P], *n.* Satiableness
sat'is-fi"a-bl[P], *a.* Satisfiable.
sat'u-ra-bl[P], *a.* Saturable.
sat'u-ra-tiv[S], *a.* Saturative.
sat'ur-nin[S], *a.* Saturnine.
sat'ur-nin-ly[S], *adv.* Saturninely.
saun'terd[P&S], *pp.* Sauntered.
sau"ro-the'rin[S], *a.* Saurotherine.
sav'a-bl[P], **save'a-bl**[P], *a.* Savable, saveable.
sav'a-bl-ness[P], *n.* Savableness.
sav'i-or[P&S], *n.* Saviour.
sa'vor[P&S], *v.* & *n.* Savour.
sa'vord[P&S], *pp.* Savored, savoured.
sawd[S], *pp.* Sawed.
sax'a-til[S], **-ile**[S], *a.* Saxatile.
sax-ic'o-lin[S], *a.* Saxicoline.
say'a-bl[P], *a.* Sayable.
scabd[S], *a.* Scabbed.
scal'a-bl[P], **scale'a-bl**[P], *a.* Scalable, scaleable.
scald[S], *a.* Scalled.
scal'lopt[S], *pa.* Scalloped.
scalpt[P&S], *pp.* Scalped.
scamp'erd[S], *pp.* Scampered.
scampt[S], *pp.* Scamped.
scand[P&S], *pp.* Scanned.
scard[P&S], *pp.* Scarred.
scarft[P&S], *pp.* Scarfed.
scarpt[S], *pa.* Scarped.
scarse[P], *a.* & *adv.* Scarce.
scar'si-ty[P], *n.* Scarcity.
scat'terd[P&S], *pa.* Scattered.
scep'ter[P&S], *v.* & *n.* Sceptre.
scep'terd[P&S], *pp.* Sceptered.
schiz"o-ne-mer'tin[S], *a.* & *n.* Schizonemertine.
school'a-bl[P], *a.* Schoolable.
schoold[S], *pp.* Schooled.
scis'sil[P&S], **-ile**[S], *a.* Scissile.
scis'sors. See CISSORS.
sci'u-rin[S], *a.* & *n.* Sciurine.
scle-ru'rin[S], *a.* & *n.* Sclerurine.
scof[P], *v.* & *n.* Scoff.
scoft[P&S], *pp.* Scoffed.
scol'ar[P&S], *n.* Scholar.
sco-las'tic[P&S], *a.* & *n.* Scholastic.
sco'li-um[S], *n.* Scholium.
scom"ber-es'o-cin[S], *a.* & *n.* Scomberesocine.
sconse[P], *v.* & *n.* Sconce.
scool[P&S], *v.* & *n.* School.
scoon'er[P], *n.* Schooner.
scoopt[P&S], *pp.* Scooped.
scorcht[S], *pa.* Scorched.
scornd[P&S], *pp.* Scorned.
scotcht[S], *pp.* Scotched.
scourd[P&S], *pp.* Scoured.
scowld[S], *pp.* Scowled.
scrab'l[P], *v.* & *n.* Scrabble.
scrach[P], *v.*, *a.* & *n.* Scratch.

scracht[P], *pp.* Scratched.
scram'bl[P], *v. & n.* Scramble.
scram'bld[P], *pp.* Scrambled.
scrapt[S], *pp.* Scrapped.
scratcht[S], *pp.* Scratched.
scrawld[P&S], *pp.* Scrawled.
screakt[S], *pp.* Screaked.
screamd[P&S], *pp.* Screamed.
screecht[P&S], *pp.* Screeched.
screend[P&S], *pp.* Screened.
screwd[P&S], *pa.* Screwed.
scrib'bla-tiv[S], *a.* Scribblative.
scrib'l[P], *v. & n.* Scribble.
scrib'ld[P], *pp.* Scribbled.
scrimpt[S], *pp.* Scrimped.
scrold[S], *a.* Scrolled.
scru[S], *v. & n.* Screw.
scrubd[P&S], *pp.* Scrubbed.
scru'ta-bl[P], *a.* Scrutable.
scuf'l[P], *v. & n.* Scuffle.
scuf'ld[P], *pp.* Scuffled.
scuft[S], *pp.* Scuffed.
scul[P], *v. & n.* Scull.
sculd[P&S], *pp.* Sculled.
sculpt, *pp.* Sculped.
sculp'til, -ile[S], *a.* Sculptile.
scum'bl[P], *v. & n.* Scumble.
scum'bld[P], *pp.* Scumbled.
scumd[P&S], *pp.* Scummed.
scund[S], *pp.* Scunned.
scurge[P], *v. & n.* Scourge.
scurged[P], *pp.* Scourged.
scur'ril[P&S], *a.* Scurrile.
scutcht[S], *pp.* Scutched.
scu'tel-lin[S], *a.* Scutelline.
scut'l[P], *v. & n.* Scuttle.
scut'ld[P], *pp.* Scuttled.
scyt'a-lin[S], *a.* Scytaline.
seald[P&S], *pp.* Sealed.
seamd[P&S], *pp.* Seamed.
seard[P&S], *pp.* Seared.
sea'son-a-bl[P], *a.* Seasonable.
sea'sond[S], *pp.* Seasoned.
se-clu'siv[P&S], *a.* Seclusive.
se-cre'tiv[P&S], *a.* Secretive.
se-cre'tiv-ly[S], *adv.* Secretively.
se-cre'tiv-ness[S], *n.* Secretiveness.
sec'til, -ile[S], *a.* Sectile.
sec'tiv[S], *a.* Sective.
sec'un-din[S], **sec'on-din**[S], *n.* Secundine, secondine.
se-cur'a-bl[P], *a.* Securable.
sed'a-tiv[P&S], *a. & n.* Sedative.
se-duc'i-bl[P], **se-duce'a-bl**[P], *a.* Seducible, seduceable.
se-du'civ[S], *a.* Seducive.
se-duc'tiv[P&S], *a.* Seductive.
se-duc'tiv-ly[S], *adv.* Seductively.
se-duc'tiv-ness[S], *n.* Seductiveness.
see'a-bl[P], *a. & n.* Seeable.
seek'a-bl[P], *a.* Seekable.
seemd[P&S], *pp.* Seemed.
seept[S], *pp.* Seeped.
see'sawd"[P&S], *pp.* Seesawed.
seethd[S], *pp.* Seethed.
seg're-ga-bl[P], *a.* Segregable.
seg're-ga"tiv[S], *a.* Segregative.
seind[S], *pp.* Seined.
sei-u'rin[S], *a.* Seiurine.
seiz[P], *vt. & vi.* Seize.
seiz'a-bl[P], *a.* Seizable.
seizd[P&S], *pp.* Seized.
sel[P&S], *vt. & vi.* Sell.
se-lect'a-bl[P], *a.* Selectable.
se-lec'tiv[S], *a.* Selective.
se-lec'tiv-ly[S], *adv.* Selectively.
self"=ac'tiv[S], *a.* Self=active.
self"=ad-just'a-bl[P], *a.* Self=adjustable.
self"=as-ser'tiv[S], *a.* Self=assertive.
self"=as-ser'tiv-ness[S], *n.* Self=assertiveness.
self"=de-fen'siv[S], *a.* Self=defensive.
self"=ef-fa'civ[S], *a.* Self=effacive.
self"=e-lec'tiv[S], *a.* Self=elective.
self"=in-duc'tiv[S], *a.* Self=inductive.
self"=lu'mi-nus[S], *a.* Self=luminous.
self"=pre-ser'va-tiv[S], *a.* Self=preservative.

self″=re-pul′siv[S], *a.* Self=repulsive.
sell′a-bl[P], *a.* Sellable.
selvs[P&S], *n. pl.* Selves.
sem′bla-bl[P], *a.* Semblable.
se′men-cin[S], *n.* Semencine.
sem″in-va′ri-an-tiv[S], *a.* Seminvariantive.
sem″i-per′me-a-bl[P], *a.* Semipermeable.
sem″i-pis′cin[S], *a.* Semipiscine.
sem″i-port′a-bl[P], *a.* Semiportable.
sem″no-pith′e-cin[S], *a.* & *n.* Semnopithecine.
se′nil[P&S], **-ile**[P&S], *a.* Senile.
sen′si-bl[P], *a.* & *n.* Sensible.
sen′sil[P&S], **-ile**[P&S], *a.* Sensile.
sen′si-tiv[P&S], *a.* & *n.* Sensitive.
sen′si-tiv-ly[S], *adv.* Sensitively.
sen′si-tiv-ness[S], *n.* Sensitiveness.
sen″so-ri-di-ges′tiv[S], *a.* Sensoridigestive.
senst[P&S], *pp.* Sensed.
sent[P&S], *v.* & *n.* Scent.
sent′ed[S], *pp.* Scented.
sen′ti-neld[S], *pp.* Sentineled, sentinelled.
sep′a-lin[S], *a.* Sepaline.
sep′a-ra-bl[P], *a.* Separable.
sep′a-ra-bl-ness[P], *n.* Separableness.
sep′a-ra″tiv[P&S], *a.* Separative.
sep-tet′[S], *n.* Septette.
sep′ul-cher[P&S], *v.* & *n.* Sepulchre.
sep′ul-cherd[P&S], *pp.* Sepulchered, sepulchred.
se-ques′terd[P&S], *pa.* Sequestered.
se-ques′tra-bl[P], *a.* Sequestrable.
ser′af[P], *n.* Seraph.
se-raf′ic[P], *a.* Seraphic.
ser′a-fim[P], *n.* Seraphim.
serch[P], *v.* & *n.* Search.
serch′a-bl[P], *a.* Searchable.
serch′a-bl-ness[P], *n.* Searchableness.
sercht[P], *a.* Searched.
se′rin[S], *n.* Serine.
se′ri-us[S], *a.* Serious.
ser′o-tin[S], *n.* Serotine.
ser′pen-tiv[P&S], *a.* Serpentive.
ser′pu-lin[S], *a.* Serpuline.
ser″ra-sal′mo-nin[S], *a.* & *n.* Serrasalmonine.
serv[P&S], *vt.* & *vi.* Serve.
serv′a-bl[P], *a.* Servable.
ser′val-in[S], *a.* Servaline.
servd[P&S], *pp.* Served.
ser′vice-a-bl[P], *a.* Serviceable.
ser′vice-a-bl-ness[P], *n.* Serviceableness.
ser′vil[P&S], **-ile**[P&S], *a.* & *n.* Servile.
ser′vil-ly[S], *adv.* Servilely.
ser′vil-ness[S], *n.* Servileness.
ser′vis[S], *n.* Service.
ses′a-min[S], *a.* Sesamine.
ses′i-in[S], *a.* & *n.* Sesiine.
ses′sil[P&S], **-ile**[P&S], *a.* Sessile.
set[S], *n.* Sett.
se-ta′ceus[S], *a.* Setaceous.
se-ta′ceus-ly[S], *adv.* Setaceously.
se-tif′er-us[S], *a.* Setiferous.
se-tig′er-us[S], *a.* Setigerous.
set′l[P], *v.* & *n.* Settle.
set′ld[P], *pa.* Settled.
set′l-ment[P], *n.* Settlement.
se-toph′a-gin[S], *a.* Setophagine.
set′ta-bl[P], *a.* Settable.
sev′er-a-bl[P], *a.* Severable.
sev′erd[S], *pp.* Severed.
sewd[P&S], *pp.* Sewed.
sew′erd[S], *pp.* Sewered.
sex′i-syl″la-bl[P], *n.* Sexisyllable.
sex-tet′[S], *n.* Sextette.
sex′til[P], *a.* & *n.* Sextile.
sfe′noid[P&S], *a.* & *n.* Sphenoid.
sfere[P&S], *v.* & *n.* Sphere.
sfer′ic[P&S], *a.* Spheric.
sfer′i-cal[P&S], *a.* Spherical.
sfer′ics[P&S], *n.* Spherics.
sfe′roid[P&S], *n.* Spheroid.
sfer′ule[P&S], *n.* Spherule.

sfinx[P&S], *n.* Sphinx.
shack″l[P], *v.* & *n.* Shackle.
shack′ld[P], *pp.* Shackled.
shad″owd[P&S], *pp.* Shadowed.
shad″ow-graf[P&S], *n.* Shadowgraph.
shad″ow-graf′ic[P&S], *a.* Shadowgraphic.
shagd[S], *a.* & *pp.* Shagged.
shake′a-bl[P], *a.* Shakeable.
shal[P&S], *v.* Shall.
shal′lo[S], *v.*, *a.* & *n.* Shallow.
shal′lowd[S], *pp.* Shallowed.
sham′bl[P], *v.* & *n.* Shamble.
sham′bld[P], *pp.* Shambled.
sham′bls[P], *n. pl.* Shambles.
shamd[S], *pp.* Shammed.
sham-pood′[S], *pp.* Shampooed.
sham′roc[S], *n.* Shamrock.
shankt[S], *a.* Shanked.
shap′a-bl[P], **shape′a-bl**[P], *a.* Shapable, shapeable.
sharkt[S], *pp.* Sharked.
sharp′end[P&S], *pp.* Sharpened.
sharpt[S], *pp.* Sharped.
shat′terd[S], *pp.* Shattered.
shawld[S], *pp.* Shawled.
sheard[P&S], *pp.* Sheared.
sheathd[S], *pa.* Sheathed.
sheavs[P], *n. pl.* Sheaves.
sheerd[S], *pp.* Sheered.
shel[P&S], *v.*, *a.* & *n.* Shell.
sheld[P&S], *a.* Shelled.
shel-lact′[S], *pp.* Shellacked.
shel′terd[P&S], *pp.* Sheltered.
shelv[P&S], *vt.* Shelve.
shelvd[P&S], *pp.* Shelved.
shelvs[P], *n. pl.* Shelves.
sher′if[P&S], *n.* Sheriff.
shift′a-bl[P], *a.* Shiftable.
shim′merd[S], *pp.* Shimmered.
shind[S], *vt.* & *vi.* Shinned.
shin′gl[P], *v.* & *n.* Shingle.
shin′gld[P], *pp.* & *a.* Shingled.
shin′gls[P], *n.* Shingles.
shipt[P&S], *pp.* & *pa.* Shipped.
shird[S], *pa.* Shirred.
shirkt[P&S], *pp.* Shirked.
shiv′erd[P&S], *pa.* Shivered.
sho[S], *v.* & *n.* Show.
shoald[S], *pp.* Shoaled.
shockt[P&S], *pp.* Shocked.
shoot′a-bl[P], *a.* Shootable.
shopt[P&S], *pp.* Shopped.
short′end[P&S], *pp.* Shortened.
shoul′derd[S], *a.* Shouldered.
shov′eld[S], *pp.* Shoveled, shovelled.
showd[P&S], *pp.* Showed.
show′erd[S], *pp.* Showered.
shriekt[P&S], *pp.* Shrieked.
shril[P&S], *v.* & *a.* Shrill.
shrild[S], *pp.* Shrilled.
shrink′a-bl[P], *a.* Shrinkable.
shrugd[P&S], *pp.* Shrugged.
shuckt[S], *pp.* Shucked.
shud′derd[S], *pp.* Shuddered.
shuf′l[P], *v.* & *n.* Shuffle.
shuf′ld[P], *pp.* Shuffled.
shund[S], *pp.* Shunned.
shut′l[P], *v.* & *n.* Shuttle.
shut′terd[S], *pp.* Shuttered.
shuv[P], *v.* & *n.* Shove.
shuvd[P], *pp.* Shoved.
shuv′el[P], *v.* & *n.* Shovel.
shuv′eld[P], *pp.* Shoveled, shovelled.
shuv′el-er[P], *n.* Shoveler, shoveller.
shuv′el-ful[P], *n.* Shovelful.
shuv′el-ing[P], *n.* Shoveling.
shuv′er[P], *n.* Shover.
shuv′ing[P], *pres. p.* Shoving.
si-al′a-gog[P&S], *n.* Sialagogue.
sic′ca-tiv[P&S], *a.* & *n.* Siccative.
sick′end[P&S], *pp.* Sickened.
si-cu′lo-din[S], *a.* Siculodine.
sid′er-o-graf[P&S], *n.* Siderograph.
sid″er-o-graf′ic[P&S], *a.* Siderographic.
sid″er-og′ra-fist[P&S], *n.* Siderographist.
sid″er-og′ra-fy[P&S], *n.* Siderography.

si'fon[P&S], *v. & n.* Siphon.
si'fond[P&S], *pp.* Siphoned.
si"fo-na'ceus[S], *a.* Siphonaceous.
si'fon-less[P&S], *a.* Siphonless.
sighd[P&S], *pp.* Sighed.
sight'a-bl[P], *a.* Sightable.
sig"il-log'ra-fer[P&S], *n.* Sigillographer.
sig"il-log'ra-fy[P&S], *n.* Sigillography.
sign'a-bl[P], *a.* Signable.
sig'na-graf[P&S], *n.* Signagraph.
sig'nald[S], *pp.* Signaled, signalled.
sig'nal-ize[P&S], *vt. & vi.* Signalise.
signd[P&S], *pp.* Signed.
sig'ni-fi"a-bl[P], *a.* Signifiable.
sig-nif'i-ca"tiv[P&S], *a. & n.* Significative.
sig-nif'i-ca"tiv-ly[S], *adv.* Significatively.
sig-nif'i-ca"tiv-ness[S], *n.* Significativeness.
sil[P&S], *n.* Sill.
sild[S], *pp.* Silled.
si-li'ceus[S], **si-li'cius**[S], *a.* Siliceous, silicious.
sil"i-qua'ceus[S], *a.* Siliquaceous.
sil'lo-graf[P&S], *n.* Sillograph.
sil-log'ra-fer[P&S], *n.* Sillographer.
sil'van[S], *a. & n.* Sylvan.
sil'verd[P&S], *pp.* Silvered.
sim'i-la-tiv[P&S], *a.* Similative.
sim'i-tar[S], *n.* Scimitar.
sim'i-tard[S], *a.* Simitared.
sim'i-us[S], *a.* Simious.
sim'i-us-ness[S], *n.* Simiousness.
sim'merd[S], *pp.* Simmered.
sim'perd[S], *pp.* Simpered.
sim'pl[P], *a. & n.* Simple.
sim'pl-ness[P], *n.* Simpleness.
sim'pli-fi-ca"tiv[S], *a.* Simplificative.
sim'pl-ton[P], *n.* Simpleton.
sim'u-la"tiv[P&S], *a.* Simulative.
sim'u-la"tiv-ly[P&S], *adv.* Simulatively.
si"mul-ta'ne-us[S], *a.* Simultaneous.
si"mul-ta'ne-us-ly[S], *adv.* Simultaneously.
sind[S], *pp.* Sinned.
sin'der[P], *n.* Cinder.
sin'ew-us[S], *a.* Sinewous.
sing'a-bl[P], *a.* Singable.
sing'a-bl-ness[P], *n.* Singableness.
sin'gl[P], *v., a. & n.* Single.
sin'gld[P], *pp.* Singled.
sin'is-trus[S], *a.* Sinistrous.
sin'is-trus-ly[S], *adv.* Sinistrously.
sink'a-bl[P], *a.* Sinkable.
sinse[P], *adv., prep., & conj.* Since.
sin'u-us[S], *a.* Sinuous.
sin'u-us-ly[S], *adv.* Sinuously.
sin'u-us-ness[S], *n.* Sinuousness.
si'on[S], *n.* Scion, cion.
sipt[P&S], *pp.* Sipped.
sis[P&S], *v. & n.* Siss.
sis'sors[S], *n. pl.* Scissors.
Sis'tin[S], **Six'tin**[S], *a.* Sistine, Sixtine.
sithe[P&S], *v. & n.* Scythe.
sit'ta-cin[S], *n.* Sittacine.
sit'tin[S], *a. & n.* Sittine.
siv[P&S], *v. & n.* Sieve.
sivd[S], *pp.* Sieved.
siz[P&S], *vi.* Sizz.
siz'a-bl[P], **size'a-bl**[P], *a.* Sizable, sizeable.
sizd[S], *pp.* Sizzed.
sizl[P&S], *v. & n.* Sizzle.
sizld[P&S], *pp.* Sizzled.
skech[P], *v. & n.* Sketch.
skech"a-bil'i-ty[P], *n.* Sketchability.
skech'a-bl[P], *a.* Sketchable.
skech'er[P], *n.* Sketcher.
skech'i-ly[P], *adv.* Sketchily.
skech'i-ness[P], *n.* Sketchiness.
skecht[P], *pp.* Sketched.
skech'y[P], *a.* Sketchy.
skep'tic[P], *n.* Sceptic.
sketcht[S], *pp.* Sketched.
skewd[S], *pp.* Skewed.
skew'erd[S], *pp.* Skewered.
ski'a-graf[P&S], *v. & n.* Skiagraph.
ski-ag'ra-fer[P&S], *n.* Skiagrapher.

ski″a-graf′ic[P&S], *a.* Skiagraphic.
ski-ag′ra-fy[P&S], **ski-og′ra-fy**[P&S], *n.* Skiagraphy, skiography.
skif[P&S], *n.* Skiff.
skil[P&S], *v.* & *n.* Skill.
skild[P&S], *a.* Skilled.
skil′ful[P&S], *a.* Skillful.
skimd[P&S], *pp.* Skimmed.
skimpt[S], *pp.* Skimped.
skind[P&S], *a.* & *pp.* Skinned.
skip′pa-bl[P], *a.* Skippable.
skipt[P&S], *pp.* Skipped.
skir′misht[S], *pp.* Skirmished.
skul[P&S], *n.* Skull.
skuld[P&S], *pp.* Skulled.
skulkt[S], *pp.* Skulked.
slab′berd[S], *pp.* Slabbered.
slabd[S], *pp.* Slabbed.
slack′end[P&S], *pp.* Slackened.
slackt[P&S], *pp.* Slacked.
slag′ga-bl[P], *a.* Slaggable.
slagd[S], *pp.* Slagged.
slamd[P&S], *pp.* Slammed.
slan′derd[S], *pp.* Slandered.
slan′der-us[S], *a.* Slanderous.
slan′der-us-ly[S], *adv.* Slanderously.
slan′der-us-ness[S], *n.* Slanderousness.
slapt[P&S], *pp.* Slapped.
slasht[S], *a.* Slashed.
slau′ter[P&S], *v.* & *n.* Slaughter.
slau′terd[P&S], *pp.* Slaughtered.
slau′ter-er[P&S], *n.* Slaughterer.
slav′erd[S], *pp.* Slavered.
sleekt[S], *pp.* Sleeked.
sleev[P], *v.* & *n.* Sleeve.
sleevd[P&S], *pp.* Sleeved.
slickt[S], *pp.* Slicked.
slid′a-bl[P], *a.* Slidable.
slid′a-bl-ness[P], *n.* Slidableness.
slid′n[P], *pp.* Slidden.
slight[S], *n.* Sleight.
slip′perd[S], *pp.* Slippered.
slipt[P&S], *pp.* Slipped.
sliv′erd[P&S], *pp.* Slivered.
slo[S], *n.* Sloe.
slo[S], *v.* & *a.* Slow.
slob′berd[S], *pp.* Slobbered.
slopt[S], *pp.* Slopped.
sloucht[P&S], *pp.* Slouched.
slowd[S], *pp.* Slowed.
slu[S], *imp.* Slew.
sluf[P&S], *v.* & *n.* Slough.
sluff′ing[S], *pres. p.* Sloughing.
sluft[P], *pp.* Sloughed.
slugd[S], *pp.* Slugged.
slum′berd[P&S], *pp.* Slumbered.
slum′ber-us[S], *a.* Slumberous.
slum′ber-us-ly[S], *adv.* Slumberously.
slum′ber-us-ness[S], *n.* Slumberousness.
slumpt[S], *pp.* Slumped.
slurd[P&S], *pp.* Slurred.
smackt[P&S], *a.* Smacked.
smalt′in[S], *n.* Smaltine.
sma-rag′din[S], *a.* Smaragdine.
smart′end[S], *pp.* Smartened.
smasht[P&S], *pp.* Smashed.
smat′terd[S], *pp.* Smattered.
smeard[P&S], *a.* Smeared.
smel[P&S], *v.* & *n.* Smell.
smeld[P&S], **smelt**[P&S], *pp.* Smelled, smelt.
smell′a-bl[P], *a.* Smellable.
smircht[S], *pp.* Smirched.
smirkt[P&S], *pp.* Smirked.
smok′a-bl[P], *a.* Smokable.
smol′der[S], *vt.* & *vi.* Smoulder.
smol′derd[S], *pp.* Smoldered.
smoothd[P&S], *pp.* Smoothed.
smoth′erd[S], *pp.* Smothered.
smug′l[P], *vt.* & *vi.* Smuggle.
smug′ld[P], *pp.* Smuggled.
snach[P], *v.* & *n.* Snatch.
snach′ing[P], *ppr.* & *n.* Snatching.
snach′ing-ly[P], *adv.* Snatchingly.
snacht[P], *pp.* Snatched.
snach′y[P], *a.* Snatchy.
snaf′l[P], *v.* & *n.* Snaffle.

snaf'ld[P], *pp.* Snaffled.
snagd[S], *pp.* Snagged.
snapt[P&S], *pp.* Snapped.
snarld[P&S], *pp.* Snarled.
snatcht[S], *pp.* Snatched.
snath[P&S], *n.* Snathe.
sneakt[P&S], *pp.* Sneaked.
sneerd[P&S], *pp.* Sneered.
sneez[P], *v.* & *n.* Sneeze.
sneezd[P&S], *pp.* Sneezed.
snick'erd[S], *pp.* Snickered.
snif[P&S], *v.* & *n.* Sniff.
snift[P&S], *pp.* Sniffed.
snipt[S], *pp.* Snipped.
sniv'el[P], *v.* & *n.* Snivel.
sniv'eld[P&S], *pp.* Sniveled, snivelled.
sniv'el-er[P], *n.* Sniveller.
sniv'el-y[P], *a.* Snivelly.
sno[S], *v.* & *n.* Snow.
snooz[P], *v.* & *n.* Snooze.
snoozd[P&S], *pp.* Snoozed.
snowd[P&S], *pp.* Snowed.
snubd[P&S], *pp.* Snubbed.
snuf[P&S], *v.* & *n.* Snuff.
snuf'l[P], *v.* & *n.* Snuffle.
snuf'ld[P], *pp.* Snuffled.
snuft[P&S], *pp.* Snuffed.
snug'l[P], *vt.* & *vi.* Snuggle.
snug'ld[P], *pp.* Snuggled.
so[S], *vt.* & *vi.* Sow.
soard[P&S], *pp.* Soared.
sobd[P&S], *pp.* Sobbed.
so'berd[P&S], *pp.* Sobered.
so'cia-bl[P], *a.* & *n.* Sociable.
so'cia-bl-ness[P], *n.* Sociableness.
so'ci-a-tiv[S], *a.* Sociative.
sod'n[P], *v.* & *pa.* Sodden.
soed[S], *pp.* Sowed.
soes[S], *3rd per. sing. pres. ind.* Sows.
sof'ish[P&S], *a.* Sophish.
sof'ism[P], *n.* Sophism.
sof'ist[P&S], *n.* Sophist.
sof'ist-er[P&S], *n.* Sophister.
so-fis'tic[P&S], *a.* & *n.* Sophistic.
so-fis'ti-cal[P&S], *a.* Sophistical.
so-fis'ti-cal-ly[P&S], *adv.* Sophistically.
so-fis'ti-cal-ness[P&S], *n.* Sophisticalness.
so-fis'ti-cate[P&S], *vt.* & *vi.* Sophisticate.
so-fis'ti-cat"ed[P&S], *a.* Sophisticated.
so-fis"ti-ca'tion[P&S], *n.* Sophistication.
so-fis'ti-ca"tor[P&S], *n.* Sophisticator.
so-fis'ti-cism[P&S], *n.* Sophisticism.
sof'is-tress[P&S], *n.* Sophistress.
sof'is-try[P], *n.* Sophistry.
sof'o-more[P], *n.* Sophomore.
sof"o-mor'ic[P], *a.* Sophomoric.
sof'tend[P&S], *pp.* Softened.
soild[P&S], *pp.* & *a.* Soiled.
so'journ[P&S], *v.* & *n.* Sojourn.
so'jurnd[P&S], *pp.* Sojourned.
so'jur-ner[P], *n.* Sojourner.
sol'derd[P&S], *pp.* Soldered.
sol'dierd[S], *pp.* Soldiered.
sol'em[S], *a.* Solemn.
so-lic'i-tus[S], *a.* Solicitous.
so-lid'i-fi"a-bl[P], *a.* Solidifiable.
so-lid'i-fi"a-bl-ness[P], *n.* Solidifiableness.
sol'stis[S], *n.* Solstice.
sol'u-bl[P], *a.* Soluble.
sol'u-bl-ness[P], *n.* Solubleness.
sol'u-tiv[P&S], *a.* Solutive.
solv[P&S], *vt.* Solve.
solv'a-bl[P], **solv'i-bl**[P], *a.* Solvable, solvible.
solv'a-bl-ness[P], *n.* Solvableness.
solvd[P&S], *pp.* Solved.
som'ber[P&S], *v.* & *a.* Sombre.
soakt[P&S], *pp.* Soaked.
soapt[P&S], *pp.* Soaped.
som'ber-ly[P&S], *adv.* Sombrely.
som'ber-ness[P&S], *n.* Sombreness.
som'brus[S], *a.* Sombrous.
som'brus-ly[S], *adv.* Sombrously.
som'brus-ness[S], *n.* Sombrousness.

som'ni-a-tiv[s], *a.* Somniative.
som-nif'er-us[s], *a.* Somniferous.
so'na-bl[P], *a.* Sonable.
so-nif'er-us[s], *a.* Soniferous.
so-no'rus[s], *a.* Sonorous.
so-no'rus-ly[s], *adv.* Sonorously.
so-no'rus-ness[s], *n.* Sonorousness.
sopt[s], *pp.* Sopped.
sor'bil[P&S], **-ile**[P&S], *a.* Sorbile.
sor'cer-us-ly[s], *adv.* Sorcerously.
so-rif'er-us[s], *a.* Soriferous.
sor'rowd[s], *pp.* Sorrowed.
sort'a-bl[P], *a.* Sortable.
sould[s], *a.* Souled.
sound'a-bl[P], *a.* Soundable.
sourd[P&S], *pp.* Soured.
sourse[P], *n.* Source.
soust[s], *pp.* Soused.
sov'er-en[P&S], *a. & n.* Sovereign.
sov'er-en-ly[P&S], *adv.* Sovereignly.
sov'er-en-ty[P&S], *n.* Sovereignty.
sowd[P&S], *pp.* Sowed.
spa'cius[s], *a.* Spacious.
spa'cius-ly[s], *adv.* Spaciously.
spa'cius-ness[s], *n.* Spaciousness.
spa-di'ceus[s], **spa-di'cius**[s], *a.* Spadiceous, spadicious.
spal'a-cin[s], *a. & n.* Spalacine.
spal"a-cop'o-din[s], *a. & n.* Spalacopodine.
spand[P&S], *pp.* Spanned.
span'gl[P], *v. & n.* Spangle.
span'gld[P], *pp.* Spangled.
spankt[P&S], *pp.* Spanked.
spar'a-bl[P], *n.* Sparable.
spard[P&S], *pp.* Sparred.
spar'kl[P], *v. & n.* Sparkle.
spar'kld[P], *pp.* Sparkled.
sparkt[s], *a.* Sparked.
spat'terd[P&S], *pp.* Spattered.
spav'ind[s], *a.* Spavined.
spawnd[s], *a.* Spawned.
speak'a-bl[P], *a.* Speakable.
speard[P&S], *pp.* Speared.
spe'cial-ize[s], *vt. & vi.* Specialise.
spec'i-fi"a-bl[P], *a.* Specifiable.
spe-cif'i-ca"tiv[s], *a.* Specificative.
spe-cif'i-ca"tiv-ly[s], *adv.* Specificatively.
spe'cius[s], *a.* Specious.
spe'cius-ly[s], *adv.* Speciously.
spe'cius-ness[s], *n.* Speciousness.
speck'l[P], *v. & n.* Speckle.
speck'ld[P], *pa.* Speckled.
speckt[P&S], *pp.* Specked.
spec'ta-cl[P], *n.* Spectacle.
spec'ta-cld[P], *a.* Spectacled.
spec'ta-cls[P], *n. pl.* Spectacles.
spec'ter[P], *n.* Spectre.
spec"tro-bo'lo-graf[P&S], *n.* Spectrobolograph.
spec"tro-bo"lo-graf'ic[P&S], *a.* Spectrobolographic.
spec'tro-graf[P&S], *n.* Spectrograph.
spec"tro-graf'ic[P&S], *a.* Spectrographic.
spec"tro-he'li-o-graf[P&S], *n.* Spectroheliograph.
spec"tro-he"li-o-graf'ic[P&S], *a.* Spectroheliographic.
spec'u-la-bl[P], *a.* Speculable.
spec'u-la"tiv[s], *a.* Speculative.
spec'u-la"tiv-ly[s], *adv.* Speculatively.
spec'u-la"tiv-ness[s], *n.* Speculativeness.
spel[P&S], *v. & n.* Spell.
speld[P&S], **spelt**[s], *pp.* Spelled, spelt.
spell'a-bl[P], *a.* Spellable.
spend'a-bl[P], *a.* Spendable.
spewd[P&S], *pp.* Spewed.
spi-cif'er-us[s], *a.* Spiciferous.
spi'cus[s], *a.* Spicous.
spic"u-lif'er-us[s], *a.* Spiculiferous.
spic"u-lo-fi'brus[s], *a.* Spiculofibrous.
spil[P&S], *v. & n.* Spill.
spild[P&S], **spilt**[P&S], *pp.* Spilled, spilt.
spi-na'ceus[s], *a.* Spinaceous.
spin'dl[P], *v. & n.* Spindle.

spin'dld[P], *pp.* Spindled.
spi-nif'er-us[S], *a.* Spiniferous.
spi'nus[S], *a.* Spinous.
spin"u-lif'er-us[S], *a.* Spinuliferous.
spi-rac"u-lif'er-us[S], *a.* Spiraculiferous.
spi-rif'er-us[S], *a.* Spiriferous.
spir"il-la'ceus[S], *a.* Spirillaceous.
spit'l[P], *n.* Spittle.
splasht[P&S], *pp.* Splashed.
splayd[S], *pa.* Splayed.
splen'dor[S], *n.* Splendour.
splen'i-tiv[P&S], **splen'a-tiv**[P&S], *a.* & *n.* Splenitive, splenative.
splin'terd[S], *a.* Splintered.
splotcht[S], *pp.* Splotched.
splut'terd[S], *pp.* Spluttered.
spoil'a-bl[P], *a.* Spoilable.
spoild[P&S], **spoilt**[P&S], *pp.* Spoiled, spoilt.
spo'li-a"tiv[P&S], *a.* Spoliative.
spon-ta'ne-us[S], *a.* Spontaneous.
spon-ta'ne-us-ly[S], *adv.* Spontaneously.
spon-ta'ne-us-ness[S], *n.* Spontaneousness.
spoold[S], *pp.* Spooled.
spoond[S], *pp.* Spooned.
spo-ra'ceus[S], *a.* Sporaceous.
spo-rif'er-us[S], *a.* Sporiferous.
spo-rip'a-rus[S], *a.* Sporiparous.
spor'tiv[P&S], *a.* Sportive.
spor'tiv-ly[P&S], *adv.* Sportively.
spor'tiv-ness[P&S], *n.* Sportiveness.
spor"u-lif'er-us[S], *a.* Sporuliferous.
spo'rus[S], *a.* Sporous.
spot'ta-bl[P], *a.* Spottable.
spraind[P&S], *pp.* Sprained.
sprawld[P&S], *pp.* Sprawled.
sprayd[S], *a.* Sprayed.
spred[P&S], *v.*, *a.* & *n.* Spread.
spred'er[P&S], *n.* Spreader.
spred'ing[P&S], *ppr.* & *n.* Spreading.
spred'ing-ly[P&S], *adv.* Spreadingly.
sprigd[S], *pp.* Sprigged.
sprin'kl[P], *v.* & *n.* Sprinkle.
sprin'kld[P], *pp.* Sprinkled.
sprite[P], *n.* Spright.
sprite'ly[P], *a.* Sprightly.
sprite'li-ness[P], *n.* Sprightliness.
spu-mif'er-us[S], *a.* Spumiferous.
spunge[P], *v.* & *n.* Sponge.
spung'er[P], *n.* Sponger.
spung'y[P], *a.* Spongy.
spurd[P&S], *a.* Spurred.
spu'ri-us[S], *a.* Spurious.
spu'ri-us-ly[S], *adv.* Spuriously.
spu'ri-us-ness[S], *n.* Spuriousness.
spurnd[P&S], *pp.* Spurned.
sput'terd[P&S], *pp.* Sputtered.
squal[P&S], *v.* & *n.* Squall.
squald[S], *pp.* Squalled.
squa'mus[S], *a.* Squamous.
squa'mus-ness[S], *n.* Squamousness.
squan'derd[P&S], *pp.* Squandered.
squar'a-bl[P], *a.* Squarable.
squasht[S], *pp.* Squashed.
squawkt[S], *pp.* Squawked.
squawld[P&S], *pp.* Squawled.
squeakt[P&S], *pp.* Squeaked.
squeald[P&S], *pp.* Squealed.
squeez[P], *v.* & *n.* Squeeze.
squeez'a-bl[P], *a.* Squeezable.
squeezd[P&S], *pp.* Squeezed.
squelcht[S], *pp.* Squelched.
squibd[S], *pp.* Squibbed.
squil[P&S], *n.* Squill.
squirmd[P&S], *pp.* Squirmed.
stabd[S], *pp.* Stabbed.
sta'bl[P], *v.*, *a.* & *n.* Stable.
stab'lisht[S], *pp.* Stablished.
stackt[P&S], *pp.* Stacked.
staf[P&S], *n.* Staff.
staft[S], *a.* Staffed.
stag'gerd[S], *pa.* Staggered.
stag-nic'o-lus[S], *a.* Stagnicolous.
staid[S], *pp.* Stayed.
stain'a-bl[P], *a.* Stainable.

staind[P&S], *pp.* Stained.
stal[P&S], *v.* & *n.* Stall.
stald[S], *pp.* Stalled.
stalkt[S], *pp.* Stalked.
stalld[P], *pp.* Stalled.
sta'mend[S], *a.* Stamened.
stam"i-nif'er-us[S], *a.* Staminiferous.
stam'merd[P&S], *pp.* Stammered.
stamp'a-bl[P], *a.* Stampable.
stam-ped'a-bl[P], *a.* Stampedable.
stampt[P&S], *pp.* Stamped.
stancht[P&S], *pp.* Stanched.
stand'ard-iz"[or **-is"**]**a-bl**[P], *a.* Standardizable, standardisable.
stan-nif'er-us[S], *a.* Stanniferous.
stan'nin[S], *n.* Stannine.
stap"e-dif'er-us[S], *a.* Stapediferous.
sta'pl[P], *v.*, *a.* & *n.* Staple.
starcht[S], *a.* Starched.
stard[P&S], *pp.* & *pa.* Starred.
star'tl[P], *vt.* Startle.
star'tld[P], *pp.* Startled.
starv[P&S], *vt.* & *vi.* Starve.
starvd[P&S], *pp.* & *pa.* Starved.
stat'a-bl[P], *a.* Statable.
sta'tiond[S], *pp.* Stationed.
sta'tiv[S], *a.* Stative.
stat'ut-a-bl[P], *a.* Statutable.
stayd[P&S], *pp.* Stayed.
steamd[P&S], *pp.* Steamed.
ste"a-tog'e-nus[S], *a.* Steatogenous.
ste"a-top'y-gus[S], *a.* Steatopygous.
ste"a-tor'ni-thin[S], *a.* Steatornithine.
sted[P&S], *v.* & *n.* Stead.
sted'fast[P&S], *a.* Steadfast.
sted'fast-ly[P&S], *adv.* Steadfastly.
sted'fast-ness[P&S], *n.* Steadfastness.
sted'i-er[P&S], *n.* Steadier.
sted'i-ly[P&S], *adv.* Steadily.
sted'i-ness[P&S], *n.* Steadiness.
sted'y[P&S], *v.*, *a.* & *n.* Steady.
steeld[S], *pp.* Steeled.
stee'pl[P], *v.* & *n.* Steeple.
stee'pld[P], *a.* & *pp.* Steepled.
steept[P&S], *pp.* Steeped.
steer'a-bl[P], *a.* Steerable.
steerd[P&S], *pp.* Steered.
steg'a-nus[S], *a.* Steganous.
steg-og'na-thus[S], *a.* Stegognathous.
ste-gu'rus[S], *a.* Stegurous.
stelth[P&S], *n.* Stealth.
stelth'i-ly[P&S], *adv.* Stealthily.
stelth'i-ness[P&S], *n.* Stealthiness.
stelth'y[P&S], *a.* Stealth.
stemd[P&S], *pp.* & *a.* Stemmed.
stem'ma-tus[S], *a.* Stemmatous.
sten'cild[S], *pp.* Stenciled, stencilled.
sten"o-co-ro'nin[S], *a.* Stenocoronine.
sten'o-crome[S], *n.* Stenochrome.
sten"o-der'ma-tin[S], *a.* Stenodermatine.
sten"o-der'ma-tus[S], *a.* Stenodermatous.
sten"o-der'min[S], *a.* & *n.* Stenodermine.
sten'o-graf[P&S], *n.* Stenograph.
ste-nog'ra-fer[P&S], *n.* Stenographer.
sten"o-graf'ic[P&S], *a.* Stenographic.
ste-nog'ra-fist[P&S], *n.* Stenographist.
sten"o-graf'i-cal-ly[P&S], *adv.* Stenographically.
ste-nog'ra-fy[P&S], *n.* Stenography.
sten"o-pet'a-lus[S], *a.* Stenopetalous.
sten"o-sep'a-lus[S], *a.* Stenosepalous.
sten'to-rin[S], *a.* Stentorine.
sten-to'ri-us[S], *a.* Stentorious.
sten-to'ri-us-ly[S], *adv.* Stentoriously.
step'dau"ter[S], *n.* Stepdaughter.
stept[P&S], *pp.* Stepped.
ster"co-ra'ceus[S], *a.* Stercoraceous.
ster'e-o-crome[S], *n.* Stereochrome.
ster"e-o-cro'mic[S], *a.* Stereochromic.
ster"e-o-cro'mi-cal-ly[S], *adv.* Stereochromically.
ster"e-o-cro'mo-scope[S], *n.* Stereochromoscope.
ster"e-o-for'o-scope[P&S], *n.* Stereophoroscope.

ster″e-o-fo-tog′ra-fy[P&S], *n.* Stereophotography.
ster″e-o-graf′ic[P&S], *a.* Stereographic.
ster″e-o-graf′i-cal-ly[S], *adv.* Stereographically.
ster″e-og′ra-fy[P&S], *n.* Stereography.
ster″e-o-plan′i-graf[P&S], *n.* Stereoplanigraph.
ster″e-o-ty-pog′ra-fer[P&S], *n.* Stereotypographer.
ster″e-o-ty-pog′ra-fy[P&S], *n.* Stereotypography.
ster′il[P&S], **-ile**[S], *a.* Sterile.
ster′i-iz″a-bl[P], *a.* Sterilizable.
ster′il-ness[P&S], *a.* Sterileness.
ster-nu′ta-tiv[S], *a.* & *n.* Sternutative.
ster-nu′ta-tiv-ness[S], *n.* Sternutativeness.
ster′tor-us[S], **ster-to′ri-us**[S], *a.* Stertorous, stertorious.
ster′tor-us-ly[S], *adv.* Stertorously.
ster′tor-us-ness[S], *n.* Stertorousness.
steth′o-graf[P&S], *n.* Stethograph.
steth″o-graf′ic[P&S], *a.* Stethographic.
stewd[P&S], *pp.* Stewed.
stich[P], *v.* & *n.* Stitch.
sticher[P], *n.* Stitcher.
stich′ing[P], *n.* Stitching.
sticht[P], *pp.* Stitched.
stich′work[P], *n.* Stitchwork.
stick′l[P], *v.* & *n.* Stickle.
stick′ld[P], *pp.* Stickled.
stif[P&S], *a.*, *n.* & *adv.* Stiff.
stiff′end[P&S], *pp.* Stiffened.
stig″ma-tif′er-us[S], *a.* Stigmatiferous.
stil[P&S], *v.*, *a.*, *n.* & *adv.* Still.
stild[P&S], *pp.* Stilled.
stim′u-la″tiv[P&S], *a.* & *n.* Stimulative.
stip″u-lif′er-us[S], *a.* Stipuliferous.
stird[P&S], *pp.* Stirred.
stitcht[S], *pp.* Stitched.
sto[S], *vt.* & *vi.* Stow.
sto′age[S], *n.* Stowage.
sto′a-way″[S], *n.* Stowaway.
stockt[P&S], *pp.* Stocked.
sto′down[S], *n.* Stowdown.
stoed[S], *pp.* Stowed.
sto′er[S], *n.* Stower.
sto″lo-nif′er-us[S], *a.* Stoloniferous.
stom′ac[S], *v.* & *n.* Stomach.
stom′ac-al[S], *a.* & *n.* Stomachal.
stom′ac-less[S], *a.* Stomachless.
stoopt[P&S], *pp.* Stooped.
stop′l[P], *v.* & *n.* Stopple.
stop′ld[P], *pp.* Stoppled.
stop′perd[S], *pp.* Stoppered.
stopt[P&S], *pa.* Stopped.
stor′a-bl[P], *a.* Storable.
storm′a-bl[P], *a.* Stormable.
stormd[P&S], *pp.* Stormed.
stowd[P], *pp.* Stowed.
strad′l[P], *v.* & *n.* Straddle.
strad-ld[P], *pp.* Straddled.
strag′l[P], *v.* & *n.* Straggle.
strag′ld[P], *pp.* Straggled.
straight′end[S], *pp.* Straightened.
strain′a-bl[P], *a.* Strainable.
straind[P&S], *pa.* Strained.
strait′end[S], *pp.* Straitened.
stran′gl[P], *v.* & *n.* Strangle.
stran′gl-a-bl[P], *a.* Strangleable.
stran′gld[P], *pp.* Strangled.
stran-gu′ri-us[S], *a.* Strangurious.
strapt[P&S], *pp.* Strapped.
stra-tig′ra-fer[P&S], *n.* Stratigrapher.
strat″i-graf′ic[P&S], *a.* Stratigraphic.
stra-tig′ra-fy[P&S], *n.* Stratigraphy.
strat″i-graf′i-cal[P&S], *a.* Stratigraphical.
strat″i-graf′i-cal-ly[P&S], *adv.* Stratigraphically.
strat″o-graf′ic[P&S], *a.* Stratographic.
stra-tog′ra-fy[P&S], *n.* Stratography.
strawd[S], *pp.* Strawed.
strayd[S], *pp.* Strayed.
streakt[P&S], **streaked**[P], *pa.* Streaked.
streamd[S], *pp.* Streamed.
strech[P], *v.* & *n.* Stretch.

strech′er[P], *n.* Stretcher.
strech′ing[P], *ppr.* & *n.* Stretching.
strecht[P], *pp.* Stretched.
strength′end[P&S], *pp.* Strengthened.
stren′u-us[S], *a.* Strenuous.
stren′u-us-ly[S], *adv.* Strenuously.
stren′u-us-ness[S], *n.* Strenuousness.
strep′er-in[P&S], *a.* Streperine.
stres[S], *v.* & *n.* Stress.
stres′ful[S], *a.* Stressful.
strest[S], *pp.* Stressed.
stretcht[S], *pp.* Stretched.
strewd[S], *pp.* Strewed.
strick′n[P], *pp.* & *pa.* Stricken.
stric′nic[S], *a.* Strychnic.
stric′nin[S], **stricnine**[S], *n.* Strychnin, strychnine.
stric′nin-ism[S], *n.* Strychninism.
stric′nism[S], *n.* Strychnism.
strid′u-lus[S], *a.* Stridulous.
strid′u-lus-ly[S], *adv.* Stridulously.
strid′u-lus-ness[S], *n.* Stridulousness.
strig′in[P&S], *a.* Strigine.
stringd[S], *a.* Stringed.
stript[P&S], *pp.* Stripped.
striv′n[P], *pp.* Striven.
stro[S], *vt.* Strow.
strob′o-graf[P&S], *n.* Strobograph.
strob″o-graf′ic[P&S], *a.* Strobographic.
stro′fe[P&S], *n.* Strophe.
strof′ic[P&S], *a.* Strophic.
strof′i-cal[P&S], *a.* Strophical.
strof′oid[P&S], *n.* Strophoid.
strol[P], *v.* & *n.* Stroll.
strolld[P], **strold**[P&S], *pp.* Strolled.
strom″bu-lif′er-us[S], *a.* Strombuliferous.
stropt[S], *pp.* Stropped.
strug′gl[P], *v.* & *n.* Struggle.
strumd[S], *pp.* Strummed.
stubd[S], *pp.* Stubbed.
stub′l[P], *n.* Stubble.
stub′ld[P], *a.* Stubbled.
stud′i-a-bl[P], *a.* Studiable.
stu′di-us[S], *a.* Studious.
stu′di-us-ly[S], *adv.* Studiously.
stuf[P&S], *v.*, *a.*, *n.* & *interj.* Stuff.
stuft[P&S], *pa.* Stuffed.
stum′ac[P], *v.* & *n.* Stomach.
stum′ac-a-bl[P], *a.* Stomachable.
stum′ac-al[P], *a.* & *n.* Stomachal.
stum′ach-er[P], *n.* Stomacher.
stu-mach′ic[P], *a.* & *n.* Stomachic.
stum′acht[P], *pp.* Stomached.
stum′ac-less[P], *a.* Stomachless.
stum′bl[P], *v.* & *n.* Stumble.
stum′bld[P], *pp.* Stumbled.
stumd[S], *pp.* Stummed.
stumpt[P&S], *pp.* Stumped.
stund[S], *pp.* Stunned.
stu″pe-fac′tiv[P&S], *a.* & *n.* Stupefactive.
stu″pe-fac′tiv-ness[P&S], *n.* Stupefactiveness.
stu-pen′dus[S], *a.* Stupendous.
stu-pen′dus-ly[S], *adv.* Stupendously.
stu′por-us[S], *a.* Stuporous.
stu′ri-o-nin[P&S], *a.* Sturionine.
stut′terd[P&S], *pp.* Stuttered.
sty′lo-graf[P&S], *n.* Stylograph.
sty″lo-graf′ic[P&S], *a.* Stylographic.
sty-log′ra-fy[P&S], *n.* Stylography.
su′a-bl[P], *a.* Suable.
sua′siv[P&S], *a.* Suasive.
sua′siv-ly[P&S], *adv.* Suasively.
sub-a′que-us[S], *a.* Subaqueous.
sub-cal′ca-rin[S], *a.* Subcalcarine.
sub″cu-ta′ne-us[S], *a.* Subcutaneous.
sub″de-riv′a-tiv[P&S], *n.* Subderivative.
sub″di-vis′i-bl[P], *a.* Subdivisible.
sub″di-vi′siv[P&S], *a.* Subdivisive.
sub-du′a-bl[P], *a.* Subduable.
sub″in-dic′a-tiv[P&S], *a.* Subindicative.
sub-ject′a-bl[P], **sub-ject′i-bl**[P], *a.* Subjectable, subjectible.
sub-jec′tiv[P&S], *a.* Subjective.
sub-jec′tiv-ly[P&S], *adv.* Subjectively.
sub-jec′tiv-ness[P&S], *n.* Subjectiveness.

sub-joind'[S], *pp.* Subjoined.
sub'ju-ga-bl[P], *a.* Subjugable.
sub-junc'tiv[P&S], *a.* & *n.* Subjunctive.
sub'la-tiv[P&S], *a.* Sublative.
sub-merg'i-bl[P], *a.* & *n.* Submergible.
sub-mers'i-bl[P], *a.* & *n.* Submersible.
sub-mis'siv[P&S], *a.* Submissive.
sub-mis'siv-ly[P&S], *adv.* Submissively.
sub-or'di-na"tiv[P&S], *a.* Subordinative.
sub-ornd'[S], *pp.* Suborned.
sub-pe'na[S], *v.* & *n.* Subpœna.
sub-rep'tiv[P&S], *a.* Subreptive.
sub-scrib'a-bl[P], *a.* Subscribable.
sub-sec'u-tiv[P&S], *a.* Subsecutive.
sub-sen'si-bl[P], *a.* Subsensible.
sub-serv'[S], *vt.* & *vi.* Subserve.
sub-servd'[S], *pp.* Subserved.
sub'stan-tiv[P&S], *a.* & *n.* Substantive.
sub'stan-tiv-ly[P&S], *adv.* Substantively.
sub'stan-tiv-ness[P&S], *n.* Substantiveness.
sub'sti-tu"tiv[P&S], *a.* Substitutive.
sub-sum'a-bl[P], *a.* Subsumable.
sub-sump'tiv[P&S], *a.* Subsumptive.
sub'til[P&S], **-ile**[S], *a.* Subtile.
sub'til-ly[P&S], *adv.* Subtilely.
sub'til-ness[P&S], *n.* Subtileness.
sub-trac'tiv[P&S], *a.* Subtractive.
sub-ven'tiv[P&S], *a.* Subventive.
sub-ver'siv[P&S], *a.* Subversive.
sub-vert'i-bl[P], *a.* Subvertible.
suc-cede'[S], *vt.* & *vi.* Succeed.
suc-ceed'a-bl[P], *a.* Succeedable.
suc-ces'siv[P&S], *a.* Successive.
suc-ces'siv-ly[P&S], *adv.* Successively.
suc-ces'siv-ness[P&S], *n.* Successiveness.
suc'cor[P&S], *v.* & *n.* Succour.
suc'cor-a-bl[P], *a.* Succourable.
suc'cord[P&S], *pp.* Succored.
suc-cum'[P], *vi.* Succumb.
suc-cumbd'[S], *pp.* Succumbed.
suc-cumd'[P], *pp.* Succumbed.
suc-cus'siv[P&S], *a.* Succussive.
suck'l[P], *vt.* & *vi.* Suckle.
suck'ld[P], *pp.* Suckled.
suckt[P&S], *pp.* Sucked.
suf'fer-a-bl[P], *a.* Sufferable.
suf'fer-a-bl-ness[P], *n.* Sufferableness.
suf'ferd[P&S], *pp.* Suffered.
suf-fice'a-bl[P], *a.* Sufficeable.
suf-fixt'[P&S], *pp.* Suffixed.
suf'fo-ca"tiv[S], *a.* Suffocative.
suf"fra-get'[P&S], *n.* Suffragette.
suf-fu'siv[P&S], *a.* Suffusive.
suf-fuze'[P], *vt.* Suffuse.
sug'ard[S], *pa.* Sugared.
sug-gest'i-bl[P], **sug-gest'a-bl**[P], *a.* Suggestible, suggestable.
sug-ges'tiv[P&S], *a.* Suggestive.
sug-ges'tiv-ly[P&S], *adv.* Suggestively.
sug-ges'tiv-ness[P&S], *n.* Suggestiveness.
su'il-lin[P&S], *a.* & *n.* Suilline.
su'in[P&S], *n.* Suine.
suit'a-bl[P], *a.* Suitable.
suit'a-bl-ness[P], *n.* Suitableness.
sul'fate[P&S], *n.* Sulphate.
sul'fa-tize[P&S], *vt.* Sulphatize.
sul'fid[P&S], *v.* & *n.* Sulphid.
sul'fin[P&S], *n.* Sulphin.
sul'fi-on[P&S], *n.* Sulphion.
sul'fo-nal[P&S], *n.* Sulphonal.
sul-fon'ic[P&S], *a.* Sulphonic.
sul'fur[P&S], *v.* & *n.* Sulphur.
sul'fu-rate[P&S], *a.* & *n.* Sulphurate.
sul'fu-ra"tor[P&S], *n.* Sulphurator.
sul'furd[S], *pp.* Sulphured.
sul'fu-ret[P&S], *v.* & *n.* Sulphuret.
sul-fu'ric[P&S], *a.* Sulphuric.
sul'fur-ous[P], *a.* Sulphurous.
sul'fur-us[S], *a.* Sulphurous.
sul'fur-y[P&S], *a.* Sulphury.
sulkt[S], *pp.* Sulked.
sum[P], *a.*, *pron.* & *adv.* Some.
-sum[P&S], *suffix.* -some.

su'mac[S], *n.* Sumach.
sum'bod"y[P], *n.* Somebody.
sumd[P&S], *pp.* Summed.
sum'er-sault[P], *v.* & *n.* Somersault.
sum'er-set[P], *n.* Somerset.
sum'how"[P], *adv.* Somehow.
sum'ma-tiv[P&S], *a.* Summative.
sum'merd[S], *pp.* Summered.
sum'mond[S], *pp.* Summoned.
sump'tu-us[S], *a.* Sumptuous.
sump'tu-us-ly[S], *adv.* Sumptuously.
sump'tu-us-ness[S], *n.* Sumptuousness.
sum'thing[P], *n.* & *adv.* Something.
sum'time"[P], *a.* & *adv.* Sometime.
sum'times"[P], *adv.* Sometimes.
sum'way"[P], *adv.* Someway.
sum'what"[P], *n.* & *adv.* Somewhat.
sum'where"[P], *adv.* Somewhere.
sun[P], *n.* Son.
sund[S], *pp.* Sunned.
sun'derd[P&S], *pp.* Sundered.
su'per-a-bl[P], *a.* Superable.
su'per-a-bl-ness[P], *n.* Superableness.
su"per-cal'en-derd[S], *a.* Supercalendered.
su"per-cil'i-us[S], *a.* Supercilious.
su"per-con-form'a-bl[P], *a.* Superconformable.
su"per-e-rog'a-tiv[P&S], *a.* Supererogative.
su-per'flu-us[S], *a.* Superfluous.
su-per'flu-us-ly[S], *adv.* Superfluously.
su-per'la-tiv[P&S], *a.* & *n.* Superlative.
su-per'la-tiv-ly[P&S], *adv.* Superlatively.
su-per'la-tiv-ness[P&S], *n.* Superlativeness.
su"per-neg'a-tiv[P&S], *a.* Supernegative.
su"per-pos'a-bl[P], *a.* Superposable.
su"per-sen'si-bl[P], *a.* Supersensible.
su"per-ser'vice-a-bl[P], *a.* Superserviceable.
su"per-vo-lu'tiv[P&S], *a.* Supervolutive.
sup'l[P], *v.* & *a.* Supple.
sup'ld[P], *pp.* Suppled.
sup'pa-bl[P], *a.* Suppable.
sup-por'tiv[P&S], *a.* Supportive.
sup-pos'a-bl[P], *a.* Supposable.
sup-pos'a-bl-ness[P], *n.* Supposableness.
sup-pos'i-ta"tiv[P&S], *a.* Suppositative.
sup-pos'i-tiv[P&S], *a.* & *n.* Suppositive.
sup-pos'i-tiv-ly[P&S], *adv.* Suppositively.
sup-press'i-bl[P], *a.* Suppressible.
sup-pres'siv[P&S], *a.* Suppressive.
sup-prest'[P&S], *pp.* Suppressed.
sup'pu-ra"tiv[P&S], *a.* & *n.* Suppurative.
su"pra-sen'si-bl[P], *a.* Suprasensible.
supt[S], *pp.* Supped.
sur'cin-gl[P], *v.* & *n.* Surcingle.
sur'cin-gld[P], *pp.* Surcingled.
sur'de-lin[S], *n.* Surdeline.
sur'fit[S], *v.* & *n.* Surfeit.
sur'fit-er[S], *n.* Surfeiter.
sur'fit-ing[S], *n.* Surfeiting.
sur-mis'a-bl[P], *a.* Surmisable.
sur-mount'a-bl[P], *a.* Surmountable.
sur-mount'a-bl-ness[P], *n.* Surmountableness.
sur-past'[P&S], *pp.* Surpassed.
sur'plis[S], *n.* Surplice.
sur'plist[S], *pp.* Surpliced.
sur-prize'[P&S], *v.* & *n.* Surprise.
sur-priz'ing[S], *pa.* Surprising.
sur-ren'derd[S], *pp.* Surrendered.
sur-veyd'[P&S], *pp.* Surveyed.
sus-cep'ti-bl[P], *a.* Susceptible.
sus-cep'ti-bl-ness[P], *n.* Susceptibleness.
sus-cep'tiv[P&S], *a.* Susceptive.
sus-cep'tiv-ness[P&S], *n.* Susceptiveness.
sus-pect'a-bl[P], **sus-pect'i-bl**[P], *a.* Suspectable, suspectible.

sus-pen'si-bl[P], *a.* Suspensible.
sus-pen'siv[P&S], *a.* Suspensive.
sus-pen'siv-ly[P&S], *adv.* Suspensively.
sus-taind'[S], *pa.* Sustained.
sus'ten-ta"tiv[P&S], *a.* Sustentative.
suth'er-li-ness[P], *n.* Southerliness.
suth'er-ly[P], *a.* & *adv.* Southerly.
suth'ern[P], *a.* Southern.
suth'ern-er[P], *n.* Southerner.
suth'ern-ism[P], *n.* Southernism.
suth'ern-ize[P], *vt.* & *vi.* Southernize.
suth'ron[P], *a.* & *n.* Southron.
sut'l[P], *a.* Subtle.
sut'ly[P], *adv.* Subtly.
swabd[S], *pp.* Swabbed.
swad'l[P], *vt.* Swaddle.
swagd[P&S], *pp.* Swagged.
swag'gerd[S], *pp.* Swaggered.
swal'low-a-bl[P], *a.* Swallowable.
swal'lowd[P&S], *pp.* Swallowed.
swampt[P&S], *pp.* Swamped.
swapt[S], *pp.* Swapped.
swarmd[S], *pp.* Swarmed.
swasht[S], *pp.* Swashed.
swayd[P&S], *pp.* Swayed.
sweet'end[P&S], *pp.* Sweetened.
swel[P&S], *v.*, *a.* & *n.* Swell.
sweld[P&S], *pp.* Swelled.
swel'terd[P&S], *pp.* Sweltered.
swerv[P&S], *vt.* & *vi.* Swerve.
swervd[P&S], *pp.* Swerved.
swet[P&S], *v.* & *n.* Sweat.
swich[P], *v.* & *n.* Switch.
swigd[S], *pp.* Swigged.
swil[S], *v.* & *n.* Swill.
swild[S], *pp.* Swilled.
swim'ma-bl[P], *a.* Swimmable.
swin'dl[P], *v.* & *n.* Swindle.
swin'dld[P], *pp.* Swindled.
swin'gl[P], *v.* & *n.* Swingle.
swin'gld[P], *pp.* Swingled.
swirld[S], *pp.* Swirled.
swisht[S], *pp.* Swished.
switcht[S], *pp.* Switched.
swiv'eld[S], *pp.* Swiveled, swivelled.
swol'n[P], *a.* Swollen.
swoond[P&S], *pp.* Swooned.
swoopt[S], *pp.* Swooped.
sylf[P&S], *n.* Sylph.
syl'la-bl[P], *n.* Syllable.
syl-vic'o-lin[S], *a.* & *n.* Sylvicoline.
syl'vi-in[S], *a.* & *n.* Sylviine.
syl'vin[S], *n.* Sylvine.
syn'a-gog[P&S], *n.* Synagogue.
syn"al-lax'in[S], *a.* & *n.* Synallaxine.
syn'cro-nism[S], *n.* Synchronism.
syn'cro-nus[S], *a.* Synchronous.
syn-eth'e-rin[S], *a.* & *n.* Synetherine.
syn'o-nym[S], *n.* Synonyme.
sy-non'y-mus[S], *a.* Synonymous.

T

-t[P&S]. -ed.
tabd[S], *a.* Tabbed.
tab'er-na-cl[P], *v.* & *n.* Tabernacle.
ta'bor[S], *v.* & *n.* Taber, tabour.
ta'bord[S], *pp.* Tabored.
tach'i-nin[S], *a.* Tachinine.
tach"i-su'rin[S], *a.* & *n.* Tachisurine.
tach'y-graf[P&S], *n.* Tachygraph.
ta-chyg'ra-fer[P&S], *n.* Tachygrapher.
tach"y-graf'ic[P&S], *a.* Tachygraphic.
tach"y-graf'i-cal[P&S], *a.* Tachygraphical.
ta-chyg'ra-fist[P&S], *n.* Tachygraphist.
tach"y-graf-om'e-try[P&S], *n.* Tachygraphometry.
ta-chyg'ra-fy[P&S], *n.* Tachygraphy.
tack'l[P], *v.* & *n.* Tackle.
tack'ld[P], *pp.* Tackled.
tack'l-man[P], *n.* Tackleman.
tackt[P&S], *pp.* Tacked.
tac"o-dom'e-ter[S], *n.* Tachodometer.

tac′o-graf[P&S], *n.* Tachograph.
tac′o-gram[S], *n.* Tachogram.
ta-com′e-ter[S], *n.* Tachometer.
tac′o-scope[S], *n.* Tachoscope.
tact′a-bl[P], *a.* Tactable.
tac′til[P&S], **-ile**[S], *a.* Tactile.
ta′cu-a-cin[S], *n.* Tacuacine.
taf″e-fo′bi-a[P&S], *n.* Taphephobia.
taf″o-fo′bi-a[P&S], *n.* Taphophobia.
ta′fi-an[P&S], *n.* Taphian.
taf-ren′chy-ma[P&S], *n.* Taphrenchyma.
taf′ri-nose[P&S], *n.* Taphrinose.
tagd[P&S], *pp.* Tagged.
taild[S], *a.* Tailed.
tai′lord[S], *pp.* Tailored.
taint′a-bl[P], *a.* Taintable.
tal″e-gal′lin[S], *a.* & *n.* Talegalline.
talk′a-bl[P], *a.* Talkable.
talk′a-tiv[P&S], *a.* Talkative.
talk′a-tiv-ly[P&S], *adv.* Talkatively.
talk′a-tiv-ness[P&S], *n.* Talkativeness.
talkt[P&S], *pp.* Talked.
tal′ond[P&S], *a.* Taloned.
tal′pin[S], *a.* Talpine.
tam′a-bl[P], **tame′a-bl**[P], *a.* Tamable, tameable.
tam′a-bl-ness[P], *n.* Tamableness.
tam′i-din[S], *n.* Tamidine.
tam′perd[S], *pp.* Tampered.
tampt[S], *pp.* Tamped.
tan′a-grin[S], *a.* & *n.* Tanagrine.
tand[P&S], *pp.* Tanned.
tan′gi-bl[P], *a.* Tangible.
tan′gi-bl-ness[P], *n.* Tangibleness.
tan′gl[P], *v.* & *n.* Tangle.
tan′gld[P], *pp.* Tangled.
tankt[S], *pp.* Tanked.
tan′na-bl[P], *a.* Tannable.
tan′ta-lin[S], *a.* & *n.* Tantaline.
ta-pei″no-ce-fal′ic[P&S], *a.* Tapeinocephalic.
ta-pei″no-cef′a-lism[P&S], *n.* Tapeinocephalism.
ta-pei″no-cef′a-ly[P&S], *n.* Tapeinocephaly.
ta′perd[P&S], *pp.* Tapered.
ta-pi″no-ce-fal′ic[P&S], *a.* Tapinocephalic.
tap″i-no-cef′a-lid[P&S], *n.* Tapinocephalid.
tap″i-no-cef′a-loid[P&S], *a.* & *n.* Tapinocephaloid.
tap″i-no-cef′a-ly[P&S], *n.* Tapinocephaly.
tap″i-no-fo′bi-a[P&S], *n.* Tapinophobia.
tap′i-no-fo″by[P&S], *n.* Tapinophoby.
tapt[P&S], *pp.* Tapped.
tard[P&S], *pp.* Tarred.
tar′if[P&S], *v.* & *n.* Tariff.
tar′iff-a-bl[P], *a.* Tariffable.
tar′nish-a-bl[P], *a.* Tarnishable.
tar′nisht[S], *pp.* Tarnished.
tar′roc[S], *n.* Tarrock.
tar′tand[S], *pp.* Tartaned.
taskt[P&S], *pp.* Tasked.
tas′seld[P&S], *a.* & *pp.* Tasseled, tasselled.
tast′a-bl[P], *a.* Tastable.
tat′l[P], *v.* & *n.* Tattle.
tat′ld[P], *pp.* Tattled.
tat′terd[P&S], *pa.* Tattered.
tau′rin[S], *a.* Taurine.
taut[S], *imp.* & *pp.* Taught.
taut′end[S], *pp.* Tautened.
tau″to-fon′ic[P&S], *a.* Tautophonic.
tau″to-fon′i-cal[P&S], *a.* Tautophonical.
tau-tof′o-ny[P&S], *n.* Tautophony.
tawd[S], *pp.* Tawed.
tax′a-bl[P], *a.* & *n.* Taxable.
tax′a-bl-ness[P], *n.* Taxableness.
tax′a-tiv[S], *a.* Taxative.
tax′a-tiv-ly[S], *adv.* Taxatively.
taxt[P&S], *pp.* Taxed.
teach′a-bl[P], *a.* Teachable.
teach′a-bl-ness[P], *n.* Teachableness.

teamd[s], *pp.* Teamed.
teas'a-bl[P], *a.* Teasable.
tea'zel[s], *v.* & *n.* Teazle.
tea'zeld[s], *pp.* Teazeled, teazelled.
tec'nic[s], *a.* & *n.* Technic.
tec'ni-cal[s], *a.* Technical.
tec"ni-cal'i-ty[s], *n.* Technicality.
tec'ni-cal-ness[s], *n.* Technicalness.
tec-ni'cian[s], *n.* Technician.
tec'ni-cist[s], *n.* Technicist.
tec"ni-co-log'i-cal[s], *a.* Technicological.
tec"ni-col'o-gy[s], *n.* Technicology.
tec'ni-con[s], *n.* Technicon.
tec'nics[s], *n.* Technics.
tec'ni-fone[s], *n.* Techniphone.
tec'nism[s], *n.* Technism.
tec'nist[s], *n.* Technist.
tec"no-cau'sis[s], *n.* Technocausis.
tec"no-chem'i-cal[s], *a.* Technochemical.
tec"no-ge-og'ra-fer[P&S], *n.* Technogeographer.
tec"no-ge-og'ra-fy[P&S], *n.* Technogeography.
tec"no-graf'ic[P&S], *a.* Technographic.
tec-nog'ra-fy[P&S], *n.* Technography.
tec"no-lith'ic[s], *a.* Technolithic.
tec"no-log'ic[s], *a.* Technologic.
tec"no-log'i-cal[s], *a.* Technological.
tec-nol'o-gist[s], *n.* Technologist.
tec-nol'o-gy[s], *n.* Technology.
tec-non'o-my[s], *n.* Technonomy.
tec"ti-bran'chi-at[s], *a.* & *n.* Tectibranchiate.
tec"to-ce-fal'ic[P&S], *a.* Tectocephalic.
tec"to-cef'a-ly[P&S], *n.* Tectocephaly.
te'di-us[s], *a.* Tedious.
te'di-us-ly[s], *adv.* Tediously.
te'di-us-ness[s], *n.* Tediousness.
teemd[P&S], *pp.* Teemed.
tee'terd[s], *pp.* Teetered.
tel[P&S], *vt.* & *vi.* Tell.
tel-au'to-graf[P&S], *n.* Telautograph.
tel-au"to-graf'ic[P&S], *a.* Telautographic.
tel"au-tog'ra-fist[P&S], *n.* Telautographist.
tel"au-tog'ra-fy[P&S], *n.* Telautography.
tel"e-a-nem'o-graf[P&S], *n.* Teleanemograph.
tel"e-bar'o-graf[P&S], *n.* Telebarograph.
tel"e-chi'ro-graf[P&S], *n.* Telechirograph.
tel"e-cryp'to-graf[P&S], *n.* Telecryptograph.
te-lec'to-graf[P&S], *n.* Telectograph.
tel'e-feme[s], *n.* Telepheme.
tel'e-fer-age[s], *n.* Telepherage.
tel'e-fone[P&S], *v.* & *n.* Telephone.
tel'e-fon"er[s], *n.* Telephoner.
tel"e-fon'ic[P&S], *a.* Telephonic.
tel"e-fon'i-cal[s], *a.* Telephonical.
tel"e-fon'i-cal-ly[s], *adv.* Telephonically.
tel'e-fon-ist[s], *n.* Telephonist.
tel"e-fo'no-graf[s], *n.* Telephonograph.
tel"e-fo"no-graf'ic[s], *a.* Telephonographic.
te-lef'o-ny[P&S], *n.* Telephony.
tel'e-fote[s], *n.* Telephote.
tel"e-fo'to[s], *a.* Telephoto.
tel"e-fo'to-graf[P&S], *n.* Telephotograph.
tel"e-fo"to-graf'ic[s], *a.* Telephotographic.
tel"e-fo-tog'ra-fy[s], *n.* Telephotography.
tel"e-fo'tos[s], *n.* Telephotos.
tel'e-graf[P&S], *v.* & *n.* Telegraph.
te-leg'ra-fer[P&S], *n.* Telegrapher.
tel"e-graf'ic[P&S], *a.* Telegraphic.
tel"e-graf'i-cal[P&S], *a.* Telegraphical.
tel"e-graf'i-cal-ly[P&S], *adv.* Telegraphically.

te-leg′ra-fone[P&S], *n.* Telegraphone.
tel″e-graf′o-fone[P&S], *n.* Telegraphophone.
tel″e-graf′o-scope[P&S], *n.* Telegraphoscope.
tel′e-graft[P&S], *pp.* Telegraphed.
te-leg′ra-fy[P&S], *n.* Telegraphy.
tel″e-i-con′o-graf[P&S], *n.* Teleiconograph.
te-lel′o-graf[S], *n.* Telelograph.
tel″e-me-can′ic[S], *a.* Telemechanic.
tel″e-mec′a-nism[S], *n.* Telemechanism.
tel″e-me″te-or′o-graf[S], *n.* Telemeteorograph.
tel″e-me″te-or″o-graf′ic[S], *a.* Telemeteorographic.
tel″e-met′ro-graf[S], *n.* Telemetrograph.
tel″e-met″ro-graf′ic[S], *a.* Telemetrographic.
tel″e-me-trog′ra-fy[S], *n.* Telemetrography.
tel-en′ce-fal[S], *n.* Telencephal.
tel″en-cef′a-lon[S], *n.* Telencephalon.
tel″e-neg′a-tiv[P&S], *a.* Telenegative.
tel″e-ob-jec′tiv[P&S], *a.* & *n.* Teleobjective.
tel″e-o-cef′al[S], *n.* Teleocephal.
tel″e-o-cef′a-lus[S], *a.* Teleocephalous.
tel″e-o-fo′bi-a[S], *n.* Teleophobia
tel′e-o-fore[S], *n.* Teleophore.
tel′e-o-fyte[S], *n.* Teleophyte.
tel″e-op′til[P&S], **-ile**[P], *n.* Teleoptile.
tel″e-os′te-us[S], *a.* Teleosteous.
tel″e-ra′di-o-fone[S], *n.* Teleradiophone.
tel″e-ster′e-o-graf[P&S], *n.* Teleostereograph.
tel″e-ster″e-og′ra-fy[P&S], *n.* Telestereography.
tel″e-ther′mo-graf[P&S], *n.* Telethermograph.
tel″e-ther″mo-graf′ic[P&S], *a.* Telethermographic.
tel″i-con′o-graf[P&S], *n.* Teliconograph.
tell′a-bl[P], *a.* Tellable.
tel′li-graf[P&S], *n.* Telligraph.
tel′lo-graf[P&S], *n.* Tellograph.
tel″lo-graf′ic[P&S], *a.* Tellographic.
tel′o-fase[P&S], *n.* Telophase.
tel″o-trem′a-tus[S], *a.* Telotrematous.
tem″e-ra′ri-us[S], *a.* Temerarious.
tem″e-ra′ri-us-ly[S], *adv.* Temerariously.
tem″e-ra′ri-us-ness[S], *n.* Temerariousness.
te-mer′i-tus[S], *a.* Temeritous.
tem″no-pleu′rin[S], *a.* & *n.* Temnopleurine.
tem″no-spon′dy-lus[S], *a.* Temnospondylous.
tem′per-a-bl[P], *a.* Temperable.
tem′per-a″tiv[S], *a.* Temperative.
tem′perd[P&S], *pa.* Tempered.
tem′perd-ly[S], *adv.* Temperedly.
tem-pes′tu-us[S], *a.* Tempestuous.
tem-pes′tu-us-ly[S], *adv.* Tempestuously.
tem-pes′tu-us-ness[S], *n.* Tempestuousness.
tem′pl[P], *v.* & *n.* Temple.
tem′pl-less[P], *a.* Templeless.
tempt′a-bl[P], *a.* Temptable.
tempt′a-bl-ness[P], *n.* Temptableness.
tem′u-len-tiv[S], *a.* Temulentive.
ten′a-bl[P], *a.* Tenable.
ten′a-bl-ness[P], *n.* Tenableness.
te-na′cius[S], *a.* Tenacious.
te-na′cius-ly[S], *adv.* Tenaciously.
te-na′cius-ness[S], *n.* Tenaciousness.
ten′ant-a-bl[P], *a.* Tenantable.
ten′ant-a-bl-ness[P], *n.* Tenantableness.
ten′derd[P&S], *pp.* Tendered.
ten′di-nus[S], *a.* Tendinous.
ten′di-nus-ness[S], *n.* Tendinousness.
ten′do-nus[S], *a.* Tendonous.

ten′e-brus[S], *a.* Tenebrous.
ten′or[S], *a.* & *n.* Tenor.
te-nor′ra-py[S], *n.* Tenorrhapy.
ten′si-bl[F], *a.* Tensible.
ten′si-bl-ness[F], *n.* Tensibleness.
ten′sil[S], **-ile**[S], *a.* Tensile.
ten′sil-ly[S], **-ile-ly**[S], *adv.* Tensilely.
ten′siv[S], *a.* Tensive.
ten′ta-cl[F], *n.* Tentacle.
ten′ta-cld[F], *a.* Tentacled.
ten′ta-tiv[S], *a.* & *n.* Tentative.
ten′ta-tiv-ly[S], *adv.* Tentatively.
ten′u-us[S], *a.* Tenuous.
ten′u-us-ly[S], *adv.* Tenuously.
ten′u-us-ness[S], *n.* Tenuousness.
ter″a-to-fo′bi-a[F&S], *n.* Teratophobia.
ter″a-tom′a-tus[S], *a.* Teratomatous.
ter-clo′rid[S], *n.* Terchlorid.
ter′cin[S], *n.* Tercine.
ter″e-bin′thin[S], *a.* Terebinthine.
ter″e-bin′thi-nus[S], *a.* Terebinthinous.
ter″e-brat′u-lin[S], *a.* Terebratuline.
ter′e-din[S], *n.* Teredine.
ter″ef-thal′ic[F&S], *a.* Terephthalic.
ter-gem′i-nus[S], *a.* Tergeminous.
ter-gif′er-us[S], *a.* Tergiferous.
termd[F&S], *pp.* Termed.
ter′mi-na-bl[F], *a.* Terminable.
ter′mi-na-bl-ness[F], *n.* Terminableness.
ter′mi-na″tiv[F&S], *a.* Terminative.
ter′mi-na″tiv-ly[S], *adv.* Terminatively.
ter′mi-to-fil[F&S], *n.* Termitophile.
ter″mi-tof′i-lus[S], *a.* Termitophilous.
tern-stre″mi-a′ceus[S], *a.* Ternstrœmiaceous.
ter-ra′ceus[S], *a.* Terraceous.
ter-ra′ne-us[S], *a.* Terraneous.
ter-ra′que-us[S], *a.* Terraqueous.
ter′ra-sfere[F&S], *n.* Terrasphere.
ter″re-mo′tiv[F&S], *a.* Terremotive.
ter′ri-bl[F], *a.* Terrible.
ter′ri-bl-ness[F], *n.* Terribleness.
ter-ric′o-lin[S], *a.* Terricoline.
ter-ric′o-lus[S], *a.* Terricolous.
ter-rig′e-nus[S], *a.* Terrigenous.
tes″sa-raf′thong[F&S], *n.* Tessaraphthong.
test′a-bl[F], *a.* Testable.
tes-ta″ce-og′ra-fy[F&S], *n.* Testaceography.
tes-ta′ce-us[S], *a.* Testaceous.
tes″ti-car′din[S], *a.* Testicardine.
tes′ti-cl[F], *n.* Testicle.
tes-tu″di-na′ri-us[S], *a.* Testudinarious.
tes″tu-din′e-us[S], *a.* Testudineous.
tet″a-nig′e-nus[S], *a.* Tetanigenous.
te-tar″to-fy′i-a[F&S], *n.* Tetartophyia.
teth′erd[S], *pp.* Tethered.
tet″ra-cam′a-rus[S], *a.* Tetracamarous.
tet″ra-can′thus[S], *a.* Tetracanthous.
te-trac′er-us[S], *a.* Tetracerous.
tet″ra-che′ni-um[F&S], *n.* Tetrachænium.
tet″ra-che′tus[S], *a.* Tetrachætous.
tet″ra-clad′in[S], *a.* Tetracladine.
tet″ra-clo′rid[S], *n.* Tetrachlorid.
tet″ra-clor″meth′ane[S], *n.* Tetrachlormethane.
tet″ra-cor′al-lin[S], *a.* Tetracoralline.
tet′ra-cord[S], *n.* Tetrachord.
tet″ra-cor′dal[S], *a.* Tetrachordal.
tet″ra-cor′don[S], *n.* Tetrachordon.
tet″ra-cot′o-mus[S], *a.* Tetrachotomous.
tet″ra-cot′o-my[S], *n.* Tetrachotomy.
tet″ra-cro′mic[S], *a.* Tetrachromic.
te-trac′ro-nus[S], *a.* Tetrachronous.
tet″ra-dac′ty-lus[S], *a.* Tetradactylous.
tet″ra-de-cap′o-dus[S], *a.* Tetradecapodous.

tet″ra-fal″an-gar′chi-aP&S, *n.* Tetraphalangarchia.
tet″ra-far′ma-calP&S, *a.* Tetrapharmacal.
tet″ra-far′ma-conP&S, *n.* Tetrapharmacon.
tet″ra-far′ma-cumP&S, *n.* Tetrapharmacum.
tet″ra-fyl′lousP&S, *a.* Tetraphyllous.
te-trag′e-nusS, *a.* Tetragenous.
te-trag′o-nusS, *a.* Tetragonous.
te-trag′y-nusS, *a.* Tetragynous.
tet″ra-lof′o-dontP&S, *a.* Tetralophodont.
tet″ra-mas′thusS, *a.* Tetramasthous.
te-tram′er-usS, *a.* Tetramerous.
tet′ra-morfP&S, *n.* Tetramorph.
tet″ra-mor′ficP&S, *a.* Tetramorphic.
tet″ra-mor′fismP&S, *n.* Tetramorphism.
tet″ra-mor′fusS, *a.* Tetramorphous.
te-tran′drusS, *a.* Tetrandrous.
tet″ra-nef′ricP&S, *a.* Tetranephric.
te-tran′y-chinP&S, *a.* & *n.* Tetranychine.
tet′ra-o-ninS, *a.* & *n.* Tetraonine.
tet″ra-pet′a-lusS, *a.* Tetrapetalous.
tet′ra-plusS, *a.* Tetraplous.
te-trap′o-dusS, *a.* Tetrapodous.
tet′ra-pusS, *a.* Tetrapous.
te-trap′ter-usS, *a.* Tetrapterous.
tet″ra-py-re′nusS, *a.* Tetrapyrenous.
te-traq′ue-trusS, *a.* Tetraquetrous.
tet′rarcS, *n.* Tetrarch.
tet″ra-sep′a-lusS, *a.* Tetrasepalous.
tet″ra-sfer′icP&S, *a.* Tetraspheric.
tet″ra-sfer′i-calP&S, *a.* Tetraspherical.
tet″ra-sper′ma-tusS, *a.* Tetraspermatous.
tet″ra-sper′musS, *a.* Tetraspermous.
tet′ra-spo″rusS, *a.* Tetrasporous.
tet′ra-sticS, *n.* Tetrastich.
te-tras′ti-cusS, *a.* Tetrastichous.
tet″ra-syl′la-blP, *n.* Tetrasyllable.
tex′tilS, **-tile**S, *a.* & *n.* Textile.
thal″a-men′ce-falP&S, *n.* Thalamencephal.
thal″a-men-ce-fal′icP&S, *a.* Thalamencephalic.
thal″a-men-cef′a-lonP&S, *n.* Thalamencephalon.
thal″a-mef′o-rosP&S, *n.* Thalamephoros.
thal″a-mef′o-rusP&S, *n.* Thalamephorus.
thal′a-mo-celeP&S, *n.* Thalamocœle.
thal″as-of′i-lusS, *a.* Thalassophilous.
tha-las″so-fo′bi-aP&S, *n.* Thalassophobia.
tha-las′si-o-fyteP&S, *n.* Thalassiophyte.
thal″as-sog′ra-ferP&S, *n.* Thalassographer.
tha-las″so-graf′icP&S, *a.* Thalassographic.
tha-las″so-graf′i-calP&S, *a.* Thalassographical.
thal″as-sog′ra-fyP&S, *n.* Thalassography.
thal-lif′er-usS, *a.* Thalliferous.
thal′linS, *a.* Thalline.
thal′lo-cloreS, *n.* Thallochlore.
thal-lof′o-riP&S, *n. pl.* Thallophori.
thal′lo-fyteP&S, *n.* Thallophyte.
thal″lo-fyt′icP&S, *a.* Thallophytic.
thal′lusS, *a.* Thallous.
tham′no-filS, *n.* Thamnophile.
than″a-to-fid′i-anP&S, *a.* Thanatophidian.
than″a-to-fo′bi-aP&S, *n.* Thanatophobia.
than″a-tog′ra-ferP&S, *n.* Thanatographer.
than″a-tog′ra-fyP&S, *n.* Thanatography.

thăn″a-to-ty′fus[P&S], *a.* Thanatotyphus.
thankt[P&S], *pp.* Thanked.
thatcht[S], *pa.* Thatched.
thau″ma-tog′ra-fy[P&S], *n.* Thaumatography.
thawd[P&S], *pp.* Thawed.
the′a-ter[P&S], *n.* Theatre.
the′a-tin[S], *a.* & *n.* Theatine.
the″a-tro-fo′bi-a[P&S], *n.* Theatrophobia.
the-at′ro-fone[P&S], *n.* Theatrophone.
the′ca-fore[P&S], *n.* Thecaphore.
the″ca-spo′rus[S], *a.* Thecasporous.
the-cif′er-us[S], *a.* Theciferous.
the-cig′er-us[S], *a.* Thecigerous.
the″co-dac′ty-lus[S], *a.* Thecodactylous.
the″co-som′a-tus[S], *a.* Thecosomatous.
the-cos′to-mus[S], *a.* Thecostomous.
thel″e-fo-ra′ceus[S], *a.* Thelephoraceous.
thel-fu′si-an[P&S], *a.* & *n.* Thelphusian.
thel-fu′sid[P&S], *n.* Thelphusid.
thel-fu′soid[P&S], *a.* Thelphusoid.
the-lyf′o-nid[P&S], *a.* & *n.* Thelyphonid.
the-lyf′o-noid[P&S], *a.* Thelyphonoid.
the-lyg′e-nus[S], *a.* Thelygenous.
the-lyg″o-na′ceus[S], *a.* Thelygonaceous.
the″ly-ot′o-kus[S], *a.* Thelyotokous.
the-lyt′o-kus, the-lyt′o-cus[S], *a.* Thelytokous, thelytocous.
them-selvs′[P&S], *pron. pl.* Themselves.
thense[P], *adv.* Thence.
the″o-fan′ic[P&S], *a.* Theophanic.
the-of′a-ny[P&S], *n.* Theophany.
the″o-fil″an-throp′ic[P&S], *a.* Theophilanthropic.
the″o-fi-lan′thro-pism[P&S], *n.* Theophilanthropism.
the″o-fil″o-sof′ic[P&S], *a.* Theophilosophic.
the″o-fo′bi-a[P&S], *n.* Theophobia.
the-of′o-bist[P&S], *n.* Theophobist.
the-of′o-rus[S], *a.* Theophorous.
the″o-fras-ta′ce-us[S], *a.* Theophrastaceous.
the″o-fyl′lin[P&S], **-ine**[P&S], *n.* Theophyllin, theophylline.
the″o-mor′fic[P&S], *a.* Theomorphic.
the″o-mor′fism[P&S], *n.* Theomorphism.
the″o-sof′ic[P&S], *a.* Theosophic.
the″o-sof′i-cal[P&S], *a.* Theosophical.
the″o-sof′i-cal-ly[P&S], *adv.* Theosophically.
the-os′o-fer[P&S], *n.* Theosopher.
the-os′o-fism[P&S], *n.* Theosophism.
the-os′o-fist[P&S], *n.* Theosophist.
the″o-so-fis′ti-cal[P&S], *a.* Theosophistical.
the-os′o-fize[P&S], *vt.* & *vi.* Theosophize.
the-os′o-fy[P&S], *n.* Theosophy.
the″o-tec′nic[S], *a.* Theotechnic.
the″o-tec′nist[S], *n.* Theotechnist.
the″o-tec′ny[S], *n.* Theotechny.
ther′a-fose[P&S], *n.* Theraphose.
ther″a-fo′sid[P&S], *a.* & *n.* Theraphosid.
ther″a-fo′soid[P&S], *a.* Theraphosoid.
ther″i-o-mor′fic[P&S], *a.* Theriomorphic.
the″ri-o-mor′fo-sis[P&S], *n.* Theriomorphosis.
the″ri-o-mor′fus[S], *a.* Theriomorphous.
the″ri-o-trof′i-cal[P&S], *a.* Theriotrophical.
ther-met′o-graf[P&S], *n.* Thermetograph.
ther-met′ro-graf[P&S], *n.* Thermetrograph.
ther″mo-a′que-us[S], *a.* Thermoaqueous.
ther″mo-bar′o-graf[P&S], *n.* Thermobarograph.
ther″mo-ca-ot′ic[S], *a.* Thermochaotic.

ther″mo-cro′ic[S], *a.* Thermochroic.
ther′mo-crose[S], *n.* Thermochrose.
ther″mo-cro′sy[S], *n.* Thermochrosy.
ther′mo-cup″l[P], *n.* Thermocouple.
ther-mof′a-gy[P&S], *n.* Thermophagy.
ther′mo-fil[P&S], *a.* Thermophile.
ther″mo-fil′ic[P&S], *a.* Thermofilic.
ther-mof′i-lus[S], *a.* Thermophilous.
ther″mo-fo′bi-a[P&S], *n.* Thermophobia.
ther′mo-fone[P&S], *n.* Thermophone.
ther′mo-fore[P&S], *n.* Thermophore.
ther″mo-fy′lic[P&S], *a.* Thermophylic.
ther″mo-fyl′lite[P&S], *n.* Thermophyllite.
ther′mo-graf[P&S], *n.* Thermograph.
ther″mo-graf′ic[P&S], *a.* Thermographic.
ther-mog′ra-fy[P&S], *n.* Thermography.
ther″mo-hy′gro-graf[P&S], *n.* Thermohygrograph.
ther″mo-met″a-mor′fic[P&S], *a.* Thermometamorphic.
ther″mo-met″a-mor′fism[P&S], *n.* Thermometamorphism.
ther″mo-met′ro-graf[P&S], *n.* Thermometrograph.
ther″mo-mo′tiv[S], *a.* Thermomotive.
ther″mo-psy-crof′o-rus[S], *n.* Thermopsychrophorus.
ther′mo-si″fon[P&S], *n.* Thermosiphon.
ther′mo=tel″e-fone[P&S], *n.* Thermo=telephone.
ther″mo-ten′sil[P&S], *a.* Thermotensile.
the″ro-ce-fa′li-an[P&S], *a.* & *n.* Therocephalian.
the-rom′o-rus[S], *a.* Theromorous.
the′ro-morf[P&S], *n.* Theromorph.
the″ro-mor′fi-a[P&S], *n.* Theromorphia.
the″ro-mor′fic[P&S], *a.* Theromorphic.
the″ro-mor′fism[P&S], *n.* Theromorphism.
the″ro-mor″fo-log′i-cal[P&S], *a.* Thermomorphological.
the″ro-mor′fus[S], *a.* Theromorphous.
the-rop′o-dus[S], *a.* Theropodous.
thi′a-sarc[S], *n.* Thiasarch.
thick′end[P&S], *pp.* Thickened.
thiev[P], *vt.* & *vi.* Thieve.
thievd[P&S], *pp.* Thieved.
thil[S], *n.* Thill.
thim′bl[P], *n.* Thimble.
thind[P&S], *pp.* Thinned.
think′a-bl[P], *a.* Thinkable.
thi-noc′o-rin[S], *a.* Thinocorine.
thi″o-an″ti-mo′ni-us[S], *a.* Thioantimonious.
thi″o-ar-se′ni-us[S], *a.* Thioarsenious.
thi″o-cro′mus[S], *a.* Thiochromous.
thi′o-fene[P&S], *n.* Thiophene.
thi″o-fe′nic[P&S], *a.* Thiophenic.
thi″o-fe′nol[P&S], *n.* Thiophenol.
thi″o-fil′ic[P&S], *a.* Thiophilic.
thi″o-fos′fate[P&S], *n.* Thiophosphate.
thi-of′thene[P&S], *n.* Thiophthene.
thi″o-naf′thene[P&S], *n.* Thionaphthene.
thirl′a-bl[P], *a.* Thirlable.
this′tl[P], *n.* Thistle.
thlips″en-cef′a-lus[P&S], *n.* Thlipsencephalus.
tho[P], *conj.* Though, tho′.
tho″ra-cos′tra-cus[S], *a.* Thoracostracous.
thornd[S], *a.* Thorned.
thor′o[S], *a.*, *n.* & *adv.* Thorough.
thor′o-fare[S], *n.* Thoroughfare.
thor′o-ly[S], *adv.* Thoroughly.
thor′o-ness[S], *n.* Thoroughness.
thrald[S], *pp.* Thralled.
thrasht[P&S], *pp.* Thrashed.
thred[P&S], *v.* & *n.* Thread.
thresht[S], *pp.* Threshed.
thret[P&S], *n.* Threat.
thret′en[P&S], *vt.* & *vi.* Threaten.
thret′en-a-bl[P], *a.* Threatenable.
thret′end[P&S], *pp.* Threatened.
thril[P&S], *v.* & *n.* Thrill.

thrild[P&S], *pp.* Thrilled.
thro[S], *v.* & *n.* Throw.
throbd[P&S], *pp.* Throbbed.
throngd[P&S], *pp.* Thronged.
throt'l[P], *v.* & *n.* Throttle.
throt'ld[P], *pp.* Throttled.
thru[S], *imp.* Threw.
thru[P&S], *a.*, *n.*, *adv.* & *prep.* Through, thro'.
thrumd[P&S], *pp.* Thrummed.
thru-out'[P&S], *adv.* & *prep.* Throughout.
thum[P&S], *v.* & *n.* Thumb.
thumd[P&S], *pp.* Thumbed.
thumpt[P&S], *pp.* Thumped.
thun'derd[P&S], *pp.* Thundered.
thu'ri-bl[P], *n.* Thurible.
thu-rif'er-us[S], *a.* Thuriferous.
thur'o[P], *a.*, *n.* & *adv.* Thorough.
thur'o-ly[P], *adv.* Thoroughly.
thur'o-ness[P], *n.* Thoroughness.
thwackt[P&S], *pp.* Thwacked.
thy'la-cin[S], *n.* Thylacine.
thy-lac'i-nin[S], *a.* & *n.* Thylacinine.
thy"la-co'le-o-nin[S], *a.* & *n.* Thylacoleonine.
thym'i-a-tec"ny[S], *n.* Thymiatechny.
thym'us[S], *a.* Thymous.
thy"re-o-fy'ma[P&S], *n.* Thyreophyma.
thy-rog'e-nus[S], *a.* Thyrogenous.
thyr-sif'er-us[S], *a.* Thyrsiferous.
thy"sa-nop'o-dus[S], *a.* Thysanopodous.
thy"sa-nop'ter-us[S], *a.* Thysanopterous.
Ti'ber-in[S], *a.* Tiberine.
ti"cho-dro'min[S], *a.* & *n.* Tichodromine.
ti'cho-rin[S], *a.* & *n.* Tichorine.
tick'l[P], *v.* & *n.* Tickle.
tick'ld[P], *pp.* Tickled.
tickt[P&S], *pa.* Ticked.
tierse[P], *n.* Tierce.
tif[S], *v.* & *n.* Tiff.
tift[S], *pp.* Tiffed.
tight'end[S], *pp.* Tightened.
ti'grin[S], **ti'ger-in**[S], *a.* Tigrine, tigerine.
til[P&S], *v.*, *n.*, *prep.* & *conj.* Till.
tild[P&S], *pp.* Tilled.
til"i-a'ceus[S], *a.* Tiliaceous.
till'a-bl[P], *a.* Tillable.
til-le"ti-a'ceus[S], *a.* Tilletiaceous.
tim'a-lin[P], *a.* Timaline.
tim'berd[S], *pa.* Timbered.
ti-mel'i-in[S], *a.* & *n.* Timeliine.
tim'or-us[S], *a.* Timorous.
tim'or-us-ly[S], *adv.* Timorously.
tim'or-us-ness[S], *n.* Timorousness.
tin'a-min[S], *a.* & *n.* Tinamine.
tin"a-mo-mor'fic[P&S], *a.* Tinamomorphic.
tin"a-mo'tin[S], *a.* & *n.* Tinamotine.
tind[P&S], *pp.* & *a.* Tinned.
tin'e-in[S], *a.* & *n.* Tineine.
tin'gi-bl[P], *a.* Tingible.
tin'gl[P], *v.* & *n.* Tingle.
tin'gld[P], *pp.* Tingled.
tink'erd[P&S], *pp.* Tinkered.
tin'kl[P], *v.* & *n.* Tinkle.
tin'kld[P], *pp.* Tinkled.
tin'seld[S], *pp.* Tinseled, tinselled.
tin"tin-nab'u-lus[S], *a.* Tintinnabulous.
tip'l[P], *v.* & *n.* Tipple.
tip'ld[P], *pp.* Tippled.
tip'staff"[P], *n.* Tipstaff.
tipt[P&S], *pp.* Tipped.
tire'graf[P&S], *n.* Tiregraph.
tire'sum[P&S], *a.* Tiresome.
tis'ic[S], *a.* Phthisic.
ti'sis[S], *n.* Phthisis.
ti"tan-if'er-us[S], *a.* Titaniferous.
ti"ta-no-the'ri-in[S], *a.* & *n.* Titanotheriine.
ti'tan-us[S], *a.* Titanous.
tith'a-bl[P], **tithe'a-bl**[P], *a.* & *n.* Tithable, titheable.

tith"o-no-graf'ic[P&S], *a.* Tithonographic.
tit'il-la"tiv[S], *a.* Titillative.
tit'l[P], *n.* Title.
tit'terd[P&S], *pp.* Tittered.
tit'y-rin[S], *a.* & *n.* Tityrine.
to[S], *v.* & *n.* Toe.
to[S], *v.* & *n.* Tow.
to'din[S], *a.* Todine.
tod'l[P], *v.* & *n.* Toddle.
toes[S], *3rd per. sing. pres. ind.* Tows.
to-fa'ceus[S], *a.* Tophaceous.
togd[S], *pp.* Togged.
toi-cog'ra-fy[S], *n.* Toichography.
toild[P&S], *pp.* Toiled.
toil'sum[P&S], *a.* Toilsome.
toil'sum-ly[P], *adv.* Toilsomely.
toil'sum-ness[P], *n.* Toilsomeness.
to'kend[S], *pp.* Tokened.
tol'er-a-bl[P], *a.* Tolerable.
tol'er-a-bl-ness[P], *n.* Tolerableness.
toll'a-bl[P], *a.* Tollable.
tolld[P], **told**[P&S], *pp.* Tolled.
tol"y-pen'tin[S], *a.* & *n.* Tolypentine.
to-mal'lin[S], *n.* Tomalline.
to-men'tus[S], *a.* Tomentous.
to-mip'a-rus[S], *a.* Tomiparous.
tongd[S], *pp.* Tonged.
ton'o-fant[P&S], *n.* Tonophant.
ton'o-graf[P&S], *n.* Tonograph.
ton"o-tec'nic[S], *n.* Tonotechnic.
toold[S], *pp.* Tooled.
tooth'ake"[P&S], *a.* Toothache.
tooth'sum[P&S], *a.* Toothsome.
tootht[P&S], *a.* Toothed.
to'parc[S], *n.* Toparch.
top'l[P], *vt.* & *vi.* Topple.
top'ld[P], *pp.* Toppled.
top"o-fo'bi-a[P&S], *n.* Topophobia.
top'o-fone[P&S], *n.* Topophone.
to-pog'ra-fer[P&S], *n.* Topographer.
top"o-graf'ic[S], *a.* Topographic.
top"o-graf'i-cal[P], *a.* Topographical.
top"o-graf'i-cal-ly[P], *adv.* Topographically.
to-pog'ra-fist[P], *n.* Topographist.
top"o-graf"o-met'ric[P&S], *a.* Topographometric.
to-pog'ra-fy[P&S], *n.* Topography.
top'o-morf[P&S], *n.* Topomorph.
topt[S], *pp.* Topped.
to-reu"ma-tog'ra-fy[P&S], *n.* Toreumatography.
tor-fa'ceus[S], *a.* Torfaceous.
tor'mi-nus[S], *a.* Torminous.
tor'siv[S], *a.* Torsive.
tor'tiv[S], *a.* Tortive.
tor'tur-a-bl[P], *a.* Torturable.
tor'tur-a-bl-ness[P], *n.* Torturableness.
to'rus[S], *a.* Torous.
tor'ren-tin[S], *a.* Torrentine.
tor'til[P&S], *a.* Tortile.
tor'tri-cin[P&S], *a.* & *n.* Tortricine.
tor'tu-us[S], *a.* Tortuous.
tor'tu-us-ly[S], *adv.* Tortuously.
tor'tu-us-ness[S], *n.* Tortuousness.
tor'u-lus[S], *a.* Torulous.
tos[P&S], *v.* & *n.* Toss.
tost[P&S], *pp.* Tossed.
tot'i-tiv[S], *a.* Totitive.
tot'terd[P&S], *pp.* Tottered.
toucht[P&S], *pp.* Touched.
tourd[S], *pp.* Toured.
to-va"ri-a'ceus[S], *a.* Tovariaceous.
towd[P&S], *pp.* Towed.
tow'eld[S], *pp.* Toweled, towelled.
tow'erd[S], *pp.* Towered.
tox"i-cof'a-gus[S], *a.* Toxicophagous.
tox"i-cof'a-gy[P&S], *n.* Toxicophagy.
tox"i-co-fo'bi-a[P&S], *n.* Toxicophobia.
tox"i-co-fy-lax'in[P&S], *n.* Toxicophylaxin.
tox-if'er-us[S], *a.* Toxiferous.
tox"i-fo'bi-a[P&S], *n.* Toxiphobia.
tox"i-for'ic[P&S], *a.* Toxiphoric.
tox"in-fec'tius[S], *a.* Toxinfectious.

tox'o-fil[r&s], *a.* Toxophil.
tox-of'i-lite[r&s], *a.* & *n.* Toxophilite.
tox-of"i-lit'ic[r&s], *a.* Toxofilitic.
tox-of'i-lus[s], *a.* Toxophilous.
tox'o-fore[r&s], *n.* Toxophore.
tox"o-for'ic[r&s], *a.* Toxophoric.
tox-of'o-rus[s], *a.* Toxophorous.
tox"o-fy-lax'in[r&s], *n.* Toxophylaxin.
toyd[r&s], *pp.* Toyed.
trace'a-bl[r], *a.* Traceable.
trace'a-bl-ness[r], *n.* Traceableness.
tra'che-o-fone[r&s], *a.* & *n.* Tracheophone.
tra"che-of'o-nus[s], *a.* Tracheophonous.
tra"che-of'o-ny[r&s], *n.* Tracheophony.
tra"che-of'y-ma[r&s], *n.* Tracheophyma.
tra"che-o-pho'nin[s], *n.* Tracheophonine.
tra"chy-car'pus[s], *a.* Trachycarpous.
tra"chy-fo'ni-a[r&s], *n.* Trachyphonia.
tra-chyf'o-nus[s], *a.* Trachyphonous.
tra'chy-lin[s], *a.* Trachyline.
track'a-bl[r], *a.* Trackable.
trackt[r&s], *pp.* Tracked.
tract'a-bl[r], *a.* Tractable.
tract'a-bl-ness[r], *n.* Tractableness.
trac'til[r&s], **-ile**[s], *a.* Tractile.
trac'tiv[r&s], *a.* Tractive.
trad'i-tiv[s], *a.* Traditive.
tra-duc'i-bl[r], *a.* Traducible.
traf'fickt[r], *pp.* Trafficked.
traf'fict[s], *pp.* Trafficked.
tra-gel'a-phin[s], *a.* Tragelaphine.
trag'u-lin[s], *a.* & *n.* Traguline.
traild[r&s], *pp.* Trailed.
train'a-bl[r], *a.* Trainable.
traind[r&s], *pp.* Trained.
tramd[s], *pp.* Trammed.
trammeld[s], *pa.* Trammeled.
tram'pl[r], *vt.* & *vi.* Trample.
tram'pld[r], *pp.* Trampled.
trampt[r&s], *pp.* Tramped.
tran'quil-ize[r], *vt.* & *vi.* Tranquilise, tranquillise.
tran-scend'i-bl[r], *a.* Transcendible.
tran-scrip'tiv[s], *a.* Transcriptive.
tran-scrip'tiv-ly[s], *adv.* Transcriptively.
transe[r], *n.* Trance.
trans-fer'a-bl[r], *a.* Transferable.
trans-ferd'[r&s], *pp.* Transferred.
trans-fixt'[s], *pp.* Transfixed.
trans-form'a-bl[r], *a.* Transformable.
trans-form'a-tiv[s], *a.* Transformative.
trans-formd'[r&s], *pp.* Transformed.
trans-fu'siv[s], *a.* Transfusive.
trans-fuze'[r], *vt.* Transfuse.
trans-fuz'i-bl[r], *a.* Transfuzible.
trans-gress'i-bl[r], *a.* Transgressible.
trans-gres'siv[s], *a.* Transgressive.
trans-gres'siv-ly[s], *adv.* Transgressively.
trans-grest'[s], *pp.* Transgressed.
tran'si-tiv[r&s], *a.* Transitive.
tran'si-tiv-ly[s], *adv.* Transitively.
tran'si-tiv-ness[s], *n.* Transitiveness.
trans-lat'a-bl[r], *a.* Translatable.
trans-lat'a-bl-ness[r], *n.* Translatableness.
trans-la'tiv[s], *a.* Translative.
trans-mis'si-bl[r], *a.* Transmissible.
trans-mis'siv[r&s], *a.* Transmissive.
trans-mis'siv-ness[r&s], *n.* Transmissiveness.
trans-mit-ta-[or **i-**] **bl**[r], *a.* Transmittable, transmittible.
trans-mut'a-bl[r], *a.* Transmutable.
trans-mut'a-bl-ness[r], *n.* Transmutableness.
trans-mut'a-tiv[s], *a.* Transmutative.
tran-spir'a-bl[r], *a.* Transpirable.
trans-plant'a-bl[r], *a.* Transplantable.
trans-pon'i-bl[r], *a.* Transponible.
trans-pon'tin[s], *a.* Transpontine.

trans-port′a-bl[P], *a.* Transportable.
trans-pos′a-bl[P], *a.* Transposable.
trans-pos′i-tiv[S], *a.* Transpositive.
trans-pos′i-tiv-ly[S], *adv.* Transpositively.
transt[S], *pp.* Tranced.
tran-sump′tiv[S], *a.* Transumptive.
Trap′pis-tin[S], *a.* Trappistine.
trapt[P&S], *pp.* Trapped.
trav′eld[P&S], *pa.* Traveled, travelled.
trav′el-er[P], *n.* Traveller.
trav′ers-a-bl[P], *a.* Traversable.
trav′erst[S], *pp.* Traversed.
trea′cl[P], *n.* Treacle.
trea′son-a-bl[P], *a.* Treasonable.
trea′son-a-bl-ness[P], *n.* Treasonableness.
trea′tis[P&S], *n.* Treatise.
treb′l[P], *v., a. & n.* Treble.
treb′l-ness[P], *n.* Trebleness.
trech′er-ous[P&S], *a.* Treacherous.
trech′er-ous-ly[P], *adv.* Treacherously.
trech′er-ous-ness[P], *n.* Treacherousness.
trech′er-y[P&S], *n.* Treachery.
tred[P&S], *v. & n.* Tread.
tred′l[P], *v. & n.* Treadle.
tred′le[S], *v. & n.* Treadle.
trel′list[S], *pp.* Trellised.
trem′bl[P], *v. & n.* Tremble.
trem′bld[P], *pp.* Trembled.
trem′el-lin[S], *a.* Tremelline.
trencht[P&S], *pp.* Trenched.
tre-pand′[P&S], *pp.* Trepanned.
tres[P&S], *v. & n.* Tress.
tres′past[P&S], *pp.* Trespassed.
trest[S], *a.* Tressed.
tres′tl, tres′sel[P], *n.* Trestle.
tre′sure[S], *v. & n.* Treasure.
tre′sur-er[S], *n.* Treasurer.
tre′sur-y[S], *n.* Treasury.
tre′zure[P], *v. & n.* Treasure.
tre′zur-er[P], *n.* Treasurer.
tre′zur-y[P], *n.* Treasury.
tri′a-bl[P], *a.* Triable.
tri′a-bl-ness[P], *n.* Triableness.
trich′e-chin[S], *a. & n.* Trichechine.
trich″o-pho′cin[S], *a.* Trichophocine.
trick′l[P], *v. & n.* Trickle.
trick′ld[P], *pp.* Trickled.
trickt[P&S], *pp.* Tricked.
tri″de-riv′a-tiv[P&S], *n.* Triderivative.
tri′glyf[P], *n.* Triglyph.
tri-glyf′ic[P], *a.* Triglyphic.
tri-glyf′i-cal[P], *a.* Triglyphical.
tril[P], *v. & n.* Trill.
trild[P&S], *pp.* Trilled.
trimd[P&S], *pp.* Trimmed.
trin′gin[S], *a. & n.* Tringine.
tri-part′i-bl[P], *a.* Tripartible.
triph′yl-lin[S], *n.* Triphylline.
trip′l[P], *v., a. & n.* Triple.
trip′ld[P], *pp.* Tripled.
trip′o-lin[S], *a.* Tripoline.
tript[P&S], *pp.* Tripped.
tri-syl′la-bl[P], *n.* Trisyllable.
trit′u-ra-bl[P], *a.* Triturable.
tri′umf[P&S], *v. & n.* Triumph.
tri-um′fal[P], *a.* Triumphal.
tri-um′fant[P], *a.* Triumphant.
tri-um′fant-ly[P], *adv.* Triumphantly.
tri′um-fer[P], *n.* Triumpher.
tri′umf-ing-ly[P], *adv.* Triumphingly.
tri′umft[P], *pp.* Triumphed.
triv′i-in[S], *a. & n.* Triviine.
tro-ca′ic[S], *a. & n.* Trochaic.
tro-chil′i-din[S], *a.* Trochilidine.
troch′i-lin[S], *a.* Trochiline.
trod′n[P], *pp.* Trodden.
trof[P&S], *n.* Trough.
tro′fy[P&S], *v. & n.* Trophy.
trog′lo-dy″tin[S], *a. & n.* Troglodytine.
trold[S], *pp.* Trolled.
trol′ly[S], *v. & n.* Trolley.
troopt[P&S], *pp.* Trooped.
trounst[S], *pp.* Trounced.
trow′eld[S], *pp.* Troweled, trowelled.
tru[S], *v., a. & adv.* True.

trub'l[P], *v. & n.* Trouble.
trub'ld[P], *pp.* Troubled.
trub'lous[P], *a.* Troublous.
trub'l-sum[P], *a.* Troublesome.
trub'l-sum-ly[P], *adv.* Troublesomely.
trub'l-sum-ness[P], *n.* Troublesomeness.
truck'l[P], *vi.* Truckle.
truck'ld[P], *pp.* Truckled.
truckt[P&S], *pp.* Trucked.
trumpt[P&S], *pp.* Trumped.
trunkt[S], *a.* Trunked.
trus[P&S], *v. & n.* Truss.
trust[S], *a.* Trussed.
trust'a-bl[P], *a.* Trustable.
try'a-bl[P], *a.* Tryable.
tryp'e-tin[S], *a.* Trypetine.
tubd[S], *pp.* Tubbed.
tu″bi-na'rin[S], *a.* Tubinarine.
tu'bu-la-rin[S], *a.* Tubularine.
tuch[P&S], *v. & n.* Touch.
tuch'a-bl[P], *a.* Touchable.
tuch'a-bl-ness[P], *n.* Touchableness.
tuch'er[P], *n.* Toucher.
tuch'i-ly[P], *adv.* Touchily.
tuch'i-ness[P], *n.* Touchiness.
tuch'ing[P], *pa., n. & prep.* Touching.
tuch'less[P], *a.* Touchless.
tuch'piece″[P], *n.* Touchpiece.
tuch'stone″[P], *n.* Touchstone.
tucht[P], *pp.* Touched.
tuch'wood″[P], *n.* Touchwood.
tuch'y[P], *a.* Touchy.
tuckt[P&S], *pp.* Tucked.
tuf[P&S], *a. & n.* Tough.
tuf'en[P], *vt. & vi.* Toughen.
tuf'end[P], *pp.* Toughened.
tuf'fen[S], *vt. & vi.* Toughen.
tuf'fer[S], *a.* Tougher.
tuf'ish[P], *a.* Toughish.
tuf'ly[P], *adv.* Toughly.
tuf'ness[P], *n.* Toughness.
tugd[P&S], *pp.* Tugged.
tum'bl[P], *v. & n.* Tumble.
tum'bld[P], *pp.* Tumbled.
tu'mor[S], *n.* Tumour.
tun[P], *n.* Ton.
tun'a-bl[P], **tune'a-bl**[P], *a.* Tunable, tuneable.
tun'a-bl-ness[P], **tune'a-bl-ness**[P], *n.* Tunableness, tuneableness.
tund[S], *pp.* Tunned.
tung[P&S], *v. & n.* Tongue.
tungd[P&S], *pp.* Tongued.
tun'neld[S], *pp. & a.* Tunneled, tunnelled.
tur'bin[S], **-ine**[S], *n.* Turbine.
tur'din[S], *a. & n.* Turdine.
turft[S], *pp.* Turfed.
tur'ky[S], *n.* Turkey.
tur'moild[S], *pp.* Turmoiled.
tur'na-ment[S], *n.* Tournament.
turnd[P&S], *pp.* Turned.
tur'ni-cin[S], *a.* Turnicine.
tur'ny[S], *v. & n.* Tourney.
tur'tl[P], *v. & n.* Turtle.
tur'tld[P], *pp.* Turtled.
tusht[S], *a.* Tushed.
tuskt[S], *a.* Tusked.
tus'soc[S], *n.* Tussock.
tu'tord[S], *pp.* Tutored.
twad'l[P], *v. & n.* Twaddle.
twad'ld[P], *pp.* Twaddled.
twangd[P&S], *pp.* Twanged.
tweakt[P&S], *pp.* Tweaked.
twelv[P&S], *a. & n.* Twelve.
twich[P], *v. & n.* Twitch.
twicht[P], *pp.* Twitched.
twigd[S], *pp.* Twigged.
twil[P], *v. & n.* Twill.
twild[P&S], *pp.* Twilled.
twind[S], *pa.* Twinned.
twin'kl[P], *v. & n.* Twinkle.
twin'kld[P], *pp.* Twinkled.
twirld[P&S], *pp.* Twirled.
twist'a-bl[P], *a.* Twistable.
twitcht[S], *pp.* Twitched
twit'terd[P&S], *pp.* Twittered.

ty'foid[P&S], *a.* & *n.* Typhoid.
ty'fus[P&S], *n.* Typhus.
ty'po-graf[P&S], *n.* Typograph.
ty-pog'ra-fer[P&S], *n.* Typographer.
ty"po-graf'ic[P&S], *a.* Typographic.
ty"po-graf'i-cal[P&S], *a.* Typographical.
ty"po-graf'i-cal-ly[P&S], *adv.* Typographically.
ty-pog'ra-fist[P&S], *n.* Typographist.
ty-pog'ra-fy[P&S], *n.* Typography.
tyr'an-nin[S], *a.* & *n.* Tyrannine.
ty-rog'ly-fin[S], *a.* & *n.* Tyroglyphine.

U

u-biq'ui-tus[S], *a.* Ubiquitous.
u-dom'o-graf[P&S], *n.* Udomograph.
ul'cer-a-bl[P], *a.* Ulcerable.
ul'cer-a"tiv[P&S], *a.* Ulcerative.
ul'cer-us[S], *a.* Ulcerous.
ul'cer-us-ly[S], *adv.* Ulcerously.
um'berd[S], *pp.* Umbered.
un"a-ban'dond[P&S], *a.* Unabandoned.
un"a-basht'[P&S], *a.* Unabashed.
un-a'bl[P], *a.* Unable.
un-a-bol'ish-a-bl[P], *a.* Unabolishable.
un"a-bol'isht[P&S], *a.* Unabolished.
un-ab-solv'a-bl[P], *a.* Unabsolvable.
un"ab-solvd'[P&S], *a.* Unabsolved.
un-ab-sorb'a-bl[P], *a.* Unabsorbable.
un"ab-sorbd'[P&S], *a.* Unabsorbed.
un-ac-cep'ta-bl[P], *a.* Unacceptable.
un-ac-cep'ta-bl-ness[P], *n.* Unacceptableness.
un-ac-ces'si-bl[P], *a.* Unaccessible.
un-ac-ces'si-bl-ness[P], *n.* Unaccessibleness.
un"ac-com'plisht[P&S], *a.* Unaccomplished.
un"ac-count'a-bl[P], *a.* Unaccountable.
un"ac-count'a-bl-ness[P], *n.* Unaccountableness.
un-ac-cu'mu-la-bl[P], *a.* Unaccumulable.
un"ac-curst'[P&S], *a.* Unaccursed.
un"ac-cus'tomd[P&S], *a.* Unaccustomed.
un"a-chiev'a-bl[P], *a.* Unachievable.
un"a-chievd'[P&S], *a.* Unachieved.
un"ac-quir'a-bl[P], *a.* Unacquirable.
un"ac-quir'a-bl-ness[P], *n.* Unacquirableness.
un"a-dapt'a-bl[P], *a.* Unadaptable.
un"a-dapt'a-bl-ness[P], *n.* Unadaptableness.
un"ad-drest'[P&S], *a.* Unaddressed.
un"ad-he'siv[P&S], *a.* Unadhesive.
un-ad-just'a-bl[P], *a.* Unadjustable.
un"ad-min'is-terd[P&S], *a.* Unadministered.
un-ad'mi-ra-bl[P], *a.* Unadmirable.
un-ad-mis'si-bl[P], *a.* Unadmissible.
un-ad-mit'ta-[or **i-**]**bl**[P], *a.* Unadmittable, unadmittible.
un"ad-mon'isht[P&S], *a.* Unadmonished.
un-a-dopt'a-bl[P], *a.* Unadoptable.
un"a-dornd'[P&S], *a.* Unadorned.
un"ad-viz'a-bl[P], *a.* Unadvisable.
un"ad-viz'a-bl-ness[P], *n.* Unadvisableness.
un-af'fa-bl[P], *n.* Unaffable.
un-af'fa-bl-ness[P], *n.* Unaffableness.
un"af-firmd'[P&S], *a.* Unaffirmed.
un"ag-gres'siv[P&S], *a.* Unaggressive.
un"a-gree'a-bl[P], *a.* Unagreeable.
un"a-gree'a-bl-ness[P], *n.* Unagreeableness.
un-aid'a-bl[P], *a.* Unaidable.
un-aimd'[P&S], *a.* Unaimed.
un-aird'[P&S], *a.* Unaired.
un"a-larmd'[P&S], *a.* Unalarmed.

un-a'lien-a-bl[P], *a.* Unalienable.
un-al-li'a-bl[P], *a.* Unalliable.
un"al-low'a-bl[P], *a.* Unallowable.
un"al-low'a-bl-ness[P], *n.* Unallowableness.
un-al'ter-a-bl[P], *a.* Unalterable.
un-al'ter-a-bl-ness[P], *n.* Unalterableness.
un-al'terd[P&S], *a.* Unaltered.
un-a-men'a-bl[P], *a.* Unamenable.
un-a-men'a-bl-ness[P], *n.* Unamenableness.
un-a-mend'a-bl[P], *a.* Unamendable.
un-a-mend'a-bl-ness[P], *n.* Unamendableness.
un-a'mi-a-bl[P], *a.* Unamiable.
un-a'mi-a-bl-ness[P], *n.* Unamiableness.
un-a-mus'a-bl[P], *a.* Unamusable.
un"a-mu'siv[P&S], *a.* Unamusive.
un-an'a-lyz"[or **-lys"**]**a-bl**[P], *a.* Unanalyzable, unanalysable.
un-an'a-lyz"[or **-lys"**]**a-bl-ness**[P], *n.* Unanalyzableness, unanalysableness.
un-an'chord[S], *a.* Unanchored.
un"an-neald'[P&S], *a.* Unannealed.
un"an-next'[P&S], *a.* Unannexed.
un-an-ni'hi-la-bl[P], *a.* Unannihilable.
un"an-noyd'[P&S], *a.* Unannoyed.
un"an-nuld'[P&S], *a.* Unannulled.
un-an'swer-a-bl[P], *a.* Unanswerable.
un-an'swer-a-bl-ness[P], *n.* Unanswerableness.
un-an'swerd[P&S], *a.* Unanswered.
un"ap-par'eld[P&S], *a.* Unappareled, unapparelled.
un"ap-peal'a-bl[P], *a.* Unappealable.
un-ap-peas'a-bl[P], *a.* Unappeasable.
un-ap-peas'a-bl-ness[P], *n.* Unappeasableness.
un"ap-por'tiond[P&S], *a.* Unapportioned.
un-ap'po-sit[S], *a.* Unapposite.
un-ap-pre'ci-a-bl[P], *a.* Unappreciable.
un"ap-pre'ci-a-tiv[P&S], *a.* Unappreciative.
un"ap-pre-hen'si-bl[P], *a.* Unapprehensible.
un"ap-pre-hen'siv[P&S], *a.* Unapprehensive.
un"ap-pre-hen'siv-ly[P&S], *adv.* Unapprehensively.
un"ap-proach'a-bl[P], *a.* Unapproachable.
un"ap-proacht'[P&S], *a.* Unapproached.
un"ap-pro'pri-a-bl[P], *a.* Unappropriable.
un-a'prond[S], *a.* Unaproned.
un-ar"gu-men'ta-tiv[P&S], *a.* Unargumentative.
un-armd'[S], *a.* Unarmed.
un-ar'mord[P&S], *a.* Unarmored, unarmoured.
un"ar-raignd'[P&S], *a.* Unarraigned.
un"ar-rayd'[P&S], *a.* Unarrayed.
un-ar-rest'a-bl[P], *a.* Unarrestable.
un-as-cend'a-[or **i-**]**bl**[P], *a.* Unascendable, unascendible.
un"as-cer-tain'a-bl[P], *a.* Unascertainable.
un"as-cer-tain'a-bl-ness[P], *n.* Unascertainableness.
un"as-cer-taind'[P&S], *a.* Unascertained.
un-askt'[S], *a.* Unasked.
un"as-sail'a-bl[P], *a.* Unassailable.
un"as-sail'a-bl-ness[P], *n.* Unassailableness.
un"as-saild'[S], *a.* Unassailed.
un"as-sault'a-bl[P], *a.* Unassaultable.
un"as-sayd'[P&S], *a.* Unassayed.
un"as-ser'tiv[S], *a.* Unassertive.
un"as-sess'a-bl[P], *a.* Unassessable.
un"as-sest'[P&S], *a.* Unassessed.
un"as-sign'a-bl[P], *a.* Unassignable.
un"as-signd'[P&S], *a.* Unassigned.

un″as-sim′i-la-bl[P], *a.* Unassimilable.
un″as-ton′isht[P&S], *a.* Unastonished.
un″a-ton′a-bl[P], **un″a-tone′a-bl**[P], *a.* Unatonable, unatoneable.
un″at-tacht′[P&S], *a.* Unattached.
un″at-tack′a-bl[P], *a.* Unattackable.
un″at-tackt′[P&S], *a.* Unattacked.
un″at-tain′a-bl[P], *a.* Unattainable.
un″at-tain′a-bl-ness[P], *n.* Unattainableness.
un″at-taind′[P&S], *a.* Unattained.
un″at-tem′perd[P&S], *a.* Unattempered.
un″at-tempt′a-bl[P], *a.* Unattemptable.
un″at-ten′tiv[P&S], *a.* Unattentive.
un″at-trac′tiv[P&S], *a.* Unattractive.
un″a-vail′a-bl[P], *a.* Unavailable.
un″a-vail′a-bl-ness[P], *n.* Unavailableness.
un″a-vaild′[P&S], *a.* Unavailed.
un″a-void′a-bl[P], *a.* Unavoidable.
un″a-void′a-bl-ness[P], *n.* Unavoidableness.
un″a-voucht′[P&S], *a.* Unavouched.
un″a-vowd′[P&S], *a.* Unavowed.
un″a-wak′end[P&S], *a.* Unawakened.
un-awd′[P&S], *a.* Unawed.
un-awnd′[S], *a.* Unawned.
un-backt′[P&S], *a.* Unbacked.
un-bail′a-bl[P], *a.* Unbailable.
un-baild′[P&S], *a.* Unbailed.
un-balkt′[P&S], *a.* Unbalked.
un-ban′isht[P&S], *a.* Unbanished.
un-bank′a-bl[P], *a.* Unbankable.
un-bankt′[P&S], *a.* Unbanked.
un-ban′nerd[S], *a.* Unbannered.
un-bard′[S], *a.* Unbarred.
un-bat′terd[P&S], *a.* Unbattered.
un-bear′a-bl[P], *a.* Unbearable.
un-bear′a-bl-ness[P], *n.* Unbearableness.
un-beat′a-bl[P], *a.* Unbeatable.
un″be-cum′ing[P], *a.* Unbecoming.
un″be-dewd′[P&S], *a.* Unbedewed.
un″be-got′n[P], *a.* Unbegotten.
un″be-liev′a-bl[P], *a.* Unbelievable.
un″be-liev′a-bl-ness[P], *n.* Unbelievableness.
un″be-lievd′[P&S], *a.* Unbelieved.
un″be-moand′[P&S], *a.* Unbemoaned.
un-bend′a-bl[P], *a.* Unbendable.
un″be-num′[P&S], *vt.* Unbenumb.
un″be-queathed′[P&S], *a.* Unbequeathed.
un″be-stowd′[P&S], *a.* Unbestowed.
un″be-trayd′[P&S], *a.* Unbetrayed.
un-bet′terd[P&S], *a.* Unbettered.
un-beu′te-ous[P], *a.* Unbeauteous.
un-beu′ti-fied[P], *a.* Unbeautified.
un-beu′ti-ful[P], *a.* Unbeautiful.
un-beu′ti-ful-ly[P], *adv.* Unbeautifully.
un″be-waild′[P&S], *a.* Unbewailed.
un″be-wil′derd[S], *a.* Unbewildered.
un-bi′ast[P&S], *a.* Unbiased, unbiassed.
un-bid′da-bl[P], *a.* Unbiddable.
un-bid′da-bl-ness[P], *n.* Unbiddableness.
un-bi″o-graf′i-cal[P&S], *a.* Unbiographical.
un-blam′a-bl[P], *a.* Unblamable.
un-blam′a-bl-ness[P], *n.* Unblamableness.
un-blancht′[P&S], *a.* Unblanched.
un-bla′zond[S], *a.* Unblazoned.
un-bleacht′[P&S], *a.* Unbleached.
un-blem′isht[P&S], *a.* Unblemished.
un-blest′[P&S], *a.* Unblessed.
un-boild′[P&S], *a.* Unboiled.
un-bookt′[P&S], *a.* Unbooked.
un-bor′derd[P&S], *a.* Unbordered.
un-bor′rowd[P&S], *a.* Unborrowed.
un-bot′tomd[S], *a.* Unbottomed.
un-bowd′[P&S], *a.* Unbowed.
un-bow′eld[S], *a.* Unboweled, unbowelled.
un-brancht′[P&S], *a.* Unbranched.

un-break'a-bl[P], *a.* Unbreakable.
un-breath'a-bl[P], *a.* Unbreathable.
un-brewd'[P&S], *a.* Unbrewed.
un-broacht'[P&S], *a.* Unbroached.
un-brusht'[P&S], *a.* Unbrushed.
un-bun'dl[P], *vt. & vi.* Unbundle.
un-bur'dend[P&S], *a.* Unburdened.
un-bur'den-sum[P&S], *a.* Unburdensome.
un-bur'i-a-bl[P], *a.* Unburiable.
un-bur'nisht[P&S], *a.* Unburnished.
un-bus'kind[P&S], *a.* Unbuskined.
un-but'terd[P&S], *a.* Unbuttered.
un-but'tond[P&S], *a.* Unbuttoned.
un-but'trest[S], *a.* Unbuttressed.
un-ca'bld[P], *a.* Uncabled.
un-cald'[S], *a.* Uncalled.
un-calkt'[P&S], *a.* Uncalked.
un-can'cel-a-bl[P], **un-can'cel-la-bl**[P], *a.* Uncancelable, uncancellable.
un-can'celd[P&S], *a.* Uncanceled, uncancelled.
un-capt'[S], *a.* Uncapped.
un″ca-rest'[P&S], *a.* Uncaressed.
un-carvd'[P&S], *a.* Uncarved.
un-cat'a-logd[P&S], *a.* Uncatalogued.
un-cen'sur-a-bl[P], *a.* Uncensurable.
un-chaind'[P&S], *a.* Unchained.
un-chalkt'[S], *a.* Unchalked.
un-change'a-bl[P], *a.* Unchangeable.
un-chan'neld[P&S], *a.* Unchanneled, unchannelled.
un-chard'[P&S], *a.* Uncharred.
un-char'i-ta-bl[P], *a.* Uncharitable.
un-char'i-ta-bl-ness[P], *n.* Uncharitableness.
un-char'terd[S], *a.* Unchartered.
un-chast'end[P&S], *a.* Unchastened.
un-check'erd[S], *a.* Uncheckered.
un-checkt'[P&S], *a.* Unchecked.
un-cheerd'[P&S], *a.* Uncheered.
un-cher'isht[S], *a.* Uncherished.
un-chewd'[P&S], *a.* Unchewed.
un-chipt'[P&S], *a.* Unchipped.
un-chis'eld[S], *a.* Unchiseled, unchiselled.
un-chopt'[P&S], *a.* Unchopped.
un-chris'tend[S], *a.* Unchristened.
un'cl[P], *n.* Uncle.
un-claimd'[P&S], *a.* Unclaimed.
un-class'a-[or i-]bl[P], *a.* Unclassable, unclassible.
un-class'i-fi″a-bl[P], *a.* Unclassifiable.
un-cleand'[P&S], *a.* Uncleaned.
un-cleard'[P&S], *a.* Uncleared.
un-cleav'a-bl[P], *a.* Uncleavable.
un-clen'ly[P&S], *a.* Uncleanly.
un-cler'gi-a-bl[P], **un-cler'gy-a-bl**[P], *a.* Unclergiable, unclergyable.
un-clipt'[P&S], *a.* Unclipped.
un-cloakt'[P&S], *a.* Uncloaked.
un-clos'a-bl[P], *a.* Unclosable.
un-cloyd'[P&S], *a.* Uncloyed.
un-coacht'[P&S], *a.* Uncoached.
un-cof'find[S], *a.* Uncoffined.
un″co-he'siv[P&S], *a.* Uncohesive.
un-coift'[S], *a.* Uncoifed.
un-coind'[P&S], *a.* Uncoined.
un″col-lapst'[P&S], *a.* Uncollapsed.
un-col'lard[P&S], *a.* Uncollared.
un-col'ord[S], *a.* Uncolored.
un″com-bin'a-bl[P], *a.* Uncombinable.
un-com'fort-a-bl[P], *a.* Uncomfortable.
un-com'fort-a-bl-ness[P], *n.* Uncomfortableness.
un″com-mend'a-bl[P], *a.* Uncommendable.
un″com-men'su-ra-bl[P], *a.* Uncommensurable.
un″com-mer'ci-a-bl[P], *a.* Uncommerciable.
un″com-mis'siond[S], *a.* Uncommissioned.
un-com'mon-a-bl[P], *a.* Uncommonable.
un″com-mu'ni-ca-bl[P], *a.* Uncommunicable.

un″com-mu′ni-ca-tiv[P&S], *a.* Uncommunicative.
un″com-pan′iond[S], *a.* Uncompanioned.
un″com-pas′siond[S], *a.* Uncompassioned.
un″com-peld′[P&S], *a.* Uncompelled.
un″com-pel′la-bl[P], *a.* Uncompellable.
un″com-pet′i-tiv[P&S], *a.* Uncompetitive.
un″com-pli′a-bl[P], *a.* Uncompliable.
un″com-pre-hen′si-bl[P], *a.* Uncomprehensible.
un-com″pre-hen′siv[P&S], *a.* Uncomprehensive.
un″com-prest′[P&S], *a.* Uncompressed.
un″con-ceald′[P&S], *a.* Unconcealed.
un″con-ceiv′a-bl[P], *a.* Unconceivable.
un″con-ceiv′a-bl-ness[P], *n.* Unconceivableness.
un″con-ceivd′[P&S], *a.* Unconceived.
un″con-dem′na-bl[P], *a.* Uncondemnable.
un″con-dens′a-[or **i-**]**bl**[P], *a.* Uncondensable, uncondensible.
un″con-denst′[P&S], *a.* Uncondensed.
un″con-du′civ[P&S], *a.* Unconducive.
un″con-ferd′[P&S], *a.* Unconferred.
un″con-fest′[P&S], *a.* Unconfessed.
un″con-fin′a-bl[P], *a.* Unconfinable.
un″con-firmd′[P&S], *a.* Unconfirmed.
un″con-fis′ca-bl[P], *a.* Unconfiscable.
un″con-form′a-bl[P], *a.* Unconformable.
un″con-form′a-bl-ness[P], *n.* Unconformableness.
un″con-formd′[P&S], *a.* Unconformed.
un″con-fut′a-bl[P], *a.* Unconfutable.
un″con-geal′a-bl[P], *a.* Uncongealable.
un″con-geald′[P&S], *a.* Uncongealed.
un″con-joind′[P&S], *a.* Unconjoined.
un″con-junc′tiv[P&S], *a.* Unconjunctive.
un-con′querd[S], *a.* Unconquered.
un-con′scion-a-bl[P], *a.* Unconscionable.
un-con′scion-a-bl-ness[P], *n.* Unconscionableness.
un″con-ser′va-tiv[P&S], *a.* Unconservative.
un″con-sid′erd[P&S], *a.* Unconsidered.
un″con-signd′[P&S], *a.* Unconsigned.
un″con-strain′a-bl[P], *a.* Unconstrainable.
un″con-straind′[P&S], *a.* Unconstrained.
un″con-tain′a-bl[P], *a.* Uncontainable.
un″con-test′a-bl[P], *a.* Uncontestable.
un″con-tra-dict′a-bl[P], *a.* Uncontradictable.
un″con-trold′[P&S], *a.* Uncontrolled.
un″con-trol′la-bl[P], *a.* Uncontrollable.
un″con-trol′la-bl-ness[P], *n.* Uncontrollableness.
un″con-tro-vert′i-bl[P], *a.* Uncontrovertible.
un″con-vers′a-bl[P], *a.* Unconversable.
un″con-vert′i-bl[P], *a.* Unconvertible.
un″con-veyd′[P&S], *a.* Unconveyed.
un″con-vulst′[P&S], *a.* Unconvulsed.
un-cook′a-bl[P], *a.* Uncookable.
un-cookt′[P&S], *a.* Uncooked.
un-corkt′[P&S], *a.* Uncorked.
un″cor-rup′tiv[S], *a.* Uncorruptive.
un-cov′erd[S], *a.* Uncovered.
un-cowld′[P&S], *a.* Uncowled.
un-crackt′[P&S], *a.* Uncracked.
un-crampt′[P&S], *a.* Uncramped.
un-crit′i-cis″[or **-iz″**]**a-bl**[P], *a.* Uncriticisable, uncriticizable.
un-cropt′[S], *a.* Uncropped.
un-crost′[P&S], *a.* Uncrossed.
un-crownd′[S], *a.* Uncrowned.
un-crusht′[P&S], *a.* Uncrushed.
un-crys′tal-lin[S], **-ine**[S], *a.* Uncrystalline.

un-crys'tal-lis″[or **-iz″**]**a-bl**[P], *a.* Uncrystallisable, uncrystallizable.
un-culd'[P&S], *a.* Unculled.
un-cul'ti-va-bl[P], *a.* Uncultivable.
un-cum'berd[P&S], *a.* Uncumbered.
un″cum-pan'ion-a-bl[P], *a.* Uncompanionable.
un-cup'l[P], *vt.* & *vi.* Uncouple.
un-cup'ld[P], *a.* Uncoupled.
un-cur'a-bl[P], *a.* Uncurable.
un-curb'a-bl[P], *a.* Uncurbable.
un-curbd'[P&S], *a.* Uncurbed.
un-curst'[P&S], *a.* Uncursed.
un″cur-taild'[P&S], *a.* Uncurtailed.
un-cur'taind[S], *a.* Uncurtained.
un-cush'iond[S], *a.* Uncushioned.
un-cus'tom-a-bl[P], *a.* Uncustomable.
un-cuv'er[P], *vt.* & *vi.* Uncover.
un-cuv'erd[S], *a.* Uncovered.
un-dampt'[P&S], *a.* Undamped.
un-dark'end[P&S], *a.* Undarkened.
un-dasht'[P&S], *a.* Undashed.
un-daz'ld[P], *a.* Undazzled.
un″de-bard'[P&S], *a.* Undebarred.
un″de-bat'a-bl[P], **un″de-bate'a-bl**[P], *a.* Undebatable, undebateable.
un″de-cayd'[P&S], *a.* Undecayed.
un″de-ceiv'a-bl[P], *a.* Undeceivable.
un″de-ceivd'[P&S], *a.* Undeceived.
un″de-cep'tiv[S], *a.* Undeceptive.
un″de-cid'a-bl[P], *a.* Undecidable.
un″de-ci'fer-a-bl[P], *a.* Undecipherable.
un″de-ci'ferd[P&S], *a.* Undeciphered.
un″de-ci'siv[P&S], *a.* Undecisive.
un-deckt'[S], *a.* Undecked.
un″de-clar'a-bl[P], *a.* Undeclarable.
un″de-clin'a-bl[P], *a.* Undeclinable.
un″de-com-pos'a-bl[P], *a.* Undecomposable.
un-ded'[P&S], *a.* Undead.
un″de-duc'i-bl[P], *a.* Undeducible.
un″de-fea'si-bl[P], *a.* Undefeasible.
un″de-fec'tiv[P&S], *a.* Undefective.
un″de-ferd'[S], *a.* Undeferred.
un″de-fin'a-bl[P], *a.* Undefinable.
un″de-formd'[P&S], *a.* Undeformed.
un″de-frayd'[P&S], *a.* Undefrayed.
un″de-lay'a-bl[P], *a.* Undelayable.
un″de-layd'[P], *a.* Undelayed.
un″de-lec'ta-bl[P], *a.* Undelectable.
un″de-lib'er-a-tiv[P&S], *a.* Undeliberative.
un″de-liv'erd[P&S], *a.* Undelivered.
un-delt'[P&S], *a.* Undealt.
un″de-lu'siv[P&S], *a.* Undelusive.
un-delvd'[S], *a.* Undelved.
un″de-mol'isht[P&S], *a.* Undemolished.
un″de-mon'stra-bl[P], *a.* Undemonstrable.
un″de-mon'stra-tiv[P&S], *a.* Undemonstrative.
un″de-mon'stra-tiv-ly[P&S], *adv.* Undemonstratively.
un″de-mon'stra-tiv-ness[P&S], *n.* Undemonstrativeness.
un″de-ni'a-bl[P], *a.* Undeniable.
un″de-pend'a-bl[P], *a.* Undependable.
un″de-pos'a-bl[P], *a.* Undeposable.
un″de-prest'[P&S], *a.* Undepressed.
un″der-tak'a-bl[P], *a.* Undertakable.
un″de-scend'a-[or **i-**]**bl**[P], *a.* Undescendable, undescendible.
un″de-scrib'a-bl[P], *a.* Undescribable.
un″de-serv'[P&S], *vt.* & *vi.* Undeserve.
un″de-servd'[S], *pa.* Undeserved.
un″de-signd'[P&S], *a.* Undesigned.
un″de-sir'a-bl[P], *a.* Undesirable.
un″de-sir'a-bl-ness[P], *n.* Undesirableness.
un″de-spoild'[P&S], *a.* Undespoiled.
un-des'tind[S], *a.* Undestined.
un″de-stroyd'[P&S], *a.* Undestroyed.
un″de-tach'a-bl[P], *a.* Undetachable.
un″de-tacht'[P&S], *a.* Undetached.
un″de-taild'[P&S], *a.* Undetailed.
un″de-vel'opt[P&S], *a.* Undeveloped.
un″de-vourd'[S], *a.* Undevoured.

un″di-af′a-nous[p], *a.* Undiaphonous.
un″di-gest′i-bl[p], *a.* Undigestible.
un-dimd′[p&s], *a.* Undimmed.
un″di-min′ish-a-bl[p], *a.* Undiminishable.
un″di-min′isht[p&s], *a.* Undiminished.
un-dipt′[p&s], *a.* Undipped.
un″dis-cernd′[p&s], *a.* Undiscerned.
un″dis-cern′i-bl[p], *a.* Undiscernible.
un″dis-cern′i-bl-ness[p], *n.* Undiscernibleness.
un-dis′ci-plind[s], *a.* Undisciplined.
un″dis-col′ord[s], *a.* Undiscolored.
un″dis-courst′[s], *a.* Undiscoursed.
un″dis-crim′i-na-tiv[p&s], *a.* Undiscriminative.
un″dis-cust′[p&s], *a.* Undiscussed.
un″dis-cuv′er-a-bl[p], *a.* Undiscoverable.
un″dis-hart′end[p&s], *a.* Undisheartened.
un″dis-joind′[s], *a.* Undisjoined.
un″dis-man′tld[p], *a.* Undismantled.
un″dis-mayd′[s], *a.* Undismayed.
un″dis-mem′berd[p&s], *a.* Undismembered.
un″dis-mist′[p&s], *a.* Undismissed.
un″dis-or′derd[s], *a.* Undisordered.
un″dis-peld′[p&s], *a.* Undispelled.
un″dis-penst′[p&s], *a.* Undispensed.
un″dis-perst′[s], *a.* Undispersed.
un″dis-playd′[p&s], *a.* Undisplayed.
un-dis′pu-ta-bl[p], *a.* Undisputable.
un-dis′pu-ta-bl-ness[p], *n.* Undisputableness.
un″dis-sem′bld[p], *a.* Undissembled.
un″dis-solv′a-bl[p], *a.* Undissolvable.
un″dis-solvd′[p&s], *a.* Undissolved.
un″dis-tem′perd[p&s], *a.* Undistempered.
un″dis-tild′[p&s], *a.* Undistilled.
un″dis-tinc′tiv[p&s], *a.* Undistinctive.
un″dis-tin′guish-a-bl[p], *a.* Undistinguishable.
un″dis-tin′guisht[p&s], *a.* Undistinguished.
un″dis-trest′[p&s], *a.* Undistressed.
un″dis-turbd′[p&s], *a.* Undisturbed.
un-ditcht′[s], *a.* Unditched.
un″di-vert′i-bl[p], *a.* Undivertible.
un″di-vin′a-bl[p], *a.* Undivinable.
un″di-vis′i-bl[p], *a.* Undivisible.
un-doomd′[p&s], *a.* Undoomed.
un-dout′ed[s], *a.* Undoubted.
un-dout′ful[p&s], *a.* Undoubtful.
un-dow′erd[p&s], *a.* Undowered.
un-draind′[s], *a.* Undrained.
un-drencht′[p&s], *a.* Undrenched.
un-drild′[p&s], *a.* Undrilled.
un-drink′a-bl[p], *a.* Undrinkable.
un-drownd′[p&s], *a.* Undrowned.
un-dubd′[s], *a.* Undubbed.
un-du′bi-ta-bl[p], *a.* Undubitable.
un-dub′l[p], *vt.* & *vi.* Undouble.
un′du-la″tiv[p&s], *a.* Undulative.
un-dumpt′[s], *a.* Undumped.
un-dur′a-bl[p], *a.* Undurable.
un-du′ti-a-bl[p], *a.* Undutiable.
un-dwin′dld[p], *a.* Undwindled.
un-eat′a-bl[p], *a.* Uneatable.
un-eat′a-bl-ness[p], *n.* Uneatableness.
un″e-clipst′[p&s], *a.* Uneclipsed.
un-ed′i-bl[p], *a.* Unedible.
un″e-duc′i-bl[p], *a.* Uneducible.
un″e-lapst′[p&s], *a.* Unelapsed.
un″e-lec′tiv[p&s], *a.* Unelective.
un-el′i-gi-bl[p], *a.* Uneligible.
un″e-lu′siv[p&s], *a.* Unelusive.
un″em-bar′rast[p&s], *a.* Unembarrassed.
un″em-bel′lisht[p&s], *a.* Unembellished.
un″em-bit′terd[s], *a.* Unembittered.
un″e-mend′a-bl[p], *a.* Unemendable.
un″em-fat′ic[p&s], *a.* Unemphatic.
un″em-ploy′a-bl[p], *a.* Unemployable.
un″em-ployd′[p&s], *a.* Unemployed.
un″em-pow′erd[s], *a.* Unempowered.

un″en-am′ord[S], *a.* Unenamored.

un″en-com′past[P&S], *a.* Unencompassed.

un″en-coun′terd[P&S], *a.* Unencountered.

un″en-cum′berd[P&S], *a.* Unencumbered.

un″en-dan′gerd[S], *a.* Unendangered.

un″en-deard′[P&S], *a.* Unendeared.

un″en-dorst′[S], *a.* Unendorsed.

un″en-dowd′[P&S], *a.* Unendowed.

un″en-dur′a-bl[P], *a.* Unendurable.

un″en-fee′bld[P], *a.* Unenfeebled.

un″en-force′a-bl[P], *a.* Unenforceable.

un″en-grost′[S], *a.* Unengrossed.

un″en-joy′a-bl[P], *a.* Unenjoyable.

un″en-joyd′[P&S], *a.* Unenjoyed.

un″en-light′end[S], *a.* Unenlightened.

un″en-liv′end[S], *a.* Unenlivened.

un″en-richt′[P&S], *a.* Unenriched.

un″en-roid′[P&S], *a.* Unenrolled.

un″en-tan′gld[P], *a.* Unentangled.

un-en′terd[P&S], *a.* Unentered.

un″en-thrald′[S], *a.* Unenthralled.

un″e-nu′mer-a-bl[P], *a.* Unenumerable.

un-en′vi-a-bl[P], *a.* Unenviable.

un-e′qua-bl[P], *a.* Unequable.

un-e′quald[P&S], *a.* Unequaled, unequalled.

un″e-quipt′[P&S], *a.* Unequipped.

un-eq′ui-ta-bl[P], *a.* Unequitable.

un″e-rad′i-ca-bl[P], *a.* Uneradicable.

un-ernd′[P], *a.* Unearned.

un-erth′[P], *vt.* Unearth.

un″es-cap′a-bl[P], *a.* Unescapable.

un″es-chew′a-bl[P], *a.* Uneschewable.

un″es-tab′lisht[P&S], *a.* Unestablished.

un″es-thet′ic[S], *a.* Unæsthetic.

un-etcht′[S], *a.* Unetched.

un″e-vad′a-bl[P], *a.* Unevadable.

un″e-volvd′[P&S], *a.* Unevolved.

un″ex-am′i-na-bl[P], *a.* Unexaminable.

un″ex-am′ind[P&S], *a.* Unexamined.

un″ex-celd′[S], *a.* Unexcelled.

un″ex-cep′tion-a-bl[P], *a.* Unexceptionable.

un″ex-cep′tion-a-bl-ness[P], *n.* Unexceptionableness.

un″ex-cep′tiv[S], *a.* Unexceptive.

un″ex-change′a-bl[P], *a.* Unexchangeable.

un″ex-cit′a-bl[P], *a.* Unexcitable.

un″ex-clu′siv[P&S], *a.* Unexclusive.

un″ex-cog′i-ta-bl[P], *a.* Unexcogitable.

un″ex-cuz′a-bl[P], *a.* Unexcusable.

un″ex-cuz′a-bl-ness[P], *n.* Unexcusableness.

un″ex-haust′i-bl[P], *a.* Unexhaustible.

un-ex′pi-a-bl[P], *a.* Unexpiable.

un″ex-pan′siv[P&S], *a.* Unexpansive.

un″ex-peld′[P&S], *a.* Unexpelled.

un″ex-pen′siv[P&S], *a.* Unexpensive.

un″ex-plain′a-bl[P], *a.* Unexplainable.

un″ex-plaind′[P&S], *a.* Unexplained.

un″ex-plor′a-tiv[S], *a.* Unexplorative.

un″ex-plo′siv[P&S], *a.* Unexplosive.

un″ex-press′i-bl[P], *a.* Unexpressible.

un″ex-pres′siv[P&S], *a.* Unexpressive.

un″ex-prest′[P&S], *a.* Unexpressed.

un″ex-pug′na-bl[P], *a.* Unexpugnable.

un″ex-tin′guish-a-bl[P], *a.* Unextinguishable.

un″ex-tin′guisht[S], *a.* Unextinguished.

un-ex′tri-ca-bl[P], *a.* Unextricable.

un-face′a-bl[P], *a.* Unfaceable.

un-fad′a-bl[P], *a.* Unfadable.

un-fal′lowd[S], *a.* Unfallowed.

un-fand′[S], *a.* Unfanned.

un-fash′ion-a-bl[P], *a.* Unfashionable.

un-fash′ion-a-bl-ness[P], *n.* Unfashionableness.

un-fash′iond[S], *a.* Unfashioned.

un-fa′therd[P&S], *a.* Unfathered.

un-fath′om-a-bl[P], *a.* Unfathomable.

un-fath′omd[P&S], *a.* Unfathomed.

un-fat′i-ga-bl[P], *a.* Unfatigable.
un-fa′vor-a-bl[P], *a.* Unfavorable.
un-fa′vor-a-bl-ness[P], *n.* Unfavorableness.
un-fa′vord[P&S], *a.* Unfavored.
un-feard′[P&S], *a.* Unfeared.
un-fea′si-bl[P], *a.* Unfeasible.
un-feignd′[S], Unfeigned.
un-feld′[S], *a.* Unfelled.
un″fer-ment′a-bl[P], *a.* Unfermentable.
un-fer′til[P&S], **-ile**[P&S], *a.* Unfertile.
un-fes′tiv[P&S], *a.* Unfestive.
un-fetcht′[S], *a.* Unfetched.
un-feth′er[P&S], *vt.* Unfeather.
un-feth′erd[P&S], *a.* Unfeathered.
un-fet′terd[S], *a.* Unfettered.
un-fe′verd[P&S], *a.* Unfevered.
un″fil-an-throp′ic[P&S], *a.* Unphilanthropic.
un-fild′[P&S], *a.* Unfilled.
un-fill′a-bl[P], *a.* Unfillable.
un-filmd′[S], *a.* Unfilmed.
un″fil-o-log′i-cal[P&S], *n.* Unphilological.
un-fil′terd[P&S], *a.* Unfiltered.
un-fin′gerd[P&S], *a.* Unfingered.
un-fin′isht[P&S], *a.* Unfinished.
un-fixt′[P&S], *a.* Unfixed.
un-flankt′[S], *a.* Unflanked.
un-flat′terd[P&S], *a.* Unflattered.
un-fla′vord[P&S], *a.* Unflavored.
un-flawd′[P&S], *a.* Unflawed.
un-fleckt′[S], *a.* Unflecked.
un-flex′i-bl[P], *a.* Unflexible.
un-fo′cust[P&S], *a.* Unfocused.
un-foild′[P&S], *a.* Unfoiled.
un-fol′lowd[P&S], *a.* Unfollowed.
un″fo-net′ic[P&S], *a.* Unphonetic.
un-forc′i-bl[P], *a.* Unforcible.
un-ford′a-bl[P], *a.* Unfordable.
un″fore-see′a-bl[P], *a.* Unforeseeable.
un-forge′a-bl[P], *a.* Unforgeable.
un″for-get′a-bl[P], *a.* Unforgetable.
un″for-giv′a-bl[P], *a.* Unforgivable.
un-forkt′[S], *a.* Unforked.
un-formd′[P&S], *a.* Unformed.
un-for′mu-la-bl[P], *a.* Unformulable.
un-fos′terd[P&S], *a.* Unfostered.
un-fould′[P&S], *a.* Unfouled.
un-frank′a-bl[P], *a.* Unfrankable.
un-frankt′[S], *a.* Unfranked.
un-frend′ly[P], *a.* Unfriendly.
un-fri′a-bl[P], *a.* Unfriable.
un-frild′[P&S], *a.* Unfrilled.
un-frus′tra-bl[P], *a.* Unfrustrable.
un-fu′eld[S], *a.* Unfueled.
un″ful-fild′[P&S], *a.* Unfulfilled.
un-fur′nisht[P&S], *a.* Unfurnished.
un-fur′rowd[S], *a.* Unfurrowed.
un-fu′zi-bl[P], *a.* Unfusible.
un-fys′i-cal[P&S], *a.* Unphysical.
un-fys′ickt[P], *a.* Unphysicked.
un-gain′a-bl[P], *a.* Ungainable.
un-gaind′[P&S], *a.* Ungained.
un-gald′[S], *a.* Ungalled.
un-gar′bld[P], *a.* Ungarbled.
un-gard′ed[S], *a.* Unguarded.
un-gar′nerd[P&S], *a.* Ungarnered.
un-gar′nisht[S], *a.* Ungarnished.
un-gar′ri-sond[S], *a.* Ungarrisoned.
un-gar′terd[S], *a.* Ungartered.
un-gath′erd[S], *a.* Ungathered.
un-gen′u-in[P&S], **-ine**[S], *a.* Ungenuine.
un″ge-o-graf′ic[P&S], *a.* Ungeographic.
un-gir′dl[P], *vt.* Ungirdle.
un-glad′dend[S], *a.* Ungladdened.
un-gleand′[P&S], *a.* Ungleaned.
un-gloomd′[P&S], *a.* Ungloomed.
un-gost′ly[P&S], *a.* Unghostly.
un-gownd′[P&S], *a.* Ungowned.
un-grant′a-bl[P], *a.* Ungrantable.
un-grasp′a-bl[P], *a.* Ungraspable.
un-graspt′[P&S], *a.* Ungrasped.
un-green′a-bl[P], *a.* Ungreenable.
un-groovd′[P&S], *a.* Ungrooved.
un-guv′ern-a-bl[P], *a.* Ungovernable.
un-guv′ern-a-bl-ness[P], *n.* Ungovernableness.

un-hackt'[P&S], *a.* Unhacked.
un-haild'[P&S], *a.* Unhailed.
un-hal'lowd[P&S], *a.* Unhallowed.
un-halvd'[P&S], *a.* Unhalved.
un-ham'perd[P&S], *a.* Unhampered.
un-hand'sum[P], *a.* Unhandsome.
un-hangd'[P&S], *a.* Unhanged.
un-har'ast[P&S], *a.* Unharassed.
un-har'bord[P&S], *a.* Unharbored.
un-har'dend[S], *a.* Unhardened.
un-harmd'[P&S], *a.* Unharmed.
un-har'rowd[P&S], *a.* Unharrowed.
un-hatcht'[P&S], *a.* Unhatched.
un-heald'[P&S], *a.* Unhealed.
un-hed'[P&S], *vt.* Unhead.
un-helmd'[S], *a.* Unhelmed.
un-helpt'[P&S], *a.* Unhelped.
un-helth'[P&S], *n.* Unhealth.
un-helth'ful[P&S], *a.* Unhealthful.
un-helth'y[P&S], *a.* Unhealthy.
un-hemd'[S], *a.* Unhemmed.
un-herd'[P], *a.* Unheard.
un-hin'derd[P&S], *a.* Unhindered.
un-hon'ord[P&S], *a.* Unhonored, unhonoured.
un-hornd'[S], *a.* Unhorned.
un-hos'pi-ta-bl[P], *a.* Unhospitable.
un-hos'til[S], **-ile**[S], *a.* Unhostile.
un-huld'[S], *a.* Unhulled.
un-hum'bld[P], *a.* Unhumbled.
un-hu'mord[P&S], *a.* Unhumored.
un-huskt'[S], *a.* Unhusked.
un"i-den'ti-fi"a-bl[P], *a.* Unidentifiable.
u'ni-fi"a-bl[P], *a.* Unifiable.
un"ig-nit'i-bl[P], *a.* Unignitible.
un"im-ag'i-na-bl[P], *a.* Unimaginable.
un"im-ag'i-na-bl-ness[P], *n.* Unimaginableness.
un"im-ag'i-na-tiv[P&S], *a.* Unimaginative.
un"im-ag'ind[P&S], *a.* Unimagined.
un"im-pair'a-bl[P], *a.* Unimpairable.
un"im-paird'[P&S], *a.* Unimpaired.
un"im-pas'siond[S], *a.* Unimpassioned.
un"im-peach'a-bl[P], *a.* Unimpeachable.
un"im-peach'a-bl-ness[P], *n.* Unimpeachableness.
un"im-peacht'[S], *a.* Unimpeached.
un"im-preg'na-bl[P], *a.* Unimpregnable.
un"im-press'i-bl[P], *a.* Unimpressible.
un"im-press'i-bl-ness[P], *n.* Unimpressibleness.
un"im-pres'siv[P&S], *a.* Unimpressive.
un"im-pres'sion-a-bl[P], *a.* Unimpressionable.
un"im-prest'[P&S], *a.* Unimpressed.
un"im-prov'a-bl[P], *a.* Unimprovable.
un"im-prov'a-bl-ness[P], *n.* Unimprovableness.
un"im-pug'na-bl[P], *a.* Unimpugnable.
un"in-creas'a-bl[P], *a.* Unincreasable.
un"in-creast'[P&S], *a.* Unincreased.
un"in-det'ted[S], *a.* Unindebted.
un-in'dext[P&S], *a.* Unindexed.
un"in-dorst'[P&S], *a.* Unindorsed.
un"in-flam'ma-bl[P], *a.* Uninflammable.
un"in-hab'i-ta-bl[P], *a.* Uninhabitable.
un"in-her'i-ta-bl[P], *a.* Uninheritable.
un"in-quis'i-tiv[S], *a.* Uninquisitive.
un"in-staid'[S], **un"in-staild'**[P], *a.* Uninstalled.
un"in-struc'tiv[P&S], *a.* Uninstructive.
un"in-sur'a-bl[P], *a.* Uninsurable.
un"in-tel'li-gi-bl[P], *a.* Unintelligible.
un"in-tel'li-gi-bl-ness[P], *n.* Unintelligibleness.
un"in-ter-change'a-bl[P], *a.* Uninterchangeable.
un"in-ter-mixt'[S], *a.* Unintermixed.
un"in-ter'pret-a-bl[P], *a.* Uninterpretable.

un″in-trencht′[s], *a.* Unintrenched.
un-in″tro-spec′tiv[s], *a.* Unintrospective.
un″in-vent′i-bi-ness[p], *n.* Uninventibleness.
un″in-ven′tiv[p&s], *a.* Uninventive.
un″in-ves′ti-ga-bl[p], *a.* Uninvestigable.
un″in-ves′ti-ga″tiv[s], *a.* Uninvestigative.
un″in-volvd′[p&s], *a.* Uninvolved.
un-ir′ri-ta-bl[p], *a.* Unirritable.
u-nit′a-bl[p], **u-nite′a-bl**[p], *a.* Unitable, uniteable.
u′ni-tiv[p&s], *a.* Unitive.
u″ni-tiv-ly[p&s], *adv.* Unitively.
u′ni-valv[s], *a.* & *n.* Univalve.
un-jagd′[s], *a.* Unjagged.
un-jard′[p&s], *a.* Unjarred.
un-jaun′dist[s], *a.* Unjaundiced.
un-jel′ous[p&s], *a.* Unjealous.
un-joind′[p&s], *a.* Unjoined.
un-jus′ti-fi″a-bl[p], *a.* Unjustifiable.
un-jus′ti-fi″a-bl-ness[p], *n.* Unjustifiableness.
un-keeld′[s], *a.* Unkeeled.
un-kild′[p&s], *a.* Unkilled.
un-kin′dld[p], *a.* Unkindled.
un-kist′[p&s], *a.* Unkissed.
un-kneld′[s], *a.* Unknelled.
un-know′a-bl[p], *a.* & *n.* Unknowable.
un-know′a-bl-ness[p], *n.* Unknowableness.
un-la′beld[s], *a.* Unlabeled, unlabelled.
un″lam-poond′[s], *a.* Unlampooned.
un-lasht′[p&s], *a.* Unlashed.
un-launcht′[p&s], *a.* Unlaunched.
un-laun′derd[s], *a.* Unlaundered.
un-lau′reld[s], *a.* Unlaureled, unlaurelled.
un-lav′isht[s], *a.* Unlavished.
un-leacht′[s], *a.* Unleached.
un-least′[s], *a.* Unleased.
un-lern′[p], *vt.* & *vi.* Unlearn.
un-less′end[p&s], *a.* Unlessened.
un-les′sond[s], *a.* Unlessoned.
un-let′terd[s], *a.* Unlettered.
un-li′a-bl[p], *a.* Unliable.
un-li′censt[p&s], *a.* Unlicensed.
un-lickt′[p&s], *a.* Unlicked.
un-lik′a-bl[p], *a.* Unlikable.
un-lik′en-a-bl[p], *a.* Unlikenable.
un-lim′berd[s], *a.* Unlimbered.
un-liq′ue-fi″a-bl[p], *a.* Unliquefiable.
un-lit′terd[s], *a.* Unlittered.
un-liv′a-bl[p], *a.* Unlivable.
un-lockt′[s], *a.* Unlocked.
un-loct′[p], *a.* Unlocked.
un-logd′[s], *a.* Unlogged.
un-lookt′[p&s], *a.* Unlooked.
un-loopt′[p&s], *a.* Unlooped.
un-lopt′[p&s], *a.* Unlopped.
un-los′a-bl[p], *a.* Unlosable.
un-low′erd[s], *a.* Unlowered.
un-luld′[p&s], *a.* Unlulled.
un-lu′mi-nus[s], *a.* Unluminous.
un-luv′a-bl[p], *a.* Unlovable.
un-luv′a-bl-ness[p], *n.* Unlovableness.
un-luvd′[p], *a.* Unloved.
un-mad′dend[s], *a.* Unmaddened.
un-maild′[p&s], *a.* Unmailed.
un-maimd′[p&s], *a.* Unmaimed.
un″main-tain′a-bl[p], *a.* Unmaintainable.
un-mak′a-bl[p], *a.* Unmakable.
un-mal′le-a-bl[p], *a.* Unmalleable.
un-man′a-cl[p], *vt.* Unmanacle.
un-man′age-a-bl[p], *a.* Unmanageable.
un-man′age-a-bl-ness[p], *n.* Unmanageableness.
un-man′gld[p], *a.* Unmangled.
un-man′nerd[s], *a.* Unmannered.
un-mapt′[s], *a.* Unmapped.
un-mard′[s], *a.* Unmarred.
un-mar′ket-a-bl[p], *a.* Unmarketable.
un-markt′[p&s], *a.* Unmarked.
un-mar′riage-a-bl[p], *a.* Unmarriageable.

un-mar'riage-a-bl-ness[P], *n.* Unmarriageableness.
un-mar'shald[P], *a.* Unmarshaled.
un-mar'vel-ous[P], *a.* Unmarvellous.
un-mas'cu-lin[P&S], **-ine**[S], *a.* & *n.* Unmasculine.
un-mas'terd[P&S], *a.* Unmastered.
un-mas'ti-ca-bl[P], *a.* Unmasticable.
un-match'a-bl[P], *a.* Unmatchable.
un-match'a-bl-ness[P], *n.* Unmatchableness.
un-matcht'[S], *a.* Unmatched.
un-med'l[P], *vi.* Unmeddle.
un-mel'an-col-y[P&S], *a.* Unmelancholy.
un-mel'lowd[S], *a.* Unmellowed.
un-melt'a-bl[P], *a.* Unmeltable.
un-mem'o-ra-bl[P], *a.* Unmemorable.
un-mend'a-bl[P], *a.* Unmendable.
un-men'sur-a-bl[P], *a.* Unmensurable.
un-ment'[P&S], *a.* Unmeant.
un-men'tion-a-bl[P], *a.* Unmentionable. [chantable.
un-mer'chant-a-bl[P], *a.* Unmer-
un-met'ald[S], *a.* Unmetaled.
un"met-a-mor'fosed[P&S], *a.* Unmetamorphosed.
un-me'terd[S], *a.* Unmetered.
un-me'zur-a-bl[P], *a.* Unmeasurable.
un-me'zured[P], *a.* Unmeasured.
un-mild'[P&S], **un-milld'**[P], *a.* Unmilled.
un-milkt'[S], *a.* Unmilked.
un-min'gl[P], *vt.* & *vi.* Unmingle.
un-min'gle-a-bl[P], *a.* Unmingleable.
un-mist'[S], *a.* Unmissed.
un"mis-tak'a-bl[P], *a.* Unmistakable.
un-mit'i-ga-bl[P], *a.* Unmitigable.
un-mixt'[S], *a.* Unmixed.
un-moand'[S], *a.* Unmoaned.
un-mockt'[P&S], *a.* Unmocked.
un-mod'i-fi"a-bl[P], *a.* Unmodifiable.
un-mod'i-fi"a-bl-ness[P], *n.* Unmodifiableness.
un-mois'tend[S], *a.* Unmoistened.
un-mol'li-fi"a-bl[P], *a.* Unmollifiable.
un-mon'eyd[S], *a.* Unmoneyed.
un-mor'tard[S], *a.* Unmortared.
un-moth'erd[S], *a.* Unmothered.
un-mournd'[S], *a.* Unmourned.
un-mov'a-bl[P], *a.* Unmovable.
un-mov'a-bl-ness[P], *n.* Unmovableness.
un-mud'l[P], *vt.* & *vi.* Unmuddle.
un-muf'l[P], *vt.* Unmuffle.
un-muld'[S], *a.* Unmulled.
un-mus'terd[S], *a.* Unmustered.
un-muz'l[P], *vt.* Unmuzzle.
un-muz'ld[P], *pa.* Unmuzzled.
un-nam'a-bl[P], *a.* Unnamable.
un-napt'[S], *a.* Unnapped.
un-nar'rowd[P&S], *a.* Unnarrowed.
un-na'tiv[P&S], *a.* Unnative.
un-nav'i-ga-bl[P], *a.* Unnavigable.
un"ne-go'ti-a-bl[P], *a.* Unnegotiable.
un-nickt'[P&S], *a.* Unnicked.
un-not'a-bl[P], *a.* Unnotable.
un-notcht'[S], *a.* Unnotched.
un-no'tice-a-bl[P], *a.* Unnoticeable.
un-no'tist[S], *a.* Unnoticed.
un-nur'isht[P], *a.* Unnourished.
un"o-beyd'[S], *a.* Unobeyed.
un"ob-jec'tion-a-bl[P], *a.* Unobjectionable.
un"ob-serv'a-bl[P], *a.* Unobservable.
un"ob-servd'[P&S], *a.* Unobserved.
un"ob-struc'tiv[S], *a.* Unobstructive.
un"ob-tain'a-bl[P], *a.* Unobtainable.
un"ob-taind'[P&S], *a.* Unobtained.
un"ob-tru'siv[P&S], *a.* Unobtrusive.
un"ob-tru'siv-ly[S], *adv.* Unobtrusively.
un"ob-tru'siv-ness[S], *n.* Unobtrusiveness.
un"oc-ca'siond[S], *a.* Unoccasioned.
un"of-fen'siv[P&S], *a.* Unoffensive.
un-of'ferd[P&S], *a.* Unoffered.
un-oild'[S], *a.* Unoiled.

un-o'pen-a-bl[P], *a.* Unopenable.
un-o'pend[P&S], *a.* Unopened.
un-op'er-a"tiv[S], *a.* Unoperative.
un"op-pres'siv[P&S], *a.* Unoppressive.
un"op-prest'[P&S], *a.* Unoppressed.
un-or'derd[P&S], *a.* Unordered.
un-or'gan-iz"[or **-is"**]**a-bl**[P], *a.* Unorganizable, unorganisable.
un-ownd'[P&S], *a.* Unowned.
un-ox'i-da-bl[P], *a.* Unoxidable.
un"ox'i-diz"[or **-is"**]**a-bl**[P], *a.* Unoxidizable, unoxidisable.
un"pac-i-fi'a-bl[P], *a.* Unpacifiable.
un-paind'[P&S], *a.* Unpained.
un-pal'a-ta-bl[P], *a.* Unpalatable
un-palld'[P], *a.* Unpalled.
un-pam'perd[P&S], *a.* Unpampered.
un-par'al-lel"a-bl[P], *a.* Unparallelable.
un-par'don-a-bl[P], *a.* Unpardonable.
un-par'don-a-bl-ness[P], *n.* Unpardonableness.
un-par'dond[P&S], *a.* Unpardoned.
un-part'a-bl[P], *a.* Unpartable.
un-part'nerd[S], *a.* Unpartnered.
un-pass'a-bl[P], *a.* Unpassable.
un-pass'a-bl-ness[P], *n.* Unpassableness.
un-patcht'[S], *a.* Unpatched.
un-pat'ro-niz"[or **-nis"**]**a-bl**[P], *a.* Unpatronizable, unpatronisable.
un-pat'ternd[P&S], *a.* Unpatterned.
un"pa-vil'iond[P&S], *a.* Unpavilioned.
un-pawnd'[P&S], *a.* Unpawned.
un-pay'a-bl[P], *a.* Unpayable.
un-peace'a-bl[P], *a.* Unpeaceable.
un-peace'a-bl-ness[P], *n.* Unpeaceableness.
un-peckt'[P&S], *a.* Unpecked.
un-peeld'[P&S], *a.* Unpeeled.
un-peer'a-bl[P], *a.* Unpeerable.
un-pen'cild[P&S], *a.* Unpenciled.
un-pend'[P&S], *a.* Unpenned.
un-pen'siond[P&S], *a.* Unpensioned.
un-pe'ple[P], *vt.* Unpeople.
un-pep'perd[P&S], *a.* Unpeppered.
un"per-ceiv'a-bl[P], *a.* Unperceivable.
un"per-ceivd'[P&S], *a.* Unperceived.
un"per-cust'[S], *a.* Unpercussed.
un"per-formd'[P&S], *a.* Unperformed.
un-per'isht[P&S], *a.* Unperished.
un"per-mis'si-bl[P], *a.* Unpermissible.
un"per-mis'siv[P&S], *a.* Unpermissive.
un"per-plext'[P&S], *a.* Unperplexed.
un-per'son-a-bl[P], *a.* Unpersonable.
un-per'son-a-bl-ness[P], *n.* Unpersonableness.
un"per-spir'a-bl[P], *a.* Unperspirable.
un"per-suad'a-bl[P], *a.* Unpersuadable.
un"per-suad'a-bl-ness[P], *n.* Unpersuadableness.
un"per-sua'si-bl[P], *a.* Unpersuasible.
un"per-sua'si-bl-ness[P], *n.* Unpersuasibleness.
un"per-sua'siv[P&S], *a.* Unpersuasive.
un"per-sua'siv-ness[P&S], *n.* Unpersuasiveness.
un"per-turbd'[P&S], *a.* Unperturbed.
un-pick'a-bl[P], *a.* Unpickable.
un-pickt'[P&S], *a.* Unpicked.
un-pic'tur-a-bl[P], *a.* Unpicturable.
un-pierst'[S], *a.* Unpierced.
un-pil'lard[S], *a.* Unpillared.
un-pil'lowd[P&S], *a.* Unpillowed.
un-pind'[P&S], *a.* Unpinned.
un-pin'iond[P&S], *a.* Unpinioned.
un-pit'i-a-bl[P], *a.* Unpitiable.
un-pla'ca-bl[P], *a.* Unplacable.
un-plankt'[P&S], *a.* Unplanked.
un-plas'terd[P&S], *a.* Unplastered.
un-plau'si-bl[P], *a.* Unplausible.
un-play'a-bl[P], *a.* Unplayable.
un-playd'[P&S], *a.* Unplayed.
un-plead'a-bl[P], *a.* Unpleadable.
un-pledgd'[P&S], *a.* Unpledged.
un-plen'isht[S], *a.* Unplenished.
un-ples'ant[S], *a.* Unpleasant.

un-plez'ant[P], *a.* Unpleasant.
un-ple'zur-a-bl[P], *a.* Unpleasurable.
un-pli'a-bl[P], *a.* Unpliable.
un-pli'a-bl-ness[P], *n.* Unpliableness.
un-plowd'[P&S], *a.* Unplowed.
un-pluckt'[P&S], *a.* Unplucked.
un-plugd'[P&S], *a.* Unplugged.
un-plumd'[P&S], *a.* Umplumbed.
un-plun'derd[P&S], *a.* Unplundered.
un-pol'ish-a-bl[P], *a.* Unpolishable.
un-pol'isht[P&S], *a.* Unpolished.
un-pold'[S], *a.* Unpolled.
un-pon'derd[P&S], *a.* Unpondered.
un-poold'[S], *a.* Unpooled.
un-por'tiond[P&S], *a.* Unportioned.
un-pos'i-tiv[P&S], *a.* Unpositive.
un"pos-sest'[P&S], *a.* Unpossessed.
un-pos'si-bl[P], *a.* Unpossible.
un-po'ta-bl[P], *a.* Unpotable.
un-pow'derd[P&S], *a.* Unpowdered.
un-prac'ti-ca-bl[P], *a.* Unpracticable.
un-prais'a-bl[P], *a.* Unpraisable.
un"pre-dict'a-bl[P], *a.* Unpredictable.
un"pre-ferd'[P&S], *a.* Unpreferred.
un-prej'u-dist[S], *a.* Unprejudiced.
un"pre-pos-sest'[P&S], *a.* Unprepossessed.
un"pre-sent'a-bl[P], *a.* Unpresentable.
un"pre-serv'a-bl[P], *a.* Unpreservable.
un"pre-servd'[P&S], *a.* Unpreserved.
un-prest'[P&S], *a.* Unpressed.
un"pre-vent'a-bl[P], *a.* Unpreventable.
un-prim'i-tiv[P&S], *a.* Unprimitive.
un-prin'ci-pl[P], *vt.* Unprinciple.
un-print'a-bl[P], *a.* Unprintable.
un"pro-cur'a-bl[P], *a.* Unprocurable.
un"pro-duc'i-bl[P], *a.* Unproducible.
un"pro-duc'tiv[P&S], *a.* Unproductive.
un"pro-fest'[P&S], *a.* Unprofessed.
un"pro-fet'ic[P&S], *a.* Unprophetic.
un-prof'it-a-bl[P], *a.* Unprofitable.
un-prof'it-a-bl-ness[P], *n.* Unprofitableness.
un"pro-gres'siv[P&S], *a.* Unprogressive.
un"pro-gres'siv-ness[S], *n.* Unprogressiveness.
un-prom'is[P&S], *vt.* & *vi.* Unpromise.
un-prom'ist[P&S], *a.* Unpromised.
un"pro-nounce'a-bl[P], *a.* Unpronounceable.
un"pro-nounst'[S], *a.* Unpronounced.
un"pro-pi'ti-a-bl[P], *a.* Unpropitiable.
un"pro-por'tion-a-bl[P], *a.* Unproportionable.
un"pro-por'tion-a-bl-ness[P], *n.* Unproportionableness.
un"pro-por'tiond[P&S], *a.* Unproportioned.
un-propt'[P&S], *a.* Unpropped.
un-prov'a-bl[P], *a.* Unprovable.
un-pub'lish-a-bl[P], *a.* Unpublishable.
un-pub'lisht[P&S], *a.* Unpublished.
un-puld'[P&S], *a.* Unpulled.
un-pum'meld[P], *a.* Unpummeled.
un-pun'ish-a-bl[P], *a.* Unpunishable.
un-pun'isht[P&S], *a.* Unpunished.
un-pur'chas-a-bl[P], *a.* Unpurchasable.
un-purst'[P&S], *a.* Unpursed.
un-pu'tre-fi"a-bl[P], *a.* Unputrefiable.
un-puz'l[P], *vt.* Unpuzzle.
un-quaft'[P&S], *a.* Unquaffed.
un-quaild'[P&S], *a.* Unquailed.
un-qual'i-fi"a-bl[P], *a.* Unqualifiable.
un-quar'terd[S], *a.* Unquartered.
un-queld'[P&S], *a.* Unquelled.
un-quench'a-bl[P], *a.* Unquenchable.
un-quencht'[P&S], *a.* Unquenched.
un-ques'tion-a-bl[P], *a.* Unquestionable.
un-ques'tion-a-bl-ness[P], *n.* Unquestionableness.
un-quick'end[P&S], *a.* Unquickened.
un-quiz'za-bl[P], *a.* Unquizzable.
un-quot'a-bl[P], *a.* Unquotable.
un-rackt'[P&S], *a.* Unracked.
un-raizd'[P], *a.* Unraised.

un-ramd′[P&S], *a.* Unrammed.

un-ran′sackt[P&S], *a.* Unransacked.

un-ran′somd[P&S], *a.* Unransomed.

un-rat′a-bl[P], *a.* Unratable.

un-rav′el-a-bl[P], *a.* Unravelable

un-rav′eld[P&S], *a.* Unraveled.

un-rav′isht[P&S], *a.* Unravished.

un-reacht′[S], *a.* Unreached.

un-read′a-bl[P], *a.* Unreadable.

un-read′a-bl-ness[P], *n.* Unreadableness.

un-re′al-iz″a-bl[P], *a.* Unrealizable.

un-reapt′[P&S], *a.* Unreaped.

un-reard′[P&S], *a.* Unreared.

un-rea′son-a-bl[P], *a.* Unreasonable.

un-rea′son-a-bl-ness[P], *n.* Unreasonableness.

un-rea′sond[P&S], *a.* Unreasoned.

un″re-buk′a-bl[P], *a.* Unrebukable.

un″re-call′a-bl[P], *a.* Unrecallable.

un″re-ceiv′a-bl[P], *a.* Unreceivable.

un″re-ceivd′[P&S], *a.* Unreceived.

un″re-cep′tiv[P&S], *a.* Unreceptive.

un-reck′on-a-bl[P], *a.* Unreckonable.

un-reck′ond[S], *a.* Unreckoned.

un-reckt′[S], *a.* Unrecked.

un″re-claim′a-bl[P], *a.* Unreclaimable.

un″re-claimd′[S], *a.* Unreclaimed.

un-rec′og-niz″[or **-nis″**]**a-bl**[P], *a.* Unrecognizable, unrecognisable.

un-rec′om-penst[S], *a.* Unrecompensed.

un″re-cov′erd[S], *a.* Unrecovered.

un″re-cuv′er-a-bl[P], *a.* Unrecoverable.

un″re-cuv′erd[P], *a.* Unrecovered.

un-red′[P&S], *a.* Unread.

un″re-deem′a-bl[P], *a.* Unredeemable.

un″re-deemd′[S], *a.* Unredeemed.

un″re-drest′[S], *a.* Unredressed.

un″re-duc′i-bl[P], *a.* Unreducible.

un″re-duc′i-bl-ness[P], *n.* Unreducibleness.

un-red′y[P&S], *a.* Unready.

un-reel′a-bl[P], *a.* Unreelable.

un-reeld′[P&S], *a.* Unreeled.

un″re-flec-tiv[P&S], *a.* Unreflective.

un″re-form′a-bl[P], *a.* Unreformable.

un″re-formd′[P&S], *a.* Unreformed.

un″re-fresht′[P&S], *a.* Unrefreshed.

un″re-fuz′a-bl[P], *a.* Unrefusable.

un″re-gain′a-bl[P], *a.* Unregainable.

un″re-gard′a-bl[P], *a.* Unregardable.

un″reg′is-terd[S], *a.* Unregistered.

un″re-herst′[P], *a.* Unrehearsed.

un-rel′a-tiv[P&S], *a.* Unrelative.

un″re-laxt′[P&S], *a.* Unrelaxed.

un″re-least′[P&S], *a.* Unreleased.

un″re-li′a-bl[P], *a.* Unreliable.

un″re-li′a-bl-ness[P], *n.* Unreliableness.

un″re-liev′a-bl[P], *a.* Unrelievable.

un″re-lievd′[P&S], *a.* Unrelieved.

un-rel′ish-a-bl[P], *a.* Unrelishable.

un-rel′isht[P&S], *a.* Unrelished.

un″re-mark′a-bl[P], *a.* Unremarkable.

un″re-markt′[P&S], *a.* Unremarked.

un″re-mem′ber-a-bl[P], *a.* Unrememberable.

un″re-mem′berd[P&S], *a.* Unremembered.

un″re-mit′ta-bl[P], *a.* Unremittable.

un″re-mu′ner-a″tiv[P&S], *a.* Unremunerative.

un-ren′derd[P&S], *a.* Unrendered.

un″re-newd′[S], *a.* Unrenewed.

un″re-nounce′a-bl[P], *a.* Unrenounceable.

un″re-nounst′[S], *a.* Unrenounced.

un″re-nownd′[P&S], *a.* Unrenowned.

un″re-pair′a-bl[P], *a.* Unrepairable.

un″re-paird′[P&S], *a.* Unrepaired.

un″re-peal′a-bl[P], *a.* Unrepealable.

un″re-peald′[S], *a.* Unrepealed.

un″re-peld′[P&S], *a.* Unrepelled.

un″re-plen′isht[P&S], *a.* Unreplenished.

un″re-port′a-bl[P], *a.* Unreportable.

un-rep″re-sent′a-bl[P], *a.* Unrepresentable.

un-rep″re-sen′ta-tiv[S], *a.* Unrepresentative.
un″re-prest′[P&S], *a.* Unrepressed.
un″re-prievd′[P&S], *a.* Unreprieved.
un″re-proach′a-bl[P], *a.* Unreproachable.
un″re-proach′a-bl-ness[P], *n.* Unreproachableness.
un″re-proacht′[P&S], *a.* Unreproached.
un″re-pro-duc′i-bl[P], *a.* Unreproducible.
un″re-prov′a-bl[P], *a.* Unreprovable.
un-rep′u-ta-bl[P], *a.* Unreputable.
un-req′ui-sit[P&S], *a.* Unrequisite.
un″re-quit′a-bl[P], *a.* Unrequitable.
un″re-serv′[P&S], *n.* Unreserve.
un″re-servd′[P&S], *a.* Unreserved.
un″re-signd′[S], *a.* Unresigned.
un″re-sist′i-bl[P], *a.* Unresistible.
un″re-solv′a-bl[P], *a.* Unresolvable.
un″re-solvd′[P&S], *a.* Unresolved.
un″re-spect′a-bl[P], *a.* Unrespectable.
un″re-spir′a-bl[P], *a.* Unrespirable.
un″re-spon′si-bl[P], *a.* Unresponsible.
un″re-spon′si-bl-ness[P], *n.* Unresponsibleness.
un″re-spon′siv[P&S], *a.* Unresponsive.
un″re-spon′siv-ly[S], *adv.* Unresponsively.
un″re-spon′siv-ness[S], *n.* Unresponsiveness.
un″re-strain′a-bl[P], *a.* Unrestrainable.
un″re-straind′[P&S], *a.* Unrestrained.
un″re-sul′tiv[P&S], *a.* Unresultive.
un″re-ten′tiv[P&S], *a.* Unretentive.
un″re-tract′a-bl[P], *a.* Unretractable.
un″re-trievd′[P&S], *a.* Unretrieved.
un″re-turn′a-bl[P], *a.* Unreturnable.
un″re-turnd′[P&S], *a.* Unreturned.
un″re-veald′[S], *a.* Unrevealed.
un″re-ver′si-bl[P], *a.* Unreversible.
un″re-verst′[P&S], *a.* Unreversed.
un″re-viewd′[P&S], *a.* Unreviewed.
un-rid′a-bl[P], *a.* Unridable.
un-rid′l[P], *vt.* Unriddle.
un-rigd′[P&S], *a.* Unrigged.
un-ringd′[S], *a.* Unringed.
un-rinst′[P&S], *a.* Unrinsed.
un-rip′end[P&S], *a.* Unripened.
un-rip′ld[P], *a.* Unrippled.
un-riv′n[P], *a.* Unriven.
un-robd′[P&S], *a.* Unrobbed.
un-rolld′[P&S], *a.* Unrolled.
un-rooft′[P&S], *a.* Unroofed.
un-rot′n[P], *a.* Unrotten.
un-rout′a-bl[P], *a.* Unroutable.
un-rubd′[P], *a.* Unrubbed.
un-ruf′[P&S], *a.* Unrough.
un-ruf′ld[P], *a.* Unruffled.
un-ru′in-a-bl[P], *a.* Unruinable.
un-ru′ind[S], *a.* Unruined.
un-sackt′[P&S], *a.* Unsacked.
un-sad′ld[P], *a.* Unsaddled.
un-sail′a-bl[P], *a.* Unsailable.
un-sal′a-bl[P], **un-sale′a-bl**[P], *a.* Unsalable, unsaleable.
un-salv′a-bl[P], *a.* Unsalvable.
un-salvd′[P&S], *a.* Unsalved.
un-sanc′tiond[S], *a.* Unsanctioned.
un-san′dald[P&S], *a.* Unsandaled.
un″sa-pon′i-fi″a-bl[P], *a.* Unsaponifiable.
un-sapt′[S], *a.* Unsapped.
un-sa′ti-a-bl[P], *a.* Unsatiable.
un-sa′ti-a-bl-ness[P], *n.* Unsatiableness.
un-sat′is-fi″a-bl[P], *a.* Unsatisfiable.
un-sawd′[S], *a.* Unsawed.
un-say′a-bl[P], *a.* Unsayable.
un-scalpt′[P&S], *a.* Unscalped.
un-scand′[P&S], *a.* Unscanned.
un-scard′[P&S], *a.* Unscarred.
un-scat′terd[P&S], *a.* Unscattered.
un-scep′terd[P&S], *a.* Unsceptered.
un-scoold′[S], *a.* Unschooled.
un-scorcht′[S], *a.* Unscorched.
un-scornd′[P&S], *a.* Unscorned.

un-scourd′[P&S], *a.* Unscoured.
un-scracht′[P], *a.* Unscratched.
un-screend′[P&S], *a.* Unscreened.
un-scrib′ld[P], *a.* Unscribbled.
un-scru′ta-bl[P], *a.* Unscrutable.
un-seald′[P&S], *a.* Unsealed.
un-seard′[P&S], *a.* Unseared.
un-sea′son-a-bl[P], *a.* Unseasonable.
un-sea′son-a-bl-ness[P], *n.* Unseasonableness.
un-sea′sond[S], *a.* Unseasoned.
un″se-duc′tiv[P&S], *a.* Unseductive.
un-see′a-bl[P], *a.* Unseeable.
un-seiz′a-bl[P], *a.* Unseizable.
un-seizd′[P&S], *a.* Unseized.
un-senst′[P&S], *a.* Unsensed.
un-sen′ti-neld[S], *a.* Unsentineled.
un-sep′ul-cherd[P&S], *a.* Unsepulchered.
un″se-ques′terd[P&S], *a.* Unsequestered.
un-serch′a-bl[P], *a.* & *n.* Unsearchable.
un-serch′a-bl-ness[P], *n.* Unsearchableness.
un-sercht′[P], *a.* Unsearched.
un-servd′[P&S], *a.* Unserved.
un-ser′vice-a-bl[P], *a.* Unserviceable.
un-ser′vice-a-bl-ness[P], *n.* Serviceableness.
un-set′ld[P], *a.* Unsettled.
un-sev′erd[S], *a.* Unsevered.
un-sew′erd[S], *a.* Unsewered.
un-shack′ld[P], *a.* Unshackled.
un-shad′owd[S], *a.* Unshadowed.
un-shake′a-bl[P], *a.* Unshakeable.
un-shap′a-bl[P], *a.* Unshapable.
un-sharp′end[S], *a.* Unsharpened.
un-shat′terd[S], *a.* Unshattered.
un-shel′terd[S], *a.* Unsheltered.
un-shelv′[P], *vt.* Unshelve.
un-shift′a-bl[P], *a.* Unshiftable.
un-shipt′[S], *a.* Unshipped.
un-shiv′erd[S], *a.* Unshivered.
un-shockt′[S], *a.* Unshocked.
un-short′end[S], *a.* Unshortened.
un-show′erd[S], *a.* Unshowered.
un-shrink′a-bl[P], *a.* Unshrinkable.
un-shund′[S], *a.* Unshunned.
un-shut′terd[S], *a.* Unshuttered.
un-sil′verd[S], *a.* Unsilvered.
un-sim′pl[P], *a.* Unsimple.
un-sin′gld[P], *a.* Unsingled.
un-sink′a-bl[P], *a.* Unsinkable.
un-skind′[S], *a.* Unskinned.
un-slack′end[S], *a.* Unslackened.
un-slackt′[S], *a.* Unslacked.
un-slan′derd[S], *a.* Unslandered.
un-slau′terd[P&S], *a.* Unslaughtered.
un-slurd′[S], *a.* Unslurred.
un-smircht′[S], *a.* Unsmirched.
un-smoothd′[S], *a.* Unsmoothed.
un-smug′ld[P], *a.* Unsmuggled.
un-snubd′[S], *a.* Unsnubbed.
un-soakt′[S], *a.* Unsoaked.
un-soapt′[S], *a.* Unsoaped.
un-so′berd[S], *a.* Unsobered.
un-so′ci-a-bl[P], *a.* Unsociable.
un-so′ci-a-bl-ness[P], *n.* Unsociableness.
un-sof′tend[S], *a.* Unsoftened.
un-soild′[S], *a.* Unsoiled.
un-sol′u-bl[P], *a.* Unsoluble.
un-solv′a-bl[P], *a.* Unsolvable.
un-solvd′[S], *a.* Unsolved.
un-sor′rowd[S], *a.* Unsorrowed.
un-sound′a-bl[P], *a.* Unsoundable.
un-sourd′[S], *a.* Unsoured.
un-span′gld[P], *a.* Unspangled.
un-spard′[S], *a.* Unsparred.
un-speak′a-bl[P], *a.* Unspeakable.
un-speak′a-bl-ness[P], *n.* Unspeakableness.
un-speck′ld[P], *a.* Unspeckled.
un-speckt′[S], *a.* Unspecked.
un-spec′ta-cld[P], *a.* Unspectacled.
un-spec′u-la″tiv[S], *a.* Unspeculative.
un-spell′a-bl[P], *a.* Unspellable.
un-speld′[S], *a.* Unspelled.
un-spild′[S], *a.* Unspilled.

un-splasht'[s], *a.* Unsplashed.
un-splayd'[s], *a.* Unsplayed.
un-spoil'a-bl[p], *a.* Unspoilable.
un-spoild'[s], *a.* Unspoiled.
un-spred'[p&s], *a.* Unspread.
un-sprin'kld[p], *a.* Unsprinkled.
un-squan'derd[s], *a.* Unsquandered.
un-squeezd'[s], *a.* Unsqueezed.
un-stackt'[s], *a.* Unstacked.
un-sta'bl[p], *a.* Unstable.
un-sta'bl-ness[p], *n.* Unstableness.
un-stain'a-bl[p], *a.* Unstainable.
un-staind'[s], *a.* Unstained.
un-stampt'[s], *a.* Unstamped.
un-stanch'a-bl[p], *a.* Unstanchable.
un-starcht'[s], *a.* Unstarched.
un-stard'[s], *a.* Unstarred.
un-star'tld[p], *a.* Unstartled.
un-sta'tiond[s], *a.* Unstationed.
un-stat'ut-a-bl[p], *a.* Unstatutable.
un-sted'y[p&s], *a.* Unsteady.
un-steept'[s], *a.* Unsteeped.
un-steerd'[s], *a.* Unsteered.
un-stemd'[s], *a.* Unstemmed.
un-stiff'end[s], *a.* Unstiffened.
un-stitcht'[s], *a.* Unstitched.
un-stockt'[s], *a.* Unstocked.
un-stop'l[p], *vt.* Unstopple.
un-stopt'[s], *a.* Unstopped.
un-stormd'[s], *a.* Unstormed.
un-stowd'[s], *a.* Unstowed.
un-straind'[s], *a.* Unstrained.
un-strait'end[s], *a.* Unstraitened.
un-strapt'[s], *a.* Unstrapped.
un-strength'end[s], *a.* Unstrengthened.
un-strest'[s], *a.* Unstressed.
un-strewd'[s], *a.* Unstrewed.
un-stuft'[s], *a.* Unstuffed.
un-stund'[s], *a.* Unstunned.
un"sub-du'a-bl[p], *a.* Unsubduable.
un"sub-merg'i-bl[p], *a.* Unsubmergible.
un"sub-mis'siv[s], *a.* Unsubmissive.
un"sub-vert'i-bl[p], *a.* Unsubvertible.
un"suc-ces'siv[s], *a.* Unsuccessive.
un-suc'cor-a-bl[p], *a.* Unsuccorable.
un-suc'cord[s], *a.* Unsuccored.
un-suck'ld[p], *a.* Unsuckled.
un-suckt'[s], *a.* Unsucked.
un-sug'ard[s], *a.* Unsugared.
un"sug-ges'tiv[p&s], *a.* Unsuggestive.
un-suit'a-bl[p], *a.* Unsuitable.
un-suit'a-bl-ness[p], *n.* Unsuitableness.
un-sumd'[s], *a.* Unsummed.
un-sund'[s], *a.* Unsunned.
un-sup'l[p], *a.* Unsupple.
un"sup-port'a-bl[p], *a.* Unsupportable.
un"sup-port'a-bl-ness[p], *n.* Unsupportableness.
un"sup-prest'[s], *a.* Unsuppressed.
un-sup'pu-ra"tiv[s], *a.* Unsuppurative.
un-supt'[s], *a.* Unsupped.
un"sur-mount'a-bl[p], *a.* Unsurmountable.
un"sur-pass'a-bl[p], *a.* Unsurpassable.
un"sur-past'[s], *a.* Unsurpassed.
un"sur-ren'derd[s], *a.* Unsurrendered.
un"sur-veyd'[s], *a.* Unsurveyed.
un"sus-cep'ti-bl[p], *a.* Unsusceptible.
un"sus-pect'a-bl[p], *a.* Unsuspectable.
un"sus-tain'a-bl[p], *a.* Unsustainable.
un"sus-taind'[p], *a.* Unsustained.
un-swad'l[p], *vt.* Unswaddle.
un-swal'lowd[s], *a.* Unswallowed.
un-swayd'[s], *a.* Unswayed.
un-swervd'[s], *a.* Unswerved.
un-switcht'[s], *a.* Unswitched.
un-syl'la-bld[p], *a.* Unsyllabled.
un-tagd'[s], *a.* Untagged.
un-taint'a-bl[p], *a.* Untaintable.
un-talk'a-tiv[s], *a.* Untalkative.
un-talkt'[s], *a.* Untalked.
un-tam'a-bl[p], *a.* Untamable.
un-tam'a-bl-ness[p], *a.* Untamableness.

un-tand′[s], *a.* Untanned.
un-tan′gl-bl[r], *a.* Untangible.
un-tan′gl-bl-ness[r], *n.* Untangibleness.
un-tan′gld[r], *a.* Untangled.
un-tapt′[s], *a.* Untapped.
un-tard′[s], *a.* Untarred.
un-tar′nish-a-bl[r], *a.* Untarnishable.
un-tar′nisht[s], *a.* Untarnished.
un-taskt′[s], *a.* Untasked.
un-taxt′[s], *a.* Untaxed.
un-teach′a-bl[r], *a.* Unteachable.
un-tear′a-bl[r], *a.* Untearable.
un-tec′ni-cal[s], *a.* Untechnical.
un-tem′perd[s], *a.* Untempered.
un-tempt′a-bl[r], *a.* Untemptable.
un-ten′a-bl[r], *a.* Untenable.
un-ten′ant-a-bl[r], *a.* Untenantable.
un-ten′derd[s], *a.* Untendered.
un-test′a-bl[r], *a.* Untestable.
un-teth′erd[s], *a.* Untethered.
un-thawd′[s], *a.* Unthawed.
un-thick′end[s], *a.* Unthickened.
un-thind′[s], *a.* Unthinned.
un-think′a-bl[r], *a.* Unthinkable.
un-thrasht′[s], *a.* Unthrashed.
un-thret′end[r], *a.* Unthreatened.
un-thresht′[s], *a.* Unthreshed.
un-thrild′[s], *a.* Unthrilled.
un-thumd′[s], *a.* Unthumbed.
un-tick′ld[r], *a.* Untickled.
un-tight′end[s], *a.* Untightened.
un-till′a-bl[r], *a.* Untillable.
un-tim′berd[s], *a.* Untimbered.
un-tith′a-bl[r], *a.* Untithable.
un-toild′[s], *a.* Untoiled.
un-tol′er-a-bl[r], *a.* Untolerable.
un-tow′erd[s], *a.* Untowered.
un-trace′a-bl[r], *a.* Untraceable.
un-trackt′[s], *a.* Untracked.
un-tract′a-bl[r], *a.* Untractable.
un-tract′a-bl-ness[r], *n.* Untractableness.
un-traind′[s], *a.* Untrained.
un-tram′meld[s], *a.* Untrammeled.
un-tram′pld[r], *a.* Untrampled.
un″trans-fer′a-bl[r], *a.* Untransferable.
un″trans-ferd′[s], *a.* Untransferred.
un″trans-formd′[s], *a.* Untransformed.
un″trans-grest′[s], *a.* Untransgressed.
un″trans-lat′a-bl[r], *a.* Untranslatable.
un″trans-lat′a-bl-ness[r], *n.* Untranslatableness.
un″trans-mis′si-bl[r], *a.* Untransmissible.
un″trans-mut′a-bl[r], *a.* Untransmutable.
un″trans-port′a-bl[r], *a.* Untransportable.
un-trapt′[s], *a.* Untrapped.
un-trav′eld[s], *a.* Untraveled, untravelled.
un-trav′ers-a-bl[r], **a.** Untraversable.
un-trav′erst[s], *a.* Untraversed.
un-treat′a-bl[r], *a.* Untreatable.
un-trencht′[s], *a.* Untrenched.
un-trest′[s], *a.* Untressed.
un-tril′[r], *vt.* & *vi.* Untrill.
un-trild′[s], *a.* Untrilled.
un-trimd′[s], *a.* Untrimmed.
un″tri-um′fant[r&s], *a.* Untriumphant.
un-trod′n[r], *a.* Untrodden.
un-trub′ld[r], *a.* Untroubled.
un-trub′l-sum[r], *a.* Untroublesome.
un-trust′[s], *a.* Untrussed.
un-tum′bld[r], *a.* Untumbled.
un-tun′a-bl[r], *a.* Untunable.
un-turnd′[s], *a.* Unturned.
un″un-der-stand′a-bl[r], *a.* Ununderstandable.
un-us′a-bl[r], *a.* Unusable.
un-u′til-iz″a-bl[r], *a.* Unutilizable.
un-ut′ter-a-bl[r], *a.* Unutterable.
un-ut′ter-a-bl-ness[r], *n.* Unutterableness.

un-ut'terd[s], *a.* Unuttered.
un-u'zu-al[p], *a.* Unusual.
un-vampt'[s], *a.* Unvamped.
un-van'quish-a-bl[p], *a.* Unvanquishable.
un-van'quisht[s], *a.* Unvanquished.
un-va'ri-a-bl[p], *a.* Unvariable.
un-var'nisht[s], *a.* Unvarnished.
un-veerd'[s], *a.* Unveered.
un-veild'[s], *a.* Unveiled.
un-vend'i-bl[p], *a.* Unvendible.
un-ven'er-a-bl[p], *a.* Unvenerable.
un-ven'omd[s], *a.* Unvenomed.
un-ver'i-fi"a-bl[p], *a.* Unverifiable.
un-ver'i-ta-bl[p], *a.* Unveritable.
un-verst'[s], *a.* Unversed.
un-viewd'[s], *a.* Unviewed.
un"vin-dic'tiv[p&s], *a.* Unvindictive.
un-vi'o-la-bl[p], *a.* Unviolable.
un-vit'ri-fi"a-bl[p], *a.* Unvitrifiable.
un-viz'ord[s], *a.* Unvizored.
un-void'a-bl[p], *a.* Unvoidable.
un-voucht'[s], *a.* Unvouched.
un-vowd'[s], *a.* Unvowed.
un-vow'eld[s], *a.* Unvoweled.
un-voy'age-a-bl[p], *a.* Unvoyageable.
un-vul'ner-a-bl[p], *a.* Unvulnerable.
un-wald'[s], *a.* Unwalled.
un-warmd'[s], *a.* Unwarmed.
un-warnd'[s], *a.* Unwarned.
un-warpt'[s], *a.* Unwarped.
un-war'rant-a-bl[p], *a.* Unwarrantable.
un-war'rant-a-bl-ness[p], *n.* Unwarrantableness.
un-washt'[s], *a.* Unwashed.
un-watcht'[s], *a.* Unwatched.
un-wa'terd[s], *a.* Unwatered.
un-wa'verd[s], *a.* Unwavered.
un-waxt'[s], *a.* Unwaxed.
un-weak'end[s], *a.* Unweakened.
un-weand'[s], *a.* Unweaned.
un-wear'a-bl[p], *a.* Unwearable.
un-weav'[p], *vt.* & *vi.* Unweave.
un-webd'[s], *a.* Unwebbed.
un-wedge'a-bl[p], *a.* Unwedgeable.
un-weend'[s], *a.* Unweened.
un-weigh'a-bl[p], *a.* Unweighable.
un-weighd'[s], *a.* Unweighed.
un-wel'comd[s], *a.* Unwelcomed.
un-welth'y[p&s], *a.* Unwealthy.
un-whirld'[s], *a.* Unwhirled.
un-whit'end[s], *a.* Unwhitened.
un-win'dowd[s], *a.* Unwindowed.
un-wingd'[s], *a.* Unwinged.
un-win'nowd[s], *a.* Unwinnowed.
un-win'sum[p], *a.* Unwinsome.
un-wisht'[s], *a.* Unwished.
un-with'erd[s], *a.* Unwithered.
un-wit'nest[s], *a.* Unwitnessed.
un-work'a-bl[p], *a.* Unworkable.
un-workt'[s], *a.* Unworked.
un-wor'shipt[s], *a.* Unworshiped.
un-wound'a-bl[p], *a.* Unwoundable.
un-wreakt'[s], *a.* Unwreaked.
un-wreckt'[s], *a.* Unwrecked.
un-wrencht'[s], *a.* Unwrenched.
un-wrin'kld[p], *a.* Unwrinkled.
un-writ'a-bl[p], *a.* Unwritable.
un-wrongd'[s], *a.* Unwronged.
un-wun'[p&s], *a.* Unwon.
un-wunt'ed[p], *a.* Unwonted.
un-wurmd'[p], *a.* Unwormed.
un-wur'thy[p], *a.* Unworthy.
un-yeand'[s], *a.* Unyeaned.
un-zel'ous[p&s], *a.* Unzealous.
up-hol'sterd[s], *pp.* Upholstered.
ur"ce-o-la'ri-in[s], *a.* Urceolariine.
u'ri-na"tiv[p&s], *a.* Urinative.
urnd[s], *pp.* Urned.
ush'erd[s], *pp.* Ushered.
u"su-cap'ti-bl[p], *a.* Usucaptible.
u-surpt'[s], *pp.* Usurped.
u-surp'a-tiv[p&s], *a.* Usurpative.
u'ter-in[p&s], **-ine**[p], *a.* Uterine.
util, -ile[s], *a.* Utile.
u'til-ize[s], *vt.* Utilise.
u'til-iz"[or **-is"**]**a-bl**[p], *a.* Utilizable, utilisable.

ut'ter-a-bl[P], *a.* Utterable.
ut'ter-a-bl-ness[P], *n.* Utterableness.
ut'terd[S], *pp.* Uttered.
uz'a-bl[P], **uze'a-bl**[P], *a.* Usable, useable.
uz'a-bl-ness[P], **uze'a-bl-ness**[P], *n.* Usableness, useableness.
uze[P], *vt.* & *vi.* Use.
u'zu-al[P], *a.* Usual.

V

vac'cin[P&S], **-ine**[P&S], *a.* & *n.* Vaccine.
vac'ci-na-bl[P], *a.* Vaccinable.
vag"i-nic'o-lin[S], *a.* Vaginicoline.
val'ly[S], *n.* Valley.
val'or[S], *n.* Valour.
val'u-a-bl[P], *a.* & *n.* Valuable.
val'u-a-bl-ness[P], *n.* Valuableness.
valv[P&S], *n.* Valve.
valvd[S], *pp.* Valved.
vam'pir-in[S], *a.* Vampirine.
vampt[P&S], *pp.* Vamped.
vam'py-rin[S], *a.* & *n.* Vampyrine.
vand[S], *pp.* Vanned.
van'gard"[S], *n.* Vanguard.
van'isht[P&S], *pp.* Vanished.
van'quish-a-bl[P], *a.* Vanquishable.
van'quisht[P&S], *pp.* Vanquished.
va'por[P&S], *v.* & *n.* Vapour.
va'pord[P&S], *pp.* Vapored, vapoured.
va'por-iz"[or **-is"**]**a-bl**[P], *a.* Vaporizable, vaporisable.
va'por-us[S], *a.* Vaporous.
va'ri-a-bl[P], *a.* & *n.* Variable.
va'ri-a-bl-ness[P], *n.* Variableness.
va'ri-a"tiv[S], *a.* Variative.
va'ri-a"tiv-ly[S], *adv.* Variatively.
va-ri'o-lin[S], *n.* Varioline.
va'ri-us[S], *a.* Various.
var'nisht[S], *pp.* Varnished.
vas'e-lin[S], *n.* Vaseline.
va"so-con-stric'tiv[S], *a.* Vasoconstrictive.
va"so-for'ma-tiv[S], *a.* Vasoformative.
veerd[S], *pp.* Veered.
veg'e-ta-bl[P], *a.* & *n.* Vegetable.
veg'e-tal-in[S], *n.* Vegetaline.
veg'e-ta"tiv[P&S], *a.* Vegetative.
veg'e-ta"tiv-ly[S], *adv.* Vegetatively.
veg'e-ta"tiv-ness[S], *n.* Vegetativeness.
veg'e-tiv[S], *a.* Vegetive.
ve'hi-cl[P], *n.* Vehicle.
veil[P], *v.* & *n.* Vail.
veild[P&S], *pp.* Veiled.
veind[P&S], *a.* Veined.
vend'a-bl[P], *a.* Vendable.
vend'i-bl[P], *a.* Vendible.
vend'i-bl-ness[P], *n.* Vendibleness.
ve-neerd'[P&S], *pp.* Veneered.
ven'er-a-bl[P], *a.* Venerable.
ven'er-a-bl-ness[P], *n.* Venerableness.
ven'er-a"tiv[S], *a.* Venerative.
ven'omd[S], *pp.* Venomed.
ven'om-us[S], *a.* Venomous.
ven'om-us-ly[S], *adv.* Venomously.
ven'om-us-ness[S], *n.* Venomousness.
ven'ti-la-bl[P], *a.* Ventilable.
ven'ti-la"tiv[S], *a.* Ventilative.
ven'tri-cl[P], *n.* Ventricle.
ven'ture-sum[P&S], *a.* Venturesome.
ven'ture-sum-ly[P&S], *adv.* Venturesomely.
ven'ture-sum-ness[P&S], *n.* Venturesomeness.
ven'tur-us[S], *a.* Venturous.
ven'tur-us-ly[S], *adv.* Venturously.
ven'tur-us-ness[S], *n.* Venturousness.
ve-ra'cius[S], *a.* Veracious.
ve-ra'cius-ly[S], *adv.* Veraciously.
ver'i-fi"a-bl[P], *a.* Verifiable.
ver'i-ta-bl[P], *a.* Veritable.
ver'i-ta-bl-ness[P], *n.* Veritableness.
ver'sa-til[S], **-ile**[S], *a.* Versatile.

ver'sa-til-ly[s], *adv.* Versatilely.
ver'si-cl[p], *n.* Versicle.
verst[p&s], *a.* Versed.
ver-tig'i-nus[p&s], *a.* Vertiginous.
ver-tig'i-nus-ly[p&s], *adv.* Vertiginously.
ver-tig'i-nus-ness[p&s], *n.* Vertiginousness.
ves'i-cl[p], *n.* Vesicle.
ves"i-co-u'ter-in[s], *a.* Vesicouterine.
ves"per-til'i-o-nin[s], *a.* Vespertilionine.
ves'per-tin[s], *a.* Vespertine.
ves'pin[s], *a.* Vespine.
vet'i-tive[s], *a.* Vetitive.
vext[s], *pp.* Vexed.
vi'a-bl[p], *a.* Viable.
vi'bra-til[s], **-ile**[s], *a.* Vibratile.
vi'bra-tiv[s], *a.* Vibrative.
vib'ri-o-nin[s], *a.* Vibrionine.
vi-ca'ri-us[s], *a.* Vicarious.
vi-ca'ri-us-ly[s], *adv.* Vicariously.
vi-ca'ri-us-ness[s], *n.* Vicariousness.
vice"=con'sta-bl[p], *n.* Vice=constable.
vice=sher'if[p], *n.* Vice=sheriff.
vic'tim-iz"[or **-is"**]**a-bl**[p], *a.* Victimizable.
vic-to'ri-us[s], *a.* Victorious.
vic-to'ri-us-ly[s], *adv.* Victoriously.
vic-to'ri-us-ness[s], *n.* Victoriousness.
vid'ū-in[s], *a.* & *n.* Viduine.
view'a-bl[p], *a.* Viewable.
viewd[p&s], *pp.* Viewed.
vig'or[p&s], *n.* Vigour.
vig'o-rus[s], *a.* Vigorous.
vig'o-rus-ly[p], *adv.* Vigorously.
vil'lain-us[s], *a.* Villainous.
vil'lain-us-ly[s], *adv.* Villainously.
vil'lain-us-ness[s], *n.* Villainousness.
vil'lan-us[s], *a.* Villainous.
vi-min'e-us[s], *a.* Vimineous.
vi-na'ce-us[s], *a.* Vinaceous.
vin'ci-bl[p], *a.* Vincible.
vin'ci-bl-ness[p], *n.* Vincibleness.
vin'di-ca-bl[p], *a.* Vindicable.
vin'di-ca"tiv[s], *a.* Vindicative.
vin'di-ca"tiv-ly[s], *adv.* Vindicatively.
vin'di-ca"tiv-ness[s], *n.* Vindicativeness.
vin-dic'tiv[p&s], *a.* Vindictive.
vin-dic'tiv-ly[s], *adv.* Vindictively.
vin-dic'tiv-ness[s], *n.* Vindictiveness.
vin'yard[p], *n.* Vineyard.
vi'o-la-bl[p], *a.* Violable.
vi'o-la-bl-ness[p], *n.* Violableness.
vi'o-la"tiv[s], *a.* Violative.
vi-pa'ri-us[s], *a.* Viparious.
vi'per-in[s], **-ine**[s], *a.* & *n.* Viperine.
vir'il[s], **-ile**[s], *a.* Virile.
vir'il-ness[s], *n.* Virileness.
vis'i-bl[p], *a.* Visible.
vis'i-bl-ness[p], *n.* Visibleness.
vi'siond[s], *a.* Visioned.
vis'it-a-bl[p], *a.* Visitable.
vis'i-ta"tiv[s], *a.* Visitative.
vi'ta-tiv[s], *a.* Vitative.
vi'ta-tiv-ness[s], *n.* Vitativeness.
vi-tres'ci-bl[p], *a.* Vitrescible.
vit'ri-fi"a-bl[p], *a.* Vitrifiable.
vit'rin[s], *n.* Vitrine.
vit'u-lin[s], *a.* Vituline.
vi-tu'per-a-bl[p], *a.* Vituperable.
vi-tu'per-a"tiv[s], *a.* Vituperative.
vi-tu'per-a"tiv-ly[s], *adv.* Vituperatively.
vi-va'cius[s], *a.* Vivacious.
vi-va'cius-ly[s], *adv.* Vivaciously.
vi-va'cius-ness[s], *n.* Vivaciousness.
vi-ver'rin[s], *a.* & *n.* Viverrine.
vi-vip'a-rus[s], *a.* Viviparous.
vi-vip'a-rus-ly[s], *adv.* Viviparously.
vi-vip'a-rus-ness[s], *n.* Viviparousness.
viz'or[s], *v.* & *n.* Visor.
viz'ord[s], *pp.* Vizored.
vo'ca-bl[p], *n.* Vocable.
voc'a-tiv[p&s], *a.* & *n.* Vocative.
vo-cif'er-us[s], *a.* Vociferous.
vo-cif'er-us-ly[s], *adv.* Vociferously.

vo-cif′er-us-ness[s], *n.* Vociferousness.
voiced[s], *a.* Voiced.
void′a-bl[r], *a.* Voidable.
void′a-bl-ness[r], *n.* Voidableness.
vol′a-til[r&s], **-ile**[r&s], *a.* & *n.* Volatile.
vol′a-til-iz″[or **-is″**]**a-bl**[r], *a.* Volatilizable, volatilisable.
vol′a-til-ness[r&s], *n.* Volatileness.
vol′i-tiv[s], *a.* Volitive.
vol′leyd[s], *pp.* Volleyed.
vol′ly[s], *v.* & *n.* Volley.
vol″ta-e-lec″tro-mo′tiv[s], *a.* Volta-electromotive.
vol′u-bl[s], *a.* Voluble.
vol′u-crin[s], *a.* Volucrine.
vo-lu′mi-nus[s], *a.* Voluminous.
vo-lu′mi-nus-ly[s], *adv.* Voluminously.
vo-lu′mi-nus-ness[s], *n.* Voluminousness.
vol′un-ta″tiv[s], *a.* Voluntative.
vol″un-teerd′[s], *pp.* Volunteered.
vo-lup′tu-us[s], *a.* Voluptuous.
vo-lup′tu-us-ly[s], *adv.* Voluptuously.
vo-lup′tu-us-ness[s], *n.* Voluptuousness.
vom′i-tiv[s], *a.* & *n.* Vomitive.
vom′i-tiv-ness[s], *n.* Vomitiveness.
vo-ra′clus[s], *a.* Voracious.
vo-ra′clus-ly[s], *adv.* Voraciously.
vo-ra′clus-ness[s], *n.* Voraciousness.
vor-tig′i-nus[s], *a.* Vortiginous.
vot′a-bl[r], *a.* Votable.
vo′tiv[s], *a.* Votive.
vo′tiv-ly[s], *adv.* Votively.
vo′tiv-ness[s], *n.* Votiveness.
voucht[r&s], *pp.* Vouched.
vowd[s], *pp.* Vowed.
vow′eld[s], *pp.* Voweled, vowelled.
voy′age-a-bl[r], *a.* Voyageable.
vul′ner-a-bl[r], *a.* Vulnerable.
vul′ner-a-bl-ness[r], *n.* Vulnerableness.
vul′pin[s], **-ine**[s], *a.* Vulpine.

W

wach[r], *v.* & *n.* Watch.
wacht[r], *pp.* Watched.
wad′a-bl[r], **wade′a-bl**[r], *a.* Wadable, wadeable.
wa′ferd[r&s], *pp.* Wafered.
wagd[r&s], *pp.* Wagged.
wa′gerd[r&s], *pp.* Wagered.
wag′l[r], *v.* & *n.* Waggle.
wag′ld[r], *pp.* Waggled.
wag′on[s], *n.* Waggon.
wag′ond[s], *pp.* Waggoned.
waild[r&s], *pp.* Wailed.
waiv[r], *vt.* Waive.
waivd[r&s], *pp.* Waived.
wald[s], *pa.* Walled.
walk′a-bl[r], *a.* Walkable.
walkt[r&s], *pp.* Walked.
wal′lopt[s], *pp.* Walloped.
wal′lowd[s], *pp.* Wallowed.
wan′derd[s], *pp.* Wandered.
wan′tond[s], *pp.* Wantoned.
war′bl[r], *v.* & *n.* Warble.
war′bld[r], *pp.* Warbled.
ward[r&s], *pp.* Warred.
warmd[r&s], *pp.* Warmed.
warnd[s], *pp.* Warned.
warpt[s], *pp.* Warped.
war′rant-a-bl[r], *a.* Warrantable.
war′rant-a-bl-ness[r], *n.* Warrantableness.
washt[r&s], *pa.* Washed.
wast′a-bl[r], *a.* Wastable.
watcht[s], *pp.* Watched.
wa′terd[r&s], *a.* Watered.
wa′verd[s], *pp.* Wavered.
waxt[r&s], *pp.* Waxed.
weak′end[r&s], *pp.* Weakened.
weand[r&s], *pp.* Weaned.

wear'a-bl[P], *a.* Wearable.
wea'ri-sum[S], *a.* Wearisome.
weav[P&S], *v.* & *n.* Weave.
weav'a-bl[P], *a.* Weavable.
wea'zend[S], *a.* Weazened.
webd[P&S], *a.* Webbed.
wed'loc[S], *n.* Wedlock.
weend[P&S], *pp.* Weened.
weighd[S], *pp.* Weighed.
wel[P&S], *v.*, *a.*, *n.* & *adv.* Well.
wel'comd[S], *pp.* Welcomed.
wel'cum[P], *v.*, *a.* & *n.* Welcome.
wel'cumd[P], *pp.* Welcomed.
weld[S], *pp.* Welled.
weld'a-bl[P], *a.* Weldable.
welld[P], *pp.* Welled.
wel'terd[S], *pp.* Weltered.
welth[P&S], *n.* Wealth.
welth'y[P&S], *a.* Wealthy.
wep'on[P&S], *n.* Weapon.
wer[P&S], *v.* Were.
weth'er[P&S], *v.*, *a.* & *n.* Weather.
weth'erd[P&S], *pa.* Weathered.
whackt[S], *pp.* Whacked.
wheeld[P&S], *a.* Wheeled.
wheez[P], *v.* & *n.* Wheeze.
wheezd[P&S], *pp.* Wheezed.
whelkt[S], *a.* Whelked.
whelmd[S], *pp.* Whelmed.
whelpt[S], *pp.* Whelped.
whense[P], *adv.* Whence.
whif[S], *v.* & *n.* Whiff.
whift[S], *pp.* Whiffed.
whimd[S], *pp.* Whimmed.
whim'perd[P&S], *pp.* Whimpered.
whipt[P&S], *pp.* Whipped.
whir[P&S], *v.* & *n.* Whirr.
whird[P&S], *pp.* Whirred.
whirld[P&S], *pp.* Whirled.
whisk'erd[S], *a.* Whiskered.
whiskt[P&S], *pp.* Whisked.
whis'ky[S], *n.* Whiskey.
whis'perd[P&S], *pp.* Whispered.
whis'tl[P], *v.* & *n.* Whistle.
whis'tld[P], *pp.* Whistled.
whit'end[S], *pp.* Whitened.
whizd[P&S], *pp.* Whizzed.
whoopt[P&S], *pp.* Whooped.
wich[P], *v.* & *n.* Witch.
wicht[P], *pp.* Witched.
wick'erd[S], *a.* Wickered.
wid'end[S], *pp.* Widened.
wid'owd[S], *pp.* Widowed.
wield'a-bl[P], *a.* Wieldable.
wier[S], *n.* Weir.
wierd[S], *v.*, *a.* & *n.* Weird.
wigd[S], *a.* Wigged.
wil[P&S], *v.* & *n.* Will.
wil'derd[S], *pp.* Wildered.
wil'ful[P&S], *a.* Wilfull.
willd[P], **wild**[P&S], *a.* Willed.
wil'lo[S], *v.* & *n.* Willow.
wim'bl[P], *n.* Wimble.
wim'en[P], *n. pl.* Women.
win'dowd[S], *pp.* Windowed.
wingd[P&S], *a.* Winged.
winkt[P&S], *pp.* Winked.
win'nowd[P&S], *pp.* Winnowed.
winst[S], *pp.* Winced.
win'sum[P&S], *a.* Winsome.
win'sum-ly[P&S], *adv.* Winsomely.
win'sum-ness[P&S], *n.* Winsomeness.
win'terd[P&S], *a.* Wintered.
wisht[P&S], *pp.* Wished.
witcht[S], *pp.* Witched.
with'erd[P&S], *pa.* Withered.
with-hold'n[P], *pp.* Withholden.
wit'nest[S], *pp.* Witnessed.
wiz'end[S], *pp.* Wizened.
wo[S], *n.* Woe.
wo'ful[S], *a.* Woeful.
won'derd[S], *pa.* Wondered.
wool'en[S], *a.* & *n.* Woollen.
work'a-bl[P], *a.* Workable.
work'a-bl-ness[P], *n.* Workableness.
workt[P&S], *pp.* & *a.* Worked.
wormd[S], *a.* Wormed.
wor'shipt[S], *pp.* Worshiped, worshipped.

wound'a-bl[P], *a.* Woundable.
wrackt[S], *pp.* Wracked.
wran'gl[P], *v.* & *n.* Wrangle.
wran'gld[P], *pp.* Wrangled.
wrapt[P&S], *pp.* Wrapped.
wreakt[P&S], *pp.* Wreaked.
wreathd[S], *pp.* & *a.* Wreathed.
wrech[P], *n.* Wretch.
wrech'ed[P], *a.* Wretched.
wreckt[P&S], *pp.* Wrecked.
wrencht[P&S], *pp.* Wrenched.
wres'tl[P], *v.* & *n.* Wrestle.
wres'tld[P], *pp.* Wrestled.
wrig'l[P], *v.* & *n.* Wriggle.
wrig'ld[P], *pp.* Wriggled.
wrin'kl[P], *v.* & *n.* Wrinkle.
wrin'kld[P], *pp.* Wrinkled.
writ'n[P], *pp.* Written.
wrongd[S], *pp.* Wronged.
wun[P&S], *pp.* Won.
wun'der[P], *v.* & *n.* Wonder.
wun'der-ful[P], *a.* Wonderful.
wun'der-ful-ness[P], *n.* Wonderfulness.
wun'drous[P], *a.* Wondrous.
wun'drous-ly[P], *adv.* Wondrously.
wun'drous-ness[P], *n.* Wondrousness.
wunt[P], *v.*, *a.* & *n.* Wont.
wunt'ed[P], *pa.* Wonted.
wurm[P], *v.* & *n.* Worm.
wurmd[P], *a.* Wormed.
wur'ry[P], *v.* & *n.* Worry.
wurse[P], *a.*, *n.* & *adv.* Worse.
wur'ship[P], *v.* & *n.* Worship.
wur'shipt[P], *pp.* Worshiped, worshipped.
wurst[P], *v.*, *a.*, *n.* & *adv.* Worst.
wurth[P], *a.* & *n.* Worth.
wurth'less[P], *a.* Worthless.
wur'thy[P], *a.* & *n.* Worthy.

X

xan'thin[P], *n.* Xanthine.
xen"o-pel'tin[P&S], *a.* & *n.* Xenopeltine.
xy'lo-graf[P&S], *n.* Xylograph.
xy-log'ra-fer[P&S], *n.* Xylographer.
xy"lo-graf'ic[P&S], *a.* Xylographic.
xy-log'ra-fy[P], *n.* Xylography.

Y

yawnd[P&S], *pp.* Yawned.
yeand[P&S], *pp.* Yeaned.
yel[P], *v.* & *n.* Yell.
yeld[P&S], *pp.* Yelled.
yel'lowd[S], *pp.* Yellowed.
yelpt[S], *pp.* Yelped.
yerkt[P&S], *pp.* Yerked.
yern[P], *vi.* Yearn.
yernd[P], *pp.* Yearned.
yield'a-bl[P], *a.* Yieldable.
yo'man[P&S], *n.* Yeoman.
your-selvs'[S], *pron. pl.* Yourselves.
yung[P&S], *a.* & *n.* Young.
yun'ker[S], *n.* Younker.

Z

zap'o-din[S], *a.* Zapodine.
zef'yr[P], *n.* Zephyr.
zel'ot[P&S], *n.* Zealot.
zel'ous[P], **zel'us**[S], *a.* Zealous.
ze'brin[S], *a.* Zebrine.
ze-nai'din[S], *a.* & *n.* Zenaidine.
zif'i-in[P&S], *a.* & *n.* Ziphiine.
zin'co-graf[P&S], *n.* Zincograph.
zin-cog'ra-fy[P&S], *n.* Zincography.
zinct[S], *pp.* Zinced.
zo'id[S], *a.* Zoide.
zo-og'ra-fy[P], *n.* Zoography.
zy-ge'nin[P&S], *a.* & *n.* Zygænine.

ADVERTISEMENTS

CPSIA information can be obtained
at www.ICGtesting.com
Printed in the USA
BVHW071033141019
561039BV00001B/191/P

9 789353 894696